Roads and Rivals

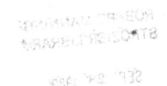

Roads and Rivals

THE POLITICAL USES OF ACCESS
IN THE BORDERLANDS OF ASIA

Mahnaz Z. Ispahani

Cornell University Press

Ithaca and London

First published 1989 by Cornell University Press.

Printed in the United States of America

Library of Congress Cataloging-in-Publication Data
Ispahani, Mahnaz Z.
  Roads and rivals.

  Bibliography: p.
  Includes index.
  1. Asia—Politics and government—1945–
  2. Roads—Asia. 3. Geopolitics—Asia. 4. Asia—
Strategic aspects. I. Title.
DS35.2.I82 1989   320.95   88-47932
  ISBN 0-8014-2220-5 (alk. paper)

The paper in this book is acid-free and meets the guidelines for permanence and durability of the Committee on Production Guidelines for Book Longevity of the Council on Library Resources.

For my mother Akhtar
and
for my father Isky

Contents

Maps

Preface

The origins of this book lie in a brief talk I was once asked to give on the strategic importance of an Asian mountain route. I was struck almost immediately that the simplicity of my assignment was deceptive. This particular route had served, and transformed, several purposes simultaneously. It had played a principal role in the region's military affairs, in its political development, in its economic growth, in its cultural change.

A recognition of this multidimensionality led me to the conclusion that the importance of land routes to state and regional politics in the developing world had not been properly addressed. The complicated facts of geography could, I believed, be profitably employed to assess the evolution of developing areas in a way they had not, to my knowledge, been discussed in recent years. The relationship between geographical and political facts, once much remarked upon by late-nineteenth-century frontiersmen and twentieth-century theorists of geopolitics and foreign policy, has provoked scant attention in current discussions of Third World regional history.

In contemporary analyses of global and regional politics, mundane geographical factors are usually either relegated to passing references in introductions or read narrowly, in only one of their many dimensions. Advances in the technologies of transport and communication since World War II have had the consequence of diminishing the importance of physical distance and access as dominant themes in state, regional, and international politics. The 1973 oil crisis revived elements of a "geopolitical" discourse in the west, focusing attention on the weighty consequences of physical distance, but still there was a failure to address the larger importance of the politics of access in the developing world. There remains a striking paucity of general works devoted to a political-geographical understanding of developing regions, where the impact of geographical factors—terrain, distance, access—on the contemporary capabilities of states remains extensive.

In this book I show how that lack may be remedied. I offer an argument for the irreducible, independent, and primary role of land routes, both as instruments of history and as tools of analysis, in the modern politics of developing areas. That role is ancient, of course, but it has persisted into the contemporary world unremarked by many students. I hope to restore the value of thinking about geographical realities as reflecting and promoting or retarding political, economic, and military processes. This book is an introductory argument for the importance of the politics of access to the domestic and foreign affairs of the countries of Asia, Africa, and Latin America.

The impact of new technologies notwithstanding, physical distance remains an essential factor in the life of developing states. I examine from the vantage point of land routes the modern history of a particular developing region, where old and new technologies and ideas coexist. Land routes are geographical phenomena whose inception, use, and demise (in the form of what I call the *antiroute*) have had a dominant impact on center-province relations within states, on interstate relations, and on the policies of great land powers toward smaller states. The acquisition or denial of access routes, it also turns out, has unintended or unexpected consequences. Transport infrastructure can outlast its builders and their intentions. Finally, routes and antiroutes constitute a pivot around which the current history of a region turns.

The multidimensionality of routes suggested to me that they might enhance an understanding of the interaction between the two facets of state policy: security and development. Again and again, I was reminded how scholars have drawn too firmly, in fact and in theory, the borders between the study of security and the study of development in Third World countries. The study of routes permitted me, indeed forced me, to trespass across those borders, to integrate what had been segregated, to interpret more accurately and completely state policies in the Third World. It broached the issues of how, when, and why security policies have impinged on policies for development, and vice versa. Many prominent studies of the interaction between security (defense) and development have been quantitative, based on a vast number of states and insecure data. Concentrating generally on weapons sales and acquisition and gross economic statistics, they have produced dramatically conflicting results. Mine is a qualitative approach, restricted in its scope, and using a single key indicator—routes—to provide more concrete, though more limited, insight into the security-development dilemma.

The geographical focus for this book is South, Central, and West Asia. In tracing the major routes or their absence, inevitably, I focus on the peripheries, on borderlands, and on zones of transition. These are areas which have been central to the acquisition of power, the pursuit of progress, and the outbreak of conflict in modern Pakistan, Afghanistan, India, and the People's Republic of China. In each case, I touch also upon early routes in order to measure continuities and discontinuities.

I hope my case for the continuing pertinence of geography has not succumbed to geographical determinism: obviously routes alone cannot alter state policies. And I hope, too, that I have committed no Braudelian indulgence. I have no doubt that future Braudels of Asia have their work cut out for them. Routes, and more generally distance and access, possess fascinating ideational, psycho-perceptual, religious, social, linguistic, artistic, and other attributes about which much remains to be written. My aims are more modest. I have confined myself to writing an exploratory essay on the political, military, economic, and geographical aspects of land routes.

The politics of access in South, Central, and West Asia is a rather untrodden field, and so I have collected evidence from a variety of writers and writings. (About the current history of some areas, like Baluchistan, Bhutan, and Tibet, there is limited information.) But this is a work of interpretation. It should stand or fall on the truth and the utility of its argument, not on the novelty of its materials. I have found new facts in a diversity of sources, but new facts are not my sole purpose. Instead I have tried to assemble disparate data and unify them with a controlling idea. My ambition is to shed new light on things that have been known in old ways.

MAHNAZ Z. ISPAHANI

Washington, D.C.

Acknowledgments

This book has been as much a personal journey as an intellectual one. For wise counsel and friendship during my time at the Fletcher School of Law and Diplomacy at Tufts University, and in Washington, D.C., I thank my teacher and constant friend Geoffrey Kemp, who first kindled and then supported my interest in this subject (indeed, in many subjects), and who has always stood by me; W. Scott Thompson, whose agile mind, feisty spirit, and confidence in my efforts helped transform long hours of research into a joy and a provocation; and Alan K. Henrikson, whose encouragement, knowledge, and exacting standards have made this, I hope, a better work.

In different ways, many people have made this book possible. My thanks go to Scheherazade Ahmed, Fouad Ajami, Rabia Ali, Zoe Baird, Barry M. Blechman, Shahram Chubin, Ambereen Dar, Leslie H. Gelb, Charles Glazer, Donna and Arthur A. Hartman, Ayesha Jalal, Anjum Katyal, Robert E. Kiernan, Robert S. Litwak, Edward N. Luttwak, Samia Ahad Mahmood, Peter Malone, Robert Meagher, Steven Miller, John Mojdehi, Michael Nacht, Nevra Neçipoglu, Janne E. Nolan, Martin Peretz, Gilberto Pimentel, the late Arnold L. Raphel, Nafis and Azhar Sadik (for a home away from home), Antoinette Sayeh, Charles N. Shane, Elizabeth Sherwood, Shirin Tahir-Kheli,

Cathryn Thorup, Phyllis Webber, Lynn Whittaker, Dean Wilkening, and Sonam Yangchen.

I am also happily indebted to the Center for Science and International Affairs at Harvard University for a two-year Research Associateship, which furnished financial, institutional, and intellectual support; to the International Fellows program of the American Association of University Women; to the Fanny Bullock Workman Fellowship of Wellesley College; and to the Exxon Fellowship at the Fletcher School. The *New Republic* was generous with its facilities and its friendship.

Holly Bailey and Roger Haydon at Cornell University Press were my excellent editors. For their efforts, and for Bill Nelson's splendid maps, I am grateful.

In a small way, I hope this book will honor the high standards of my grandfather, the late Mirza Abol Hassan Ispahani, and my uncle Syed Hashim Raza. I hope it will also honor the woman who was my first teacher and is my firm friend, my grandmother, Ghamar Ispahani.

With their devotion and spirit of play, Tiny Grimes and Stuff Smith allowed me to approach each day at the wordprocessor gladly. Iraj Ispahani, Lalehnaz Ispahani, and especially Farahnaz Ispahani (who toiled in the labyrinth of my notes) deserve loving thanks for the trust they reposed in me. Lise Hartman's confidence in my project was as unwavering as her affection. This book is a tribute to her talent as a critic and her genius as a friend.

Without my cherished Leon Wieseltier's gifts of imagination, rigor, sweetness, patience, and love, there would be no book. I thank him for the way he is with me.

This book is for my parents. In their support of the intellectual progress and professional careers of their daughters, they have few peers in Pakistani culture. My father has always respected and encouraged my every endeavor; his astute judgment, keen generosity, and loving interest were never far away. (In Karachi, he is my man on the scene.) This book is a tribute, too, to my mother's conviction that a woman's most powerful resource is a fine education, and to her determination that her daughters have one. It was she who imbued in me her own vivid sense of the beauty and the value of the life of the mind.

M. Z. I.

1

Routes and States

Before 1979, the name "Afghanistan" was hardly heard in the Western world. Who knew this borderland of Central and South Asia, home to great cities of antiquity, ancient crossroads between empires of the East and the West? It had long been perceived as a distant and obscure country. But less than a hundred years ago, in Afghanistan and its environs, a brutal competition for strategic access was played out between competing empires.

Who knew Baluchistan before the Western oil crises of the 1970s and the concurrent outbreak of tribal revolt there? Who considered it before the outbreak of the modern Afghan wars? Even within the framework of Pakistan—and before its inception, of British Imperial India—most Baluch territory had languished in geographical and political obscurity. Only recently have its physical routes and its political map been transformed.

Who knew, finally, the majestic mountain borderlands where China and Pakistan meet, where China and India meet, where Tibet, Nepal, and Bhutan lie, where today runs that much-heralded successor to the Silk Route, the Karakoram Highway? Completed in 1978 with much fanfare, the highway was fully opened to foreigners in 1986. In the contested lands through which it runs, India and Pakistan have sacrificed hundreds of lives, since 1984, to win the nearby massive Siachin Glacier. Why has this remote, desolately beautiful, and dangerous terrain been snatched from oblivion? Why have neighbors come to see this high road as a grave regional threat or a powerful regional symbol?

The past one hundred years have transformed the borderlands of South, Central, and West Asia. From isolated peripheries that evoked no more than an occasional imperial heavyhandedness, these lands have gradually metamorphosed into areas of consuming strategic interest. The events that brought them to international attention are the culmination of a long series of historical adventures, old and new. And in these adventures, geography and history have affected each other to a remarkable degree. The tyranny of terrain remains a stubborn reality. In fact, perhaps the most informative perspective from which to observe the evolution of these borderlands is a political-geographical one—specifically, the politics of the region's land routes.

Routes and Antiroutes

A route is both a geographical and a political idea, both an end and a means. Routes create access, and access, as Jean Gottman observes, has been a "central problem" in human history. It lies at the heart of man's relationship to his environment, and it is a matter as much political as geographical. Access in space, as Gottmann says, has been "organised at all times in history to serve political ends, and one of the major aims of politics is to regulate the conditions of access."[1] Routes may be seen most abstractly as a form of regulation. A route may define a country or an area and make it available to the purposes of man.

This book is based on the idea of access. I shall argue first that it is possible to evoke the political-geographical evolution of a region by an examination of routes of access. I shall make use of the facts of physical access to determine the politics of access in a particular region and in particular states. Second, since routes perform in both the crucial spheres of state activity, security and development, they are an ideal instrument by which also to reveal the qualitative relationship between these two facets of state policy.

Opposing the route is what I call the *antiroute*—any natural or artificial constraint on access. Antiroutes may serve the same human purposes as routes. But antiroutes create pressure against movement—they limit, restrain, or "channel" it—where routes facilitate broader movement. Mountains and deserts, legal boundaries and tariffs that raise the cost of crossing them—all are forms of the anti-route. (Lord Curzon remarked that the earliest frontiers "erected a barrier or created a gap," that is, restricted movement and access.)[2] What routes move, and what antiroutes prevent from moving, are people and goods within and across frontiers. Routes are the means for the centralization of the state, for the distribution of resources, and for the conduct of war. Transport infrastructure is critical to the definition of the modern state. Routes are also the means for the movement of ideas, transmitting what has been called the "iconography" of the state, the dominant culture and ideology of the political center, to its peripheries.[3]

Routes take many forms. They cross land, sea, and air; they may be natural geophysical features or the physical constructs of men.[4] The attributes of physical routes have not changed through time: roads and railroads still can define the territorial reach and physical capabilities of the state and are integral to the achievement of its political, economic, and military potential. Whatever its form, a route is a function of the characteristics of its environment and of technological advances in the modes of transportation and communication.

Land routes, in particular, are important and useful for historical analysis in the modern world. They have meaning and function in the vital areas of state life—in the economy, in politics, in the dissemination of ideas and ideologies, in internal security, external defense, and the pursuit of foreign policy goals. They are integral to the formation of states and empires, and to their continuation and expansion. Transport infrastructure defines, in a sense, the material conditions for a state's internal and external capabilities.

In developed countries, air power and nuclear weapons, on the one hand, and the virtual elimination of the problem of accessibility, on the other, may lead us to conclude that the problem of distance has ceased to be. But such a conclusion is false. Physical distance remains fundamental to the political, economic, and security concerns of developing countries, where terrain and topography still pose no small obstacle to the expansion of state power. Furthermore the few major routes that do exist have a disproportionate impact on state policies. By creating a historical map of routes one can chart the political evolution of a developing area.

In the nineteenth century, the importance of major arteries of commerce and warfare was evident to scholars and statesmen. Routes of transport impinged on the extent of political and of economic interests. For the conduct of war, routes across land have been indispensable. But broader regional analysis that relies on the facts of physical access has attracted few supporters among students of state politics and international affairs since World War II.

The advent of nuclear weapons and the need to quickly "develop" the former colonies so that they might "catch up" with the modernized West focused attention on technology and the technological imperative. This, in turn, made geographical factors in developing countries appear less significant. Yet these reputedly antiquated or anachronistic factors—territory, terrain, resources, distance, routes—remain immensely relevant to the policies of such countries as Pakistan, Afghanistan, the People's Republic of China, and India. Geography has yet to be confounded by technology. Indeed, as I hope to demonstrate, the modern history of routes resurrects the traditionally important role of geographical constants in South, Central, and West Asia. The primacy and vitality of routes, which were undisputed characteristics of earlier historical periods, remain relevant—in fact, essential—to state policy in a developing world where jet engines and space satellites coexist with the bullock and the wheel.

An argument for the stubborn significance of the facts of physical access in modern regional history should not be conceived of as an essay in geographical determinism or geographical reductionism. Routes must be understood, of course, within the contexts—political, economic, military, ideational, and geographical—which accord them their significance. But it is the danger of underemphasizing geography, not the danger of overemphasizing it, that threatens contemporary analysis.

Interest in land routes brings other analytical benefits. It reveals some basic and occasionally overlooked truths about the ever-shifting balance between security and development in developing countries. Routes are "dual-capable"; that is, in all their attributes they function in, and stand at the nexus of, security and development. Thus the study of the politics of routes can furnish a salutary corrective to one of the most wasteful errors in the analysis of the developing world: the persistent segregation of the study of security from the study of development. For the study of routes, such a segregation makes no sense. Rather, the study of routes requires an evaluation of the impact of security considerations on those of development, and vice versa.

A paucity of infrastructure in former colonies is a problem that affects those concerned with security and those concerned with development—in short, the state's elite. Not just the armed forces but the political nation-builders and the economic integrators are concerned with routes. Territory must be secured from external penetration; large land masses and disparate peoples must be bound together. Without land routes, borders cannot be defined and secured; political, economic, and geographical peripheries and their peoples cannot be linked politically and economically with, or be controlled by, the state center. Without routes, in sum, it is difficult to forge a state or to assert and maintain a national identity—witness the myriad consequences of the thousand mile physical rift between West Pakistan and its erstwhile other half, now Bangladesh. In the age of airwaves and cassettes, routes continue to be paths along which ideologies travel; Trotsky's train in Russia (and Lenin's train from Switzerland) and TANU's Landrovers in Tanzania are not things of the past. For security, for development, for the administration of state policies, routes are essential, and they serve, consequently, as a rewarding analytical tool.

With the advent of newly independent states in Asia and in Africa, academic and policy-making priorities became attached either to the old "problem of security" or to the new "problem of development." Certainly it is necessary for the purposes of specific micro-analyses to separate the two realms. But so considerable a schism developed between the two "competing" interests that their interconnections became subdued, ignored, or lost. Moreover, the few scholars who have linked the study of the two fields have concentrated their talents on one problem and one perspective: the impact of military expenditures (particularly the sale and acquisition of arms) on economic growth. But their work suffers, I shall argue, from the problems of generalizations about countries where hard data are clearly inadequate to the task at hand.

Study of the politics of routes in the South, Central, and West Asian borderlands not only restores a necessary awareness of the historical relationship between security and development but also provides an understanding of their contemporary relationship. This book focuses on the points of linkage and overlap, on the friction and the tense interaction, between these two theaters of policy. Over time, I shall show, there has been a tendency for security concerns to win out over those of development. Insecurity, in fact, has often urged development.[5] In the building of major routes, security concerns have generally had primacy. Indeed, in those instances when considerations of socioeconomic development have dominated those of military security, the result has been a loss of security. This point is most dramatically manifested in modern Afghanistan. There, a centuries-old policy that accorded higher priority to state and ruler security than to economic expansion was reversed, and the result was the loss of territorial and national integrity.

Newly independent states, faced with the dilemma of security versus development, have acted most often when strong security concerns intervene. Strategically insignificant areas have witnessed little development. Where a periphery takes on strategic importance, however, the infrastructure of access begins to emerge, even to flourish. Of course, a route can have both strategic and developmental consequences; it is likely that benefits will ensue for both policy areas. In most of the cases under consideration here, however, calculations of security have provided the impetus for development; where this has not been the case, a decrease in security has resulted.

Finally, routes have a more general utility for the student of the Asian borderlands. Routes are what sociologists might call a "strategic research site" for virtually all the geopolitics of the region. Routes amount, as Alan K. Henrikson has said, to a "skeleton, or X-ray," of the politics of countries and regions.[6] As one charts the course of routes and antiroutes across time, for example, it becomes possible to assess the transition from imperial questions of trade and strategy to postimperial questions of development and security. The history of routes illustrates the impact of war and trade on regional evolution across many forms of political organization. In effect it "maps" relationships within and between Pakistan, Afghanistan, India, the Himalayan states, and China—particularly in their frontier lands—and thus suggests the possibilities for integration, growth, and defense in these states. Finally, it is perhaps most illuminating with regard to the evolving political and geographical status of traditional peripheries and zones of transition.

It is hardly possible to understand the modern national and regional dilemmas of these Asian states without an understanding of the geographical constraints they face now and have faced in their colonial or imperial past. In the earlier era antiroutes (borders and boundaries) were put in place, and territorial disputes initiated, which continue to trouble rulers today. Without some understanding of the frontier defense policies of British India, for example, or a knowledge of Russia's march into Central Asia, it is difficult to understand Pakistani-Afghan, Afghan-Soviet, Pakistani-Indian, Sino-Pakistani, Sino-Indian, or Indo-Soviet political-geographical relations or the role of access routes in the Soviet invasion of Afghanistan. To start the discussion of modern events in each chapter, therefore, I sketch this history with an eye to the pertinence of routes.

The Dimensions of Routes

Routes, and the access they create, may be systematically conceptualized as having five dimensions: geographical, political, economic, military, and ideational.

Geographically, distance may be measured as sheer physical distance, but it may also be measured in terms of the time and effort its conquest requires. Vanquishing distance is fundamental both to history and to geography—there can be no differentiation of space without movement along defined paths.[7] As paths spread, so does the extent of geographical knowledge. Physical distance is conquered by routes, which overcome natural barriers and topographical constraints; it is conquered, that is to say, in direct relation to advances in the technology of transport and communications and to the sheer will of state-builders. Increased technological prowess leads to increased mobility and carrying capacity and to lower costs. Massive wars, of great logistical complexity, can now be fought at vast distances from the homeland. This conquest of distance also provides the geographical basis for the foundation of political units and for the efforts of those units to transform their internal and external environments.

Politically, routes help determine the potential of states. To define themselves—to develop territorial identities—and to differentiate themselves one from another, modern states must delimit territory and control access by outsiders.[8] They establish antiroutes. Internally, state and national integration also proceeds by routes, but in a different manner. Whereas states cannot come into existence without the ability to deny access, they cannot be physically consolidated and politically sustained without the ability to expand access—without the extension of the authority and the legitimacy of the center to the peripheries. Political integration requires the creation of access. In the development of a coherent polity, the infrastructure for movement, for access to the source of power, must exist. Without routes, internal disintegration or political fragmentation results.

Access routes are extremely useful if a state is to expand its political potential outward. They permit the establishment of political and diplomatic contacts, of alliances between states with common or complementary interests. Indeed, it is often on routes that the maintenance and expansion of such coalitions depend. Neighboring states with linked routes possess the greatest potential for collaboration, though geographical proximity is never a guarantee of alliance. In fact, neighborhood and enmity are commonly witnessed together. For example, although physical routes exist between India and Pakistan and between the Soviet Union and China, there is little access. Radically different views of politics or ideology—perceptual distance—separate these states. Movement between them is strictly controlled. Finally, in developing states, decisions about the creation of major routes are always made in the political arena.

Since ancient times, trade routes have brought together pastoral nomads and settled populations. Pack animals once lumbered from China to the Middle East, India, and even Rome, carrying basic foodstuffs, luxury goods, and religious belief. Plunder and payments to ensure safe passage were the trappings of power in territories outside the control of a central power. Urban populations, especially those located in large cities, were often at the mercy of transport and trade: as William McNeill notes, they "suffered catastrophe with any prolonged interruption of food supply. . . . [They] survived only on the strength of a smoothly functioning transport system capable of bringing food from afar."[9]

The stubborn importance of routes to economic intercourse and political centralization was well stated by Brooks Adams in 1902. Man, he argues, needs food and defense, and few communities have succeeded in feeding and arming themselves entirely from their own resources. So men have warred, though mostly they have traded, in order to balance needs and resources. Trade has required junctions, or "fairs," for the exchange of goods: "No fair can thrive unless accessible, and none can be accessible with approaches closed either by defects or robbers; hence some system of road-building and police must precede centralized trade. . . . Nor can business be transacted without a tribunal to decide disputes."[10] From this process emerge separate administrative—political units. In Adams's view, trade, through the gradual evolution of institutions and routes, gives rise to civil societies.

Transport geographers and modern economists disagree regarding the exact causal relationship between improved routes and economic development. They dispute whether investment in transport is a precondition, or a catalyst for development, or one in a set of permissive inputs. They view differently the relative merits of improving existing arterial routes as opposed to expanding low-grade, feeder roads, the impact of new routes on center-periphery links and on regional economic disparities, and the value of investments in routes as opposed to those in directly productive projects. They concur, however, in the importance of transport projects to the national economic planning of developing states.[11]

In their development plans, governments emphasize different goals at different times; they may emphasize one sector over another, one region over another, depending on their priorities. All their choices, however, involve some consideration of access: whether it exists, is sufficient, must be created, in which direction, and for what primary or tangential uses. When a decision is made to open a mine, build a factory, expand rural production, or increase access to urban or foreign markets, it immediately poses questions and demands decisions be made regarding transport requirements and constraints.

States also use routes in the formation of domestic regional economic programs. A state may ignore the development needs of a particular area, thus depriving it of infrastructure; another may consciously attempt a program of overall regional development, creating transport links specifically to lessen regional differences. Often young states build "developmental" roads and railway lines for the purpose of promoting settlement and traffic.[12]

Developing countries pursue economic strategies which nearly always incorporate both trade and foreign aid. Important in the attempt to obtain optimum economic benefits from trade with other states are control over and expansion of routes. States also attempt to regulate the direction and quantity of trade with different partners through tariffs, quotas, exchange rates, customs duties, transit rights, and the like, that is, by creating antiroutes.

To increase their economic productivity, security, and market size, states may also form integrated regional groupings in which conditions of access are eased for member-states relative to nonmembers.

Such regional integration policies often involve the joint expansion of physical channels of communication and transport. The Southern African Development Cooperation Conference (SADCC), the Regional Cooperation for Development (RCD) group in South and West Asia, and the Development of Islamic Countries Transport Organisation (DICTO) are examples. It is yet to be seen whether the South Asian Association for Regional Cooperation (SAARC), which includes Pakistan, India, Sri Lanka, Bangladesh, Nepal, Bhutan, and the Maldives, will pursue joint infrastructure and communications projects, therby signaling commitment to regional economic integration.

Foreign aid is often apportioned for routes. The inadequacy of financial resources in most developing countries, or their low technological capability leads them to raise funds and expertise for road and rail construction from foreign governments and international institutions. Donor-states with a plethora of political, economic, and military interests in developing countries, as well as the International Monetary Fund (IMF) and the World Bank with their narrower, "developmental" perspectives, receive many requests for infrastructural aid. Transport projects are large. They involve high expenditures and long periods of gestation. Decisions in support of them are big decisions, and to complicate matters, the criteria for donor and recipient may not necessarily coincide. The specific domestic, political, economic, or strategic interests of the recipient may or may not complement the global strategic or political access requirements of important donor-states or the technical assessments of international institutions.

In decisions on foreign infrastructural aid, therefore, economic, political, strategic, and geographical concerns intersect. Routing assistance may be provided, for example, to foster economic and political stability in the recipient state. It may be refused if the recipient's regime is repugnant to the donor, or if the routes to be developed are of no strategic value to the donor or of some strategic value to its opponent. Thus the economics of transportation or the development needs of the recipient state are by no means the only rationales for route construction. Indeed, infrastructural aid can be viewed as part of the broader arms trade. The infrastructure of access is also "dual-use": depending on its location and specifications, it can be an instrument of economic development or a tool of internal security or external defense.

Thus, for example, when it proposed solutions to the problems of reduced Western accessibility to bases and of low-intensity conflict in the Third World, the 1988 report of the U.S. Working Group of the Commission on Integrated Long Term Strategy, of the Department of Defense, showed how, in the sphere of infrastructural aid, security and development interests can become entangled. It argued that since physical infrastructure such as roads and bridges plays an important role in Third World conflicts, the United States should provide military engineering support in "developing an engineer force structure to provide both combat support . . . and a capability to conduct civic action and other nation building tasks." American security aid and the military could become involved in a pioneering program consisting of "leading edge reconstruction work" in repairing roads, bridges, and other physical infrastructure in areas of high risk and conflict inside Third World countries. A combination of security assistance, U.S. Agency for International Development, and economic support funds could be used for these purposes. Such construction work would also give American military engineers "training otherwise denied them in building roads and airstrips" while being responsive to "host government's interests and consistent with the U.S. Ambassador's general plan for developmental assistance."[13]

Militarily, routes provide the state with means for internal control and for the expansion of its external security interests. In developing countries, the concept of security incorporates both the need for internal consolidation and the need for defense against external threats. To constrain centrifugal forces, routes must permit not only peaceful means of integration but coercive ones as well. The center must have access to the political (which often coincides with the geographical) periphery, not only to transmit a dominant ideology and culture but also to facilitate the effective deployment of troops and the extension of governmental writ. Routes built by the central government can thereby threaten the security of the traditional power structure in peripheries. They may also function as useful socioeconomic bribes to placate restless peoples and lure them away from local masters. Finally, a state's control of routes to its peripheries must be stronger than the control exercised by a neighboring state if the former is to exercise real political and administrative control.

For successful defense against external threat, forces must be mobile within a state. The antiroutes must be held strong, and the routes secured to provide speedy, efficient deployment of forces to meet threats from many directions—important attributes for most developing countries, located in unstable regional environments and often enmeshed in territorial disputes with neighbors. Good routes have always been vital for the active defense of borders and for troop mobility within the state. In the Roman Empire, for instance, border defense and the successful maintenance of territorial security focused on a logistical and protective infrastructure: watchtowers, outpost forts, signal communication networks, troop bases, and, of course, roads. These, as Edward N. Luttwak has written, "were the essential elements of the system." The roads served as "axes of penetration beyond the border as well as rearward routes for communication, reinforcement, troop circulation, and supply . . . as patrol routes against infiltration and small-scale incursions . . . as interprovincial highways."[14]

The importance of routes is more obvious in warfare than in peace-time. Routes are vital to both the tactical aspects of battle and the strategic aims of war and conquest. In the time of Athens and Persia, war and a ruler's reach were circumscibed principally by the require-ments of transport and provision. With new technologies of transport came innovation in wartime: the conception of the Schlieffen Plan before World War I, for example, was closely linked to the con-tingencies of railroad timetables and planning. During the American Civil War the railroad permitted, for the first time, the movement of armies consisting of over a hundred thousand men who could fight for years with supply lines stretching hundreds of miles away.[15] Logistical constraints such as modes of transport and communication, as Geoffrey Kemp and John Maurer point out, "define and determine the scope of military operations to a far greater extent than is usually admitted by military historians interested in describing battles and campaigns. . . . Changes in the means of transportation can have a revolutionary impact on strategy because accepted notions of time and space governing the movement of military forces are trans-formed."[16]

The search for access has often played a major role in the expan-sionist claims of states or their aims in war. Examples are the German quest for *Lebensraum* and the arguments of some Russians (in the nineteenth century) and some Afghans (in the twentieth century) that access to the sea is essential for the long-term security of the state.

Lack of access to the sea creates a high degree of insecurity for land-locked states. Today, there are twenty-five independent, land-locked states, nineteen of which are developing and fifteen of which are among the least developed countries in the world. Despite international covenants safeguarding the right of transit to the sea (across which the bulk of trade moves), and treaties of trade and transit with their neighbors, all land-locked states face higher strategic, political, and economic risks owing to their geographical location. Interior peripheries of coastal states suffer similar problems: high transport costs, inadequate facilities, maintenance, and management, delays in transit, higher costs of insurance, storage, and interest on loans, and higher risks of loss, damage, or theft.[17]

In the formation of strategic alliances and security ties, routes of access are again significant. The U.S. containment policy of the 1950s and 1960s, which gave birth to such organizations as SEATO, CENTO, and ANZUS, centered on the acquisition of strategic and political access by the United States and its denial to the Soviet Union. The territories of SEATO and CENTO members formed a land cordon to thwart access by the Soviet Union. These pieces of land might also have served as bases, facilitating American strategic access; their owners, in turn, would gain access to American military and economic resources. The spatial consequences of such alliances are evident both in the patterns of movement and communication which develop between geographically distant friends and in the patterns of development within the territories of the smaller allies; bases built for naval or army use, for instance, can alter patterns of land use, civilian employment, and settlement.

This basic rationale for relationships between the United States, the Soviet Union, and their smaller, weaker friends across the globe remains today. In a nuclear world, access remains a primordial issue. If the root interest of developing countries in forging security ties with great powers is to address their own local concerns, to contain domestic or regional threats, then a dominant concern of great powers is their need for political, economic, and strategic access. After the evolution of a nuclear balance between them, the United States and the Soviet Union shifted their conventional battleground to the developing countries of Asia, Africa, and Central America; consequently the projection of power and influence, the gaining of access to resources and facilities and their denial to an opponent, have become important security tasks. Bases and knowledge of internal routes in regions of perceived interest remain cardinal to U.S. and Soviet military planning.

Access has always been essential to the security of global powers. Access to grain supplies played a critical role in the grand strategy of

Athens, Rome, and Byzantium. In the nineteenth century, Britain required access to overseas food supplies and raw materials in order to feed and employ its own people.[18] In 1973 countries in the Western world deemed access to the oil resources of the Persian Gulf a vital national economic and strategic interest.

Finally, routes facilitate the flow of ideas. Although this book focuses on the politics of physical access, the powerful relationship of access and ideas should be at least noted.[19] To be sure, in the modern era the movement of ideas involves new and different forms of distance, yet routes across land, sea, and air remain surprisingly basic and persistent in their transmission (cassettes, radios, television, and satellites notwithstanding). And even as these modern technologies enter the war of ideas in developing countries, the incompleteness of physical access, particularly in the political-geographical peripheries of Third World states, continues to affect the advance of ideas. Without physical routes, the consolidation of ideological control is more difficult. In the building of nation-states, in the ideological wars between superpowers, and in a national revolution like Ayatollah Khomeini's, the spread and the control of ideas are fundamental to the political strategies of states. To disseminate both the idea of the state and its ideology, a developing country must overcome distance. To extend national beliefs and attitudes, for example, rural roads must be built. To the spread of information, to the exposure of peripheries to the orthodoxy and the administration of the center, such roads are necessary.

Geography and Politics

This book explores the politics of physical access in South, Central, and West Asia. I hope to revive the usefulness of a political-geographical perspective for studying state, regional, and international politics; and for grasping the continuities, discontinuities, and pivotal events in a region's modern history.

The concerns of political geographers address both goals of independent states, what Norman Pounds calls self-preservation and welfare.[20] These goals incorporate all the policies, internal and external, that affect the total strength or weakness of a state. Pounds stresses an integrated approach to the concerns of the nation-state. In 1950 Richard Hartshorne described the purpose of any state as to bring together "all the varied territorial parts into a single organised unit." Such a task requires the extension of an infrastructure of transport and communications across the territory of the state. On the material plane, then, states may be characterized by their "circulation" systems, or systems of transport and communication which permit the movement of men, goods, and ideas within the state and between it and other parts of the world.[21]

An emphasis on the important role of routes, access, and distance in the study of state and region is supported by Stein Rokkan's use of the center-periphery model in the study of political development. In order to differentiate political systems, according to Rokkan, one must first determine the structure of the space they control, that is, the territory, the political center, and the peripheries. Next, to study the transactions between center and peripheries "over distance," one must consider (1) the physical conditions of transport and communication, that is, distance and barriers; (2) the "technological conditions for movement," that is, horses, roads, ships, aircraft; and (3) the military, economic, and cultural conditions that enhance or inhibit contact. In sum, he argues, "geography and the technology of transportation determine the potential reach of efforts of expansion; the balance of military power, the directions and the character of trade routes, the affinities and the differences in codes of communication determine the actual reach of such efforts."[22]

To study the politics of routes is to employ the "movement" factor in analyses of power relationships. It is to incorporate a view in which the movement of men, material, and ideas provides the focal point for assessing changes in geopolitical patterns. Such a focus addresses geographical realities as they are changed by technological advances, new or different political ideologies, the redistribution of peoples, or the emergence of new patterns of trade and aid.[23] This movement factor forms a centerpiece of modern theories of geopolitics.

I stress the distinction between geopolitics and *Geopolitik*. Confusion over the precise meaning of geopolitics has arisen in large part due to its association with *Geopolitik*, the German military "science" founded on the theory of the state as an organic entity.[24] Geopolitics has been expounded by such theorists of international relations as Halford Mackinder, Alfred Thayer Mahan, and Nicholas Spykman. These men viewed the historical evolution of power relationships from the perspectives of both politics and geography. As Colin Gray points out, such an approach can, "when not abased, . . . direct attention to factors of enduring importance."[25] In an era of technological advance and change, the symbols of historical continuity and geographical meaning are too readily neglected. They are certainly not inconsequential to political history.

The control, use, and expansion of routes were a mainstay of earlier geopolitical deliberations. From their theories of the importance of mastery over sea routes, land routes, or air routes, the geopoliticians developed broad frameworks to explain the past, present, and future distribution of international political and military power. "A geographical-historical perspective on global strategy" is made possible, as Mackinder said, when matters are "regarded from the point of view of human mobility, and of the different modes of mobility."[26] In drawing on geopolitics, I do not mean to argue for geographical determinism. It is the analysis of the relevance of routes to the course of political, economic, and military history which may be usefully applied to the affairs of state and region in the developing world.

Spykman, in "The Geography of Foreign Policy," discussed at length the historical role of transport and communications in a state's integration, growth, and external policies. His views remain pertinent to developing states. "Effective centralized control," he said, depends primarily on two factors: "On the existence of an effective system of communication from the center to the periphery, and on the absence or the successful counter-balancing of centrifugal forces of separatism." Topography is a great barrier to political unification, and until it is overcome by "artificial means," that is, route construction, integration and state power are distant goals. Roads and railroads have always, by their expansion or decline, affected the significance of a state's location. They have also been historically important as integrative, political, and strategic forces. "From the beginning," Spykman says, "governments have strengthened their control over territory by supplementing the natural means of communication and attempting to overcome the barriers posed by topography"; large states have built routes "for strategic and political reasons long before the economic significance of outlying areas justified such construction."[27] The growth of states and empires is paralleled, then, by an expansion in their routing systems, and conversely, their decline is often marked by the neglect of these same systems.

The proposition that geographical phenomena such as routes are analytically and historically important, however, is not as uncontroversial as it might seem. The argument for the use of a geopolitical, or political-geographical, perspective lost authority with political analysts and political actors after World War II. One reason was the association of the idea with *Geopolitik*. The other, more substantial reason was the accumulation of nuclear arsenals. Historical geopolitics seemed to be set aside, and there emerged a new detachment from the time-honored relationship between geography and politics. The physical environment, it seemed, could no longer constrain men from their universal destruction. The strategic continuities with the past appeared to have been severed.[28] The future was to be a very new kind of history. The reality that commanded contemporary attention in the West was the rate of technological progress. This was the outstanding phenomena of the postwar era, before which the traditional analysis had to give way.

In 1957, John Herz announced that the centuries-old characteristic of the nation-state—its territoriality, which he defined as its identification with a specific piece of land surrounded by a "wall of defensibility"—was bound to vanish. The nation-state, he said, was about to become obsolete. Nuclear weapons had transformed the relationship between a government, its territory, and its people. It was no longer possible to contemplate the idea of a government able to defend the national territory. Some years later Harold Sprout and Margaret Sprout also rang the death knell for geopolitics. In a nuclear world, they argued, there was no longer room for the conventional, earthbound concepts of "location, space, distance, and geographical configurations." By 1960 these could be strategic variables only in "increasingly obsolescent frames of reference."[29]

The conflict in Vietnam, fought at a great distance, inspired still another reconsideration of the relationship of geography to politics. In his anti-isolationist essay "Illusions of Distance," Albert Wohlstetter suggested that distant powers no longer suffered a "comparative disadvantage" in war owing to massive advances in the technology of transport and communication. These advances had so reduced the economic costs and so increased the capacity for long-distance haulage that a proximate and a nether power could reach a given point with equivalent effort. Linear theories of strength weakening with distance had become invalid. The new revolution in transport technology also had the effect of expanding the "geographical extent of interests." Yet in the 1970s, following the discovery that the Persian Gulf was a "vital national interest" for the United States, logisticians, military planners, and the Congress of the United States, all became enmeshed in debates about how to overcome the distance of seven thousand air miles—how to gain bases, how to counter the advantages of proximity enjoyed by the Soviet Union. The geographical extent of interests was already global moreover, during the time of the European empires. The access routes of Britain, France, Germany, and Italy crisscrossed the globe; roads and railroads, new sea routes, and faster ships were deployed to secure political interests that themselves derived from the ability to traverse the furthest oceans and deserts. The relationship between geography, technology, and political interests is an old one.[30] The 1973 oil embargo by producer-states in the Middle East and Persian Gulf brought to the fore the question of defending American interests and economic power, and Western society in a distant region. Strategists were rudely awakened to the prospect that nuclear weapons had not altered politics and strategy permanently. The focus shifted to traditional issues—to resources, routes, location, barriers, and access. When the Rapid Deployment Force (RDF), now renamed the Central Command, was first initiated, the burning issue was a classical one: How do we resolve the dilemma of access?

Assessing the new situation, Geoffrey Kemp argued that "new trends"—the diffusion of power, the importance of scarce resources and a growing interdependence, the changing pattern of overseas base rights, and the new maritime regime being proposed under the Law of the Sea Treaty—had resurrected "the importance of geography and resources as factors in military thinking and [made] us more sensitive to the geostrategic perspectives of regional powers." In the new map of power relations, "knowledge about the whereabouts of food, energy and mineral resources, the location of small islands, patterns of sea and air lines of communication, and the impact of arms transfers on regional power balances may become as necessary a tool for analysis as familiarity with the acronyms of nuclear warfare has been in the recent past."[31]

In the 1980s technological advances again came to be viewed as palliatives to the dilemma of securing global access. In 1988 the U.S. Working Group of the Commission on Integrated Long Term Strategy recommended that, given adverse political changes in the Third World which were making the retention of U.S. bases abroad increasingly difficult, technological alternatives to land bases should be initiated.[32] This movement beyond bases, however, is not yet a reality; and if it ever becomes one, the question of physical access to distant territories will have been only reformulated, not made obsolete.

It is an irony of history that as the nuclear world was being invented and discoursed upon, scores of "underdeveloped" former colonies were experiencing the birth pangs of statehood. These new states were constrained by their untamed environment, by their lack of resources, by the diversity of their peoples. Their leaders were concerned with survival and with conventional security. In the developing regions of the world, the territorial state whose demise Herz announced in 1957 had been born only a few years earlier or was yet to be born. It was inchoate, with an entire history of territory, peoples, and work yet to be written. Here, the plain facts of geography were (and are) integral parts of territorial continuity and coherence, central to the binding of peoples into a unitary community and to the expansion of newly national economies.

Foreign and security concerns, too, were prominently circumscribed by geography. Zulfiqar Ali Bhutto, father of Pakistan's nuclear program, observed that "geography continues to remain the most important single factor in the formulation of a country's foreign policy. . . . Territorial disputes . . . are the most important of all disputes. . . . Many relations can be changed and influenced, but not the reality of the presence of a geographical neighbour."[33] These words were written in 1969. Ten years later Afghanistan was invaded by Soviet troops by air and across land routes built by Soviets and Afghans together. An ancient mountain redoubt was pierced, a conventional invasion and occupation realized, in a region that houses two great nuclear powers, the Soviet Union and China, and two near-nuclear powers, India and Pakistan. The intimate connection between political and geographical elements remains ascendant.

Security and Development

In the post–World War II period of new states, socioeconomic and political development became a key responsibility in territories that had just acquired definition, leaders, and goals. The immediate geographical aspects of statehood and of aspirations to nationhood were much in evidence—the impetus to retain the legally bounded territorial existence of the state, to defend controversial territorial claims, to bind heterogeneous populations from physically, economically, and politically different regions into a whole, to master the hindrances posed by an unforgiving environment with a low technological capability. Still theories of development paid insufficient heed to the interaction of political with geographical factors. They lost sight of the locational specificity, the textured particularity of a country or a region, the knowledge of how men mold or are molded by their physical environments.

One example of this general bias against the recognition of security concerns in the study of economic development is provided by theories of industrialization.[34] Industrial location theory may consider factors of cost-effectiveness, efficiency, proximity to population centers, and transportation links, but strategic factors are sometimes paid scant attention. Still, industries are sited with strategic considerations in mind. The location of the Yugoslav steel industry, for example, was a subject of much concern after 1948; as F. E. I. Hamilton notes, "the threat of attack from the north and east resulted in the location of some capacity in strategically more isolated and more secure areas [in 1949] in the mountainous central and southwestern regions. . . . After 1948, development [at Smederevo] was discouraged because of its proximity to the vulnerable northeastern frontier."[35] The economic calculus of cost and benefit is rarely sufficient to determine the nature of large-scale economic infrastructure projects in developing countries.

Some writers have tried to address directly the relationship between security (or defense) and development. Broadly speaking, they work from two perspectives. First is the popular argument that expenditures on security are detrimental to—or, at best, neutral in their effects on—development. (This view is often accompanied by the perception that in the long run, all the components of development will bolster security.) Second is the argument that assured security is a precondition for expanded efforts in development: resource-poor countries in insecure environments (the habitat of most developing states) will tend to survival first and to growth only later. Such broad conclusions about so many countries, however, cannot be pursued satisfactorily through quantitative analysis because of the inadequacy of available statistical data. Since the acquisition and expansion of access is primary to the definition of both security and development, a qualitative study of land routes might better evoke a narrower yet more textured understanding of the dynamic relationship between the two faces of state policy.

The processes of generating progress and power in a state are immutably tied to the creation, restriction, or control of access. Development requires the enhancement of physical and political accessibility. It acts upon and broadens the social, economic, and political potential of a state's territory and a nation's people. It denotes increases in the physical reach of the state and its capacity for political negotiation with or control of its peripheries, in the number and range of persons, tribes, and ethnic, religious, and other primary groups that respond similarly to a national idea, and in aggregate economic productivity and distributive capacity. State security requires a reduction in perceptions of external threat to specific frontiers, firm external antiroutes, and the vanquishment of internal antiroutes—in other words accessibility to and control over its peripheries by the political center ("ruler" or "regime").

Many writers have approached the relationship between security and development in a unidirectional and unidimensional way, concentrating on the impact of arms sales and military expenditures on development. The disarmament and development school has focused on the impact of increased weapons sales by developed countries and increased weapons purchases by developing countries. Adverse effects on growth have been charted. In 1972 a United Nations Group of Experts on the Economic and Social Consequences of Disarmament argued that if less were spent on defense, the result would be a "disarmament dividend," which could be "redirected to raise standards of living and to promote faster growth." Similarly, in 1982 the Independent Commission on Disarmament and Security Issues, headed by Olaf Palme, used macro-statistical data to demonstrate the adverse economic and social consequences of military spending and reiterated the point that expenditures on the defense sector detract directly from the opportunities for progress in the development sector. Nicole Ball has frequently argued that expenditures on defense, even those that might have both positive and negative effects, ultimately have a negative effect on development.[36]

Emile Benoit has challenged such conclusions. He maintains that states which spend large amounts of money on the defense sector can also have rapid rates of growth. Benoit studied forty-four developing countries between 1950 and 1965 and argued that defense expenditures had both positive and negative effects on the potential for economic growth, with the positive effects triumphing. He noted, too, that defense programs could contribute to development "by helping to maintain public order and internal and external security. In addition, they may contribute in other ways to strengthening national unity against divisive forces of tribal and regional loyalties (nation-building effects)."[37] His study provoked others: one concluded, on the basis of further statistical analysis, that in "relatively resource unconstrained" countries, defense expenditures "may play an important and positive role in increasing growth." And David K. Whynes argued that domestic military expenditures and international military aid "represent a net economic cost to the Third World, in spite of the variety of potential benefits which might accrue as a result of related industrial and manpower developments." The debate has continued: in 1987 A. F. Mullins, Jr., produced a quantitative study that first eliminated the possibility that new states might resemble their European precursors in which the need for military power drove development, and development itself produced the goods necessary for the creation of military power. According to Mullins, Benoit was wrong: new states with the largest GNPs, the best GNP growth rates, and particularly those which made the "greatest overall economic progress across the period are states that paid proportionately the least attention to military capability." Furthermore, some states choose outside patrons and their arms rather than internal development as the path to military strength. Mullins concluded—again on the basis of a statistical measurement of military and development capability—that only by restraining arms transfers into the developing world might the new states "exit from the present trap" in which they are "open to the devastation of war" and simultaneously inhibited in the "fundamental foundations of the development process."[38]

Benoit's and successor studies are often too wide (in the use of multicountry, macro-statistical data) and too narrow (in the definition of the constituent elements of development) to generate particular conclusions about the multifaceted relationship between security and development. Benoit defined development, even economic development, too strictly. Economic development is a notion much broader than the dollar value of gross national product or the gross domestic product, and military expenditures are linked to more than arms procurement. Most important, the broad interaction between security and development cannot be measured solely in terms of economic variables; it should also include political, social, and geographical factors.

The problems of security and development are rooted in the fundamental premise of state viability or, what comes to the same thing, territorial-political integrity. This geopolitical coherence is the first requirement in the pursuit of political identity, economic growth, and distribution of wealth. It is the essence of internal and external security, and is not to be taken for granted (as witness Nigeria and Biafra, Pakistan and Bangladesh, Vietnam, Laos, and Cambodia).

For many Third World writers and political elites, the need to retain independence, and therefore security, is of the first order of importance regardless of a state's wealth or poverty. They think that the need for development cannot reduce the requirement for security. According to Syed Shaukat Ali, "defence and national security are a pre-condition of development. In a situation where there is no security, external or internal, little mobilisation and development of resources can take place." He calls defense spending an "insurance premium," with beneficial spin-offs, and even suggests that "development at the cost of defence may make a country a more tempting prize for the aggressor and therefore a greater security risk."[39]

K. Subrahmanyam argues that the presence of poverty in developing countries does not imply that defense expenditures should necessarily be made subordinate to those for development. Economic development may be a leading policy aim for the government of India, but, he points out, national security is a necessary condition for the achievement of that goal: it is important to posit an integrated view of defense and development. The "schizophrenic approach," as he calls it, appeared natural only when defense was the responsibility of the state and economic growth that of the private sector. His plea for an integrated analysis is based on the notion that "a nation state is more vulnerable during the period of its development," and so, it becomes essential that "special attention be paid to questions of national security."[40]

In Iran, Stephanie Neuman found the Iranian elite of the 1970s believed that development could not be realized "without internal and external security." Here too, investments in defense were regarded as insurance premiums safeguarding the nation's "independence, wealth, and development."[41]

Despite their disagreements, these writers address the dual role of transport routes. For example, defense programs, according to Neuman, often foster "new communities in sparsely populated areas of the country. Roads, water supply, ports, housing, electricity and communications serve the military as well as the civilian sector." The spur roads built off the twenty-eight-mile highway between the newly developed Khatimi Air Force Base and Isfahan connected villages "that have existed in semi-isolation for hundreds of years."[42]

Research on questions of security and development, as Neuman correctly notes, suffers from a "unidimensional definition of military expenditures and economic development"; at present, she suggests, the "comparative case study method may be the only methodological option open."[43] I wish to build on Neuman's criticism, using a multi-disciplinary, nondeterministic approach to assess three geographically linked case studies from a political-geographical perspective.[44] Routes are an exemplary vehicle for such an undertaking. As ends, viewed as systems of access and nonaccess, they define internal relations between center and periphery, and external relations with other states. As means, they permit us to grasp the impact of security concerns on those of development and vice versa.

I employ two constants, one geographical, the other theoretical. The frontier lands of modern Pakistan lie at the heart of this story: they are a pivot between South, Central, and West Asia, lively actors in regional dramas, and the focus of pressure by great land powers (the Soviet Union and China) and the great sea power (the United States). And routes, the key concept in this work, are the single category of analysis across the region.

This work encompasses the lands that stretch from Iran and Baluchistan, from the mouth of the Persian Gulf and the shores of the Arabian Sea, to the peaks of the Hindu Kush, the Karakorams, and the Himalayas. These are the rimlands of the subcontinent, stretching from the Pakistan-Iranian frontier along the Afghan-Pakistani border to those northern parts of the subcontinent touched by China: the Northern Areas (in Pakistani parlance), Kashmir, the Aksai Chin, and (although I exclude them from detailed consideration), India's northeastern territories, Sikkim, Nepal, and Bhutan.[45]

All these lands experienced empire in the premodern era, specifically the imperial rivalry between Great Britain and Russia during the nineteenth century. The routing strategies of empire—their boundary-making, their geopolitical deliberations—have touched all these states, affecting their size, shape, nationalistic moods, and quarrels. Yesterday's routing controversies are the political and military dilemmas of today.

As the great empires of the past took a deep and abiding interest in the affairs of this region, so too do today's superpowers evince a keen

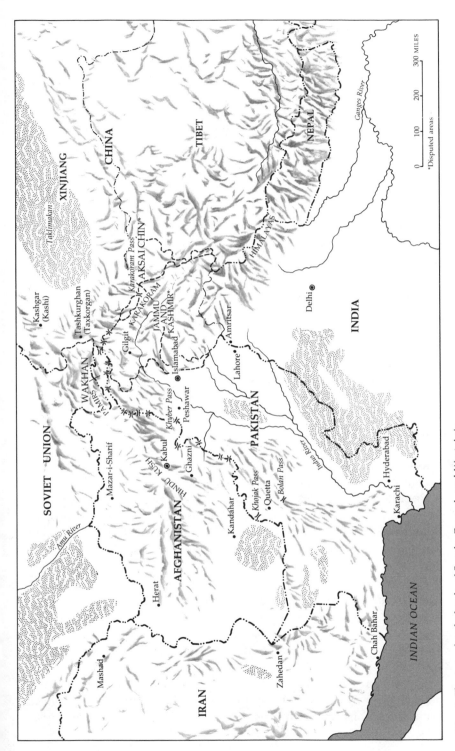

Map 1 The inner borderlands of South, Central, and West Asia

and pointed concern. The area where Central Asia, the subcontinent, and the lands of the Persian Gulf jostle together are of political-geographical interest to the Soviet Union, China, and the United States. The new and the old coexist. Two important regional actors, the Soviet Union and China, are international nuclear powers; India and Pakistan are inchoate nuclear states. Nevertheless, a conventional invasion was recently successful, and a guerrilla resistance continued in 1988.

All these states, large and small, face similar problems of security and of development. There are no advanced industrial democracies here. From China to Pakistan, the region's states have territorial-political quarrels with their neighbors; they all perceive their environment as highly threatening. Physical security and continuity within particular geographical configurations are live concerns. There are too few resources and technological skills and an abundance of human needs. All these states face the pressing requirement for defense and the vulnerability arising from low levels of development.

The three case studies of this book set out to explore somewhat varied aspects of routes and politics, security and development. I ask three questions of all three cases: What role have routes played in the historical and modern evolution of the region? Have factors of security dominated factors of development in the construction of major routes, or vice versa, and with what national, regional, or global effects? Can the politics of routes provide an X-ray of the geographical-political evolution of the region?

Although Pakistan is the hub of this tale, my story is not confined to a single state; it travels with the routes themselves, across South, Central, and West Asia. Each case begins with a profile of the premodern history of routes: this analysis suggests that traditional political-geographical constructs remain useful to chart the continuities and discontinuities in regional history.

The first case study examines Pakistan's western borderlands—Baluchistan and beyond, where South Asia and the lands of the Persian Gulf intersect. It explores relations and transactions between the Pakistani center and the Baluch periphery, focusing on internal and regime security, political integration, route development, and social change.

The second case study assesses the role of routes in Afghanistan's policies of security and development and in its political-geographical evolution. It also moves across Afghanistan's southern boundary to

Pakistan, where Central and South Asia blend. The issues of trade and foreign infrastructural aid are examined mainly in relation to the external security policies of the state.

The third case study discusses the routes that connect the heart of Chinese Central Asia—the cities of Xinjiang—and Tibet with the rimlands of the subcontinent. It examines the rationales, purposes, and achievements of a great regional power, China, in its dealings with the states of the Himalayas and the Karakorams. It discusses the relationship of route building to war, to alliances, and to regional political and strategic maneuvers, and the impact of these features on the economic development and integration of the borderlands.

The Region

The spatial setting of this book is the vast tracts of land—encompassing deserts, mountains, valleys, and rivers—which comprise the western, northwestern, and northern borderlands of the Indian subcontinent and the southern frontier lands of Central Asia. The relevance of routes is immediately apparent in this land mass. In its topography, commerce and war have tended historically to flow across the narrow breaches in the great antiroutes that mottle the region. A geographical overview of South, Central, and West Asia identifies the physical, economic, cultural, political, and military linkages between the borderlands. Land routes of ancient and modern vintage have perpetuated these ties in a region of great barriers and make it pointless to consider parts of the borderlands separately.

The Asian geopolitical system is composed, Alastair Lamb suggests, of three main zones: the Russian, the southern, and the Chinese.[46] It is in the borderlands of these three zones that this book is set. The roads I study belong mainly in Afghanistan, Baluchistan, and the North West Frontier Province of Pakistan, the modern Chinese provinces of Xinjiang and Tibet, Nepal, Bhutan, and the disputed Northern Areas, the Aksai Chin, and Kashmir.

The mountain ranges across these lands are the most formidable in the world. As an antiroute they have no peer. Yet the region has also witnessed, throughout its history, the insinuation of routes—channelers of movement—across these high barriers. Natural routes exist, awesome passes with treacherous defiles that offer some possibility for movement. Men have created a few great highways, too: the

ancient Silk Route (or rather routes) as well as the Karakoram Highway, a majestic feat of modern engineering across which com-
paratively little traffic moves.

These territories are dominated by deserts, a massive complex of
mountain ranges, and the basins and valleys of Asia's most magnificent rivers. The huge desert ring of arid, scorched lands that often
suck the rivers dry before they reach the sea begins in the east with
the Taklimakan Shamo in Xinjiang. Above it lies the Gobi, the Desert
of Stone. To the west, in Soviet Central Asia, lie the Kizil Kum or Red
Sands, which extend east and northward as far as the delta of the Syr
Darya. To the southwest are the Kara Kum or Black Sands, bounded
by the Aral Sea and the delta of the Amu Darya. Only the brief respite
of an oasis or two separates these sands from the deserts of the
Iranian plateau and of the Indian subcontinent.

This same plateau holds the arid, windswept deserts of Sistan in
present-day Iran, and Baluchistan, the westernmost province of
Pakistan. Across the fertile lower Indus Valley we approach the great
Indian desert of Rajasthan—the Thar Desert—running northeastward
from the Rann of Kutch for about four hundred miles. North of the
Thar Desert, beyond the Himalayas, we return to the Taklimakan
Desert of Xinjiang. The underbelly of this desert chain is the Indian
Ocean.

Studding the lands encircled by desert and extending beyond them
into Tibet, Nepal, and Bhutan are the mountains, the greatest being
the Himalayas, the center of the world and the throne of the gods in
Hindu poetry and myth. From east to west the mountains embrace
the subcontinent, fanning out across the country we know as
Afghanistan, breaking the monotony of the flat Iranian deserts, and
separating the high, cold lands of Central Asia from the subcontinent.
The Himalayas or "Abode of Snow" are the southern buttress of the
Tibetan Plateau; they run for fifteen hundred miles like an arched
shield across the north of India. Nestled between these mountains
and a lesser range, the Pir Panjal, is the Vale of Kashmir. Adjacent to
the Himalayas stand other clusters of high peaks, the Karakoram or
Black Gravel Range and the Pamirs. Protecting northern Kashmir and
Gilgit, the Karakoram range ranks among the world's most forebod-
ing terrain. Extending for about two hundred fifty miles, the range
boasts the greatest number of high peaks in the world—thirty-three at
over 24,000 feet, culminating in K-2 or Mount Godwin Austin (28,250
feet). Northwest of the Karakorams lie the great Pamirs, the "Roof of

the World." Radiating from the Pamirs to the north are the Tian Shan, or Heavenly Mountains, and the Hindu Kush range. The mountains of the Hindu Kush stretch for a distance of four hundred miles. Standing at altitudes of 12,000 to 19,000 feet, they form the main watershed between the Amu Darya and the Indus River. The face of the mountains is flecked with passes, and together, as barrier and route, they form the dominant motif in the Afghan landscape.

These mountains merge with the more arid western mountains. At the northern rim of the Iranian Plateau run the Kopet Dagh, which possess the characteristics of both desert and steppe. South of them is the Safed Koh Range, often snowcapped and averaging about 12,000 feet above sea level. And splicing the northeast Baluchistan Plateau are the Sulaiman Mountains, which continue north to south for three hundred miles. Among other mountain formations are the Bugti and Marri Hills, which squat southeast to northwest and bear the names of Baluch tribes. The Kirthar Hills form the western boundary of the lower Indus plain.

As if not content with possession of the world's most empty waste-lands and its most daring peaks, the region also boasts some of its mightiest rivers. Here flow the Syr Darya and the Amu Darya, which has its source in the Pamirs. The land of the Amu Darya, the vener-able Oxus, is the land of modern Afghanistan. To the south lies the valley of the Indus River, fertile and rich. This channel reputedly gave its name to the subcontinent—it was Sindu the Divider to the an-cients—and for centuries was considered the furthest known point on earth, the ultimate frontier. Like the other great rivers of Asia, the Indus rises in the Himalayas, high in the Tibetan Plateau. From these northernmost reaches it flows for five hundred miles in a north-westerly direction, turns southwestern at Leh, crosses the Ladakh range, and flows through the world's most daunting gorges. South-east of Gilgit, the Indus is joined by the first of its major tributaries and hurtles downward for a thousand miles toward the sea. The enormous drainage basin of the Indus system is the heartland of Pakistan.[47]

These stark topographical realities have shaped human interaction. Until European empires expanded into the Turkestan–Iran–North-west Indian subsystem—introducing political frontiers and bound-aries, cartographical and technological advances such as the arrival of rail power in India in 1853—lines of control between different peoples and states were hazily defined and ever-shifting. The international traffic of peoples and wares overland was greater, in relative terms, than in modern times. As the age of empire came to a close, boundaries were demarcated and then fell into dispute. The new states closed their borders. India and China went to war, Pakistan and India did the same (the former falling into a crisis with Afghanistan, too), China severed its ties with the Soviet Union, and this last state invaded Afghanistan in 1979–80. All these conflicts were linked to quarrels or concerns over frontier territories, lines of political control, territorial definition, and, of course, routes. The ancient geographical barriers were no longer necessary to constrict movement; political forces sufficed. Yet the modern era witnessed the creation of new routes that ran across untrodden terrain as well as the old imperial boundaries and gave rise to their own politics.

2

Baluchistan and Its Environs: The Motives for Access

What is now the Pakistani province of Baluchistan was long isolated, impoverished, internally fragmented, and strategically inconsequential. Yet the Baluch insurgency of 1973 threatened the national stability of Pakistan. (Already the Baluch had perplexed the Shah in neighboring Iran.) After the Soviet invasion of Afghanistan, this danger was compounded by new requirements for the province's external defense. Not only was there a rapid influx of about 700,000 refugees from Afghanistan—about 100,000 Baluch, the rest Pakhtuns—but Soviet forces had direct access to Pakistani territory.[1] By 1980 Baluchistan had become a strategic periphery.

Pakistani governments were not alone in taking a new approach to Baluchistan. From its bases in southern Afghanistan, the Soviet Union, which had once evinced a keen interest in access to Baluchistan, could now exert pressure on the province through the threat of cross-border attacks or the instigation of indigenous revolt. The Soviet entry into Kabul also reawakened U.S. interest in South Asia. Some U.S. circles came to perceive Pakistan's western borderlands as a likely stop on the Soviet Union's southerly line of march or as a potential area for fine harbors from which to help protect U.S. interests in the Persian Gulf. The Makran Coast of Baluchistan, abutting the Persian Gulf, spans nearly five hundred miles of the shores of the Arabian Sea. The port of Gwadar, in particular, began to loom large in the perceptions of local and foreign statesmen.

The Baluch themselves live in the territories of northeastern Iran, around Herat in Afghanistan, near Mari (Merv) in Soviet Turkmenistan, and, of course, in Pakistan.[2] From the Pakistani province of Baluchistan they have spread into the neighboring provinces of Sind, the North West Frontier Province (NWFP), and the Punjab. The Baluch have also settled in Oman, Iraq, Jordan, Syria, and Saudi Arabia. The Middle Eastern oil boom lured many Baluch, especially from the Makran Coast (which has historical ties to the Gulf), to settle in the Arab Gulf states; others have gone as far as East Africa. Estimates of their population vary, but a 1984 study placed 3.7 million Baluch— about 70 percent of the entire Baluch population—in Pakistan.[3]

The province of Baluchistan, incorporated in 1970, is Pakistan's largest, with an area of about 134,000 square miles. It is also Pakistan's most thinly populated province and, demographically, its most complex. Roughly three million people live there, including the Brahui tribes, Jats, Gujars, Tajiks, Turkomen, Hazaras, Jamotes, Makranis, and Pakhtuns. The main Pakhtun tribes, concentrated in the northern parts of Baluchistan, are the Kakars, Tarins, Panris, and Achakzais. The isolation and extreme poverty of the province have contributed to a migration out: more than half of the Baluch live in the provinces of Sind and Punjab. Baluchistan's considerable resources include gas, coal, and oil, which was first discovered in 1873.

The most durable single force in Baluchistan's history has been its desolate and uncompromising terrain and its consequent inaccessibility. Baluchistan's geography has largely circumscribed its political history. Natural barriers, or antiroutes, have conditioned the political, military, and economic strategies attempted in Baluch lands by successive overlords. The politics of Baluch routes have mirrored the major events in the evolution of the region. Baluchistan's history can be captured by its arterial history.

Baluchistan encompasses the eastern part of the Iranian Plateau. Its coastline runs along the edge of the Persian Gulf and along the land routes linking the Middle East, Central Asia, and the subcontinent. "There is little or no natural difference," as the geographer Oscar Spate has put it, "between the desert basins of northwest Baluchistan and of Sistan, or between Iranian and Baluchi Makran; and for the

Map 2 The Province of Baluchistan and its environs. The insert is based on a map in Joseph E. Schwartzberg, ed., *A Historical Atlas of South Asia* (Chicago: University of Chicago Press, 1978).

most part the frontier peoples straddle the actual boundary."[4] Since ancient times, traders passing from Persia to India have traversed Baluch lands. In many aspects, Baluchistan's early history parallels its contemporary circumstances. Before the coming of modern European imperial powers, Baluchistan was a farther geographical and political periphery of empires to its east, west, and north. Its location prevented the exercise of effective control from without, and the area's physical environment retarded effective integration within. Today it remains on the periphery of modern states—Iran and Pakistan. And even now, it is only slowly being brought into the mainstream of national socioeconomic and political life.

For centuries the harshness of the dusty red Baluch lands has aborted the schemes of men, both native and foreign. The topography—mountains, hills, vast expanses of desert and saline marshes—has contributed to the scattering of population, to the low level of tribal integration, and to the prevention of successful conquest or control by invading forces. The debilitating heat of Baluchistan's cities led one Englishman to exclaim: "O God, when thou hadst created Sibi and Dadhar, what object was there in conceiving hell?" The land is mostly sand, black pebbles, and rock. The dry hills, dark mountains, dusty deserts, murky swamps, sun-cracked basins, and jagged coastline with its "hammerhead peninsulas" conspire to create a sense of geographical separateness and hostility, which has cramped political, economic, and social processes.[5] Only three places are conducive to large human settlements: the city of Quetta stands in one, the depression of Sibi between the Sulaiman and the Kirthar ranges is another, and the Kalat Basin, to the west of the Kirthar Range, is a third.

Nature is hard in Baluchistan. There is little rainfall and much geological uncertainty. Earthquakes are frequent: as recently as 1935, an earthquake killed more than twenty thousand people and destroyed Quetta. In the long summer months the hot simoon and the *bad-e-sad-o-bist-roz* (wind of one-hundred-twenty days), which storms through the zone between Iran's Elburz mountains and the central peaks of Afghanistan, wield a destructive force across the land. The northwesterly *gorich* wind, hot in the summer and cruelly cold in the winter, sweeps constantly across western Baluchistan. The winter winds have been described as like a "keen-edged blade, to the dividing asunder of bones and marrow."[6]

The Baluch themselves have a close relationship with their hard milieu. One Baluch bard describes the intimacy thus: "Mountains were forts of the Baluch, high peaks their comrades, hills their army, trackless furrows their friends, spring water their drink, leaves of the dwarf-palm their cup, thorny bushes their bed, and stony ground their pillow."[7]

Baluchistan has been ruled by Afghan, Arab, Persian, and Mughal. Egyptians and Greeks have traversed these parts; Sikh and Sindhi have overrun these frontiers. Since antiquity, Baluchistan has commanded many of the high roads from Arab, Persian, and Turkic lands to the subcontinent. Although commercial contacts flourished periodically, however, Baluchistan's inhospitable topography bode ill logistically and militarily for any entering force. The land's most famous victim was perhaps Alexander the Great. His armies are said to have passed through Las Bela and Makran and journeyed across the Mula Pass. Alexander lost nearly three-quarters of his force while trying to leave India through Baluch territory.[8]

Between the eighth and the tenth centuries the Arabs ruled the coastal areas but had no effective control over the rest of Baluchistan. They raised Baluchistan to the status of a major trade route: the Makran coastal region became a "great commercial highway" and remained, after their departure, a center of trade between the Persian Gulf and India.[9] The Arab invasion of Baluchistan and Sind, however, was limited. They were unable to extend their conquests further into the subcontinent. Not until the arrival of Mahmud of Ghazni, through the passes of the North West Frontier, would Muslim rule be established over the farther Indian plains.

With the decline of Arab rule, Baluch lands changed hands often, reflecting the ebb and flow of neighboring empires. From 1594 onward, Baluchistan was an official possession of the Mughal Empire, although its rulers were never able to exercise real control from Delhi. As the core of the Mughal Empire began to rot in the eighteenth century, Baluchistan slipped from their grasp. Afghan, Persian, then British sovereignty followed. Despite the intrusions of so many peoples—intrusions aimed usually at guarding lines of communication—few invaders stayed long or displayed much interest in the region.

As the Makran Coast of Baluchistan has been drawn toward Persia and the Gulf, so the northern parts of Baluchistan have experienced the tug of the lands and the people to the north. The location and direction of natural routes played no small role in forging these bonds. The passes of northern Baluchistan permitted Central Asian peoples to reach Baluch soil. From the fourteenth century onward,

Baluchistan's history was closely linked with the movement of peoples from southern Afghanistan.

Baluchistan may be entered from the north through a host of mountain routes, including the Bolan, Khojak, Gomal, Tochi, and Mula passes. The sixty-mile-long Bolan Pass is to Baluch history what the Khyber Pass is to that of the North West Frontier. Across it have come Central Asian conquerors and much of the region's trade. Fear of invasion through the Bolan Pass shaped British strategic policy in Baluchistan in the nineteenth century. Seasonal migrants from the north entered across the pass, journeying through Baluchistan to find work in the Indian plains. One group of migrant tribes stayed to make this land their own and to endow it with their name: the Baluch.

Who the Baluch are, and where they came from, are questions shrouded in myth and speculation, although Baluch and non-Baluch writers have constructed elaborate genealogies. Some scholars point to Iran as their original home; others, to the Arab lands; and Baluch traditions and poetry claim Aleppo, in Syria, as the starting point of their eastward migration.[10]

Baluchistan's environment placed natural obstacles in the path of Baluch tribal organization. No single group of tribes rose to exercise full political and administrative control over any substantial part of the country. Their history is inflected, rather, with factionalism, fragmentation, and war. Brian Spooner, an anthropologist (for decades the only kind of scholar working on Baluchistan), has suggested a compelling explanation for the eternal political and military fragmentation of the country: the "marginal" location of Baluch lands. The topographical constraints, the inadequacy of arable or pasture lands, and the dispersion of the nomads, especially in the face of remarkable transportation and communication difficulties, promoted Baluch divisiveness. The few tribal confederations that did rise were crushed by others—with one brief exception. Under Nasir Khan (1741–1805), whose rule has been lauded as the "Augustan Age of the Khanate," roads, caravansaries, and mosques were built, and a measure of centralized administration fostered. Nasir Khan, however, was never wholly sovereign. At various times he acknowledged Nadir Shah of Persia and Ahmad Shah Durrani of Afghanistan as his overlords.[11]

Baluchistan's internal trade also was insignificant. What trade there was came across the passes on its way to or from Persia, India, and Central Asia. Under British rule, the fishing villages of Gwadar and Pasni on the Baluchistan coast were the centers of a small maritime trade with the rest of their Indian possessions. Both villages also possessed postal and telegraph offices, and every two weeks ships belonging to the British India Steam Navigation Company would call with the mails.[12]

In Baluchistan, then, geography has toyed with history. Peripheral location and physical environment hindered local dominance and the embrace of proximate empires. Indigenous tribal federations rose and fell like a metronome keeping the time of local history. Neither Persian nor Afghan nor Mughal bound Baluchistan, either politically or economically, to them. Baluchistan did not excite much interest in neighboring empires: it was strategically unimportant. A financial link—tribute—was enough.

The Great Game in Baluchistan and Its Environs

In the late nineteenth century the British Empire, advancing westward across India, became Baluchistan's first true imperial possessor. During these years the British and the Russians were at serious play in their Great Game of routes. As a result, the British assumed ever-expanding interests along India's frontiers.

Baluchistan was important in the mental maps of India's rulers because it became the last western frontier of British India, bordering upon sites of pressing danger—Afghanistan and Russian Central Asia, Persia and the Persian Gulf region.[13] These were the lands contested in the Great Game. British policy consisted largely of preventing other powers, especially Russia, from gaining access to India. It was a policy embodied in the building or the denial of routes.

The British emphasized the antiroute—denying access, sketching buffer zones, drawing boundaries that raised the costs of free movement. Inside Baluchistan a circumscribed policy of route-building—to support the demands of imperial frontier defense—was adopted. The British guarded control of all the sea routes and devised stratagems to defend all possible land avenues of advance toward India. The historical and geographical connections of Baluchistan with southern Persia, the Persian Gulf region, and Afghanistan were not lost on them. Until the late eighteenth century the Persian Gulf lands had sparked little debate or imperial interference in local trade, feuds, and piracy. During the nineteenth century, however, the colonial powers—Britain, Russia, Germany, and France—maneuvering a careful balance between European and Eastern politics, all participated in the race (real or perceived) to capture, or to deny to others, the routes to India.

By the late 1800s Lord Curzon was announcing that India, without which "the British Empire could not exist," was threatened. The British were disturbed by Russia's advance across Central Asia toward Afghanistan and growing Russian influence at the Persian court in Tehran. For them, one of the most troublesome aspects of Russia's political and commercial efforts in Persia was the establishment of exclusive—and unexploited—railroad concessions. From the 1870s onward, numerous proposals to build roads and railroads in Persia were put forward by traders and businessmen, civilian and military engineers, the governments of Russia, Britain, Germany, and others. As elsewhere in the Great Game, so in Persia the Russian perceptions of British intentions and plans showed a marked similarity to British perceptions of those of their opponent. Imperial rivalry between Britain and Russia resulted in the absence of a major railroad in Persia in the late nineteenth and early twentieth centuries. The two powers collaborated, however, to ensure that no third party gained transport rights in Persia.[14]

Russian policy in Persia vacillated between encouraging its concessionaries to seek the favor of the Shah and opposing the construction of routes altogether. Its merchants and traders were eager to exploit Iranian and even Indian markets, but the terrain was so perilous, and the transport so rudimentary (only camels or donkeys could cross the mountains), that the high risks and high transit costs doubled or tripled the price of Russian merchandise.[15] The demands of trade provided the impetus to improve access, but political and military priorities intervened to dampen commercial enthusiasm.

The Russian government suspected the British of trying to gain railroad concessions from Naser ed-Din Shah (1848–1896) and of expanding their commercial and political influence into north Persia. In 1890 the director of the Asiatic Department of the Russian Ministry of Foreign Affairs argued that "the main concern of Russia . . . should be to prevent the British from constructing railways anywhere in Persia." The head of the Russian Foreign Ministry asked "by what means could Russia continue to prevent the British from building railroads in Persia?" In 1889 the Shah was forced to promise Russia the exclusive right to all railroad concessions for the next five years. The Shah was later asked to extend the moratorium on railroad construction by other powers until 1900, 1910, and once more until 1917.

Meanwhile the Russians would create, review, and then abandon their own plans for railroads in north Persia. (They did complete a road from Qazvin to the Bay of Anzali in October 1899.) The Russian military thought it best to "keep Persia completely without railroads"; if this became impossible for political reasons, they suggested the most useful route would run from Tehran to the Caucasus.[16]

A concession obtained by the British to begin a railroad from Mohammareh on the Karun River to Khorramabad, and northward to Jolfa, aroused Russia's anger. The memorandum received by the British ambassador at St. Petersburg read in part: "The proposed railroad is situated in the neutral zone, and according to Article 3 of the Convention of 1907, we cannot deny England the right to demand such a concession for herself. The terminal of this line is, however, situated in closest proximity to our zone of influence; the line would be injurious to our economic interests and would, therefore, be very unfavourably received by public opinion." Persian economic development interests were given short shrift, of course. Barring the few rail miles built by Britain from Zahedan to the border of its Baluch possessions, and a short military line built by Russia from its border to Tabriz, Persia saw no railroads until the construction of the Trans-Iranian railroad under Reza Shah Pahlavi in 1938.[17]

Britain's concerns, which mirrored Russia's, were well expressed by Lord Curzon. He viewed Russia's insistence on exclusive railroad concessions in Persia as the "obvious and necessary means" of advance by a state "hampered in warfare by being mainly a land power, [which] has long been on the search for a new seaboard, and has directed covetous eyes upon the Persian Gulf." Russian incursions into Sistan, the British thought, could "revolutionize at once the conditions" upon which the "whole system of Indian defence has been built up." Curzon called Sistan a terra media "through which any power desirous of moving southwards from Meshed, particularly any power that is covetous of an outlet upon the Indian Ocean, must pass." Not only would possession of Sistan place the Russians at the doorway of Baluchistan, it would also provide the shortest possible rail route linking the Transcaspian Railroad with the Indian Ocean and would present fewer difficulties for the Russians than the alternative Afghan route.[18]

Curzon suggested a British railroad to meet the Russian threat and uphold British economic dominance in southeastern Persia: "Of all the possible suggestions for countering Russian menace to India by pacific and honourable means, the construction of such a railway is at once the least aggressive, the cheapest, and the most profitable." The railroad would enhance British commercial and political influence in southeastern Persia and provide a new defensive flank next to Afghan territory. "The railways into South Persia that Russia aspires to lay in the future" said Curzon, "should be laid beforehand by Great Britain." Given Sistan's contiguity to Baluchistan, the opening up of the area by railroad was viewed as being of the utmost importance. Curzon suggested that the existing British railway to and beyond Quetta could supply the starting point of a railroad into Sistan, and he outlined its strategic benefits: it would deter Russian operations against Herat in western Afghanistan and "checkmate the flank movement" against Baluchistan. This rail line, he thought, might even be linked by a southerly branch to Gwadar on the Makran Coast of Baluchistan or to Bandar Abbas on the Persian Gulf. When the British began construction on the Nushki-Sistan railroad, the Russian press and Russian officials voiced loud objections.[19]

The two powers continued to thrust and parry into the twentieth century. Routes and antiroutes were at the forefront of the Great Game. In the late 1800s the British settled on the approximately 497-mile-long Goldsmid Line as the boundary between Persia and the British Empire in India, which turned the Baluchis into subjects of different states and left over a quarter of Baluch territory within Persia. The boundary was never properly demarcated, however, nor was it particularly effective. In time, Curzon would come to argue that, as Afghanistan's mountainous terrain was being transformed into a buffer, so too Persian lands should become an antiroute. This notion was enshrined in the Anglo-Russian accord of 1907: Persia was divided into spheres of influence, with the northern segment reserved for Russia and the southern for Britain. This partition systematically foreclosed threats ensuing from the manipulation of access in Persia.

Apart from establishing spheres of influence in southern Persia and in Afghanistan, the British acquired, held, and protected many territories in order to ensure the security of the land and sea routes leading to and from their empire in India. They took Cape Colony from the Dutch and set up naval bases at Gibraltar, Malta, and Cyprus. When they could not prevent construction of the Suez Canal, they acquired it, and Egypt and Sudan too. They established control over Somaliland and Aden and cultivated good relations with the

Arab states of the Middle East and Persian Gulf. British policy makers responsible for western India were, however, particularly wary about route developments toward the Persian Gulf coast. India's defense depended on "undivided control of the territories and waters of the Gulf." This concern has been called the "mainspring of British policy" there.[20]

Route developments across West Asia became a cause of controversy, debate, and diplomatic negotiation between the four leading European imperial states. Access by any foreign power to the Persian Gulf shores by land or by sea route, for commercial or military purposes, was discouraged by British leaders in India and in England. Despite the attraction of lucrative opportunities for commerce, such proposals for access were eventually always denied.[21] British scepticism was nicely evident in the confusing entanglements over the Berlin-Baghdad railway, the Baghdadbahn, which became the object of tense diplomacy before World War I.

At the time, Germany's *Drang nach Osten* was the present and considerable danger. With a concession from the Ottomans in Turkey, the Germans intended the Berlin-Baghdad railroad to revive the "central route" of medieval trade, the land routes used before the Portuguese dragged commerce out to sea. The first public notices of the proposed railroad emerged in Constantinople (Istanbul) in 1899. A twenty-five-hundred-mile, transcontinental line, it would run from Constantinople on the Bosphorus to Basra on the Shatt al-Arab. The Berlin-Baghdad Railroad would, in Edward Mead Earle's words, "open to twentieth-century steel trains a fifteenth-century caravan route. It was to replace the camel with the locomotive."[22]

The plentiful strategic opportunities for German use of the line in the event of a war with Britain were outlined by one German publicist, Paul Rohrbach: "If it comes to war with England, it will be for Germany simply a question of life and death. . . . England can be attacked and mortally wounded by land from Europe in only one place—Egypt. The loss of Egypt would mean . . . the end of her dominion over the Suez Canal and of her communications with India and the Far East. . . . We can never dream, however, of attacking Egypt until Turkey is mistress of a developed railway system in Asia Minor and Syria."[23]

Russia and Britain both had difficulties with the German railroad. The Russian military establishment declared that it was impossible to reconcile the Baghdad Railroad "with Russia's strategic interests," especially in Persia. The British insisted that Germany recognize their special interests in the Persian Gulf and refrain from seeking a terminus for the railroad there. Lord Curzon was a zealous opponent of the German route. Upon hearing about the proposed railroad, Curzon had, in his inimitable style, promptly undertaken the "protection" of Kuwait and awarded it a British resident adviser, so that when a German mission visited Kuwait in 1900 to discuss a rail terminus and port facilities, they found an amir who refused to talk.[24]

Although the economic benefits of the Berlin-Baghdad railroad for the British Empire were evident, political and strategic considerations, principally the security of routes proximate to western India, were more important than commercial benefits. "Control of the Persian Gulf, an outpost of Indian defence, became" according to Earle, "the keynote of British resistance to the Bagdad Railway." In the 1914 agreement that was finally reached to permit construction of the railroad, the Germans had to agree that the line beyond Basra could not be built without British permission and abandoned their hopes of acquiring a port on the Persian Gulf.[25] Such contests for the control of West and Central Asian routes lay at the hub of the politics, diplomacy, and strategy of European Empires.

Awareness of the geopolitical connections between Persia, the Gulf, and Baluchistan remained a cornerstone of British policy through the mid-twentieth century. Sir Olaf Caroe, one of the last British guardians of India's frontier, argued for these old links in his influential book *Wells of Power* (1951). The Persian Gulf and the Gulf of Oman were a single sea channel, he argued; the "political assessor must reckon them as one right down to Karachi." The new state of Pakistan, he said, "with its seaport and airport at Karachi and its long coastline of Baluchistan, stands at the mouth of the larger Gulf, and is vital to the reckoning." Baluchistan was "an empty porch to the Pakistan mansion, but porches, "though empty, must be held by the owner of the house."[26] The Soviet invasion of Afghanistan in the late twentieth century would reassert these regional linkages on the mental maps of local and foreign policy makers. And as it had earlier, the geopolitical competition between outside powers would generate a new game of routes in the region.

Baluchistan under British Rule

The British became involved in Baluchistan as a result of an eternal quandary of land empire: Where should the final frontier be drawn?

This search for the perfect antiroute in India's western and north-western reaches brought Britain to Baluchistan. British soldiers moved across Baluchistan during the First Afghan War in 1839 and occupied parts of the country until 1842 in order to protect land lines of communications and logistics routes. This war, with the Second Afghan War of 1878–1880, brought home the need to control not only the North West Frontier but also the Baluch areas if the British were to keep the tribes at bay and adequately deter threats from the north.

Inside Baluchistan, British administrative policy aimed at securing their new Indian frontier, but little more. Routes were developed for the narrowly defined purpose of securing British military transport and communications. A physical infrastructure was built—roads, rail-roads, military cantonments (and pleasant retreats, such as Ziarat, for British officers)—to support the exigencies of imperial frontier defense. Military need was paramount; the blandishments of development, of which there were some, were incidental. In effect, the British form of governance and defense in Baluchistan sustained territorial control without integrating the land either politically or economically with the rest of the empire. In this the British progressed only a step further than previous empires.

Baluch lands were incorporated under three different styles of administrative control, each with a set of infrastructure programs (or the absence of such programs). A small strip of northern territory situated alongside Afghanistan—about 9,476 square miles—became British Baluchistan. It was administered directly, and its physical infrastructure was relatively highly developed. It was created out of the annexed city of Quetta and its environs in 1876; Pishin and Sibi, ceded by the Afghans in the Treaty of Gandamak of 1879, and the Zhob Valley, taken in 1891. About 78,034 square miles were left under the nominal control of the khanates of Kalat, Las Bela, Kharan, and Makran. And about 44,345 square miles were called Agency Territories. These areas were occasionally acquired and controlled by British officers. They were administered under the rubric of the Sandeman system, in which central points in Kalat and the tribal areas were occupied in force and linked by fair roads, while local sardars were authorized to govern matters internal to the tribes. These areas were also the least developed.[27] In Baluchistan, the British followed a policy of creeping annexation of territory and gradual control of the tribes. The area was not pacified until the last decade of the nineteenth century.

Economic progress in Baluchistan was a side-effect of British mili-

tary building. The Sandeman system of political dominion emphasized a policy of divide-and-rule. Thus it reinforced the land's
historical fragmentation and its schism-ridden tribal organizations.
According to Olaf Caroe, Baluchistan seventy years after Sandeman
was "scarcely distinguishable" from its earlier state because of the
"static" nature of this British system. Unlike in British ventures in the
Punjab or Bengal, little economic gain accrued to the British from this
remote periphery. No income taxes were imposed, and the taxes
levied were low compared to those in other parts of India. In Baluchistan the British actually found themselves out of pocket. Population centers developed in areas that hosted a garrison or stood along
an important British military communications route. No major ports
were developed or used as export facilities. Even the water supplies at
Quetta, Sibi, and Loralai were conceived from military need. Subsidies were paid to the sardars, who also received special privileges,
pensions, and grants. No expenditures were made to improve the lot
of the tribesmen themselves: illiteracy remained prevalent, and the
Baluch had few contacts with the rest of India.[28]

Within British Baluchistan lay the Bolan Pass and Quetta and,
eventually, nearly all the important works built by the British. To
guard the routes from Herat and Kandahar, the British constructed
fortified cities at Quetta, Fort Sandeman, Mach, and elsewhere, as
well as a sturdy but limited infrastructure of access. The British
viewed the Bolan Pass as one of the two gates of India. (The Khyber
was the other.) It was to protect this route that Quetta, today the
provincial capital of Baluchistan, was built. The imperial strategist Sir
Thomas Holdich observed that "all roads south of Herat lead to
Quetta." During the debates around the time of the Second Afghan
War about the imperial frontier in the borderlands, discussion had
centered on the location of the "scientific frontier"—the Kabul-
Ghazni-Kandahar line. Questions had arisen about how many routes
across the mountain ranges could be kept open and defended by the
limited British forces in India. Some held that if Kandahar, inside
Afghanistan, was not retained by the British, it could be used as a
launching-pad for an invasion of India through the Bolan Pass.[29]
When Kandahar was not taken, the importance of securing the Bolan
route gained currency with British strategists, who argued for the
garrisoning of Quetta. From Quetta, the British would be able to
threaten the flank of any foreign army attempting to enter India. No
action was taken until 1876, however, because Baluchistan was largely

uncharted. In that year, as the Russians moved across Central Asia and as Anglo-Afghan relations showed a marked deterioration, Quetta was finally occupied. By 1877, British troops were stationed there.

The predominance of Quetta in British strategy was entirely a function of its location. At 5,500 feet above sea level, the city is rimmed by a circle of dark, desolate hills. It lies between the Bolan Pass and the Khojak Pass (50 miles northwest of Quetta.) Both portals have attracted the attention of many an invader. Quetta also commands all the southern approaches to the valley of the Indus. Here the British made an extensive military investment, developing large tracts of land to house 25,000 troops. A service industry grew to meet the needs of the frontiersmen. John Jacob of Sind made Quetta the cornerstone of frontier policy; and for the British, Quetta became "one of the great strategical positions in the world."[30] Quetta was made the hub of road and rail networks in Baluchistan. Located in the northern reaches of the territory, it was transformed into an artificial center. From Quetta roads began to radiate in many directions. Often, points not linked with each other were connected to the city. The southern portion of Britain's army in India was posted with reference to Quetta along the Bolan way and distributed through the Bombay and Madras presidencies. From Karachi reinforcements could then be easily deployed from sea, creating a rapidly mobile force along the frontier.

Control of Baluchistan's routes and passes served a further purpose: the security of commerce. The Bolan route was a leading artery of trade between Central Asia and the subcontinent. The tribes, who made their livelihood by raiding, were the bane of British administrators. Yet it was only after the Second Afghan War, which made the Bolan route critical for military logistics, that the British took control of the access route with the paid-for support of local sardars. The Gomal Pass, another well-traveled route close to the Bolan Pass, also became a British concern when tribal raids blocked trade there. As Quetta had been erected in defense of the Bolan Pass, so the British built Fort Sandeman to safeguard the Gomal Pass. The protection of these few access routes governed British policy toward Baluchistan. The areas around the passes were garrisoned, fortified, and developed. Cities were raised, and a route network was put in place.

The Second Afghan War was the catalyst for these British activities. Militarily, the war had been a tough lesson in the hazards of logistics. Because the British lacked good rail lines, they virtually exhausted the

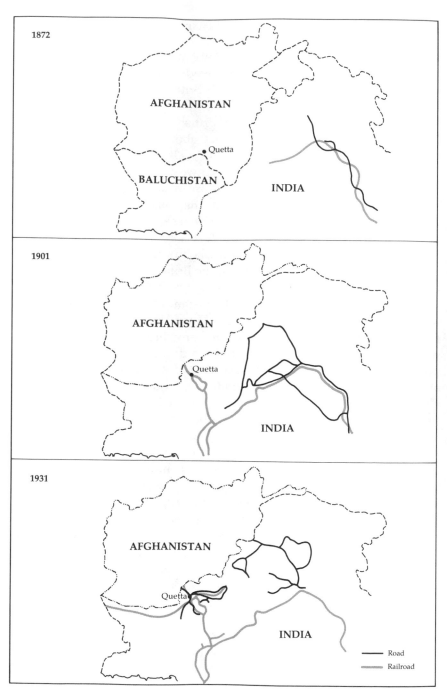

Map 3 British route construction in Baluchistan. Based on road and rail maps in Joseph E. Schwartzberg, ed., *A Historical Atlas of South Asia* (Chicago: University of Chicago Press, 1978).

supply of camels in Sind and the Punjab in order to transport troops and supplies. Sir Robert Sandeman alone gathered twenty thousand camels to work in relays the long stretch of road to Kandahar. Thirty to forty thousand camels perished as a result of overwork, costing the British government about £200,000.[31]

This Afghan misadventure taught the British never again to let logistics decide the outcome of a war. They began to build a road and railway network in and around the Bolan route. The Sind-Pishin Railway was a child of the Afghan War. Begun in 1879, it ran 312 miles from Jhatpat across the Harnai Valley to Chaman, by the Khojak Pass; a branch line connected Bostan and Quetta. The railway was completed in 1892. After 1885 the Bolan road was metaled and bridged. In 1889 the road was completed to Quetta; in 1893, to Chaman. The British, in sum, expended great thought, effort, and expense in building a routing infrastructure. Despite the obstacles of Baluch terrain, British perseverance—and many thousands of Indian lives—paid off; on 27 March 1887, for example, the train ran successfully on the line from Sibi to Quetta. In 1905 the ninety-mile line from Quetta to Nushki was opened, much to the chagrin of the Russians. It would later be extended to Nokundi near the Anglo-Persian border.[32]

The 1908 British Imperial Gazetteer for Baluchistan records that "all the railways and the best of the roads have had their origin in strategical needs." Noting a "continual increase" of roads linking "remote parts with the railways and the Punjab" since the beginning of the British occupation, the gazetteer states, however, that the "principal extension has taken place in the north-east corner of the Province. In the south and the west no cart-roads exist, and many of the routes are barely practicable even for camels." British routes were built "primarily to facilitate the movement of troops in times of emergency." The government of independent Pakistan later noted that other transport and communications requirements needed for socioeconomic development had been "totally ignored." In fact, among the important roads the British bequeathed to Pakistan at independence, only two were in Baluchistan, and both came from Quetta. The first was to Kalat, the second to Sukkur.[33]

What the British achieved in Baluchistan was only a small advance on the accomplishments of preceding empires. By constructing road and rail and an efficient system of political subordination, the British integrated Baluchistan territorially into their Indian Empire and exercised effective control over strategically necessary areas. They did nothing purposeful, however, to alter existing patterns of local economic or political activity. If anything, they reinforced traditional patterns of feudal overlordship and divisiveness among the tribes.

The British interest in Baluchistan had little to do with economics. Any economic benefits were unintended spin-offs of strategic policy for the frontier. Existing access routes were defended through new construction; forts, military towns, roads, and railroads were hastily constructed to ease the rapid deployment of military personnel. The British concern with Baluchistan's location and with the defense of the entrances to western India created a pattern of routes that skewed the map, ignoring western and southern Baluchistan as oases of progress sprouted in the frontier zone to the north. Baluchistan would remain a periphery, undeveloped, isolated, and increasingly discontented. Not until this periphery posed a political and strategic threat to the new Pakistani center would it rise to prominence in the minds of policy makers at home and abroad. Only then would the map of Baluchistan, and its politics, begin to change.

Territorial Integration and Governmental Neglect, 1947–1971

In 1947 Baluchistan faded into relative strategic obscurity. The new Pakistani state, incomparably weaker than the British Empire, had not only to shoulder the security of the subcontinent's western and northwestern frontiers but also to face a historically unprecedented enemy to the east, the newly independent state of India. As Pakistan and India became the focus of each other's strategic anxieties, Baluchistan was no longer the most sensitive frontier.

To compound the hazards of regional insecurity was Pakistan's prodigious poverty. The new state had few funds and little ability to cultivate its resources. Still, the priorities of self-government differed from the priorities of empire: Pakistan was to become a nation-state, and it was to develop. For Pakistan to retain its free and independent status, territorial integration was a minimal requirement. Baluchistan mattered to the extent that the concept of the nation-state mattered, but in the early postpartition years the development of the region was slighted.

The economic and political development of peripheries, Brian Spooner argues, has always been "difficult except as the result of direct interest from an external power . . . Unless they are important for communications, mineral deposits, or other strategic considerations, such interest is not exerted. The investment required to achieve or maintain political control is not justified."[34] Spooner's historical point is buttressed by patterns of arterial development in Baluchistan during British rule and throughout the life of the Pakistani state.

Between 1947 and 1971 this area minimally endangered the security interests of the political center. A periphery insufficiently threatened from outside or from within is prone to underdevelopment, and such proved to be the case in Baluchistan. Its relative isolation and backwardness, as well as the old patterns of Baluch tribal life, were preserved. Accessibility remained low. Few developmental routes were built in south and west Baluchistan, and only an occasional road was cut to extract resources or to quell the minor revolts that broke out during the 1950s and 1960s. Baluchistan's impermeability would have important repercussions for government policy and for regional geopolitics during the 1970s and 1980s.

The legacy of empire had been Baluch territories more backward than the rest of the country but that also contained a vivid internal economic imbalance. As a military center under the Raj, Quetta and its environs had made economic progress. In the new Pakistan, governments preserved Quetta's importance as a national military center and as the province's political center, for the danger from the north had not quite receded. Today the Quetta-Pishin area (where Pakhtuns make up over 60 percent of the population) is one of the smallest and yet most advanced districts of Baluchistan. Manufacturing industry is located in Quetta, and the district is the most urban and most literate in the province. Districts such as Sibi, on the other hand, which house large Baluch tribes, have very low rates of urbanization and literacy.[35]

For twenty-four years, Baluchistan remained an isolated periphery whose relative strategic inconsequence had major repercussions on its development. The magnitude of the new eastern danger from India caused fears for the Baluch antiroute to fade. The principal threat, in the perception of Pakistani defense planners, no longer emerged from Pakistan's location next to Afghanistan and southern Iran. Concern focused, as Shirin Tahir-Kheli notes, on the "absence of defensive terrain, the lack of depth, and the 1,100 mile length of the border with India." Ninety percent of West Pakistan's population and infrastructure—its roads, railroads, industry, canals, and cities—lie close to the Indo-Pakistani border. According to one senior Pakistani military officer, "India's capture of twenty-five miles would wipe out Pakistan because our communication, irrigation, industry and population pattern are all together within that depth."[36] To a lesser extent, there was concern about Afghan intrusions in the North West Frontier and Baluchistan. Relations with Iran to the west, however, were good. On the mental maps of Pakistani leaders, Baluchistan (barring its northern tracts) was a backwater. Its few major routes languished in disrepair.

The central government's policies in the early postpartition years concentrated on the territorial integration of Baluchistan. After 1947 it moved to assert Pakistan's national identity by depriving the princely Baluch states of their independent status.[37] Kalat, Las Bela, and Makran acceded to Pakistan—after a struggle. In 1948 Prince Abdul Karim Khan, brother of the Khan of Kalat, led a revolt against the Pakistani government. It was crushed. Ten years later the now-deposed Khan led another revolt, but it too was subdued. Although the government had permitted the princely states a degree of autonomy in 1952 by grouping them in the Baluchistan States Union, in 1955 they were amalgamated into one political, administrative, and geographical unit—West Pakistan.

The One Unit Plan led to heightened political conflict and to sporadic fighting between the central government and the Baluch, which peaked in 1968. In 1970 the One Unit Plan was abandoned, and Baluchistan was accorded the status of a province. A central element of intercourse between center and periphery was the use of the army, time and again, to extinguish the fires of revolt. But the Pakistan Army could not properly resolve the conflict between the political center and the Baluch tribesmen, largely because of earlier policies of benign neglect. Baluchistan's untraveled tracts, its routelessness, allowed the guerrillas to avoid direct contact with army units.

The paucity of hard data makes it difficult to generalize about the economy of Baluchistan during this period. But Baluchistan was, and remains, Pakistan's least developed and most backward province. It was, and is, much less developed than the Punjab and Sind. Until recently the coal and natural gas produced in the province were used across Pakistan but played no consequential role in the economy of Baluchistan itself. The development program spurred by General Ayub Khan in the 1960s affected the main line of economic activity—Karachi-Lahore-Peshawar—and the rich green fields of the Punjab. According to a later government's report, "no significant development took place" in Baluchistan between 1955, when all Baluch territory was incorporated under a standard national administrative structure, and 1970—despite the fact that both the Second and the Third Five Year Plans had given it special mention. Under Zulfiqar Ali Bhutto, another government report on Baluchistan complained that "inadequate transportation" was "one of the main reasons for the underdevelopment of this region." The roads were few and in bad condition.[38]

Baluchistan's distance from the mainstream of national life was confirmed by and reflected in the approach of the Pakistani political center to the creation of access. One key to altering historical conditions in Baluchistan—a physical infrastructure that could unlock the land—was not used. Existing road projects lingered, and apart from some resource-related construction and the RCD Highway between Iran and Pakistan, few major road-building ventures were undertaken, especially in the coastal areas.[39] The hazards of terrain, domestic financial constraints, and the lack of an external threat combined to triumph over the creation of access.

In these years the Pakistan Army did build a few routes to ease movement into fractious parts of Baluchistan. One case of army road building is mentioned by a writer who twice visited the home of the Bugti sardars. Sylvia Matheson records that in March 1957 a rough road of sorts existed to Dera Bugti, though it was not much more than a camel track with some of the largest stones removed. The trip—forty-four miles long—took two-and-a-half to three hours. When she returned in 1965 a new, much shorter route had recently been built by the Pakistan Army. It cut travel time by one hour. The area around the new road had been occupied by the army, however, and virtually sealed off to civilian traffic.[40] Road building following independence, then, was sporadic, a variant on British themes. The few major routes that were built primarily addressed, and highlighted the importance of, internal security, regional association, and resource extraction.

As intermittent road building continued, the Baluch tribes pursued their longstanding opposition to construction. In 1967, for example, the Marris resisted—without success—the army's attempts to carve routes through their territory.[41] Similar situations prevailed in Baluchistan and in the North West Frontier Province (NWFP). Although there are salient differences in the tribal structures of Pakhtun and Baluch society, the Pakhtun being more democratic and individualist, the inhabitants of both peripheries resisted routes through their territories. Road building by the new state threatened the tribes even more than had that of imperial predecessors. The imperialists had sought to control tribal chiefs but not to alter tribal life. Baluch opposition flared often, and most dramatically, in violent tribal demonstrations against the roads that were the dominant symbol of the Pakistani state's attempt to extend its authority into the periphery.

Administration, too, was complicated by Baluchistan's inaccessibility, and it did not deviate from the norm established by the British. Until 1970, three administrative zones existed, exactly as the British had organized Baluchistan. A small part of the country had a normal civil administration and a police force. Another was divided into political units monitored by tribal levies; the third, which mainly consisted of vast, inaccessible tracts of land, was run by the sardars. Until the mid-1970s, the writ of the central government covered only 134 square miles, 0.1 percent of the land area of the province.[42]

Governmental neglect, combined with the anticenter proclivities of particular Baluch tribal leaders and Baluch student organizations, slowly radicalized Baluch sentiment. These groups advocated positions ranging from demands for provincial autonomy to the establishment of a new state, Greater Baluchistan. The first extant map of this future state was drawn up by Mir Abdul Aziz Khan Kurd in his capacity as first general secretary and founder of the Baluch movement known as the Organisation for the Unity of Baluchistan. The map was published in the weekly *Al-Baloch*, issued at Karachi on 20 August 1933.[43] This version of Greater Baluchistan incorporated Iranian Baluchistan, the province of Sind, and parts of the NWFP and the Punjab populated mainly by the Baluch, as well as all of British-controlled Baluchistan and the territories of the princely states. Claims for Free or Greater Baluchistan also spawned maps that included large portions of eastern Iran all the way up to the border with Soviet Turkmenistan. In 1973 the Pakistani government reported the capture of maps of "Liberated Baluchistan" which showed a state stretching from the Soviet border with northeastern Khorasan, in Iran, to the Persian Gulf.[44]

The Years of Reckoning, 1971–1977

After 1971 events changed the position Baluchistan occupied on the mental maps of Pakistani and regional officials. As Baluchistan became difficult to manage domestically and prominent strategically, its changing status encouraged development projects. New pressures favored what might be called security-propelled development and a high level of military and economic transactions between center and periphery. Progress in Baluchistan was spurred by a combination of events, interests, and personalities: the rash of internal and regional security concerns that emerged with the 1971 dismemberment of Pakistan, Zulfiqar Ali Bhutto's notions of his place in Pakistan and Pakistan's place in the region, and the newly acquired power and old fears of the Shah of Iran. To this potpourri of concerns were added Afghan and Soviet dabbling in the affairs of the Baluch.

When Bangladesh broke away from Pakistan in 1971, it added a political dimension to its existing physical separation from West Pakistan. Prior to secession, Pakistan had been, in political-geographical terms, a most unhappily constructed state. Its two land masses were separated not only by a distance of one thousand miles but by a thousand miles of Indian territory. The locations of East and West Pakistan also gave rise to different political-geographical perspectives. From Dhaka the states of Southeast Asia drifted naturally into view, whereas from Karachi it was the states of the Middle East which stood on the horizon.[45] Only India was visible from both cities. Without bonds of social, economic and political justice, or even proximity to tether the two wings of Pakistan together, ideology was not enough. Following the severance of the eastern territory Bhutto, Pakistan's new leader, proposed a revised geopolitical perspective that placed Pakistan along the Middle East-Gulf-subcontinent axis—the same axis of which the British had conceived. Baluchistan again became a frontier in focus. Bhutto said: "The severance of our eastern limb by force has significantly altered our geographic focus. This will naturally affect our geopolitical perspective. The geographical distance between us and the nations of Southeast Asia has grown. . . . [Our interest] is within the ambit of South and Western Asia. It is here that our primary concern must henceforth lie."[46]

Connections between the Pakistani province of Baluchistan and the Iranian province of Sistan va Baluchistan rose again to the fore. But Iran was no longer a wasting, weak Persian Empire. Instead, it was a strong, vigorous regional power. Reza Pahlavi, the Shah of Iran, played a dominant role between 1971 and 1977, both in his own Baluch lands and in those belonging to Pakistan. The Shah recognized and feared the historical links between his own coastline and

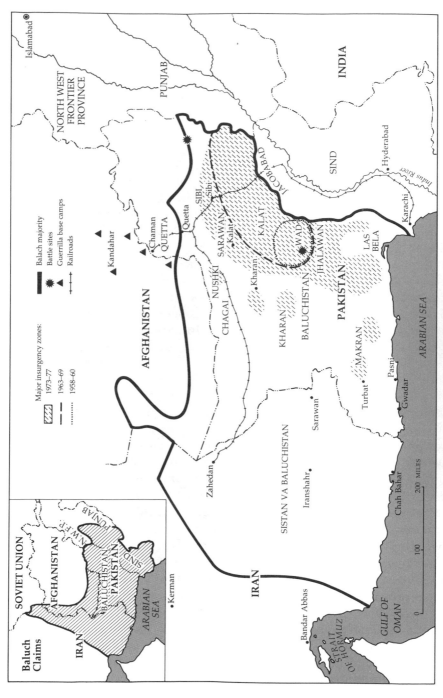

Map 4 Baluch lands and Baluch territorial claims. Adapted from maps in Selig Harrison, *In Afghanistan's Shadow: Baluch Nationalism and Soviet Temptations* (Washington, D.C.: Carnegie Endowment for International Peace, 1981).

the Makran Coast. The role routes played in his security-propelled development policies inside Iran presaged the role routes were to play inside Pakistani Baluchistan.

As Bhutto formulated an iron-fisted approach to the Baluch, looking westward for support of his policies, so the Shah was looking eastward. Conscious of his role as the "policeman of the Gulf," and dreaming of a regional market and a security sphere stretching from Iran to India, the Shah found Baluch lands assuming an unusual regional significance. His own Baluch population in Sistan va Baluchistan was restless, ignited by domestic grievances as well as by Iraqi propaganda.[47] A major military project, the naval complex at Chah Bahar, was also housed in this troubled province. By the early 1970s events here, as well as those in neighboring Baluchistan, took on pressing urgency. Together, Bhutto's and the Shah's concerns combined to produce a forceful suppression of the Baluch insurgency and a simultaneous move toward the socioeconomic development of Baluchistan. Part of this development took the form of investments in an infrastructure of access.

In Iran's Baluch territories fitful rebellions had broken out during the 1950s and 1960s. Opinions on how to deal with the roughly one million Baluch differed. In January 1977 Premier Amir Abbas Hoveyda asked: "There are not very many of them, are there? But they happen to live in a strategic part of the country. Should we let them use this accident of geography and history to provoke us into devoting resources to develop that wretched part of the country?" The Shah, however, heeded different words which suggested that economic progress could quiet the Baluch.[48] In the early 1970s he ordered the construction of a physical infrastructure in Sistan va Baluchistan. The security of a strategic periphery would be brought about through a specific development strategy.

During the 1970s, Iran's Baluch lands witnessed a rapid improvement of transport and communications facilities, as well as an increase in the number of troops stationed there. Route building in Sistan va Baluchistan, as Selig Harrison shows, left something to be desired in terms of social, political, and even economic advantages for the Baluch. Whereas millions of dollars were spent connecting Zahedan, the provincial capital, with the port of Chah Bahar on the coast, the rest of the province—dominated by desert, mountain, and scrub—did not receive comparable attention. For example, one road, the only link between Sarawan (which has a population of 90,000) and the nearest city, Khash, one hundred miles away, was left a dirt track. In fact, the new military road to Chah Bahar itself bypassed many important points of settlement. Military-related road building and port development, however, did have some economic spin-offs: wages of construction workers, for example, rose from 10 tumans per day ($1.50) before 1973 to 50 tumans per day ($7.50) in 1978.[49]

Once the British had become concerned about, and ultimately intervened in, a weak neighbor, southeastern Persia; now the Shah began to exert pressure in the reverse direction. He had blocked Soviet movement toward Iran, but Afghanistan and Pakistan were small, relatively weak independent states. As the Shah saw it, those ways now lay open. He saw the Pakistani province of Baluchistan as doubly threatened, by Soviet expansionism and by internal revolt. His sense that Iran's own security was threatened by transborder linkages with Pakistan induced his interference in Baluchistan's affairs. According to Bhutto, the Shah "felt strongly that letting the Baluch [in Pakistan] have provincial self-government was not only dangerous in itself, for Pakistan, but would give his Baluch dangerous ideas."[50] New freedoms could travel, fast and easily, across the border between Iranian and Pakistani Baluch lands.

In an interview given in April 1973, the Shah announced that any threat to the integrity of Pakistan would be met by a "protective reaction" from Iran. To another journalist the Shah posed this question: "If we don't assume the security of this region, who will do it?"[51] Iranians even speculated about taking responsibility for Baluchistan before any untoward incident occurred. Some influential Iranians toyed with the idea that Iran should coordinate with the Pakistanis a military arrangement whereby Iran would have control over the conduct of affairs in western Pakistan, in order to preempt fragmentation and a land grab by the Soviet Union.[52]

There was cooperation and a commonality of interest between the Shah and Bhutto during the Baluch insurgency that broke out in 1973.[53] The Shah gave Bhutto military assistance—men and equipment—and economic aid. Iranian Huey-Cobra helicopters and Iranian pilots were loaned to the Pakistan Army. Work on the RCD Highway was also stepped up. At the April 1974 meeting of CENTO, the recommendation was put forward that road links between Turkey, Iran, and Pakistan should be improved with special priority accorded to the construction of a new road from Chah Bahar to Zahedan and to improved links between Chah Bahar and the Makran coastal town of Turbat in Pakistan.[54]

Neither Pakistani nor Iranian leaders saw the Baluch problem as solely an internal crisis. The Soviets and the Afghans continued to manifest an interest in access to Baluchistan. The Afghans included Baluchistan in their proposed state of Pakhtunistan, which would provide them with economically vital access to the sea. Pakhtunistan was to be composed of lands from the NWFP and Baluchistan and, within the latter, of lands from Kalat, Makran, Las Bela, and Chagai.[55] Afghanistan also demonstrated its devotion to the cause of the Baluch by elevating Baluchi to the status of a national language even though it housed only a hundred thousand citizens of Baluch origin.

Since the time of Amir Abdur Rahman (1880–1901), who had admonished his sons to try to improve land-locked Afghanistan's economic opportunities by taking Baluchistan, Afghans of differing ideological stripes have either pursued Pakhtun claims or supported claims to a Baluch state. Speaking to a large gathering in August 1979, Hafizullah Amin, then president of Afghanistan, reasserted its ties to the Baluch coastline. "Our revolution is revered, and welcomed," he said, "from the Oxus to the Abasin, from the mountains of Pamir to the beaches of Gwadar in Pakistan." Another Afghan leader, Babrak Karmal, later said that his country "principledly advocates the right of the fraternal Pushtun and Baluchi peoples to express their free will, which should themselves take decisions on their future." In September 1985, he declared: "The unity of Pushtuns and Baluchis is also a guarantor of freedom, progress, unification and national maturity for the Pushtuns and Baluchis."[56] The Afghans' position on Pakhtunistan, however, has not endeared them to many Baluch who already resent Pakhtun domination of their northern territories. Although both Pakhtun and Baluch nationalists oppose the Pakistani center, their goals conflict, and their territorial ambitions are for two separate states, one Pakhtun and the other Baluch. The territorial claims of some proponents of the former engulf those of the latter.

The Soviet Union's interest in Baluchistan has endured although policies toward the Baluch have not always been consistent.[57] During Britain's sojourn in India the Russians evinced a keen desire to cultivate their influence in Persian and British Baluchistan. In 1920, a group of Baluch journeyed to the Baku Conference arranged by the Soviets in support of the cause of eastern nationalist movements.

According to a 1927 report by Mir Ahmad Yar Khan, then the crown prince of Kalat and an officer in the British Indian Army, the Baluch in Iran and Afghanistan, "influenced by the Russian propaganda from across the border, were leaving their homes and moving in small groups to the Marv and Ashkabad regions in Russia." During 1945–46, a report of the British consulate in Zahedan also asserted that the Russians were active, particularly in the dissemination of propaganda in the Baluch coastal area of Makran.[58]

Contemporary Soviet policy toward Baluchistan has been at best ambivalent. The Soviets do not appear to include Baluchistan within the boundaries of an Afghan-sponsored state of Pakhtunistan. Nor have they overtly supported Baluch independence movements. In fact, they condoned Bhutto's counterinsurgency. Still, they have never disavowed an independent Baluchistan, for such a weak state with magnificent harbors on the Arabian Sea would offer the Soviet Union great advantages.[59]

Pakistan's location is strategically alluring to any global power with interests in Central, South, and West Asia. The Soviet Union is no exception. Pakistan's Baluch coastline lies at the mouth of the Persian Gulf, and its northern areas lie close to the Soviet Pamirs and the Chinese province of Xinjiang. Since the partition of the subcontinent Moscow has often promoted the concept of economic cooperation between India, Pakistan, Afghanistan, and the Soviet Union. It has also indicated a desire to link its own extensive road and rail network with those of India and Pakistan, through Afghanistan, where it perfected an elaborate logistics and transport infrastructure.[60]

In the first quarter of 1948, immediately following the partition of the subcontinent, Mir Ahmad Yar Khan, now the khan of Kalat, wrote that one of the dangers facing Pakistan came from Russia, "pressing its demand of access to the port of Gwadar" on Baluchistan's Makran Coast. A spate of rumors and accusations about the Soviet interest in the Baluchistan coast, and in a north-south route leading to it, resurfaced in the 1960s. In the Indian Lok Sabha, members of parliament raised questions about the alleged development of a Soviet naval base at Gwadar. The Indian government responded that, although the Soviets were reportedly assisting in the development of the port, they were not constructing a naval facility there. In 1970 the Soviets were reported to have completed a strategic highway through Afghanistan to Karachi. A correspondent for the London *Times* said: "For the present the road link through Pakistan is likely to be used not as a terminal to a naval base, but merely for the delivery of food, naval stores or fuel to Soviet units cruising the Indian Ocean, or possibly for the discreet replacement of submarine crews or marine commandos."[61] The road was said to have been a much shorter and quicker route than the long sea haul from Vladivostok. These reports were unsubstantiated, and the Pakistanis quickly denied their veracity.

Still, the Soviet Union had tried to get permission to build both the route and the port. Requests for access were turned down by the government of Pakistan.[62] In 1969 the Soviets asked permission to build a highway from Chaman on the Afghan-Pakistan border toward one of the five still undeveloped port cities (Gwadar, Pasni, Ormara, Jewani, and Somniani) on the Makran Coast. Of these five towns, Gwadar is the largest and has the finest natural harbor (with a sea depth of thirty-two feet). The Soviets further suggested they would be happy to assist Pakistan in a five-year project for the expansion and improvement of Gwadar.[63]

North-south routes across Baluchistan and the use of a port on the Makran Coast would have had many strategic advantages for the Soviet Union. The acquisition of land routes could serve purposes beyond the exercise of influence in, or control over, Baluchistan. It could give the Soviets access to sea routes, expanding their reach across the sea lanes of the Strait of Hormuz and the northern Indian Ocean. It could permit the Soviet Navy to operate at long distances from its shores for extended periods of time; service more ships, which in turn would allow an increase in Indian Ocean patrols; and raise the level of Soviet missions along the shipping routes so vital to the West.[64]

A Soviet presence at Gwadar would have obvious military implications for the passage of events in the Persian Gulf and Iran. Yet it has been argued that the Soviet interest in Gwadar is mainly economic and "only potentially strategic": the Soviet Union specializes in overland transportation systems. Its railways parallel the role of sea lanes for other nations—nearly 80 percent of its foreign commerce travels by rail or by pipeline. Thus, the offer of a route to Gwadar may quite plausibly have been motivated by commercial goals.[65] But routes can serve dual purposes simultaneously, and it is potential military disaster rather than potential economic gain for which political and military leaders must plan. The Pakistanis turned down Soviet offers to cooperate in the creation of access. The development of the Makran Coast was left to another decade and to a worsening geopolitical reality.

Soviet-built tunnels and highways in Afghanistan, begun in the

1950s and linked to the Afghanistan-Pakistan border, had—before the invasion of Afghanistan—cut the time it took to reach the borders of Baluchistan from Soviet Central Asia to a mere eighteen hours. After the winter of 1979, that time was reduced to zero. The Soviets stood at the frontier of Baluchistan, highlighting the regional significance of Pakistan's—and particularly Baluchistan's—location.

As the 1970s progressed, then, Baluchistan acquired political and strategic significance. Its geopolitical status was transformed from that of a useless, irksome backwater to a vital beachhead. Meanwhile, war scarred Baluch lands.

Inside Baluchistan, 1973–1977

The years from 1973 to 1977 saw an insurgency in Baluchistan born of the contradictions between Bhutto's urge to control the provinces and the political aspirations of some Baluch tribal, youth, and military organizations. In these years land routes played an important role both at the tactical level of the evolution of the insurgency and at the more consequential level of the conflict between the political center and its periphery.

The crux of the legal, political, and ultimately military confrontation between Bhutto and the elected representatives of Baluchistan was the tense relation between the former's efforts to create a centralized administration in a unitary state and Baluch demands for a measure of distance from the political center. As in many former colonies, this was a struggle between the new elite of the center and the old elite of the periphery. Bhutto's philosophy of national development would not accommodate Baluch claims for political diversity and for the retention of traditional forms of social hierarchy. Segments of Baluchistan's tribal political leadership felt they had little say in the exploitation and distribution of resources culled from their land.

The beginnings of the insurgency dated from Bhutto's dismissal of the elected provincial government in Baluchistan, the coalition government of the National Awami party (NAP) and the Jamaat-e-Ulema-e-Islami (JUI).[66] This coalition had governed Baluchistan from late April 1972 until its dismissal in February 1973. From the start the question of routes was embedded in the clash between center and periphery, between tribe and nation-state. When Bhutto evicted the NAP-JUI politicians, he accused them of having interfered with his attempts to modernize Baluchistan through road-building projects.[67] As the insurgency gained momentum, between 1973 and 1975, Bhutto made three offers of amnesty, but no agreement was reached on ending the war. On 2 August 1974, for example, he asked for the surrender of tribal irregulars and threatened that if it were not forthcoming, he could "blow the mountains to bits."[68] Direct Federal rule was imposed in December 1975 and January 1976.

On 8 April 1976 Bhutto made his most sweeping move: he announced the abolition of the sardari system. He officially divested the tribal chiefs of their traditional overlordship and of all the wealth and privilege to which they had been entitled. In one fell swoop he sought to transform the hierarchy of Baluch tribal society. This attack on the traditional rights of the sardars only increased Baluch intransigence.

The war in Baluchistan was bloody. By late 1974, Selig Harrison estimates, about 70,000 soldiers of the Pakistan Army were fighting in Baluchistan and 55,000 Baluch had entered the field. Casualties were high: close to 8–9,000 combatants as well as hundreds of women and children were killed in four years of heavy fighting. Although the guerrillas—relatively untrained and disorganized—suffered heavy losses, the army was unable to win a victory on the ground. Airpower, using first Chinook and then Huey-Cobra helicopters (gifts of the Shah) was more effective. In a bloody round of battles in the fall of 1974 the Baluch insurgents suffered heavy losses, and many of them dispersed to protected sites inside Afghanistan.[69]

Routes, of course, have historically been pertinent to insurrection. Knowledge of uncharted terrain and of the location of the rough, natural routes that traverse it, has always been a weapon of the guerrilla. Similarly, the construction of roads and mobility permits the counterinsurgent to deny the guerrilla the advantages of inaccessibility. Building sturdy logistical routes into valued hinterlands has been a traditional "developmental" device to preempt or to vanquish insurrection.

Encounters between soldier and guerrilla during this war were circumscribed by the problems and possibilities posed by Baluchistan's terrain. All conflicts, large and small, are, in important senses, wars of logistics. But where the ground is more difficult and less known—as in Afghanistan, Baluchistan, the Karakoram, and the Himalayan borderlands—logistics become more complex and more salient factors in conflict. Also, in Baluchistan routes symbolized more than means of transport and supply. In the eyes of some Baluch tribal leaders, they were the instruments of the center's efforts to dominate economic extraction, political progress, and social change.

Tribesmen and soldiers frequently fought along the major transport routes. The insurgents tried to block or destroy existing routes. The soldiers' task was twofold: to protect lines of transport and communication, particularly those related to the exploitation of coal, gas, and oil; and, by building roads, to attack the guerrillas in their mountain redoubts. It was a war in which even shepherds participated, "burying binoculars in the belly-wool of their sheep" while conducting reconnaissance for fighters in the hills.[70] In the early stages of the conflict systems of transport were the focus of attack. Non-Baluch personnel of the Pakistan Western Railway were attacked, and railway guards were kidnaped. The press release issued by the government after a party of Dir Scouts was ambushed in 1973 accused "NAP-trained guerrillas" of conducting subversive activities that concentrated on blocking railway tracks, shooting at trains, removing fishplates, and destroying telephone wires. One of the first forays of the Pakistan Army into Baluchistan, in fact, took place when the rebels attacked a transport route.[71]

The Marri tribe, earlier the bane of the British, formed the backbone of the revolt. The neglect of transport as well as water, sewage, and electrical infrastructure in the 1950s and 1960s stimulated Baluch anger and resentment toward the center but also led to the inability of the Pakistan Army to penetrate Baluchistan, to put down the revolt, to claim victory. At a time when the central government needed accessibility for pacification and control, it faced the consequences of previous government policies toward Baluchistan.

The Bolan route was, as in the time of the British, a regular target for the tribesmen. The army manned posts along the route, in some areas as little as a mile apart, to protect the trains. Using a "blockhouse" strategy whereby forts and outposts were strung along the main lines of transport and communication, it tried to secure the passage of military vehicles and commercial trains. The Pakistan Railway even tried to outmaneuver the guerrillas by canceling all trains in the early morning. The trains were armed. The Bolan Express traveling from Karachi to Quetta, for example, made a special stop at Sibi to collect an armed bogey before journeying through the mountains.[72]

As dominant symbols of intrusion by the center, these trains attracted intense tribal attention. The Marris concentrated their efforts against the Bolan Express, aiming to prevent the transport of coal mined in the heart of Marri territory, in Harnai, for use outside their lands. By the middle of 1974, the guerrillas had cut the main roads that connected Baluchistan with neighboring provinces, were disrupting coal shipments to the Punjab, and were hindering road-building efforts in areas of oil exploration. Said Khair Buksh Marri, sardar of the tribe, "We saw what happened in the Bukti areas, where they have 'developed' Sui gas, 80% of which goes out of Baluchistan to make others rich." The Baluch Peoples Liberation Front (BPLF) flaunted their success in having prevented, for five years, the completion of 36 miles of oil-related roads. Ultimately, even though the soldiers rebuilt these roads, guerrilla tactics proved successful. AMOCO, a foreign corporation, withdrew from Baluchistan.[73]

Transport routes also brought to a head the conflict between Bhutto's interest in development for the purpose of corroding the Baluch tribal structure and enhancing his grip on a significant periphery, on the one hand, and the tribal sardars' view that development plans, and the exploitation of oil, coal, and gas, were attempts to exploit Baluchistan's people and resources to serve the purposes of Punjab, Sind, and the NWFP, on the other. Transport routes played an important role in this conflict over whether development should be pursued for its own sake, for the purposes of internal security, for the consolidation of the dominance of the center over the periphery, or for regional security.

The main thrust of Bhutto's view was to modernize Baluchistan and thereby destroy the power of the sardars. According to Bhutto, himself of Sindhi feudal stock, the insurgency was no more than the revolt of sardars against socioeconomic change that threatened their wealth and privilege. This plausible hypothesis was rejected by the sardars and other Baluch dissident groups involved in the controversy.[74] They pointed instead to Bhutto's well-known dislike of sharing power and to his inability to abide by the results of the first free and fair elections ever to be held in Pakistan.

Bhutto also feared the further territorial-political disintegration of Pakistan. The 1971 secession of Bangladesh added new concerns about provincialism and separatism. And where it appeared that the idea of national identity was losing its grip, as in Baluchistan, Bhutto sought to replace its integrational pull by tangible force and the creation of physical access. Requirements for the perpetuation of the state, for internal security, and for the exercise of authority by the center over the provinces coalesced with the interest in Baluchistan's natural resources, as reasons to develop Baluchistan.

When it came to Baluch lands, Bhutto seemed to believe that the key to Pakistan's survival in its post-1971 form lay in the suppression of the social system of the periphery and in the forward assertion of central control. Glossing over the fact that thousands of soldiers were in Baluchistan, under his orders, he told Selig Harrison in 1977 that, unlike the military approach used by General Ayub Khan, his approach sought to destroy the sardari system through the momentum generated by economic development: "The *sardars* realize they are done for if we can do it, if we can get roads in, schools in, hospitals in. That is why they are opposing us. They know that if we destroy the *sardari* system, we will destroy Baluch identity, or at least begin the process of destruction."[75]

The solution to the problems of security, as Bhutto interpreted them, was sought in military maneuvers and in economic development, particularly in transport infrastructure. The new roads to be built under the government's scheme would bring Baluch tribesmen into increasing contact with the rest of the country and destroy their narrow isolation. From 1972 onward, the government accorded top priority to roadbuilding in Baluchistan.[76]

The Bhutto government touted its expenditures on the development of Baluchistan. Prior inattentiveness to the area could not be emphasized sufficiently: Bhutto pointed to the only major road project initiated in Baluchistan after independence, the RCD Highway, which had lingered for over twelve years. The increased allocation of progressively larger sums was meant to indicate the center's "concern for the province" and its "anxiety to remove the disparity between Baluchistan and the other provinces."[77]

The transport and communications sector (with much of the infrastructure built by the army) received the highest priority. In October 1974, the Bhutto government issued a White Paper to justify its stance on Baluch affairs. It described the missions of the army in Baluchistan: "The military presence in Baluchistan in aid of civil power has a dual purpose: preservation of law and order and economic development."[78] This latter role was assigned to the army because it was the only source of manpower in society sufficiently organized to transform the physical infrastructure of Baluchistan. As the insurgency spread, the road-building efforts of the Pakistan Army became the vanguard of efforts at development. According to the

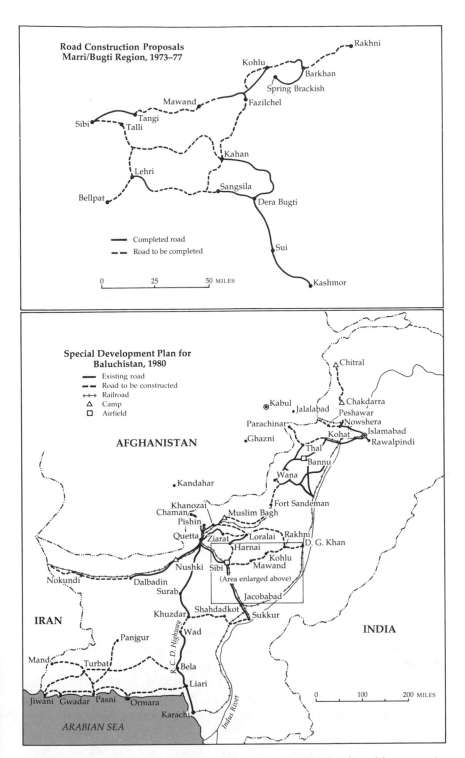

Map 5 Road-building projects in Baluchistan, 1973–77 and 1980. Adapted from maps in Government of Pakistan, *White Paper on Baluchistan* (Rawalpindi: Printing Corporation of Pakistan, 1974), and Government of Pakistan, *Special Development Plan for Baluchistan* (Islamabad, 1980).

government, the army "has assigned the highest priority to road construction because without roads the rugged mountains will never yield to the will of economic planners."[79]

Socioeconomic change was the government's weapon against the power of the sardars. It was to be brought about through electrification, education, and the creation of physical access. Roadbuilding would also permit the army to penetrate the interior. The increased ability of the tribesmen to move freely, it was thought, would lessen their dependence upon the sardars, decrease "block voting," and alter their political affiliations. A much larger percentage of the Baluch population would be able to come to the polling booths of their own accord. In the general elections of 1970, for example, the lack of roads was deemed "an important factor in keeping over sixty percent of the voters away from the polling booths." The majority of the tribesmen who reached these booths were transported by their sardars. New roads would create new voting patterns. This, some surmised, was another reason for the sardars' opposition to the new roads.[80]

In the fifteen months following the dismissal of the NAP-JUI government in February 1973, army engineers constructed 550 miles of roads in Baluchistan. Roads were built in areas of especial turbulence, where there was oil, and as links between Baluchistan and its neighbors. Roadbuilding followed the trail of the coal mines in the Marri areas and of the gas fields of Sui in the Bugti areas. The center aggressively pursued the development of Baluchistan's resources in a period of insurrection and in areas of anti-center resistance.[81]

There was disagreement among Baluch leaders on these center-directed development projects. Some of them argued that Baluch needs would be best served by supporting the center's economic development programs and later initiating a political struggle. Others suggested that accepting Bhutto's economic lead would compromise the Baluch movement for increased political rights.[82]

The debate focused on roads. That some sardars took exception to the center's road-building program is evident. That they physically opposed attempts to push roads into the tribal heartland of Baluchistan is clear, too, as witness guerrilla attacks against railroads and road construction. But Bhutto and these leaders represented the grounds for Baluch hostility differently. Bhutto felt that the querulous sardars feared the impact of new roads on vested tribal interests and traditional modes of political and social control. His government attributed Baluchistan's lack of routes to the policy of the sardars to "keep their feudal preserves closed to commerce and the traffic in men and ideas that would threaten their power." Bhutto told a story of having offered one imprisoned sardar—Khair Buksh Marri—his freedom, in return for a promise to end his opposition to the government. The sardar responded that he would do so, on condition that "the building of roads in the Marri area was stopped."[83]

The Baluch leadership viewed Bhutto's security-propelled development program as an attempt not to modernize Baluchistan but to control it. According to Marri, his opposition was not to the notion of development per se but to its "exploitative and political character" under Bhutto's guidance: most of the roads built by the army in Baluchistan were "not for our benefit but to make it easier for the military to control us and for the Punjabis to rob us. The issue is not whether to develop, but whether to develop with or without autonomy." Anyhow, talk of development in the midst of a bitter war was not trustworthy. Apart from differences in education policy (where the Pakistani government was more forthcoming), Selig Harrison concludes, Pakistan and Iran followed "broadly similar" economic policies toward Baluch lands, "neglecting many critical areas, such as water development, while giving disproportionate attention to others, notably road construction, for military reasons."[84]

Land routes were enmeshed, then, in a classic center-periphery dispute, born of the attempt to hold diverse peoples under a single umbrella of statehood. Access to and in Baluchistan became the unglittering prize. Bhutto's fears for Pakistan's internal security, his insistence on center-determined provincial development, and the Shah's internal and regional security concerns, clashed directly with the demands of Baluch opposition leaders for broader political and social influence, both in Baluchistan and in Pakistan, and for the right to determine when, where, and how their resources would be exploited and used, and their physical infrastructure built.

Baluchistan after the Soviet Invasion of Afghanistan

In the 1970s, as a truncated Pakistan attempted to cope with the trauma of a second partition, the potential for a loosening of Baluchistan's ties to the central government was particularly sensitive. Pakistan's perennial incohesiveness resulted in a development program for Baluchistan. After the Soviet invasion of Afghanistan in December 1979, however, a new Pakistani government, headed by General Zia ul-Haq, again pursued the rapid development of Baluchistan. The need to enter the provincial heartland and to improve relations with the Baluch had become especially urgent. With the Soviets on the borders, the continued advantages of security-propelled development were vigorously asserted.

When the Soviets entered Kabul, Baluchistan was launched into strategic prominence. It came to occupy an important position on the mental maps of policy makers from Tokyo to Washington. Once more, its importance derived from its location. From Afghanistan the Soviets were thought to threaten Western oil and other regional interests. As early as 1948, Harry Hodson had described the Gulf region as a borderland where great interests meet and clash. The area of overlap, he said, stretched in a rough arc from Kashmir to the North West Frontier, Afghanistan, Iran, and Egypt. This curve embraced the Gulf region "as closely and as neatly as the Turkish crescent embraces the Star." For Hodson, this was the Arc of Danger.[85] The geopolitics of Olaf Caroe and Harry Hodson influenced a new generation of thinkers when Afghanistan fell to the Soviets; cries rang out in Anglo-American circles about the "arc of crisis" and the "arc of danger." This arc or, more properly, this crescent embraced Pakistan, reviving old fears about the subcontinent's western frontier. Maj. Gen. M. Rahim Khan, then head of Pakistan's Ministry of Defence, announced that "for the first time in the life of Pakistan, we have to look at our western defenses." In one of many such allusions, the American undersecretary of state James Buckley referred to Pakistan in Senate testimony as "an essential anchor of the entire Southwest Asian region."[86]

In the superpower competition for global strategic access, the Soviet Union had acquired, through its invasion of Afghanistan, a set of air and land (and potentially sea) routes that could complicate U. S. military planning and logistics in the Indian Ocean–Persian Gulf region. Any Soviet approach toward the Makran Coast in Baluchistan would worsen matters. U. S. policy in the wake of the Soviet invasion was reactive. Pakistan's geographical assets, its locational significance for the United States (so vivid during the Cold War years), became attractive to Jimmy Carter and Ronald Reagan. Soviet contiguity to Pakistan made U. S. policy more sensitive to Asian geopolitics. Washington aggressively concerned itself with forcing the

Soviets to withdraw their troops from Afghanistan through the training and supply of Afghan mujahideen groups operating from bases inside Pakistan. U. S. analysts also considered the denial of Baluchistan to the Soviets and mulled over the province's potential usefulness for U. S. forces. They drew attention to the large port city of Karachi and the small port towns of the Makran Coast as possible basing areas for the prepositioning of supplies and equipment in the event of a military contingency in the Persian Gulf.

Writing in 1980, Admiral Thomas Moorer called for the establishment of a naval base at Gwadar. Referring to Gwadar as an "excellent, if undeveloped," potential naval facility, Moorer and Alvin Cottrell argued that the harbor was much better suited topographically and financially to be a naval base than other possibilities in the vicinity of the Gulf of Oman. According to these writers, Bhutto had offered the use of Gwadar to the United States in 1973–74, in exchange for a lifting of the U. S. arms embargo then in effect.[87]

Another analyst, Francis Fukuyama, outlined the grounds for revived U. S. ties to Pakistan. Such a political and military attachment would be especially valuable, he suggested, in light of the dangers potential in a Soviet acquisition of Baluchistan. Soviet access to "a port yet to be built" in Baluchistan or to Karachi would place the Soviet Navy at the head of the Gulf, far closer to U. S. lines of shipping than their present base at Aden. The Soviets could use Pakistani facilities for direct operations in the Persian Gulf or as ports for the supply of aid to their friends in the region. According to Fukuyama, however, Pakistan's "geopolitical position" could be turned to the advantage of the United States, since its territory could serve as an important "entrepot for an RDF moving into the Persian Gulf from the east, i.e., from Diego Garcia or the Phillipines." Both distance and deployment times for the RDF could be decreased, and arrangements could be made for the emergency transit of heavy equipment, aircraft and supplies.[88]

As in imperial times, then, Baluchistan and its environs had become the staging grounds for a new game of routes. The problems of access—enhancement as well as denial—preoccupied the United States. They were important to its renewed political-military association with Pakistan, an association that was to result in U.S. economic aid for the infrastructural development of Baluchistan. As a new strategic frontier was demarcated, first by the Soviet Union and then by the United States, the routes of Baluchistan rose to prominence.

The Soviet presence in Afghanistan created a serious conventional threat to Pakistan's northwestern borders. In its brief yet deeply troubled history—three wars with India, a civil war, and an insurgency—Pakistan had never faced such a dangerous combination of external threats: India, the Soviet Union, and Afghanistan were all hostile. Pakistan's leaders saw the security of the NWFP and Baluchistan as jeopardized. Military threats to Pakistani security now conceivably included a Soviet cultivation of insurgency and terrorism in the border provinces, a combined Indo-Soviet attempt to splinter Pakistan into three territories: one part would become a newly independent state of Baluchistan, another would be incorporated into Afghanistan, and a third into India; and sporadic crossborder aerial and land-based incursions by Soviet and Afghan military forces. In the fall of 1981 Lieutenant-General Fazle-Haq, then governor of the NWFP, pronounced the long-term goal of the Soviet Union as a warm-water port on the shores of Pakistan: "They will make a strategic thrust to get access to a warm water port in our Baluchistan province."[89]

Faced with simmering discontent inside Baluchistan and a new external threat, Zia's government became preoccupied with peacemaking and development in the province. It would take no small effort to calm the Baluch, a few of whom continued to voice extreme anticenter sentiments. Said Jamil Bugti, son of Akbar Bugti (sardar of the 100,000-strong Bugti tribe), "If we heard that the Russians were going to invade Pakistan tomorrow, we would send them a cable saying please do not wait that long. Come today."[90] Astutely, Zia withdrew the army from Baluchistan and offered financial compensation, amnesty, and release to Bhutto's Baluch antagonists.

The next response of the military government to the new dangers facing the province took the form of a Special Development Plan for Baluchistan (SDP). This document circulated among international aid agencies and foreign governments. The SDP decried (as previous governments had done) the earlier lack of interest in the progress of Baluchistan. The most notable feature of the SDP was its emphasis on the provision of a transport and communications infrastructure for the region.

The SDP's recommendations intended both to give the Baluch a sense that their development needs were being considered and to contend with the security threat to Pakistan's borderlands. In the Preface to the SDP, Ghulam Ishaq Khan, then deputy chairman of the

Planning Commission, made the case for a development policy influenced by considerations of external and internal security. First, however, he averred it had always been the aim of government policy to develop backward areas. There is limited evidence to support the contention, despite repeated public pronouncements to this effect. The deputy chairman then pointed out that "the pursuit of this objective has acquired added significance in so far as . . . Baluchistan and the NWFP, [sic] are concerned in the wake of recent events in Afghanistan."

Before 1980 the Fifth Five Year Plan for the economic development of the country was to have made adequate provisions for these provinces, but the new strategic reality altered the needs of development. In 1980 the government considered it necessary to "reinforce" the plan with the SDP, which contained schemes that would make "an immediate, visible and direct impact on living conditions." The Baluch were to benefit from speedily established economic and social programs. Investments were to be made in physical infrastructure; as the Preface concluded: "The construction of some of these facilities will also serve the incidental purpose of strengthening the defense of the western border of Pakistan."[91] After 1980 Baluchistan received more government funding per capita than any other Pakistani province.

Zia referred to Baluchistan in that year as "the most sensitive area of Pakistan." Such statements accompanied the rapidly rising interest in the development of Baluchistan. Gone were the days when this land was lost in its own shadows. Zia echoed Hoveyda's words: "Given the military importance of Baluchistan . . . we obviously cannot think of it as having something in particular to do with the Baluch. They have a provincial population equal to one third of the population of one city in the Punjab, Lahore. They have coal, gas, and oil that the whole country needs. We are one country and the Baluch are part of our country."[92] Integration and development were the arguments of the nation-state, as well as its weapons for internal and external security.

Zia's economic program for Baluchistan did not differ much from Bhutto's in its essentials. Although his political approach was more subtle, the general mimicked his predecessor's stance on social change in Baluchistan. Transport infrastructure was emphasized. Each new road and school was viewed as weakening the sardars and concomitantly increasing the control of the central government.[93] Whereas Bhutto had claimed credit for the road building undertaken during the insurgency, Zia's government insisted that those earlier accomplishments must be credited to the army and therefore to the military government. In fact, said his government, not enough had been done under Bhutto for transportation. A government publication complained that although no "meaningful development [of Baluchistan] is possible without a network of roads," the condition of the roads there "for many years up to 1977 continued to be anything but satisfactory." Zia's government, however, "has laid the top-most priority on the construction of roads."[94] Once more, Baluchistan was to be made accessible.

The military government's public goals were to remove provincial perceptions of economic deprivation; to lay the physical infrastructure required for growth; and to integrate the province's economy and polity with the rest of the country. The construction of routes served all these purposes.

It was the high cost of building transport infrastructure in Baluchistan's inhospitable terrain, the government argued, that had deterred development in the past. Now, however, the "added significance" of the Soviet invasion of Afghanistan might convince foreign donors that this key land-bridge urgently needed a physical foundation for development. The political and military interests of external powers in the revived game of access in South, Central, and West Asia would provide the financial means for opening up and developing the economy of Baluchistan.

The 1980–81 Annual Development Plan for Baluchistan allotted the largest amount for the transport and communications sector. Rs. 82.972 million ($4.6 million) were awarded to these schemes.[95] Among the proposed roadworks were Makran's coastal routes. The roads from Liari to Ormara and the whole route from Karachi to Pasni and onward to Gwadar and Turbat were to be improved. The coastal areas were also to be provided with electricity. This attentiveness to Makran accorded well with the geopolitical perspectives of both Pakistani and foreign governments, which linked the consequences of enhanced mobility and access in the western edges of the subcontinent to the security of Pakistan and the lands of the Persian Gulf.

In the Special Development Plan, too, the transport and communications sector was allocated the highest level of funding—about $535 million. A blizzard of road-building proposals followed on the heels of Afghanistan's collapse to the Soviets, which the Pakistani government viewed as a powerful stimulant to the generosity of foreign, anticommunist, aid donors. Improvements in road and rail, however, were based upon primarily economic and social justifications. According to the plan:

> The construction and improvement of roads and other transport facilities will require highest priority in order to strengthen links between major settlements within the Province and between these settlements and their potential trading centres in other Provinces. It is quite clear that unless the pre-requisite of building a transport system which integrates hitherto inaccessible or not easily accessible areas with the rest of the Province and other regions is completed, it would not be possible to attract private investments in the Province nor to set up profitable public sector units. In fact, even provision of education and health facilities will be rendered difficult and the strategic goal of furthering social mobility hampered.[96]

Although the SDP emphasized the development of backward areas, also scattered through it were references to the military rationales for routes. The proposed all-weather routes were to open up remote areas, assist in the development of mineral resources, and ease trade. They also had a security component. The importance of the Zhob-Dhanasar road, for example, which would link northern Baluchistan with the frontier, "in facilitating trade and commerce as well as military requirements justifies its high priority," said the SDP. The existing 149-mile shingled Khuzdar-Kharan road was deemed unsuitable for "heavy vehicles." A black-topped road was thought necessary to connect Kharan via Khuzdar with divisional headquarters at Quetta. This road would not only facilitate civilian traffic but would also be of "considerable strategic importance as ultimately Kharan is going to be connected with RCD Highway section between Quetta and Taftan."[97]

The SDP program had a wide scope. The routes proposed included sections of the RCD Highway and roads linking Baluchistan with the NWFP, as well as with other provinces and with Iran. The Makran coastal routes were again to be improved. The roads built by the army in the Marri-Bugti areas during the insurgency were now deemed inadequate. Zia's government lamented the area's continued isolation and poverty, and proposed more roads. A new, three-section, 404-mile railway line between Karachi and Bela was also suggested. Finally, funds were requested for road-building and maintenance equipment for the improvement of roads and tracks. Many of the provincial routes were tracks or fair-weather roads that required both upgrading and maintenance.

The timing and location of the proposed routes indicate their importance not only to Pakistan's economic, but also to its security, calculations. There was a need to open up the oil-rich Marri-Bugti areas, to improve links between army quarters at Quetta and major points in Baluchistan, to permit better access from other provinces into Baluchistan, and to secure the mobility of troops across an east-west line. Baluch routes had become important to deployment in the event of a two-front war—a possibility that now had to be considered. One Pakistani division, previously a reserve force, was turned into a "front-line" force against the Soviet threat to Baluchistan. Roads and infrastructure for "moving forces from one front to another" were planned.[98]

Some Baluch opposition leaders were uncomfortable with Zia's plans. They felt the government's advocacy of rapid development had come too late to soften the Baluch consciousness of injustice. They also remained well aware that the controlling grip of the center would travel along the very roads being built in the name of socioeconomic progress. Even as the programs for development were being implemented—a national grid station to provide Quetta with Sui gas (for the first time), a large airport capable of handling wide-bodied jets, television inaugurated—there remained disaffected Baluch who questioned what they termed the government's "misguided priorities in development."[99]

One focus of their suspicions was the Rs. 742 million ($41.2 million) Sibi-Kohlu-Rakhni-Kahan road construction project. The key sector of the route, being built by the National Logistics Cell under the auspices of the government of Baluchistan, was to run through the heart of Marri territory. To these Baluch, the money could have been spent far more profitably elsewhere, to benefit a much larger number of people, rather than on an uneconomical route through desolate terrain known only to a few thousand Marri tribesmen.[100] According to the government, however, the road was essential to the economic development of this impenetrable and backward area, particularly for the expansion of oil exploration activities.

International financial and aid organizations usually appraise investment projects on an economic basis using cost-benefit analyses. They rarely accomodate political or strategic criteria in their determinations. One such prominent organization, approached by Zia, scrutinized the proposals of the SDP in a staff report. On the grounds of economic infeasibility, and on the grounds that the proposed projects would bring little immediate relief to the inhabitants of Baluchistan (which was the purpose of the SDP as described in its Preface), it considered a number of projects presently unnecessary. In particular, these international analysts felt they could not recommend the construction of many of the land routes proposed by the government of Pakistan.

The staff report suggested the government's routing policy should focus on road maintenance and improvement. It supported the government's contention that the difficult topography and climate of Baluchistan, and the inadequacy of transport routes, were making the development of the region costly and laborious. There was little industrial progress and few small-scale enterprises in the province; all were rendered inefficient by the inadequacy of infrastructure.

Yet the conclusions drawn by these economists did not precisely coincide with those of the government of Pakistan. Although improvements in transport and communications were necessary over the long term, the staff report argued, the road and rail construction promised few immediate benefits for the general population. In Baluchistan, traffic volumes were light; most provincial roads did not see more than two hundred vehicles per day. In the staff report's assessment, barring a few exceptions, only rudimentary new routes should be built. Any broader improvements in transport infrastructure could not be justified on economic grounds. The huge transport investments proposed by the government of Pakistan were unlikely to improve the routine economic conditions of Baluchistan's people in any substantial fashion. As alternatives to the Pakistani-proposed road and rail schemes, the international aid organization suggested that existing roads be improved, bottlenecks removed along the main interprovincial and regional networks, and air services expanded. Such efforts would more readily and more speedily alleviate the problems of Baluchistan's inhabitants than the time, effort, and cost involved in planning and building large road and rail networks.[101]

The World Bank and the United Nations High Commission for Refugees (UNHCR) did, however, finance some road improvement schemes in the province. In 1986, for example, about 18 percent of all work on Baluchistan's roads was carried out by Afghan refugees and financed by UNHCR. The refugees upgraded 9.3 miles of the Quetta-Chaman road at a cost of $1.8 million. Another $21 million was spent by the World Bank on upgrading the Pishin-Surkhab road and on providing better access to markets for the Khanozai farmers and their produce.[102]

Zia found backers for the SDP despite cautious economic reviews.

States in the Middle East, Europe, East Asia, and North America had become concerned about the wider consequences of the Soviet invasion for Pakistan and about the special vulnerability of Baluchistan. They saw Pakistan as poised on the edge of a precipice. And Baluchistan's lack of routes, its potentially excellent harbors along the Makran Coast, internal discontent, and the presence of the Soviet Union on its borders were all objects of worry to regional states, particularly those in the Gulf, and to distant powers with global interests. The war in Afghanistan guaranteed a steady and substantial flow of economic, military, and potentially dual-use infrastructural aid into Pakistan.

Some seventeen foreign governments and donor agencies became active in Baluchistan. They included Kuwait, the United States, West Germany, Canada, Japan, Great Britain, France, the European Economic Community, the World Bank, the Asian Development Bank, the International Labor Organization, UNHCR, United Nations Development Program (UNDP), and the World Food Program. Cooperation was most extensive between Pakistan and the states of the Middle East and the Persian Gulf, which were intimidated by the Soviet Union's proximity to Baluchistan's shores; and between Pakistan and the United States, which was contesting with the Soviet Union a global game played, by the latter's choice, in these borderlands.[103]

The Arab states were quick to extend financial aid for projects inside Baluchistan. For example, the Kuwait Fund for Arab Economic Development (KFAED) gave Rs. 315 million ($17.5 million) in foreign exchange loans to facilitate the construction of a 214-mile-long gas pipeline within Baluchistan. Reportedly the fund also agreed to invest $400 million in two irrigation projects and one venture to generate electricity. In 1987 Pakistani and Kuwaiti finance ministers discussed other likely projects for KFAED funding, including further improvements of the coastal roads and a dam.[104]

The largest aid commitment in Baluchistan was made by the United States. The new coincidence of U. S. and Pakistani strategic interests led to the provision of foreign aid for Pakistan's development and, specifically, to discussions regarding the country's new border defense requirements. These perceived commonalities of strategic interest supported a large U.S. investment in infrastructural aid to Pakistan.

When war broke out in Afghanistan, Pakistan requested financial aid and modern weapons in order to create the military infrastructure required to fulfill two purposes: prevent a spillover of the Afghan war into Pakistan by providing a credible frontier defense and protect against Soviet-sponsored insurgency in Baluchistan. Initially the Pakistani government quoted a figure of $1.5 billion as necessary to build the land arteries—chiefly roads and railways—needed for the rapid movement of troops and supplies up and down the Durand Line boundary between Afghanistan and Pakistan. The border zone is modestly peopled, littered with passes, and comprised of large unprotectable tracts. There were barely any good roads in the mountainous east or in the arid desert to the west. Nor did any north-south routes extend across the region. In the NWFP and Baluchistan what few good routes existed were of British vintage. Airfields were also rare, and communications, where they did exist, were rudimentary. According to Maj. Gen. M. Rahim Khan, a million soldiers would be required to effectively patrol the borders alone.[105]

In 1980, considering its frail military network in the borderlands, Pakistan asked for infrastructural aid. The outlay for Baluchistan requested in the Special Development Plan and the plan's socioeconomic goals should be assessed in the context of the enormous new security requirements of Pakistan's land forces. Zia's government urged a U. S. contribution to construct a logistics infrastructure in the NWFP and in Baluchistan. It made astute proposals about particular forms of aid—a reflection based on historical memory of the politics of routes and of the multifaceted role routes have played in the hard terrain of these provinces. The Pakistanis argued that monies for transport would have a most positive political impact, since these could help to foster the economic development of the provinces. As Francis Fukuyama also noted, such funds would be useful and "politically less provocative "because although they would have direct military utility, they could be disguised as economic aid. What the Pakistanis did not mention was that although the government was eager for roads that served development, such roads would also facilitate the army's "control over ethnic or tribal separatism." Assessing the perils of transport aid for the United States, however, Fukuyama warned that north-south routes in Baluchistan "designed to carry the Pakistanis north may also serve to drive the Russians south. . . . There is little point in improving naval access to the Baluchistan coast if it is simply to become a Soviet base in a number of years."[106]

As of 1987, the United States had agreed to provide Pakistan with two substantial aid packages—$3.20 billion in 1980 and $4.02 billion in 1987—which included monies for road building. The United States Agency for International Development (USAID) became the most active foreign development corps in Baluchistan. Of the total 1980 aid package to Pakistan, $1.6 billion was allocated for economic development. Of this latter sum, $250 million—the largest amount of U.S. money ever to filter into Baluchistan—was set aside for nineteen major projects in the province.

The improvement of physical infrastructure along the Makran Coast has been a feature of the USAID program, and more than $100 million have been allocated to the coastal areas. Seventy million dollars have been set aside for large-scale projects such as a water reclamation plant. Millions more have been awarded to build and improve roads linking the towns along the coast. One Pakistani newspaper noted that the United States had been "very interested in building a road network along the Makran area." In 1985 USAID was spending $40 million on a road project linking Bela (already linked to Karachi) to Turbat (already linked to Gwadar by a passable road). According to USAID officials, this road was one of the few projects "specifically requested" by the Pakistani government. "This is not a Cam Ranh Bay project," said one U.S. aid official.[107] Two years later, USAID was reportedly funding a five-hundred-mile-long highway that would originate at Karachi, wind along the Makran Coast, and terminate at the Iranian border.[108] Some Pakistanis grumble that "not much has actually filtered down to the common man." Workers in other aid and refugee assistance programs have also suggested that "there are far more important needs in Baluchistan—drinking water for example, and health care—than a new road."[109]

The United States denied any connection between its road-building efforts in Baluchistan and its larger military policies for the region, particularly those relating to the deployments of CENTCOM in the Persian Gulf. In October 1987 the U.S. ambassador to Pakistan, the late Arnold Raphel, gave an interview to the *Daily News*, an English-language Pakistani newspaper, in which he responded to questions about the role USAID was playing in Baluchistan:

> Next year, we are spending 40 million dollars in Baluchistan which is at the request of the Government of Pakistan and of the province. A large component of that 40 million dollars is for health and education. We're now sending about 100 students a year from Mekran to the United States. Plus, a lot of it is for road building. But these are roads that the

Government of Pakistan has come to us and said "we want a road from Turbat to Sibi" and we've said "okay, we'll help you do it" but there is no connection to Centcom at all.[110]

Still, the U.S.-Soviet competition in these borderlands has brought the old Makrani fishing town of Gwadar to prominence. It has come to be seen as a symbol of the barter in which large and small states have traditionally engaged: access for money and arms. In the region, talk has been rife about roads being built to and from Gwadar, its port facilities being developed, airports being constructed. Lawrence Lifschultz, an American journalist, quoted Lieutenant-General Rahimuddin Khan, then chairman of the joint chiefs' committee, as saying that twenty-three airports (both new and upgraded) now exist in Baluchistan. These included facilities at the Makran coastal towns of Jiwani, Pasni, and Gwadar, at Turbat further inland, and at Quetta. Lifschultz also noted reports of a new air base under construction in the Chagai region near Afghanistan.[111] Although the full extent of U.S.-Pakistani military cooperation in the 1980s is uncertain, Pakistan has reportedly provided aircraft refueling sites for the U.S. Central Command, as well as docking facilities for U. S. ships at Karachi. According to a Pentagon official, Pakistan has granted "refuel and rest facilities," "from time to time, on a case by case request basis," for U.S. maritime forces traveling to the Persian Gulf. (This report was denied by Pakistan's ambassador to the United States, Jamsheed K. A. Marker.)[112] The Pakistani government has banned foreigners from Gwadar.

India has voiced concern about the links between U.S. interests and Pakistani facilities. One writer warned that "any extension of bases by Pakistan to the United States—naval facilities at Gwadar, air bases, surveillance operations, or the prepositioning of arms and supplies for the Rapid Deployment Force—would seriously affect Indo-U. S. relations and would exacerbate tension between India and Pakistan." Pakistani opposition politicians also charged that General Zia had granted base-rights to the United States on Baluchistan's Makran Coast and that Gwadar figures prominently in the regional strategies of both the Gulf Cooperation Council (GCC) and the Central Command.[113]

Both Zia's government and U. S. officials denied the presence of U.S. military facilities on the Makran Coast.[114] Pakistan avers that, as it is a nonaligned state, "No foreign forces are allowed to use any strips or ports in Pakistan. There are also no U.S. listening posts on Pakistan's soil to monitor Soviet missile tests or for any other purpose." The U.S. State Department has said: "The U.S. has not asked for and the Government of Pakistan has not offered base rights." Ambassador Raphel specifically denied U.S. involvement in Gwadar. He told *Dawn*, a Pakistani English-language newspaper, that "no matter how often I say we don't have bases in Gwadar and go and look, that's the same story that appears every month in the newspapers." The foreign advisers whose presence in Gwadar has been officially documented are Japanese. In 1979 the Pakistani government requested Japanese equipment and materials on a grant basis for the Coast Fisheries Development Project.[115]

These occurrences and debates illustrate the immutability of the politics of access at the national, regional, and global levels. The Soviet entrance into Afghanistan gave rise to this tangled geopolitical dance over the Makran Coast and the listless but vitally located port of Gwadar. The politics of routes raised Gwadar to a prominent position on the mental maps of Pakistanis and foreigners concerned with the military prospects of the region. Gwadar may be remote from the centers of strategic and political discourse, but its fate became their intimate concern.

A Soviet military withdrawal from Afghanistan presages a decline in Baluchistan's prominence on the mental maps of American policy makers. While Soviet forces remained in Afghanistan, sixty miles from Quetta, the United States made substantial contributions to the economic development of Baluchistan. A Soviet troop withdrawal, however, will reduce U.S. concerns for the Pakistani province. Still, with fewer bases worldwide, the United States does face perennial problems of long-distance supply, especially in the neighborhood of West Asia. Future requirements for regional access, and a recognition of the historical linkages between the lands of Baluchistan and West Asia, will temper the diminution of American interests in these parts. For the states of the region, proven Soviet mobility and the revival of the links between events in Central Asia, and South and West Asian realities should ensure continued attention to the land routes and sea ports of Baluchistan.

As long as Pakistani concerns remain about the anticenter strain in Baluch politics (which, to a great extent, has been quieted in the last decade) and about the course of future events inside Afghanistan and in West Asia, the state will pursue the construction of routes in north, south, and west Baluchistan. The Afghan war has clearly shown the province's easy permeability across the hundreds of passes which cut through the borderlands. Future political, military, or economic chaos in the north is likely to flow into Baluchistan and the NWFP. (In 1988 there were still nearly one million Afghan refugees in the environs of Quetta.) Pakistan's political center must have expanded military and economic access to Baluch territory.

Baluchistan's old cross-border links with revolutionary Iran, and its links to the Arab states of the Gulf, will also continue to focus attention on the affairs of the province. The ancient ties between Iran's and Pakistan's Baluch areas have troubled the revolutionary regime of Ayatollah Khomeini as they troubled his predecessor, the Shah. While the Shah wanted to keep the radicalism of Pakistan's Baluch out of his areas, Khomeini has wanted to stem the flood of Iranians fleeing across the border into Pakistan. In the 1980s the Baluchistan border has seen the exodus of thousands of Iranians fleeing military service, the Iran-Iraq war, or religious persecution. Anti-Khomeini factions have entered Pakistan in search of locales from which they might disturb Iran. They have carried their war into the cities of Quetta and Karachi. Iran has also been discomfited by the easy infiltration of Baluch (and other) narcotics traders into its territory. Its leaders now argue that, "in view of the two countries' particular strategic location," Iran-Pakistan economic cooperation, antinarcotics efforts, and agreements to expand road transport across Baluchistan have become increasingly important. The rail route from Quetta to Zahedan is to be revived.[116]

Today, as in Baluchistan's early and imperial history, the politics of land routes are an obsessive concern. In varying degrees, access has promoted social, political, and economic change. As long as foreign strategic interest and economic assistance continues, more routes will be carved through Baluchistan, continuing to reduce the political restraints imposed by distance.

Expansion of access inside Baluchistan will increase the territorial reach of the Pakistani center, thereby further frustrating any local or externally supported movements, for Baluch autonomy. For the center, the new "developmental" routes also symbolize efforts to bring socioeconomic change to the structures of Baluch life. It has been the center's hope that the gradual disintegration of its rival, the old order of the periphery, when it comes, will entice the diverse inhabitants of Baluchistan into the political processes of the nation-state. By wrecking the traditional Baluch hierarchies, a more unitary national identity might be forged. For this the infrastructural development of Baluchistan must proceed.

The level of economic transactions between the Pakistani center and Baluchistan has often been linked to the level of internal insecurity or external threat perceived by the center. Changes in access map the peaks and troughs in transactional levels between center and province from the 1950s to the 1980s. Improvements in transport infrastructure and in extractive technologies, an increase in political linkages, and the modest reduction of social barriers to increased contact between the Baluch and the rest of Pakistan, that is, alterations in the conditions of access, have been brought about to fulfill not only the economic but also the political and security purposes of the Pakistani state.

Developmental advances in the physical infrastructure of Baluchistan have been prompted, then, not only by the demand of the center for the resources of the periphery but also by the need for coherence and security by the Pakistani center, by the perception of a neighboring power that the region was faced with the dangers of Soviet domination, by the armed intrusion of a global power into Baluchistan's northern neighbor, Afghanistan, by the impact of a regional war, and by the global U.S.-Soviet competition. As the rival superpowers make peace, and Afghanistan is freed from Soviet control, Baluchistan may well see a reduction in external interest.

The politics of routes in the Baluch periphery shows how insecurity can foster development. The timing and nature of route building projects reveal this pattern of security-propelled development. The vitality of routes to both security and development has allowed the Pakistani center and its friends abroad to blur the distinctions between economic and military purposes and to introduce economic progress while improving their strategic environment in this borderland of Asia.

A remote political and geographical periphery to the many empires and states that have possessed it, Baluchistan is finally, if slowly, opening up, and its people are being exposed to the currents of national life. Still, enormous tracts of land remain outside the purview of the central government. National politics now enters the major cities and towns of Baluchistan, but the routeless marches of the region remain home to still-isolated tribal people.

3

Afghanistan, Pakistan, and the Soviet Union: The Price of Access

In 1979 the Soviet Union invaded Afghanistan. In December of that year, Soviet aircraft landed at Bagram air base and Kabul International Airport, and Soviet ground forces traveled into Afghanistan along the road from Kushka to Kandahar and from Termez through the Salang Tunnel to Bagram and Kabul. The Soviet invasion resulted in the death of an estimated one million Afghans (out of a population of barely fifteen million) and the forced migration of nearly five million Afghan refugees and mujahideen—mostly Pakhtuns—across the controversial twelve-hundred-mile-long Durand Line, into the North West Frontier Province (NWFP) and Baluchistan in Pakistan, Iran, and India. To Pakistan's own ten million Pakhtun citizens were added millions more from Afghanistan.[1]

When the Soviets moved southward, Pakistan became a "front-line" state, facing a strategic quandary notable even by the turbulent standards of its national and regional history. Not only did it have to cope with the external threat to its borders, but it also had to contend with the strains on its domestic economy, polity, society, and environment caused by Afghan refugees and mujahideen. The routes across the Hindu Kush and the Durand Line carried the conflict into Pakistan. The impact could be seen in the rival slogans on the walls of Peshawar, in the spread of cheap and plentiful weaponry (which reached as far south as the Arabian Sea port city of Karachi), in the heroin trade, in the bombings and acts of sabotage that afflicted the NWFP, in the atmosphere of political tension, and in the new conflicts over local economic assets between Afghans and Pakistanis. The Durand Line failed to shield the subcontinent from the consequences of war in Afghanistan.

These dramatic events would not have been possible without the existence of particular routes and the circumvention of particular anti-routes. The routes provided the Soviet Union with physical access to Afghanistan from the north and the Afghans with continuous access to Pakistan. It is in the history of access to and from Afghan territories that the origins of Afghanistan's modern predicament may be found. This is saying something much less obvious than the fact that the Soviets needed roads for successful conquest. Afghanistan's present subordination shows how a great power can exploit the decision of a small country to risk its security for the sake of development by accepting important infrastructural aid.

Route and barrier have been pivotal to contemporary Afghan efforts to pursue integration, economic growth, and national security. The significant events that led to the Soviet involvement in Afghanistan—the legacy of the Great Game, the making of the Durand Line, and the Afghan-Pakistani quarrel over the future "state" of Pakhtunistan—were all caught up in the web of Central and South Asian routes.

Most striking in recent years is the unprecedented transformation of the infrastructure of access in these difficult lands. The longstanding lack of access inside Afghanistan, and the longstanding use by that country of access southward through the subcontinent, were both reversed to a dangerous degree in the decades following the 1950s. The historical pattern of land routes across Afghanistan and the North West Frontier of Pakistan has had a profound impact on geographical and political evolution.

The changing directions of commerce, the patterns of human movement, of religion and ideas, the question of the tribes, the growth of empires and their clashes, the very configuration of present-day states, and the dilemmas of security and development they face—all

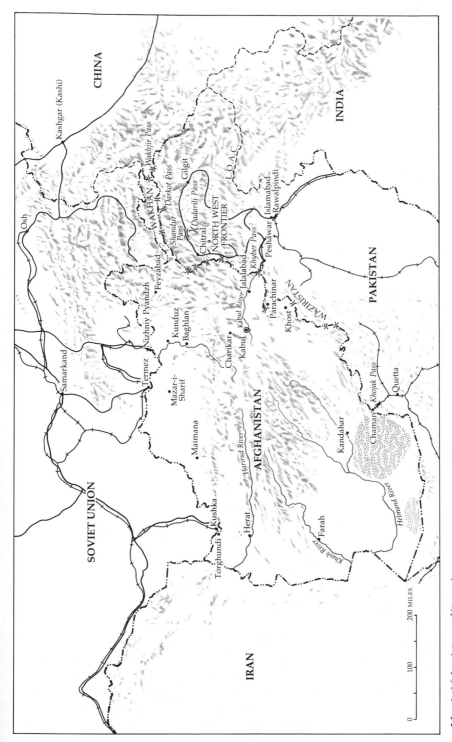

Map 6 Afghanistan and its environs

have been inextricably tied up with the same problem. Routes have lent structure to the movement of trade and of war. The many barriers and few routes in these borderlands have defined the southward movement of political and economic currents from Central Asia to the subcontinent. The routes leading into the northwestern reaches of the subcontinent have historically originated in the basins and oases of Turkestan and in Iran. All have had to strike their way through the defiles of the Hindu Kush or its sister ranges to enter South Asia.

The history of routes in Afghanistan is a microcosm of its larger political, economic, and strategic quandaries. Successive invasions have colored the composition of Afghanistan's peoples and linked its political, military, and economic history with those of the Central and South Asian heartlands. They have been made possible by the sparse land routes that wind their way through a tortuous landscape. Afghan lands are serrated by mountain ridges, and many parts are thirsty for water. The country possesses a jagged, uneven plateau intersected by a few rivers, basins, lakes, and deserts. The Amu Darya runs more than 500 miles in the north. Afghanistan's other rivers include the Helmand (625 miles), the Harirud (530 miles), and the Kabul (285 miles).

Modern Afghanistan is home to many nationalities. Before 1980, the estimated population of fifteen million was about 50 percent Pakhtun (in the southern crescent of the country), 25 percent Tajik (in the north), 9 percent Uzbek (also in northern Afghanistan), and another 9 percent Hazara (in central Afghanistan). Other prominent groups included roughly 800,000 Aimaq, 600,000 Farsiwan, 200,000 Brahui, 125,000 Turkomen, 100,000 Baluch, and 100,000 Nuristanis. A few thousand Kirghiz and Pamiri lived in the Pamirs, Badakhshan, and Wakhan; also present were small numbers of Qizilbash, Kohistanis, Gujars, Jat Gujis, "Arabs," Hindus, Sikhs, and Jews.[2]

The Hindu Kush mountain range spreads across the center of the country; its eastern peaks are the tallest. Other mountain ranges— importantly, the Safed Koh—emerge from the Hindu Kush. The range has witnessed the passage from Turan and Iran of conqueror, merchant, and pilgrim. These mountains are a formidable barrier, and yet they have also provided occasional channels of access or, more theoretically, have been both route and antiroute. Their passes have been the foremost avenues of communication, trade, and con- quest. They include the Kotal-e-Shebar northwest of Kabul; the Kilik, Wakhjir, Baroghil,and Kachin passes in the eastern mountains; and the Mula, Bazarak, Bamian, and Haji Gak passes in the western mountains. Although the Hindu Kush passes have permitted a modest, continuous interaction between the peoples of the fertile agricultural valleys that the mountains separate, overland communication between north and south has generally been difficult to establish and to maintain. Even today, this geographical divide contributes to Afghanistan's fragmented economy and polity.

There is another important sense in which the Hindu Kush has acted as antiroute. The mountains restrict large and sustained movements, denying that breadth of control of the lands on both sides which would permit the establishment of state or empire encompassing the territories of modern Afghanistan and Pakistan. Many great men have invaded both territories, but none has established enduring rule.[3]

Once Afghanistan stood at the epicenter of great civilizations, empires, and trade routes across land—routes that stretched from the Mediterranean to China. (Its remoteness in the minds of Europeans and Americans is the result of the perspective, and the new world, born of sea-power.) Afghan lands were the critical intermediate zone between Iran, Turan, and India. They straddled the line of march for would-be conquerors of the Indus and Gangetic plains. The need for expansionist empires to control or to block routes of access made Afghanistan the centerpiece of what was, essentially, a Great Game of routes.

The eastern defiles of the Hindu Kush are filled with passes leading into Pakistan's frontier territories. These hilly lands, with their wide flood plains and basins, are the middle ground between the highland massif of Central Asia and the Indian plains. Here are located the barriers that separate the two areas, as well as the routes that connect them.[4] Among the more important routes to Pakistan are the Tochi, Kurram, Gomal, Bolan, and Khyber passes. Today the wide, low, and thirty-three-mile-long Khyber Pass occupies a preeminent position on the mental maps of those who observe the frontier. It begins south of the Kabul River at Jamrud, ten miles from the oasis of Peshawar—the first target of invaders bent on taking the Punjab or advancing toward Delhi—and continues in a northwesterly direction into Afghanistan. Across the dry, cracked hills of the pass stand the high fortresses of Pakhtun tribesmen. From the Khyber road, to which the writ of nontribal rulers has always been restricted, these ancient strongholds seem impervious to the laws and the politics of the empires and states that have sought entry into Pakhtun territory.

Although the Khyber has developed legendary status, historically it was not the only pass of high importance. Its mythic quality in Western literature stems in large measure from the paramountcy accorded to it by Britain's imperial strategists. The Khyber Pass was viewed as commanding the line of control from Peshawar to Kabul and featured prominently in the disasters of the First Afghan War (1838–42).

Other passes have been used, however, particularly those to the north which permit movement along the Kunar River and across the lower Swat valley, through Bajaur and Swat. Alexander the Great is thought to have entered India across this way. The Kurram Pass, lying below the Khyber and beyond the Safed Koh range, is also worthy of note. It was infamous during the Mongol raids in the region. In their time the British continued to keep an eye on it; guarding its entrance inside the subcontinent today are the military cantonments they built—Parachinar and Thal.

The frontier lands that these passes join have long been inhabited by the Pakhtun tribes. These tribes have maintained an intimate connection with their mountainous terrain. Democratic men among themselves, they have shown a warlike face to any who have dared force their obedience. Since the tribes control the passes, and hence the trade and military routes across the frontier, all would-be conquerors of India have met the Pakhtuns, negotiated with them, or warred with them. (The 200,000-strong Afridi tribe, for example, has long "guarded" the Khyber Pass.)

The powerful Mughal dynasty tried, until the eighteenth century, to vanquish the tribes of the frontier, but to no avail. Like Alexander before him, Babur, the first Mughal, managed to traverse the frontier, but he could not set up any administration over the tribes. In the early 1580s, Akbar the Great forced the first great road across the frontier— only to suffer a devastating defeat at the hands of the Yusufzai tribe in 1586. His chief engineer, Qasim Khan, did build a road across the Khyber over which wheeled vehicles could travel. It has been recorded that "a road hard to negotiate even by horses and camels, after Qasim Khan's improvements could be passed with ease by wheeled carriages." Still, Mughal lines of communication were constantly attacked, and as Olaf Caroe notes, "regular administration, with all the detail of the Mughal revenue system, hardly reaches beyond the towns and lands adjacent to the highways."[5] In this sphere, too, little has changed. Today the writ of the government of Pakistan extends mainly along the few highways which snake through tribal territories.

Tribal independence from state authority continues in a form barely more subdued than that of centuries past.

Geopolitically, India's conquerors focused on land. The Mughals, for example, were so strongly oriented toward the consideration of land routes that they gave little thought to the potential dangers of the growing mobility of vessels at sea.[6] This Indian dynasty would receive its death blow not from some landward danger, as it had feared, but at the hands of merchant-conquerors who came across the water. Still, there was a logic to Mughal concerns. As their own empire in India expanded, the seafaring British would also come to adopt the traditional concepts of Asian strategy, which centered on the control of land routes. And in the nineteenth and early twentieth centuries they were to become a protagonist in that most famous of all land wars, the Great Game.

The Great Game of Routes: Russia, Britain, and Afghanistan

In the late 1800s the imperial contest between Russia and Britain imposed severe stresses on a small, land-locked, politically volatile country. Afghanistan was hemmed in between the two growing powers. The impact of their imperial conflict would be clearly reflected in the physical map of Afghanistan. With the departure of the British from India in 1947, Afghanistan lay virtually devoid of good routes (particularly railroads), impoverished, and distanced from the world.

The British did not have to conquer the defiles of the Hindu Kush in order to gain control of India. As they began to extend their control, however, they discovered that their most unpredictable frontier lay by these mountains. The danger of a clash with the Russian Empire to the north of the Hindu Kush concentrated British strategic minds on the northwestern frontier lands of the subcontinent. During the British era, imperial boundaries were set and zones of control were established where Central and South Asia meet.

The nineteenth and early twentieth centuries saw the ancient struggle to control the land routes from Central into South Asia acted out in its boldest historical form. The Great Game, played by Russians and Britons across the deserts, mountains, and plains of the region, was in essence a struggle for control over routes across land—and it was strikingly continuous in strategic terms with the exercises in empire that preceded it. The interests and the intrigues of the gameplayers bequeathed Afghanistan its present territorial form, not necessarily conforming to any natural frontiers or to any particular ethnic or demographic features. It created a quandary for Afghanistan's kings regarding the balance between external security and domestic concerns, it sowed the seeds of a persistent quarrel between Afghanistan and Pakistan—through the establishment of the Durand Line boundary—and it consequently foreshadowed new forms of controversy in the postimperial era. New routes and barriers gave rise to new politics. Antiroutes, as much as the routes themselves, shaped the politics of access between modern Afghanistan and Pakistan. And in 1979, long after the creators of the Game had perished, the Soviets won a military victory, albeit short-lived, in the Great Game of routes.

The diligent strategists of the nineteenth century sought to establish or deny access in such a manner as to compartmentalize the Central and South Asian borderlands for the purposes of territorial control and administration. The frontiers would make direct and open conflict between the two advancing imperial systems unlikely. The struggle over access emerged not only in the creation of routes but also in their denial: in the drawing of boundaries and in the creation of that preeminent antiroute, the buffer state. The buffer was Afghanistan, its status confirmed by the Anglo-Russian Convention of 1907.

RUSSIA: THE SEARCH FOR ACCESS

The sequential pattern of Russian occupations of the oases of Central Asia was paralleled by their focus on the development of efficient land lines of communication. Railroads were the Russian forte. British imperial strategists were fearful of the implications of this emphasis on route development for the defense of India. From the Central Asian khanates, which they rapidly subjugated, the Russians sought to extend their transport routes toward neighboring Afghanistan.

The Russian railroad advance into Central Asia had both strategic and economic motives, and corresponding benefits. Not only were rail lines the means for tactical conquest and the retention of physical control; they also featured in the Russian attempt to make the Central Asian khanates economically dependent on the Russian core. This nineteenth-century policy would find a precise parallel in the Soviet penetration of Afghanistan during the twentieth century. Then, too, Russians argued that their routing strategy was intended solely to advance the economic development of the area. Prince Gortchakov insisted in his well-known circular of 1864 that Russia sought only some calm resting place for its frontiers, within whose bounds commerce and civilization would be safe and would flourish.[7]

Whatever its economic and protective political motives might have been for the conquest of Central Asia, Russia progressed across the new transport network toward Afghanistan, altering the military and political balance in the region. The old barriers to mobility—desert and mountain—were overcome, and a new strategic reality was presented to the British in India.

Russia's historical interest in India and its desire to push vigorously southward to a port on the Indian Ocean have provoked unending debates. Some writers have argued that the Russians never seriously considered the invasion of the subcontinent in the nineteenth century: they were well aware of the insurmountable logistical difficulties involved. Yet it was also generally conceded at the time that if the Russians were to take or absorb Afghanistan, they would win the Game.[8] Judgments about Russian intentions—historical or contemporary—notwithstanding, it is certain that the advance of specific routes, the creation of accessibility and mobility in particular directions, necessarily alters the geographical environment and can give rise to new social, economic, political, and strategic facts.

Russia's construction of railroads in Central Asia made the British fear for their lines of communication along the North West Frontier. A brief glance at Russia's primitive logistics before the railroad prompts the conclusion that without it the Russians could not have integrated the khanates with the Russian heartland, consolidated their hold on the oasis states, or threatened their use as points from which to approach India.

As late as 1880, Russia had no railroads in Central Asia. Camels and horses were the means of communication. These means of transport, along with scarce supplies, posed a formidable problem for campaigns in the desert steppe. Fresh horses and camels might not be available. There was an acute shortage of water. Force movements were dictated by the open nature of the steppe. A military expedition in Central Asia has been described as "only a caravan or train, following no regular route, always suffering from want of water or fuel and liable at each halt to have its horses and camels driven away, and consequently to be deprived of its means of advancing"; an expedition of this sort was but "an escort for the protection of its own baggage and train."[9]

The railroad altered this situation. In the mid-1880s a railway connecting the Caspian Sea to the Asian heartland was constructed. Russian strategists (most importantly General Annenkov) argued for the connection of the furthest Turkic outposts with the Caucasus. In 1881, one hundred sixty miles of rail were laid, and in May 1888, the eight-hundred-seventy-nine-miles-long route from the Caspian to Samarkand was opened.

Building the Transcaspian Railway was no simple task. The technical work, and a large portion of the manual work, was undertaken by military men, who had to overcome enormous obstacles of topography and environment. There was, first, a terrible scarcity of water, and for the first one hundred ten miles there was no drinkable water at all. Two hundred miles of shifting, billowing sands confounded the military engineers. The coal needed to fire the construction lines was not to be found. But these difficulties were surmounted. In Lord Curzon's words: "The construction of the railway means the final Russification of the whole Turkoman steppes from Khorasan to Khiva, and from the Caspian to the Oxus."[10] The Turkomen were placed under Russian rule, Persia was endangered, and British trade in Persia and Afghanistan was steadily replaced by Russian merchandise.

From Samarkand rail lines were built to Tashkent and to Andhijan in Ferghana. Another line connected Merv (Mari) to Kushk (Kushka) on the Afghan frontier. The branch line to Kushk was militarily necessary because Kushk was the site for storage of railway materials necessary to extend the line. The railhead at Kushk, according to a senior Russian official, was built "solely for strategic purposes," and the minister of finance recommended it be connected to British railroads in India, through Afghanistan.[11] The extension to Kushk brought Russian troops and supplies within seventy miles of Herat, inside Afghanistan. In 1979 it was from Kushk that the Soviets launched their ground offensive into Afghanistan.

Prior to the 1880s, vast tracts of independently held and difficult terrain had lain between Russia and British India, serving as an antiroute between the two powers. With the completion of the Transcaspian Railway and the subjugation of the khanates, Russian routebuilding stirred an imperial game of routes. As one party advanced along a newly built route, the interest of the other lay in holding construction at bay. Russian route building, reconnaissance of terrain, assessment of tribal relations, and investigation of feasible new political-military ties and trading outlets along the Central and South Asian frontier zones urged a British response, as did their attempts to initiate direct trade connections with the Punjab and Kashmir.

Despite the fact that none of them became operational, Russian plans for the infiltration of Afghanistan and for the invasion of India were made often, and were promoted by men of such stature that the fear of attack became commonplace in the strategic consciousness of Britain's frontiersmen. These threats affected British routing policies in India and in Afghanistan. The plan presented in 1791 to the Empress Catherine by M. de St. Genie, advocating the invasion of India along the Bokhara-Kabul route, was followed in 1800, and again at Tilsit in 1807, by discussions between Napoleon and Tsar Paul regarding the former's notion of weakening Britain in Europe by destroying her in the colonies, particularly in India. Other plans followed: at the start of the Crimean War came General Duhamel's submission to Tsar Nicholas, that Russia

> can attack England in her only vulnerable point, in India, and thus force her to assemble so great a force in Asia as to weaken her action in Europe. History teaches us that nearly all the Powers which conquered India found their way to it through Central Asia and Persia, and that the roads by which Alexander the Great, Genghis Khan, Tamerlane, Sultan Baber, and lastly Nader Shah, broke into India are now also open; they pass through Khorassan and Afghanistan, whether they lead from Persia or from the Oxus. The towns of Candahar and Cabul are the gates of the Indies.[12]

Although in the Gortchakov-Granville agreement of 1872–73 the Russian chancellor had assured Britain that his country viewed Afghanistan as completely outside its sphere of influence, there followed further plans of invasion routed through Afghanistan. In 1878, for example, General Skobelev conjured up the most detailed plan of invasion yet. The routes from the Caspian, via Bokhara, and from Ferghana southward were all to be used in a three-pronged attack. Although the scheme was never put into practice, Lord Curzon noted that Skobelev was the most powerful Russian general in Central Asia and that he considered it worth his while to map out such a complex plan of operations.[13] It is not surprising, then, that the British, watching and listening from their outposts on the Indian frontier, should fret about the combined effect of new railroads and old invasion plans.

The British response to Russia amounted to a strategy in Afghanistan and inside India's North West Frontier which focused on the control and manipulation of access. British policy was five-pronged: the denial or circumvention of access routes that the Russians might attempt to control; the imposition of buffer status on Afghanistan; the attempt to influence route development within Afghanistan; the establishment of the Durand Line boundary between that state and British possessions in India; and the protection of the boundary through the construction, inside the frontier, of a network of strategic routes and military outposts.

British authorities in India and in London viewed attempts to build an intercontinental routing system, especially one that would have increased the mobility of troops and the movement of supplies across Afghanistan, as "strategically dangerous" to the stability and the security of India's frontier. Such a system could ease Russian attempts to menace the Indian frontier and, perhaps more important, it would force Britain to increase its investment in men and material to safeguard an already troublesome frontier.[14]

In 1903, Sir Arthur Balfour determined that "so long as it [Afghanistan] possesses few roads and no railways, it will be impossible for Russia to make effective use of her great numerical superiority at any point immediately vital to the Empire."[15] Afghanistan was to be inaccessible and impermeable, denying the possibility of swift, surprise movements across its frontiers. British trepidation over Russian railroad construction contributed largely to the formation of this Afghan buffer. It should also be noted, in view of what was to transpire fifty years later, that the British thought it wise for the Afghans to maintain minimum economic contacts with their northern neighbor.

Still, some proponents of the Forward School of British military strategy, as well as British citizens with economic interests, pressed for an extension of rail lines across Afghanistan. According to the Forward School, securing the British line of defense into Afghanistan required that railroads be constructed within that country. The suggestions of the Intelligence Branch of the government of India in 1891, regarding Afghanistan, are indicative of this perspective: they recommended that the Amir of Afghanistan guarantee the improvement of communications between India and Kandahar and Kabul, and supply the British with information about "roads and routes all over Afghanistan."[16]

In the final years of the nineteenth century, private citizens of Europe (including Britons), as well as agents of the Russian government, also made many proposals for the construction of rail lines in the Central Asian periphery. These lines would intrude into Afghan territory and connect the transport networks of the British with those of the Russians. In each case the British government set aside positive economic assessments and vetoed the projects. The supreme consideration was strategic. For example, a proposal to link Paris with Calcutta via Orenberg, Tashkent, Balkh, and Peshawar was approved by the Russians. Judged an economically sound proposal, it was then rejected by the British. General Annenkov proposed the connection of British and Russian railroads across Afghanistan. The route he specified would have linked Paris to India through Warsaw, Moscow, Baku, Herat, Kandahar, and Quetta. In 1906 the Russian newspaper *Novoe Vremya* also promoted these linkages between British and Russian rail.[17]

Inside India, however, Britain's officers were content with the roughly six-hundred-mile gap between the two railway systems. Lord Curzon said that although he found Annenkov's proposals "worthy of consideration," he felt that a host of factors, including "past history" and the "prejudices of the two countries," militated against cooperation in route building.[18] Where there was no trust, there would be no access.

In May 1905, British routing policy was enunciated again:

Russia [is] making steady progress toward Afghanistan and railways [are] under construction which could only be strategic. . . . A war on the North-West Frontier would be chiefly a problem of transport and supply. We must therefore allow nothing to be done to facilitate transport. Any attempt to make a railway in Afghanistan in connection with the Russian strategic railways would be regarded as an act of direct aggression against us. . . . As long as we say resolutely that railways in Afghanistan should only be made in time of war, we can make India absolutely secure. But if, through blindness or cowardness, we permit the slow absorption of the country, if strategic railways are allowed to creep close to our Frontier, we shall have to maintain a much larger army.[19]

Debate persisted about the merits of linking the railroads through a new network in Afghanistan, but traditional political and military preoccupations continued to triumph over the economic merits of the propositions. By 1905 the British were firmly set on a buffer policy. The outbreak of World War I served only to confirm their stance.

AFGHANISTAN

Inside Afghanistan, too, there was an unavoidable trade-off between the requirements of territorial and "ruler" security and the interests of economic growth and political integration. Foreign infrastructural aid was turned down for the sake of survival. The pressures on Afghanistan, a main artery in this game of routes, from Britain to the south and the Russians to the north pushed its rulers to take drastic measures: they denied themselves an advanced, large-scale routing network in order to preserve their freedom.

A nucleus of independent Afghan power first arose from the conquests and unification policies of a Saddozai Pakhtun, leader of the Abdali tribes—Ahmed Shah Durrani (1747–73).[20] By 1750 his territories encompassed all the lands south of the Hindu Kush up to the Indus River. Afghanistan's boundaries, however, which defined the territorial limits of the Amir's writ, emerged as a product of Afghan wrangling and Anglo-Russian negotiation and engineering. The northern border with Russia was first established in 1886. By 1888 it had been demarcated.

In 1895 the Anglo-Russian Joint Pamir Commission settled Afghanistan's eastern border, including within that country, and against the wishes of the Amir, the Wakhan ridge. This is a strip of narrow and strategically significant land bounded by the Pamirs, China, and the northern reaches of the subcontinent. Coveted by Russia since 1891, it owns numerous passes of entry into Hunza and Chitral in the northern subcontinent. Wakhan was forcibly inserted inside Afghanistan as part of the buffer between the imperial powers. When the buffer fell to Soviet power in the next century, the rationale behind its original inclusion in Afghan territory came once again to the fore: Wakhan posed old dangers to the modern rulers of the North West Frontier and China.[21]

In 1893 the British authorities and Amir Abdur Rahman agreed to set up the Durand Line, delineating the southern line of responsibility for the maintenance of law and order. This line divided British and Afghan zones of influence and responsibility in the tribal borderland. According to a British frontiersman of the time, Robert Issaq Bruce, the Durand Line was established mainly to facilitate British control over the tribes: "No measure has been carried through since our occupation of the Punjab so pregnant of possibilities for the pacification and strengthening of our frontier, and the civilization and attaching of the Border tribes to our rule."[22] This artificial antiroute was an awkward contrivance that would embitter Afghanistan's relations with Pakistan and spur the geopolitical reorientation of twentieth-century Afghanistan.

Abdur Rahman, Amir of Afghanistan (1880–1901), an astute autocrat with a penchant for cruelty, held conflicting views about the merits of the Durand Line. At various times he desired, and at others he uncomfortably acquiesced in, a boundary that would distinguish his tribal possessions from those of the British. Foremost among his considerations in agreeing to the new antiroute were the need to limit the expansion of British rail and road communications (which were mushrooming along the frontier), to stamp out tribal rebellions and raids, and to acknowledge Britain's control of his southern access routes across which flowed Afghanistan's trade, spare parts, gasoline, and, most important, arms and ammunition. His own interests in the matter were not entirely material, because he could not resist. In the past, the Afghans had occasionally vanquished the British: during the First Afghan War, for example, all but one of the British members of the invading force perished. Still, resisting the British was no small task. As one British officer put it, "We advance, we absorb, we dominate, we destroy independence."[23]

Artificial antiroutes are best formed with some reference to natural barriers. The Durand Line, however, conformed to little geographical and no ethnic logic. It divided tribal lands and even tribes. An absurdity was perpetrated upon the 400,000-strong Mohmands; those in the Mohmand hills were cut off from those settled in the valleys of Kunar and Jalalabad. The Pakhtun tribes were neither consulted nor involved in any aspect of the negotiations. They would also pay no heed to the closure symbolized by the boundary.

The Durand Line was an implausible line of separation and closure. If its objective was to reverse the patterns of movement and allegiance across the passes, it did not, and could not, succeed. The tribes continued to move freely across the boundary. (In the Afghan war of the twentieth century, this antiroute was in effect erased.) Nor were Amir Abdur Rahman and his successors ever satisfied with the documents they had signed. Although the agreement was confirmed by Habibullah in 1905, Amanullah in 1921, and Nadir Shah in 1930, the Afghans never relinquished their desire to reunify Pakhtun tribal territories and to expand the territorial limits of Pakhtun rule southward to the sea. In the middle of the twentieth century, arguments over the validity of the Durand Line were to prompt controversy between Afghanistan and Pakistan over the creation of a state called Pakhtunistan.

All these activities—negotiation and agreement, demarcation and delimitation—surrounding Afghanistan's external boundaries reflected a keenly felt need to set up artificial antiroutes, which, through accepted legal authority, could establish separate spheres of influence and, as the buffer state was to do, could restrain the advance of British and Russian power toward one another. During these maneuvers, Afghanistan was, as Amir Abdur Rahman delicately described it, "like a poor goat on whom the lion and the bear have both fixed their eyes."[24]

Mistrustful of both the Russians and the British, the Afghan Amirs evolved policies for security and economic growth which denied major routes within their territory. The Amirs sacrificed economic advance to the survival of both the state and the ruler. The domestic politics of the early Afghan state was a struggle for the definition of spheres of control between the ruler of the state and the leaders of the tribes. Kabul's governors generally adhered to the policy of noninterference in the affairs of powerful tribes. The evolution of the Afghan state, as Olivier Roy suggests, was "bound up with the search on the part of the state bureaucracy [hukumat] for autonomy from the tribes." Initially, he says, it was the tribes that saw the state as "existing on the periphery," and the "historical mission of the Afghan state may be summarised as an attempt to reverse this relationship in order to pass from the periphery to the center."[25]

An arm's-length approach to tribal affairs required Afghan Amirs to hesitate before striking paths into tribal territories. In fact, Afghan domestic policy regarding rail and road construction in the outlying areas coincided with the British policy of access denial. Although Abdur Rahman followed an ugly policy of pacification toward the tribes, which included execution, deportation, and resettlement, few Amirs would risk stirring Pakhtun revolt. These tribes considered route building—especially by the British—as an intrusive attempt to control their land, their leaders, and their economy. For them, as one modern historian notes, the railways were seen "variously as a sinister plot to advance the centralizing schemes of the Afghan government at their expense or as a direct British military threat."[26] Today the tribes hold similar suspicions. Each new effort to cut a route in the borderlands of Afghanistan and Pakistan occasions a new and often violent quarrel with local tribes.

Still, Afghan and British policies were founded on different rationales. The British concern was with Russia and the Pakhtun tribes of the northwestern subcontinent. The Afghan concern was with Britain and Russia, as well as with the tribes. Afghanistan's harsh terrain made it difficult for any invader to hold the entire country. Amir Abdur Rahman was not prepared to create an infrastructure of access (however beneficial it might be to the economy) which would increase the mobility of troops, Russian or British, or the more efficient movement of supplies necessary to hold Afghanistan. He opted, in fact, to follow what Vartan Gregorian describes as a policy of "aloofness, isolation and deliberate underdevelopment."[27]

This is not to argue that Abdur Rahman was not interested in modernization. Among his other achievements, he systematized the Afghan monetary and revenue systems and hired foreign experts, physicians, printers, geologists, and engineers. Within Afghanistan, he attempted to improve trade routes between Kabul and Balkh; Kabul, Ghazni, and Herat; Herat and Kandahar; Jalalabad and Kafiristan; and Kabul and Peshawar. Even in this domestic sphere, however, he believed in the strict control of access: for example, inhabitants of Kabul needed a special pass to travel beyond the city limits.[28]

The Amir believed that the only solution to the threat of foreign encroachment on Afghan land lay in the denial of access. His views on route building—and on railroads in particular—echoed those of Frederick II of Prussia, who espoused the view that good communications only made a country easier to overrun.[29] Thus, when members of the Forward School proposed a railroad linking Kandahar with Herat, Abdur Rahman reacted quickly and angrily: he refused even to consider the proposal. And when the British built the Khojak Tunnel within their new Indian frontier and completed construction of a railway up to New Chaman near the border with Afghanistan, the Amir accused them of plunging a "knife into my vitals." In a policy continued by his successor, the Amir forbade his subjects to make use of the railway for trading purposes. The caravans that traded between Kandahar and Quetta were forced to journey across the mountains and to deposit their goods at the first outpost on the southern side of the Khojak Tunnel. Any Afghan who rode the railway was to suffer the punishment of death. In consequence the volume of traded goods fell by about two-thirds.[30]

Abdur Rahman thought that railways, these "most important means and necessary factors of trade," should be delayed "until such time as we shall possess a sufficient army for the protection of our kingdom." Where insufficient military capability existed to guard against the perils of access, insufficient reason existed to encourage the presence of routes. Abdur Rahman had carefully thought through the problem of rail construction:

> Railways ought to be opened, at first, in the interior of Afghanistan, quite away from the boundaries of the neighboring powers, and should run only between one town and another in the country itself. By-and-bye, however, when the country is strong enough to defend itself against all foreign aggression, then the railway lines may be joined on to those of the neighboring countries in such a manner that the lines will be put in connection with whichever Power is less hostile than the other.[31]

Abdur Rahman's successors followed modified versions of his policy. Habibullah (1901–19) made some improvements on the principal Afghan trade routes, but he considered no railroads. He, too, rationalized his country's impoverishment as the "price of independence"; a British railroad, he said, would be like a "spear pointed at the heart of Afghanistan." Habibullah also saw additional benefits in rejecting access: the country would incur no foreign debt, nor would it be dependent in any way on a foreign country. During his tenure, a British sympathizer, Sir J. D. Rees said, "As to the Ameer's reluctance to admit railways into his territories, I confess, I sympathize heartily with it, for I believe the coming of the railways would mean the end of independent Afghanistan."[32] Amanullah (1919–29) repaired a few old roads, built a handful of new ones, and even made unrealized plans for a railroad. It was to be built in the interior, with tracks to border regions to be laid in the distant, uncertain future.

By 1933, the network of routes in Afghanistan was no spur to economic development. With an area of 250,000 square miles, Afghanistan possessed 1,800–2,000 miles of roads, very few of good quality. The Great Game had created a convergence in British and Afghan routing policy. As long as their country was militarily weak and sandwiched between two expanding empires, Amir Abdur Rahman and his successors followed a policy of deterrence designed to raise the costs of entry, occupation, and control for invaders. When security was the prime component of state policy and the responsibilities of development did not press upon a ruler, such an approach to access could be used effectively to ensure the survival of the ruler and his territory.

THE INDIAN FRONTIER

Britain's two-tiered routing response to Russia was not restricted to Afghanistan. Not only were foreign rail and road projects blocked in Afghanistan but the British also constructed roads and railroads, forts, and cantonments, along the North West Frontier. They sought to decrease the turbulence wrought by the tribes of the frontier without directly administering all Pakhtun lands: so small was the number of troops with which they had to control all India, they could not even consider mastery over the Pakhtuns. In the latter part of the nineteenth century and into the twentieth century, therefore, British defenses were based on the establishment of a mixed system of effective logistics and political negotiation.

Lord Curzon's scheme for the defense and control of the frontier hinged on three propositions: that tribal levies be raised to patrol their own lands; that British troops be deployed further inland, away from the immediate border areas; that new roads and rail lines be cut to permit the rapid deployment of troops and supplies to the frontier. Where overland access from Afghanistan was relatively easy, a few vital forts—such as the one at Malakand in the north—were built. These were then linked to Peshawar and Rawalpindi by metaled road and rail. During the Afghan wars of the nineteenth century, some Pakhtun tribes on the British side of the frontier had abetted the Afghans, giving an additional incentive to British construction in tribal territory.[33]

British route building in the frontier lands was extensive. Peshawar was linked to Jamrud by a broad-gauge railway and with Landi Kotal by a road through Mullagori territory. Mahsud tribal territory was penetrated by roads. Routes were also carved out in Waziristan, and the British built a thirty-two-mile-long metal road through the Khyber Pass. Among the military cantonments erected were those at Wazirabad, Rawalpindi, and Peshawar. These posts were linked by roads. The two hundred-mile-long North West Frontier road from Khushalgarh to Dera Ismail Khan, via Kohat and Bannu, was begun in 1885 and completed in 1892. Other important military roads of the period include those completed in 1890 in northwestern Baluchistan from Dera Ghazi Khan to Loralai via Fort Munro; the Murree-to-Kohat route, completed in 1891; and the 127-mile Kaghan Valley military road, which was required to transport supplies to the garrisons at Chilas and Gilgit. These routes did not initially (and in some cases did not ever) promote either trade or agriculture. Road building during the entire two decades leading up to 1901 promoted strategic goals.[34] In 1925 the British ran a railroad through the Khyber Pass.

The borderlands were divided into a province and some tribal territories. In November 1901 the establishment of the North West Frontier Province was announced. It incorporated the districts of Peshawar, Kohat, and Hazara and the trans-Indus portions of Bannu and Dera Ismail Khan, which were transfered from the Punjab. The Pakhtun tribes threatened the British with a loss in the Great Game, since they could, and frequently did, disrupt British communications and movement along the borderland. Early British strategies for coping with the tribes proved unsuccessful. Numerous campaigns, bloody expeditions, and endless, futile blockades were instituted—to little avail. On 5 March 1923, Sir Denys Brays, the British foreign secretary, enunciated a new policy of peaceful penetration. He pointed to the source of tribal autonomy: "In their inaccessibility" he said, "lies their strength." More routes were advocated. The British tried to insinuate their control deeper into the tribal areas "through a road system."[35] A hectic period of bridge, road, and railroad construction followed. This infrastructure became the core of the British system of frontier defense and pacification, applauded for its military and economic benefits: "The construction of these roads will facilitate the pursuit of raiding gangs, further the interests of commerce, and lead to increased mobility."[36]

The building of roads and railroads, however, seldom met with a happy response from the tribes, and the British were required to shed blood in the service of their routes. The tribes of the periphery rose, as the Amirs of Afghanistan had always feared they would. Of the

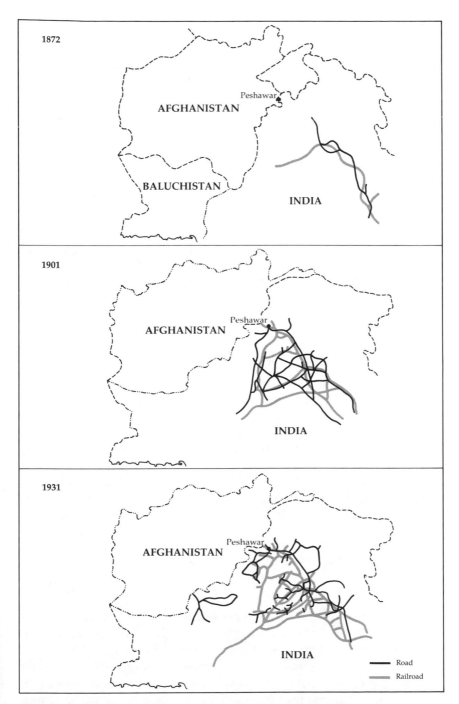

Map 7 British route construction in the North West Frontier. Based on road and rail maps in Joseph E. Schwartzberg, ed., *A Historical Atlas of South Asia* (Chicago: University of Chicago Press, 1978).

many uprisings of the period, among the worst were those of 1909, 1933, and 1935. Initial construction work on the Loi-Shilman railway, for example, was abandoned because it caused the Mohmand tribe to rise in revolt. One observer predicted that continued work on that railway would have provoked a conflagration.[37]

In the *Civil and Military Gazette* of August 1935, however, the British were still waxing enthusiastic about the potential benefits that roads could provide for the tribes. They suggested yet another launching of "road construction projects side by side with the plans for economic development of the country through which the proposed road passes," which "will give a new orientation to the thoughts of the tribesmen on the reasons underlying the road programme."[38] But new roads continued to meet with new revolts. Construction threatened the political and economic autonomy of the tribes, as well as their independence of action.

The Great Game of routes left an indelible imprint on the geopolitical evolution of the region. It was deepest in Afghanistan. Most of the major decisions—by the British, the Russians, and the Afghans—to build or not to build routes were based on considerations of security. Maps tell the story: there stands, in the imperial era, a virtually routeless, poor, but independent Afghanistan; while to its north and to its south, road and rail networks are approaching it. In the years after the partition of the subcontinent, Afghanistan, landlocked, encircled, and dependent upon southern routes previously controlled by the British Empire, would seek an outlet from its historical dilemma. Afghanistan would clamor against the Durand Line and demand a new state be etched from the territory of nascent Pakistan.

Modern Afghan Geopolitics: Trade, Transit, the Tribes, and Aid

In this story of routes the impress of the imperial politics of access upon the frontier lands of contemporary Afghanistan and Pakistan is apparent. In the postimperial period Afghanistan, in its pursuit of foreign and security goals, and in its ambitious development plans for increased trade and economic growth, inevitably faced new dilemmas about how to balance the old requirements for security with the new responsibilities for development. Traditional, historical, and geographical constraints still bound state behavior, but new opportunities also became evident.

PAKHTUNISTAN

The Afghan argument for a state called Pakhtunistan to be carved out of Pakistan has been on one level an argument for the right of all cultural, ethnic, and linguistically distinct minorities who form "nations" to a separate statehood. In the developing world, colonial boundary-making left societies torn apart or forced together. Numerous ethnolinguistic peoples were placed within a single state or divided across many states. In these newly configured states the repeated claim to self-determination—to nationhood—is not trivial, and it is extremely dangerous to ruling elites. The policy of the new political center in these states promotes, at least verbally, the political integration of the peripheries and a unitary national identity. For these central governments, the limits to self-determination have been set. For the minority peoples most often resident in economic and geographical peripheries, however, self-determination often continues to be a live concept.

Inside the subcontinent Pakhtun nationalists, led by the late Khan Abdul Ghaffar Khan, the "Frontier Gandhi," have made demands ranging from greater Pakhtun self-governance to an independent Pakhtunistan. In 1947 a meeting of Ghaffar Khan's "Khudai Khidmatgars" (God's Servants) called for the establishment of an independent Pakhtunistan. Still, Ghaffar Khan's Pakhtunistan was comprised of the North West Frontier Province; he did not envision its association with Kabul.

Afghanistan also does not claim a Pakhtun state that would incorporate the entire Pakhtun "nation," both its own Pakhtuns and those of Pakistan—only the latter. Historically, the Afghan Amirs maintained close political, military, and economic links with the Pakhtun tribes who roam the lands to the south of the Durand Line. But in the era of the nation-state both Pakistan and Afghanistan laid claim to the allegiance of many different peoples and tribes. Afghanistan's ethnological argument, in fact, could be read as inimical to its own interests, since the country houses so many different ethnic groups with links to the lands beyond Afghanistan.

The Afghans have also made territorial claims based upon the lands acquired by Ahmed Shah Durrani in the eighteenth century. The claim is disputed by those who argue that a legal agreement was signed by Amir Abdur Rahman and Sir Mortimer Durand and more-over that Ahmed Shah Durrani's conquests extended far beyond the lands claimed—at one stage they reached close to Delhi.[39]

On another, more concrete level, however, the Afghan pursuit of Pakhtunistan may be interpreted as originating in the search for economically precious access routes. Afghanistan's active cultivation of the scheme has centered on the importance to a landlocked country, that lacks control over routes to open waters, of the acquisition or control of routes leading southward through Pakistan to the Arabian Sea.

The Afghan claims for Pakhtunistan extend across the NWFP and Baluchistan to the Arabian Sea shoreline of southern Pakistan. Afghan territorial demands have varied, but they always include the Pakhtun areas of Pakistan. Often lands beyond the NWFP are also involved. In 1951 the Afghan journal *Anis*, a semiofficial publication, printed a map of Pakhtunistan which included Chitral, the NWFP, and the Pakhtun-occupied areas of Baluchistan stretching to the Indus.[40] The incorporation of Baluchistan, whose Pakhtun inhabitants are gathered mostly around Quetta, and which contains a number of different ethnic groups, makes sense only if we consider the proposal in the light of Baluchistan's valuable maritime frontier.

In 1952 the Afghan Information Bureau in London published a long tract detailing the territory, resources, and potential of a Pakhtunistan that incorporated the areas between the Afghan-Pakistan border and the Indus river, "which is the natural and historical border of the Indian subcontinent" (thereby denying the validity of the Durand Line), and the lands from Chitral in the north to Baluchistan in the south. According to the tract, the new state would have significant economic advantages because it would be "bound on the west by the river Indus, the banks of which river from the borders of Kashmir down to the Arabian Sea, have always been considered one of the most fertile regions of the world." One-hundred-ninety-thousand square miles were claimed. The text is careful to reiterate that the future state of Pakhtunistan "has the advantage of access to the sea in Baluchistan which is obviously a factor of great importance in the future trade of the country." Perhaps the most authoritative definition of Pakhtunistan came when, in 1969, the Afghan government issued a postage stamp that depicted the future country. The map on the

Map 8 Afghan territorial claims for Pakhtunistan

stamp included the NWFP and Baluchistan in the territories of Pakhtunistan.[41]

Since the time of Amir Abdur Rahman, the rulers of Afghanistan have recognized the economic, political, and military vulnerabilities inherent in their country's land-locked location. In the nineteenth century they were limited to the denial of peripheral routes within Afghan territory in order to sustain the minimal security goal of an independent existence. British control of the NWFP and Baluchistan provided little scope for the southward penetration of Afghan influence. Still, Afghans were aware even then of the desirability of the acquisition of southern access routes. Abdur Rahman pondered the way in which imperial constraints on his kingdom restricted its economic opportunities. At the turn of the century, he wrote:

> Afghanistan ought to secure a footing upon the ocean. . . . The southwestern corner of Afghanistan is very close to the corner of the Persian Gulf and the Indian Ocean, and from this only a small, plain plateau of ground between Kandahar, Baluchistan, Persia, and part of Karachi [sic]. . . . I always had a great fancy for a little piece of this sandy desert . . . of great value if annexed to Afghanistan in order to bring the country in touch with the ocean. . . . If Afghanistan had access to the ocean there is no doubt that the country would soon grow rich and prosperous. . . . If no favourable opportunity occurs in my lifetime to bring about this purpose, my sons and successors must always keep their eyes on this corner.[42]

The Afghans pursued their interest in this little piece of sandy desert during on-again, off-again negotiations with Germany which began as early as 1915. The Germans wanted Afghan support for the weakening of the British in India. With little fondness for their overbearing southern neighbor, the Afghans were willing to talk, but at a price. If one is to provoke the ire of a powerful neighbor, it is wise to seek enormous compensation. The Afghans demanded, in return for their help in the ouster of the British, guarantees of Afghan independence and assistance in the acquisition of access routes to the sea.[43]

In 1915 a German emissary promised Amir Habibullah "territorial concessions along the Indian Frontier and a free port at Karachi"; and between 1939 and 1941 the Afghans negotiated with the Germans once more regarding "the possible territorial changes resulting for Afghanistan from the war," including the "British possessions in the southeast and south to Karachi."[44] Although the joint venture came to naught, the two countries maintained good relations through World War II.

In 1947, as the subcontinent was divided into the new states of India and Pakistan, the Afghans sought to assert their ideological and territorial claims. They argued with the Interim Government of India that when the British departed, the 1893 Durand Line Treaty should lapse automatically and large portions of the future state of Pakistan thereby "revert" to Afghanistan. On 21 June 1947, less than two months before the creation of Pakistan, the Afghan prime minister, Mohammed Hashim Khan, insisted that his country's future neighbor Pakistan "will realise that our country with its population and trade, needs an outlet to the sea, which is very essential. . . . If the nations of the world desire peace and justice . . . it will be easy for us to get an outlet to the sea."[45]

The Afghans informed the British that Pakistan must be made to continue the Afghan right of transit from the Khyber to Karachi. And in November 1947 an Afghan envoy returned home from a visit to Pakistan and broadcast the following Afghan demands on the new state: the Pakhtun tribal areas must form a "free, sovereign province," and Afghanistan must be given access to the sea through the provision of either "an Afghan corridor in West Baluchistan" or a "free Afghan Zone in Karachi."[46] Once the strong northward pressure exerted by the British died away, in sum, Afghanistan began to press its claim—through propaganda, mass demonstrations, armed clashes, and the severance of diplomatic relations—for a zone of access through Pakistani territory. In August 1949 a group of Afridi Pakhtun tribesmen formally launched the new state of Pakhtunistan.

The Soviet Union has supported Afghan proposals for a referendum on the question of Pakhtunistan. It first "expressed sympathy" for Afghan claims during the December 1955 visit of Nikita Khrushchev and Nikolai Bulganin to Kabul. In the Joint Soviet-Afghan Communiqué of 4 March 1960, issued at Kabul, a Soviet spokesman said that the problem of Pakhtunistan demands the "application of the principal of self-determination on the basis of the UN Charter."[47]

In Soviet writings of the 1950s all Pashtu-speakers were regarded as Afghans, and both Soviets and Afghans neglected the economic ties between the Pakhtuns of the NWFP and the rest of the subcontinent. Still, the Soviets have sometimes qualified their support for Pakhtunistan. For example, they have never "declared" themselves on the issue of Afghan claims to non-Pakhtun areas such as Gilgit, Chitral, and southern Baluchistan.[48] When in pursuit of better ties with Pakistan, the Soviets have also tried to avoid entanglement in the politics of Pakhtunistan. And when their larger interests have been at stake, as in the 1988 Geneva talks to secure the withdrawal of Soviet troops from Afghanistan, they have been swift to take umbrage at Afghan attempts to jeopardize negotiations by raising the Pakhtunistan issue.

As a result of their territorial dispute Afghanistan and Pakistan followed mutually antagonistic foreign, security, and economic policies. Afghanistan's interest in Pakhtunistan led to a policy of ideological and territorial aggrandizement, and relations between the two states were hostile. Afghanistan trifled with Pakistan's territorial integrity, for example, by expanding ties with Pakhtun tribal leaders inside the Pakistani frontier, playing host to them in Kabul, paying them large subsidies, founding schools for them, infiltrating the tribes with agents, and directing a barrage of propaganda against Pakistan.[49] There is a sad irony here: Afghanistan's hostile security relations with Pakistan were balanced by its economic dependence on its southern neighbor for the movement of population and goods. The numerous routes of migration and trade which cut across the boundary between the two countries were heavily traveled, and the Afghan economy was dependent on the viability of these routes. Yet Afghanistan treated Pakistan as a neighbor to be challenged.

AFGHANISTAN'S TIES WITH PAKISTAN

Afghanistan's location and terrain have resulted in internal fragmentation, poverty, and heavy reliance on foreign trade. Before the Soviet Union's invasion in 1979, northern Afghanistan had only 3.7 miles of rail. This predicament was shaped by the exigencies of the Great Game, the high cost of construction imposed by Afghanistan's terrain, and the difficulties of choosing a track gauge. Because it is landlocked, Afghanistan has relied on three main outlets for economic intercourse with the rest of the world: through Iran to the west, through the Soviet Union to the north, and through Pakistan to the south (each possesses a different railroad gauge). The rail networks of these three countries are reached by road. The Iranian railhead at Mashad is about 195 miles from Herat. The Soviet railhead at Kushka is 65 miles north of Herat; and Mazar-i-Sharif in northern Afghanistan is near two branches of the Soviet railroad at Termez. The Pakistani railway at Quetta lies 130 miles south of Kandahar.

Both the Soviet and Pakistani routes have been heavily used. The Soviet Union has offered Afghanistan improving terms for the shipment of its goods through the provision of transport linkages to the Pacific (via Vladivostok), to northern Europe and the United States (via Leningrad), and to southern Europe (via the Black Sea ports). Afghanistan has also been economically dependent on Pakistan's road and rail routes to the port at Karachi. There are two main ways: the Peshawar-Karachi route and the Chaman-Karachi route. The former is better traveled—over two-thirds of Afghanistan's transit trade through Pakistan moves across the Khyber in this direction.

Afghanistan's need for the Pakistani transport network was owed to the legal import-export transit trade that flowed through Karachi, the unrecorded transactions of illegal frontier trade, and the movement of peoples in the seasonal migration of Afghan nomads into Pakistan. The transit trade through Pakistan was regulated by five-yearly Transit Trade Agreements between Afghanistan and its neighbor. The agreements commited Pakistan to grant all the necessary facilities to Afghan goods traveling along its road and rail systems, as well as at the port of Karachi. The transit trade in the export category included food, crude materials, chemicals, manufactured goods, and machinery and transport equipment. The import category included food, beverages, tobacco, mineral fuels, animal and vegetable oils, manufactured goods, and transport equipment. Before the border closures, about 175 railway wagons filled with dried fruits and nuts also traveled through Peshawar to India between November and February each year. Between September and December truckloads of fresh fruit also moved into India.[50]

The frontier smuggling trade, which involved local Afghan items such as dried fruit and karakul and foreign goods ranging from electronic equipment to hosiery and cosmetics, brought a healthy profit to the Afghan government and continues unhindered in the tribal belt of Pakistan. Exact statistics are not available of course, but one calculation made during the 1960s estimated that goods worth Rs. 4–5 crores ($2.2 to $2.78 million) found customers in Pakistan. The value of goods smuggled into Pakistan and into Iran (which consisted mainly of sheep) has been conservatively estimated by another source at about one-fifths of the value of Afghanistan's total commercial trade.[51] These goods were transferred across the Durand Line freely; as one Afridi tribesman put it, "You might call what we do smuggling. But to us it's just trade."[52] Since import tariffs were high in Pakistan, goods such as radios, tires, and rayon were imported into Afghanistan and then smuggled back into Pakistan to be sold at tribal village markets or in the bazaar in Peshawar.

Both countries avert their gaze and smuggling flourishes, although Pakistan suffers loss of revenue. Still, the Pakistani government placates the tribes (they have stressed the income and employment opportunities the trade creates), and the Afghan government earns valuable foreign exchange. By preventing depopulation, smuggling also bolsters the economic life of the region. Customs revenue lost to the government of Pakistan has been balanced by the monies saved on additional law enforcement efforts in the area. A government official said: "If we didn't provide the tribes with a source of living, they would become criminals. . . . Now our tribesmen can't afford not to be a part of Pakistan. They are too much committed through trade and the real estate they have been able to buy outside the tribal area."[53] For all these reasons, the first illegal duty-free markets were reportedly endorsed by the Pakistani authorities. Moreover, the Pakistanis, like the British before them, cannot properly monitor or control the trading arrangements of the tribal heartland, which has few roads and numerous passes. They try to enforce—often unsuccessfully—only a few modest rules: for example, smuggled items must be carried on the caravan tracks rather than along the main roads.

Another source of Afghanistan's reliance on cross-boundary routes was the seasonal movement of the Afghan nomads, the powindahs, into Pakistan. (The Afghans argue that the Durand Line endangered the livelihood of these migrants.) Even at the high point of Anglo-Russian rivalry, the powindahs crossed the passes and made their way to the Indus plains and beyond, sometimes as far east as Bihar and Bengal. Historically, these nomads have been important carriers in the caravan trade that traveled from Central to South Asia.

Each year before 1980, roughly 200,000–300,000 powindahs, mainly Ghilzai Pakhtuns, would move—whole villages with their animals. In the autumn months the powindahs crossed into Pakistan through the Tochi, Gomal, Kurram, Khyber and other passes. They meandered across the Durand Line to winter in the plains of the subcontinent, searching for work and pastureland, returning to Afghanistan with the advent of spring. Their seasonal migration had been called "the greatest remaining mass movement of men and animals in [the] world."[54] Until the hostility between Afghanistan and Pakistan affected their routes, the powindahs were free to move across the Durand Line without passports or visas.

These forms of dependence upon Pakistan were exceptionally important to Afghanistan's economic viability, especially because of the significance of trade to the Afghan economy. And it was in the theater of trade that Afghanistan's radical political and geographical realignment would be acted out. The Afghans were to reorient their trade and, gradually, their other domestic and foreign involvements, when Pakistan, in effect, closed off Afghanistan's access to the southern trade routes.

In Afghanistan, foreign trade had long been considered the "sole viable path to economic growth". According to one estimate made in 1960, "Trade provided the earliest access road to the riches of the world without which no Afghan King or private investor could hope to increase the country's productive capacity. Because trade has been the traditional and most natural way of adding to the meager resources, it has assumed increasing importance as development efforts have become more intensive."[55] A large proportion of Afghan trade traveled through Pakistan. Between 1955 and 1960, the years of the first and second border closures, the total value of Afghanistan's foreign trade through Pakistan was calculated to be approximately $21 million in 1955; $25 million in 1956; $43 million in 1957; $40 million in 1958; $47 million in 1959.[56]

As the main source of taxes, and therefore of government financing, monies from trade were vital to the economy. Heavy duties on traded goods were the main source of revenue. By implication, this dependence on trade taxes required that for income to be predictable or to rise, trade must be regular or must be increased.[57] Any disruption or severance of trade routes would have a doubly disruptive impact on the Afghan economy. An untimely, unpredictable gap between the financial resources needed to reach development targets and the expected revenues from trade would hamper development plans.

STRUGGLE OVER ROUTES:
THE BORDER CLOSURES

The verbal (and, on occasion, the physical) contest between Pakistan and Afghanistan over the issue of Pakhtunistan expressed itself in a series of actions that damaged beyond repair any hopes of cooperation between the two neighbors. The 1950s and 1960s saw hostilities ranging from propaganda warfare to the sacking of consulates. Yet the greatest damage in political, economic, and strategic terms, was done when the struggle for a Pakhtun state became a conflict over access to, and denial of, routes.

A focus of the Great Game thus became a focus of this smaller game. Territorial sovereignty, trade, transit, and the tribes were the stakes. Since its inception Pakistan had been plagued by Pakhtunistan; (India increased the pressure by supporting the Afghan claim. In 1965, the deputy minister of external affairs, Dinesh Singh, promised India's full "support for the legitimate aspirations of the Pakhtoon people."[58]) As a response to Afghan pressure for access in the south, the Pakistanis manipulated Afghanistan's need for the trade, transit, and migratory routes that ran through their territory. Afghanistan's southern routes were blocked, access was sporadically denied to the port of Karachi, and Pakistan thereby fastened a grip on the Afghan economy.

The closure of the Afghan-Pakistan border and the blockade of routes led the Afghans to consider alternative routing strategies and promoted the expansion of road systems linking Afghanistan to the Soviet Union. This reaction was to lead to a redirection of Afghanistan's economic and then political flows, and finally to a loss of the country's independence.

Pakistan took these measures in response to Afghanistan's irredentist claims. Hindsight makes it clear that these early failures of two weak states to promote a conciliatory regional diplomacy sowed the seeds of a crisis in Central and South Asian security. The Pakhtunistan quarrel caused Kabul to look to the Soviets for economic and political support. In 1979 Afghanistan would fall to the Soviet Union. During the long Soviet occupation, the Pakhtuns of Afghanistan would move south into Pakistan—spurring new economic and political schisms there—and westward, into Iran. Soviet access to southern Afghanistan in the 1980s would also contribute to a new strategic situation in West Asia—in Iran and the Persian Gulf.

The United States, a prominent donor of infrastructural aid to Afghanistan, deemed itself too geographically distant to insinuate itself successfully between the small country and its giant neighbor. Its efforts to reconcile Afghan with Pakistani interests also failed. And so the culmination of a series of events which began in the routing

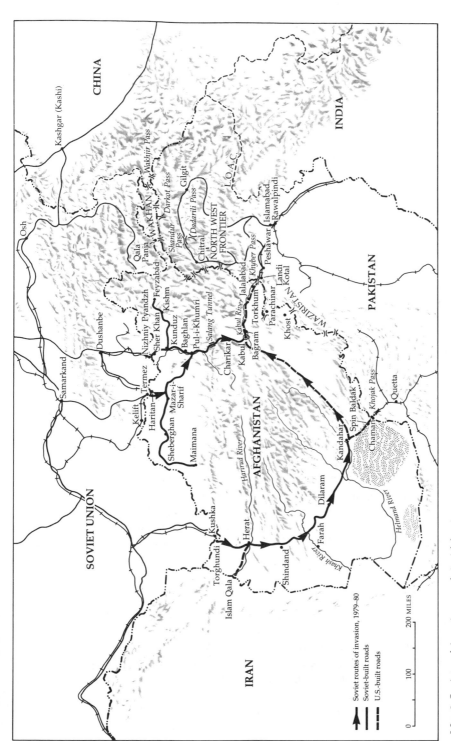

Map 9 Soviet and American roads in Afghanistan

CHINA

Kashgar (Kashi)

INDIA

SOVIET UNION

Osh

Samarkand

Dushanbe

Kelift

Termez

Haritan

Nizhniy Pyandzh

Sher Khan

Kunduz

Baghlan

Pul-i-Khumri

Salang Tunnel

Kishm

Feyzabad

Qala Panja

WAKHAN

Wakhir Pass

Dirkot Pass

Gilgit

Shandur Pass

(Dadarili Pass)

Chitral

NORTH WEST FRONTIER

L.O.A.C.

Charikar

Kabul

Kabul River

Jalalabad

Torkhum

Khyber Pass

Bagram

Peshawar

Islamabad

Rawalpindi

Landi Kotal

Parachinar

Khost

WAZIRISTAN

PAKISTAN

Sheberghan

Mazar-i-Sharif

Maimana

Harirud River

AFGHANISTAN

Kandahar

Spin Baldak

Chaman

Khojak Pass

Quetta

Dilaram

Farah

Khash River

Helmand River

Torghundi

Kushka

Islam Qala

Herat

Shindand

IRAN

Soviet routes of invasion, 1979–80

Soviet-built roads

U.S.-built roads

0   100   200 MILES

war between Afghanistan and Pakistan confirmed Amir Abdur
Rahman's worst fears.

Three times, in 1950, 1955, and 1961, Afghanistan's promotion of
Pakhtunistan led to responses from Pakistan which ranged from
moderate interference in the movement of Afghan goods traveling the
Kabul-Karachi route to complete closure of the border. In pushing for
Pakhtunistan, the Afghans miscalculated the support they would
receive from Pakhtuns within Pakistan and the ability of the government of Pakistan to make good its threats. Landlocked Afghanistan's
rights of transit could be readily manipulated by the coastal state.

In the early years of the conflict, Afghan imports and exports
traveling through Pakistan were inconvenienced. A few problems
resulted from administrative chaos in post partition Pakistan. The
port at Karachi was congested and inefficient. Other transit problems
could have been deliberately caused. For example, Afghan goods
faced long delays in shipment and high demurrage costs. The
Pakistan authorities placed a ceiling on the number of rail cars requisi-
tioned to ply the roads northward from Karachi. Afghan merchandise
was often damaged; on occasion it failed to arrive in Kabul; and
sometimes the permission needed to export certain products from
Afghanistan was denied.[59]

In 1950 the Afghans became very agitated about Pakhtunistan, and
Pakistan's responses became more aggressive. In July of the previous
year the Afghan parliament had rejected the validity of the Durand
Line; in August 1950 Pakhtunistan flags were hoisted in Kabul; and
on 30 September 1950 the Afghans raided Pakistani frontier areas. In
retaliation, the Pakistanis slowed down the flow of essential goods
into Afghanistan. They stopped Afghan gasoline imports for nearly
three months. The official Pakistani justification was a legal-technical
one: Afghan lorries were not deemed roadworthy because they failed
upon inspection to conform to the specifications of the government of
Pakistan.[60]

In 1955 the Pakhtunistan issue again became inflamed. The border
between Pakistan and Afghanistan was closed for almost five months,
and no Afghan goods were allowed to travel on Pakistani roads. This
time the furor arose when Pakistani authorities, for constitutional and
political purposes, decided to restructure the country's internal politi-
cal-administrative boundaries. All the provinces of West Pakistan
were amalgamated into a single unit. The scheme, announced on 27
March 1955, incorporated, of course, the NWFP.

The Afghans viewed this inclusion as a threat to the status of the NWFP as the core area of Pakhtunistan. Afghan mobs attacked Pakistani missions in Kandahar, Kabul, and Jalalabad. Then the Pakistanis moved. They closed the trade routes to Afghan men and material, and diplomatic relations were cut. This rupture of the southern roads was an early catalyst for the reorientation of Afghanistan's trade towards the Soviet Union.

Even though full diplomatic relations were restored in 1956, the course of Afghan-Pakistan relations was never steady. Neither country could count on the continued good behavior or the promises of the other. In fact, another crisis was already brewing. Between 19 and 21 May 1961 Afghan irregulars raided the Pakistani frontier near Bajaur, seventy miles north of Peshawar. In September diplomatic relations were again terminated. Pakistan requested the closure of its consulates in Afghanistan, and Mohammed Daoud Khan responded by insisting on the closure of the border. Afghanistan denied itself the use of Pakistani roads and railroads at a critical juncture: two of its main export crops were scheduled to be shipped through Pakistan to India. To ward off domestic violence, the Afghan government purchased the grape and pomegranate crops grown by especially troublesome tribes. And the Soviet Union stepped in with offers to purchase and ship the crops out of Afghanistan. Goods and equipment supplied by foreign assistance programs, and required to continue development projects in Afghanistan, were also stuck in Pakistan.[61]

Between 1955 and 1961 the Pakistanis and the Americans had become increasingly concerned about Soviet activities inside Afghanistan. Particularly worrisome was the ongoing Soviet road-construction program. As early as 1956 a U.S. representative had warned Daoud that "Soviet economic aid was laying a logistical infrastructure for invasion."[62] In 1959 Pakistani military leaders told U.S. officials they feared a "Soviet drive through Afghanistan towards the warm water ports on the Arabian Sea." General Ayub Khan, then president of Pakistan (and a Pakhtun), voiced a similar fear: "Extensive road building and airfield construction in Afghanistan would enable sizable Military Forces to march into West Pakistan's plains at short notice. The time is not far off when these roadbuildings in Afghanistan can be a real threat to the entire subcontinent." In this round of the routing controversy, Pakistan took a somewhat more moderate stand. The government announced it would "honour its international obligations to keep Afghan in-transit goods flowing."[63] But the Afghans, having found a new friend, halted the movement of their own products.

If Pakistan did not restrict the movement of Afghan material, however, it did hinder the movement of Afghan men, restricting the entry of about 75,000 Afghan powindahs into Pakistan. When some migrating tribesmen tried to force their way across the unguarded passes, scuffles with Pakistani frontiersmen ensued. The tactic employed by the Pakistanis was simple yet unacceptable to the Afghans, who had to defend their stance on Pakhtunistan: Pakistan required the powindahs to produce travel documents and innoculation certificates. Such papers implied the legal closure and the territorial compartmentalization of the Durand Line. The nomads, of course, possessed no passports. If the Afghan government had provided them, the Pakistanis would have promptly stamped a visa, thereby certifying the existence of a legitimate antiroute and forcing the government of Afghanistan to accept the Durand Line. Stuck in Afghanistan throughout the year, the nomads added to the economic woes of the Afghan government, already suffering from the dislocation of its trade. (Inside Afghanistan, the nomads began to fight among themselves for winter grazing lands, and Afghan farmers resisted their intrusions.)[64]

Not until 1963 did the mediation of the Shah of Iran temper the hostility and briefly reconcile the policies of the squabbling neighbors. The Tehran Agreement of May 1964 brought about the restoration of full diplomatic ties. The border was reopened, and normal trade was resumed. Yet by now the repeated border closures had already had their most serious consequences for Afghanistan: they had contributed to the increased economic reliance of the Kabul government on Soviet aid and on Soviet routes.

Although Pakistani finances were affected by the border closures, the impact was localized. Both the Peshawar and the Rawalpindi chambers of commerce complained to the central government that the lack of trade with Afghanistan was having a negative impact on their local economies. The transit trade from Afghanistan was a source of income to goods handlers, including laborers, clearing and forwarding agents, truck owners, and drivers. During the 1960s, when the borders were open, Pakistan earned an estimated Rs 2.54 crores ($1.41 million) per annum.[65] It was in Afghanistan, however, that the impact was felt on a national scale. Because of the country's reliance on foreign trade (to fund its domestic projects), a high proportion of which was transacted through Pakistan, the closures hampered the Afghan economy.

The full impact of the denial of access to the sea can be gauged by Afghan responses to the crises and by statistical shifts in Afghanistan's trade with both Pakistan and the Soviet Union. Afghanistan had suffered a similar fate during World War II, when its cordial relations with the Axis powers (especially with Germany) had raised the ire of the British, those master manipulators of Afghan trade. At that time Afghanistan had found its southern routes blockaded, and it was not at liberty to choose a relationship with its northern neighbor. Now, however, it was. Afghanistan's leaders embarked on a mission to acquire alternative—and secure—trade routes that could replace the Pakistani road and rail network.

AFGHANISTAN'S SEARCH FOR ALTERNATIVE ROUTES

Afghanistan's quest for alternative trade routes did not involve overtures to the Soviet Union alone. Afghan governments made sporadic attempts through the 1970s—by which time it was too late—to open up other, western routes. These efforts to diversify access suggest an Afghan interest in averting dependence on the Soviet Union. They also point to an Afghan attempt not to squander the country's historic strategic assets—its rugged and inhospitable northern regions. Afghanistan approached both the United States and Iran for assistance in building alternative external trade routes, but it was to achieve some success with these parties (especially Iran) only after two decades of Soviet road building inside its territories.

Afghanistan shares a four-hundred-ninety-seven-mile border with Iran. Its rulers wanted new roads and railroads linking its cities to Iran's port at Chah Bahar on the Persian Gulf coast. In the post–World War II era, and despite a long history of cultural and political contacts, transport links between Afghanistan and Iran had lain in disrepair, suffering a lack of use. The condition of the routes reflected the state of Afghan-Iranian political and economic relations. One traveler has described them as "non-existent": the "converging lines of rock and pot holes—one cannot honestly call them roads—which lead up to the border are clearly intended to discourage rather than facilitate traffic . . . and the same is true of the customs posts and visa formalities on either side of the border."[66]

After the border closure of 1961, however, the Afghan foreign minister, Prince Naim, approached President John F. Kennedy for financial support to develop routes across Iran which would substitute for the routes through Pakistan. The Afghans were interested in a project that would require construction of about 3,600 miles of roads in Iran, through Zahedan to Chah Bahar, as well as extensive port facilities.[67] The United States felt the distances were too long, the cost too high, and the route too difficult to build. Kennedy's response was negative: he thought the route through Iran was "usable to a point but too expensive," and he suggested instead that Afghanistan try to mend fences with Pakistan. He asked Naim to consider the source of greatest danger: "That arising from complete dependence on the Soviet Union or that from some adjustment with Pakistan to enable goods to flow again."[68] Thus, improved overland routes to the west were not realized. Although Afghanistan and Iran did conclude a five-year transit agreement in January 1962, the lack of good routes between the two countries kept trade more expensive than that which moved through Pakistan or the Soviet Union.[69]

More than a decade later, the Shah of Iran decided to shoulder responsibility for the region's security. In his attempt to wean Afghanistan from Soviet influence, he made a lordly offer of aid for Afghanistan's development—with specific provision for transport infrastructure—and for the cultivation of new regional markets incorporating their two countries, as well as India and Pakistan. The Afghans were willing to listen. By the mid-1970s, talks between the two countries on the development aid requirements for the protection of Afghan security were well under way.

In 1973, Iran and Afghanistan signed agreements to end their dispute over the waters of the Helmand and to expand their air links and facilities for Iran Air and Ariana Afghan Airlines. In May 1974 discussions were held regarding the construction of a transit route linking Afghanistan to the port of Bandar Abbas on the Persian Gulf. The port would serve as a new, duty-free export outlet for Afghan goods.[70] In October 1974 Iran donated $10 million for feasibility studies, including estimates on the construction of a new railroad. It was to be Afghanistan's first other than the few miles of rail which linked Kushka to Torghundi on the northern border.

In 1975 the Shah offered Afghanistan a $2 billion aid package, a large portion of which was to build the railroad. Kabul was to be linked with Kandahar via Ghazni. A branch line was to link Herat to the Soviet border, and another was to wind its way through Zahedan to the Iranian port of Bandar Abbas. The 1,128-mile railroad would have a line running to Islam Qala and onward to Mashad, where it would join the Iranian rail network. Another branch would run from Kandahar to connect with the Pakistani railroads at Quetta. The cost was estimated at $1.7 billion, and plans were approved in 1977.[71] When the Shah's rule collapsed, these plans met a premature end.

It would be wrong to think that this railroad was conceived or could have been constructed in time to reorient Afghan patterns of trade or direction of political influence or to have any other discernible impact on the level of Soviet involvement in Afghanistan. The Soviets' political, military, and economic influence was pervasive by the mid-1970s, and their physical accessibility to Afghan centers was excellent.

Intent on pursuing their quarrel with Pakistan, the Afghans had created a dangerous security dilemma for themselves. In essence, they had sacrificed present economic security to achieve future economic and strategic access, as well as an unlikely ideological victory in the shape of Pakhtunistan. With the failure of their attempts to balance their reliance on the Soviet Union with a reliance on Iran or on the United States, the Afghans embarked on a routing policy that sacrificed security for development. The only option that remained open to them, as they perceived their dilemma, was the cultivation of ties with the Soviet Union.

Beginning in 1955, Soviet aid flowed into Afghanistan in ever-increasing quantities. Yet the United States was already a donor of aid, providing financial and technical assistance for transport infrastructure and other large-scale ventures such as the colossal Helmand Valley project. What was the role of a geographically distant sea-power in a region of the world to which it had little access? What did the United States hope to accomplish by the provision of transport aid to a country so far from itself and so close to the Soviet Union?

U.S. AID AND U.S. ROADS IN AFGHANISTAN

The United States was the first country to be approached by Afghanistan for economic aid and, later, for arms. It was also the first country to turn Afghanistan down. The Afghans were looking, in the late 1940s and early 1950s, for sufficient economic and political attention from the United States to balance increasing Soviet attention. Although Afghanistan persisted through the early 1950s in its attempts to entice a U.S. military interest, the United States felt itself to be too far away, Afghanistan of too little consequence, and its own emerging security relationship with Pakistan too important to make strong ties with Afghanistan a workable proposition. This American preoccupation with supporting Pakistan contributed to Afghanistan's growing reliance on the Soviet Union. Ambassador Robert G. Neumann (1966–73) later said that John Foster Dulles turned down the Afghan request for military aid because, in view of Afghanistan's "location and poor communications, an enormous logistics effort would have had to be undertaken by the U.S. where the risk of escalating the Cold War would have been high."[72]

Even at the height of the Cold War, therefore, the United States did not think much of Afghanistan's strategic relevance to its global concerns. (After 1980, this perception would suddenly be reversed; talk of the Great Game would be revived.) In that earlier time, the U.S. military was not overly enthusiastic about promoting a relationship with Afghanistan. A prescient 1950 study for the Joint Chiefs of Staff stated: "Afghanistan is of little or no strategic importance to the United States. . . . Its geographic location coupled with the realization by the Afghan leaders of Soviet capabilities presages Soviet control of the country whenever the international situation so dictates."[73]

There was an apparent contradiction between these U.S. perceptions of Afghanistan's strategic value and political future and the content of U.S. aid programs. U.S. infrastructural aid—which enhanced Afghanistan's permeability to its northern neighbor—was born of a confusion in assessments of interest and policy. If U.S. policy makers thought they might compete with the Soviet Union for equality in political, economic, or military influence in Afghanistan—accruing from the donation of infrastructural aid—then they misunderstood the interaction between such aid, trade, influence, and location. The formula would work positively for a proximate power such as the Soviet Union but had little chance of benefiting the United States. When U.S. money and men increased the accessibility of Afghanistan's southern cities to the Soviet Union, U.S. goodwill was working against its own long-run interests.

It was apparent that U.S. concern with Afghanistan related in the main to U.S. concerns with the country's neighbors. In 1954 the National Security Council (NSC) felt that Soviet aid to Afghanistan indicated a "possible Soviet intention" to assert its control over the small state, thus ending its "buffer status." Such a takeover would create "undesirable consequences" for Turkey, Iran, and Pakistan by increasing their defense burdens, by raising the threat of Soviet access to the port of Karachi, and by driving a wedge between the three countries.[74]

Two years later another executive policy paper stated: "U.S. policy must have as its fundamental objective in Afghanistan denial of the area to Soviet control." Still, it continued, "because of proximity and trade and communications ties, Afghanistan is more susceptible to Soviet influence than to that of the United States."[75] The recommendation was to encourage the strengthening of Afghanistan's political and economic ties with Pakistan, especially by improving transport facilities through the latter country, in an attempt to improve conditions for the resolution of the Pakhtunistan dispute. Better relations with Iran were also encouraged to enable Afghanistan to decrease its dependence on the Soviet Union.

Another memorandum dealing with Afghanistan, this time from the Bureau of Budget, recommended in 1959 "removing impediments to expanded trade with Pakistan and India" and "intensifying efforts to improve transport facilities through Pakistan."[76] In South and Central Asia, then, the United States tried to promote a transport assistance program that would facilitate better regional relations and open Afghan territories. It failed, however, to place this strategy in the context of the region's larger, internal dynamics. On their own, successful American efforts to open up southern Afghanistan were both undermined and made dangerous by failed American efforts to increase Afghan-Pakistani transport cooperation and to support the building of an Afghan-Iranian route.

U.S. officials thought Afghanistan a country of "no strategic importance" which should nevertheless be denied to the Soviet Union. Few policies were pursued, however, in support of the latter objective. For example, transport infrastructure could have been excluded as a ready beneficiary of U.S. development assistance, or the Afghan plan to build an alternative route through Iran could have been more actively encouraged. Since Afghanistan was hostile to Pakistan, U.S. suggestions that the Afghans rely on the latter's roads and railroads did not adequately address the region's political realities. These proposals were unworkable and unreliable tools with which to solve the regional dilemmas of access.

If Afghanistan's political strategy—especially under the leadership of Daoud—was to elicit U.S. aid by encouraging economic assistance from the Soviet Union, it worked, though only in the short term. The calculus of benefits from the Afghan perspective, however, appears more understandable (albeit more risky) than that from the U.S. perspective. Given the assessments of Afghanistan's strategic and political importance to the United States made by Presidents Carter and Reagan after 1980, American competition and sometimes even cooperation with the Soviet Union in the building of routes in the latter's vicinity would seem an ill-fated effort.

In fact, the 1954 NSC report had argued that more aid to Afghanistan—other than for the improvement of ties with Pakistan—could have adverse consequences, such as an expensive and "ultimately useless" bidding contest with the Soviet Union. It could even cause the Soviet Union to try countermeasures dangerous to Afghan independence. Still, the United States decided to compete.[77] It set to work, initially through its International Cooperation Administration (ICA), on major transportation and other projects for the development of Afghanistan.

Transport infrastructure was one of the top two components of Soviet economic aid to Afghanistan. In the U.S. aid program, it was one of the top three priorities. Some minor transport-related projects were suggested by the National Security Council, such as provision of more rolling-stock along Afghan-Pakistani trade routes and storage facilities for Afghan goods. But inside Afghanistan, U.S. development assistance agencies granted substantial funds and know-how to construct hard-surfaced roads in the southern parts of the country. These roads linked up with Soviet-built roads in the north, and together they formed a ring of highways that encircled the heart of Afghanistan.

Some writers have argued in support of U.S. route building in Afghanistan. Their arguments, however, fail to consider Afghan geopolitics. Leon Poullada says, for example, that the failures and inefficiencies of U.S. aid projects gave the Soviets an opportunity to tempt Afghanistan with better financial and technical offers. Poullada approvingly cites the mandate of Henry Byroade, U.S. ambassador to Afghanistan, which was to "get the American program going." Apparently Byroade became so frustrated "with the incompetence and the delays of the aid administration that he imported the Army Corps of Engineers to finish a lagging road program."[78] Of course, it is possible—likely, in fact—that if the United States had not built the great southern routes, the Soviets would have completed the task. Still, the assessment that the United States could not, and should not, try to "win" in a country next door to the Soviet Union appears incompatible with these American efforts. What would ultimately save the Afghans from the Soviet Union was not the roads that the United States built inside Afghanistan—these facilitated Soviet control after 1980—but the hundreds of natural routes that cut through Afghanistan's hilly south and into Pakistan.

The geopolitical assessment of aid differs for proximate and distant powers. Distance matters. A cursory review of the region's history could have foretold the military futility of U.S. transport assistance programs and their military utility for the Soviet Union. The British, even as they stood at Afghanistan's borders, had created a buffer to protect their interests in India. Within Afghan territories, they had declined a contest of route building with the Russians. If the notion of "competition" kept U.S. transport aid programs to Afghanistan alive, it was founded on a false understanding of the dynamics of distance.

The United States built the main arterial routes in southern Afghanistan. Between 1950 and 1971, U.S. grants and loans totaled $286 million (with an additional $126.8 million under the PL-480 food aid program). Of that amount, $130.4 million went to construct transport infrastructure. The United States built the 367.5 miles of highway from Kabul to Kandahar and on to Spin Baldak on the border with Pakistan. By 1964 more than half the route from Kabul to Kandahar had been surfaced with asphalt by the United States Agency for International Development (USAID). The 140-mile asphalt road from Kabul to Torkhum was built with U.S. assistance, as was the 76.5 mile road from Herat to Islam Qala on the Iranian-Afghan border (this road branches off from the Soviet-built highway from Kushka to Kandahar). During construction of the major Kabul-Kandahar highway, one U.S. official in Afghanistan commented that the project was "extravagant in the extreme" and built largely "for political reasons."[79]

The United States not only helped complete the circle of roads started by the Soviet Union, it also worked with the Soviets on other infrastructure projects. Together, the two powers built Kabul airport. The Soviets built the airstrips and erected the buildings, the Americans installed the communications and electronic equipment. The fate of another airport—Kandahar International—demonstrates the ambiguous nature, and the potentially deleterious consequences, of infrastructural aid for a distant donor country. Opened in 1962, it was built with U.S. funds—ICA provided $10 million in grants and $5 million in loans—reportedly to act as a possible "recovery base" for U.S. bombers in a war with the Soviet Union. In 1976 only six thousand passengers used the airport, then operated as an alternative landing site when bad weather closed Kabul airport. In 1980 the Soviets turned the airport into their most important southwestern base. A more poignant commemoration of the U.S. adventure in Afghanistan is a minor bridge built by an American engineer, across which the Soviets ran their northern road at Dilaram—Heart's Ease.[80]

After the Soviet Union had become master of Kabul, the United States decided to improve Pakistan's western and northern borderland routes. In 1986, for example, U.S. officials reportedly agreed to provide 80 percent of the estimated $70 million required to construct a five-mile road and tunnel across the 10,000-feet-high Lowari Pass near the border with Afghanistan. The monies were to come from the 1987 U.S. aid package of $4.02 billion, and when completed, the new route would link Chitral with points south.[81] Writing in the mid-1960s, the geographer David Dichter had commented that although improved communications would "dominate any future economic development of Chitral," and there had been "a lot of talk recently on the part of the Pakistan Government about tunnelling through the Lowari in order to connect Chitral for the whole year with the lowlands," it was "extremely doubtful, in view of the small economic returns expected from such a costly project" whether such improvements would take place.[82] Efforts made in the 1970s were limited by financial constraints.

SOVIET INFRASTRUCTURAL AID AND
CHANGING PATTERNS OF TRADE

During the nineteenth century, British pressure and Afghan policy had limited Russian involvement in Afghanistan. The Amirs of Afghanistan, even more distrustful of the Russians than they were of the British, had kept their transport capabilities in the peripheries at a minimum and discouraged strong trading ties with their northern neighbor. Still, the Russians never stopped pressing the Afghans for trade concessions and improved communication and transport links. From the time of General Annenkov's proposals until 1919, when they urged the construction of a railroad from Kushk to Herat, the Russians tried repeatedly to foster new routes between the two states.[83] Each time either the British or the Afghans rejected Russian offers.

Conditions changed, however, after 1947 regenerating Soviet-Afghan relations in a new, more intricate, and eventually more deadly form. The road map of Afghanistan was to change dramatically, precipitating and reflecting these changed relations. By 1972, with assistance from the Soviet Union and the United States, the country possessed 1,553 miles of paved roads, linking south with north and east with west, along with 10,750 miles of other motorable roads, as compared to roughly 1,790 miles of "barely usable tracks" in 1932.[84]

The political and economic requirements of Afghanistan's rulers had changed, as had their opportunities. When the British ruled India, the Kabul government had no mandate urging development. Progress and modernization were not important responsibilities of Afghanistan's Amirs. The banner of development was raised with the advent of nationalist movements to power in the new countries of the developing world. Earlier, in Afghanistan, a traditional autocracy had negotiated benefits for the tribes, but economic expectations and political largess were both on a scale much smaller than today's. Abdur Rahman could choose to keep his country routeless so that it would remain free, and his own.

After 1945 the new rulers of Afghanistan, especially Daoud, had new domestic goals: economic development and modernization. When Pakistan blocked the passage of Afghan goods and migrants, it made clear the need for foreign economic assistance and new channels of access for Afghan trade. In seeking ties with the Soviet Union, Afghan leaders insisted that their need to attain higher standards of living was more important than their political predilections.[85] Afghanistan's earlier concentration on its security problems was now balanced by its need to attend to national development. Sour relations with Pakistan and a fruitless search for alternative routes through Iran created opportunities for the Soviet Union. Within Afghanistan, the warnings of its nineteenth-century rulers were set aside.

Like nearly all developing countries, Afghanistan suffered a resource gap. It could not meet its expenditures on planned development projects without foreign assistance to supplement its meager budget. Trade, so vital an element in prospects for growth, was also more vulnerable than in other developing countries because Afghanistan was land-locked and possessed both difficult terrain and a frail transport network. It was a needy case and, from the Soviet

Union's point of vantage, strategically and conveniently located. It became the first major noncommunist beneficiary of the Soviet Union's foreign aid program for developing countries in the years following 1953.

Each time Pakistan curtailed Afghan use of the southern routes, the Soviet Union stepped in with offers of financial assistance, particularly for transport and overland trade. In 1950, the year Pakistan interfered with Afghan gasoline supplies, the Soviet Union and Afghanistan signed the first of many renewable trade and transit agreements. In 1953 the Soviets gave Afghanistan a $3.5 million credit to build grain silos, a flour mill, and a bakery. In July another aid agreement was signed between the two countries, this time for technical and financial assistance for the construction of a $1.2 million gasoline pipeline that crossed the Amu Darya into the Soviet Union. Four gasoline bulk storage tanks were also to be built across Afghanistan. These projects were directly related to southern border closures and Pakistan's ability to halt, at will, Afghan food and gasoline supplies. The grain silos could store strategic reserves, and the pipeline and fuel tanks could import Soviet gasoline and store Afghan oil in the event of a cut-off.[86] In October 1954, part of a $2.1 million Soviet loan was earmarked for a small but evocative venture in which the United States would not participate—the paving of Kabul's streets.

The major Soviet aid flows to Afghanistan began in 1955. The border closure of that year was followed by an Afghan request for increased shipment of duty-free goods across Soviet territory and for the shipment of Western imports through the Soviet Union. Another trade and transit agreement was signed. The Soviets responded to the Afghan routing crisis by developing special facilities for the speedy, and duty-free, transit of Afghan goods through their territory.[87]

Still, since the northern roads were generally primitive, time and cost were much higher for goods moving northward rather than through Pakistan. There was no harbor on the Afghan side of the Amu Darya, nor did roads exist capable of moving heavy trucks to the river. Only small boats could be used on the river, only camels on the road tracks.[88] As with trade along Iranian routes, expanded trade agreements could not compensate for the lack of road, rail, and harbor facilities. The Soviets set out to rectify this problem. Owing to the mountainous terrain, road building in Afghanistan promised to be a costly and laborious venture. From the scale of their enterprise it might be believed that Soviet motives involved more than a desire for skins and dried fruit.

Between 15 and 19 December 1955, Nikita Khrushchev and Nikolai Bulganin visited Kabul. Their arrival, as one writer has said, marked a "revolution" in the "rate and course of Afghanistan's modernization."[89] It also marked the transformation of the Afghan buffer and the historical function of the Hindu Kush: no longer would it be a formidable antiroute. Now the Soviet investment in infrastructure began in earnest. It erased Afghanistan's physical impenetrability. Afghanistan was awarded a thirty-year, $100 million loan at an annual interest rate of 2 percent. The funding included money for a military airbase at Bagram (which was put to good use in 1980), and a portion was reserved for the construction of roads in northern Afghanistan. Among the projects discussed by the Afghans and the Soviets were roads from Kunduz to Pul-i-Khumri and port facilities at Sher Khan on the Amu Darya north of Kunduz, which faced a Soviet railhead at Nizhniy Pyandzh.

This investment in access was paralleled by growing Soviet involvement in other Afghan institutions. Between 1950 and 1959 the Soviets provided $246.2 million in aid, mainly in the form of long-term loans. Between 1950 and 1960, too, Afghanistan's dependence on the Soviet Union for weapons rose from zero to 100 percent, from about 10 percent to 90 percent for petroleum products, and from 17 percent to nearly 50 percent for total foreign trade.[90]

Since the modern Soviet-Afghan relationship began, the Soviet Union had focused on Afghanistan's northern areas, that is, on the lands adjacent to Soviet Central Asia. Between the mid-1950s and the 1970s, Soviet road building and infrastructure development was concentrated in regions proximate to Soviet river ports, railheads, and cities along the fifteen-hundred-mile-long common border. These programs tightened the Soviet Union's economic and military hold on its southern neighbor.

Soviet generosity extended mainly to the northern areas and to road construction that linked up with their own transport networks. The Soviets built asphalt roads from Kabul to Sher Khan on the Soviet border. The road from Kabul to Jabal-us-Seraj extends for 47.8 miles; from Jabal-us-Seraj to Doshi it is 66.5 miles long; and from Doshi to Sher Khan Bandar, it is 133.5 miles long. These roads link central Afghanistan to the Soviet border along the Amu Darya, following roughly a straight line.[91] Construction faced enormous difficulties, since numerous ravines and rivers mark the region. The completed all-weather route across the Hindu Kush was opened by Alexei Kosygin in September 1964.

In his memoirs, Nikita Khrushchev refers to U.S.-Soviet competition in Afghanistan, and to the consequent importance of Soviet roads. He accuses the United States of putting pressure on Afghanistan by "giving credits, building roads. . . . In its desire to encircle us with military bases, America threw itself all over . . . Afghanistan." By 1955, Khrushchev believed that the U.S. was "penetrating Afghanistan with the obvious intent of setting up a military base there." He decided, therefore, to help the Afghans construct a few hundred miles of road close to the Afghan-Iranian border.

> It cost us a hefty sum since we had to tunnel through the mountains. However, because Afghanistan didn't have railroads, such a highway would be a main artery, carrying the economic lifeblood of the country. The road also had great strategic significance because it would have allowed us to transport troops and supplies in the event of war with either Pakistan or Iran.
>
> It was up to us to persuade the King and his government that we wouldn't misuse the road—that it would serve the cause of peaceful economic development. It took some time for the ice to melt entirely and for the Afghan leaders to understand that we weren't pursuing mercenary or military goals in their country.[92]

Around this time the anthropologist Louis Dupree reported that some observers, "particularly Pakistanis, Turks, and Iranians," referred to the Soviet road and the U.S.-built Kabul-Jalalabad road, with which it intersects, as the "Moscow to Delhi Highway." Dupree posed a question: "Logically, however, just how strategic is a road in the era of possible nuclear warfare, with effective missiles soon to be operational?" He asked this question in 1960; the conclusive answer came almost two decades later.[93]

To make the most effective use of their northern routes, the Soviets undertook a costly ($638 million), time-consuming (6 years), and dangerous construction project: the 1.7-mile Salang Tunnel. At a height of 11,000 feet, the tunnel is 17 feet wide and 25 feet high; it reduces traveling distance by 126 miles. Built to conform to the requirements of both vehicular and caravan traffic, including camels and donkeys, the tunnel is the major entrance for people and goods moving across the Hindu Kush. Before the tunnel was completed in 1964, and especially in the winter months, the mountains had blocked the meeting of northern and southern roads.[94] Their barrier function was now eroded. During the Soviet occupation of Afghanistan in the 1980s, the Salang Tunnel was the primary logistics and supply route for Soviet troops and material. It was also the main route by which Soviet troops withdrew to Termez in 1989.

In 1959 the Soviets awarded grants and technical assistance for another road in Afghanistan, and the contract for the project was signed on 11 January 1960. A 425-mile highway was built linking the Soviet border town of Kushka to Torghundi, onward to Herat, and then to Kandahar in the south. (At this time the Soviets also agreed to build the Shindand military airfield.) The cost of construction was roughly $140 million, of which $129 million was an outright grant. The manner in which the road was built and the route it followed make it appear that other than economic considerations prevailed in planning and construction. The highway did reduce previous traveling distance—but only by sixty miles—and in doing so bypassed important centers of human settlement, including the city of Farah. The Kushka-Kandahar road is concrete-surfaced, and reportedly its bridges are built to carry extra heavy loads. This road would link up with the U.S.-built road between Kabul and Kandahar. The economist Marshall Goldman referred to it as "an outstanding example of the cooperative use of foreign aid by the two countries."[95] In 1961, when the dispute with Pakistan resulted in yet another border closure, work on the road was speeded up.

The British had been allergic to any development of the Kushka-Kandahar route because, with control of that route, Russian access to Quetta in Baluchistan became feasible. By 1980 such Soviet roads had altered conditions of access which had prevailed in the Central and South Asian borderlands for hundreds of years. The roads brought their makers to the frontiers of Pakistan's Pakhtun and Baluch territories.

As economic assistance projects, these roads were creating a new political and strategic framework for Afghanistan. In 1967 Marshall Goldman wrote that the Soviets seemed "determined to prove" that they could "encourage economic development without undue . . . interference." A 1971 World Bank mission, however, viewed the matter differently: some Communist and Western projects were said to have been "dictated as much by strategic or ideological considerations as economic ones." Earlier, in 1961, another observer, the historian Arnold Toynbee, offered this perspective on road building in

Afghanistan: "These new roads promise to reinstate Afghanistan in her traditional position in the World. They are her economic bonus from the present political competition between the Soviet Union and the United States. The bonus is valuable, but the accompanying risk is high. Roundabouts are strategic as well as economic assets, and strategic assets are tempting political prizes." In the same year, Toynbee also warned that the "struggle in Afghanistan is taking various forms; road-building is one, and there again the Russians seem to be getting the best of it."[96]

The road-building agreements made between the Soviet Union and Afghanistan during this time included some disturbing provisions. In the border agreement of 18 January 1958, for example, Article 21 stipulated that "on forty-eight hours notice either side could examine those parts of international bridges linking the two countries that were located on the other side's territory." In effect, the Soviets could track any "suspicious" developments on the Afghan side. The 30 May 1959 agreement regarding construction of the Kushka-Kandahar road preceded another agreement for the construction of three bridges. Afghan engineers subsequently commented that these bridges—built, as was usual, under the supervision of Soviet engineers—had carrying capabilities far higher than what was required to move the heaviest Afghan civilian traffic. U.S. military attachés noted that the load limit of the bridges was precisely the weight of the heaviest Soviet battle tank.[97]

In 1965 the Soviets worked on the reconstruction of the road from Pul-i-Khumri—about one hundred miles north of Kabul—via Mazar-i-Sharif to Sheberghan. At the time, Afghan citizens worried that these highways were wide enough and strong enough to carry troop transports and tanks.[98] In the 1970s work proceeded apace in the northern areas: on the Sheberghan-Maimana road (estimated to cost $200,000), the Kunduz-Khanabad-Kishm road (estimated to cost $150,000), and other asphalt highways. The Soviets also gave over $2.1 million to cover repairs and maintenance of the vital Salang Tunnel and highway. Mazar-i-Sharif was linked to Termez.

Among the Soviet Union's other infrastructure projects were Kabul and regional airports, pipelines for the transport of natural gas to the Soviet Union, and a new $50 million project—agreed to in October 1978—for a rail and road bridge over the Amu Darya at Haritan. Like the new highways, the pipelines served to transfer Afghan resources (in this case, natural gas) northward. In October 1967 Afghanistan began to export natural gas to the Soviet Union and by January 1977 had shipped 23 billion cubic meters through the pipeline.[99]

Soviet efforts expanded considerably after 1980. The "much acclaimed expenditure on roads and communication," said one source, "is being directed in its entirety to strengthening strategic links with the USSR." Six regional airports and numerous Afghan-Soviet routes were completed in 1981 alone. According to other sources, the postinvasion period also saw a broad range of infrastructural activities concentrated in northern Afghanistan. In 1982 the road and rail bridge, which carried fuel pipelines, was built over the Amu Darya. Reportedly, the Soviets also began to build their first railroad inside Afghanistan in the vicinity of Kushka—the fulfillment of a Russian ambition since 1919. The projected cost to the Soviets was 3.1 billion rubles. By 1985 they were also said to be working on the initial stage of another rail project, laying tracks to Pul-i-Khumri.[100]

Thus the Great Game of routes came full circle. When Pakistan, Britain's fragile successor on the subcontinent's northwestern frontier, denied Afghanistan's people and commerce a southern outlet, and when the United States kept its distance, Afghanistan turned to the north. It soon became linked by new routes to the Soviet Union and dependent upon the Soviet Union for its trade. Out of the conflict over Pakhtunistan emerged a pattern: the Soviet Union would extend its hand to Afghanistan after a rupture with Pakistan. In the Afghan-Pakistan crisis in 1961, for example, the Soviets forestalled financial disaster for the Afghans by airlifting fruit to Soviet Central Asian markets. The fruit, Afghanistan's main export, would otherwise have rotted on the roads.

Soviet road building brought in a great deal of money and Soviet products. It also brought many Soviet citizens, who came to administer the construction projects from start to finish. No Afghan firm was capable of building major roads. A U.S. officer's report from Afghanistan in the mid-1950s said that "all road and bridge plans and blueprints in the Ministry of Public Works have been turned over to the Soviet engineers." Other observers described one road project thus:

> All decisions on the planning and construction were made entirely by Soviet engineers, aided by extensive Soviet staffs. All the road-building machinery was imported on credit from the Soviet Union, which also provided the steel for the bridges and even the nails for the wooden structures. These are all processed on the spot by Russian engineers

and technicians, the Afghans providing only the stone and laborers. The Russians have also sent along their own doctors.[101]

For the Kushka-Kandahar highway project, the Soviets brought in three thousand men, along with geologists, geographers, historians, linguists, ethnographers, and folklorists. By 1979 there were over 3,700 Soviet and East European economic and technical advisers in Afghanistan. An estimated 5,000 Afghan students had studied at Soviet academic institutions, 1,600 at Soviet technical institutions. Roughly 3,725 Afghan military men had been trained in the Soviet Union.[102]

Soviet road building, in sum, brought access to the Afghan core. The Soviets gained economic clout, political power, and strategic access. The roads also reoriented the flow of Afghan trade. The Amirs of Afghanistan had not promoted trade with Russia because they were anxious about the consequences of economic dependence on their neighbor. Russian trade offices had not been welcome in the nineteenth and early twentieth centuries; apart from a brief period of fairly cordial relations in the 1920s, Soviet trade consulates were not permitted on Afghan soil. Until the fracas with Pakistan the Afghans basically continued to follow a "closed border policy" in the north. Trade did exist: the Soviet share of Afghan trade rose from 7 percent in 1924–25 to about 24 percent in 1938–39, but this too came to an abrupt halt during World War II.[103] After the war Afghan dependence on the southern routes became nearly total.

By 1952, however, trade between Afghanistan and the Soviet Union had doubled, and a Soviet trade office had opened in Kabul. Afghan-Soviet trade was rapidly rising. In 1950 only 17 percent of all Afghan trading activities took place in conjunction with the Soviet Union. Between 1950 and 1956 the Soviet portion of Afghan trade more than doubled, increasing over 30 percent in 1956 alone (the year following the five-month-long border closure between Afghanistan and Pakistan). From 1961 onward the rise became rapid and continuous. In 1977–78, 43 percent of all Afghan exports went to the Soviet Union. On the Soviet side the numbers were smaller, but the trend was the same. In 1946 Soviet trade with Afghanistan had a total value of 0.1 million rubles; by 1957 it had risen to 34.9 million rubles; by 1966 the figure was 82.9 million rubles. A parallel decline was observed in Afghanistan's transit trade through Pakistan. In the late 1960s the transit trade had fallen absolutely as well as relatively.[104]

Between 1954 and 1967 Soviet economic aid in grants and credits to

Afghanistan reached $570 million, with only India and Egypt among developing countries receiving larger sums. The Afghan government's Five Year Plans for development—of which the first two (1957–66) gave top priority to the construction of transport routes—received substantial support from the Soviet Union. The 1956–61 plan got 60 percent of all foreign aid donated for its implementation from the Soviet Union and the 1961–66 Plan got 50 percent of its foreign funding from the Soviet Union.[105] These two plans were laid out during the worst conflicts between Afghanistan and Pakistan.

The 1,553 miles of paved roads constructed between 1956 and 1972 in Afghanistan also reduced transport costs, which in turn provided benefits for domestic and foreign trade. The increase in domestic trade during the late 1960s and early 1970s was reflected in a decrease in interregional price differentials for major commodities. Still, domestic levels of trade remained low, and so the economic benefits derived from the new routes were not substantial. Traders and transport entrepreneurs benefited, not rural Afghans. Between 1959 and 1968 import prices also fell by 40 percent while export prices rose by 15 percent. The resulting improvement in commodity terms of trade was due in considerable part to the decline in transport costs, although these remained quite high.[106]

Neither the Afghan government nor the Soviet Union was overly attentive to the construction of small but important roads connecting rural areas with urban centers and with one another. Given its complex, fragmented terrain and its dispersed population, Afghanistan required numerous cheap, low-volume roads. For similar reasons, these roads were costly to construct. Highways, of course, were even costlier. The efforts of both the Soviet Union and the United States gave Afghanistan an excellent national highway system, but the country remained devoid of minor routes. What few rural roads were constructed were below standard, and certain towns and areas, such as Feyzabad, were not even connected to the main trunk routes.[107]

The roads required to link villages to the main highways still needed much improvement in the late 1970s. The construction of these feeder roads was still being ignored. The economist Maxwell Fry concluded that improvements in transport infrastructure were "motivated primarily by strategic necessities" and did not particularly benefit rural communities.[108] This deficiency in transport links perpetuated the disjointed nature of the Afghan economy, which has been described as "a wide sea dotted with islands of economic activity, each one more or less limited to its own local market, primarily because of inadequate transportation."[109] It also militated against the political integration of peripheral tribes and the state's control of outlying areas. Rarely was an Afghan government based in Kabul able effectively to penetrate and to monitor the countryside. The Soviets would learn this historical lesson and suffer its consequences during the 1980s, when they attempted to subdue the mujahideen in Afghanistan's mountain valleys.

In 1977 Louis Dupree had delineated the pattern of Soviet economic aid projects: "Note that the majority of Soviet projects, including the building of roads, are geared to increasing exports from Afghanistan to Russia, which to some observers sustains the bogey that the Soviets will ultimately dominate Afghanistan through economic pressure."[110] That ultimate domination was brought about by military force, but prior to 1979 Afghanistan was economically independent of the Soviet Union only in a very limited sense. Moreover, its trade and route dependence on the Soviet Union had wider meaning for Afghan national security. The Soviet Union had entangled Afghanistan in a complex set of (primarily extractive) economic relationships. Through their infrastructural efforts across Afghan territories, and through the many links they built with their own lands, the Soviets actively promoted the nondiversification of Afghan economic dependence. Afghan vulnerability grew in direct proportion to the increase in Soviet accessibility. As the requirements of development grew, so did those for an increase in trade revenues; as Soviet-Afghan trade increased, so did Afghanistan's economic and political dependence upon the Soviet Union. Defense ties were fastened in December 1978 when the leader of the Communist Peoples Democratic Party of Afghanistan (PDPA), Nur Mohammed Taraki (who ousted Daoud in a coup on 27 April 1978), and Leonid Brezhnev signed a treaty of friendship and cooperation which said, among other things, that Afghanistan and the Soviet Union would have mutual consultations and take appropriate measures to ensure one another's security, independence, and territorial integrity.

A related matter sheds further light on the Soviet commitment to Afghanistan's domestic interests. When the Afghan government requested financial assistance and technical help in the construction of a gas pipeline within Afghanistan, for the use of its urban population, the Soviets replied that such "internal projects were not feasible" and argued that the mountainous terrain precluded building such a lengthy pipeline. The Soviets, of course, as Dupree notes, had already linked their own core areas with Central Asia by an even lengthier pipeline than the one in question, and that pipeline had traveled over equally difficult terrain.[111]

The Soviet Union's exploitation of Afghanistan's gas resources matches its efforts in the field of transport infrastructure and focuses our attention on the Soviet concern with the northward reorientation of Afghan economic resources. In 1986 a sixty-mile pipeline carrying Afghan gas supplies to Soviet Central Asia was opened. Yet apart from two domestic gas plants inside Afghanistan, the Soviets did not encourage Afghanistan to use its own gas resources. Afghan gas has been exported to the Soviet Union at prices far below the international rate.[112] The Soviet Union also continued through the 1980s to emphasize the development of northern Afghanistan: of the twenty separate economic agreements made between Afghanistan and the Soviet Union in 1987, more than half involved projects—ranging from footwear factories to the exploitation of gas fields—in the northern areas.

Afghan Dilemmas and Afghan Routes

Afghanistan's land-locked location and terrain combined with its leaders' foreign policy goals to create a quandary regarding the reconciliation of security with development policies. The path of progress followed by the Afghan governments of the postimperial era ended with the loss of their independence. A reversal took place in modern Afghan national policy: modernization needs were accorded precedence over the nation's security. The cumulative result was the loss of security. Heavy reliance on the Soviet Union for economic aid created both a large burden of economic debt and a spiraling political reliance upon the holders of the purse-strings. Afghanistan's modern rulers could no longer balance security and development as their predecessors had done. Whereas earlier Amirs had been forced by British power to sacrifice control of their southern possessions, the new leaders extended their territorial claims, in the form of Pakhtunistan, into Pakistan. Earlier Amirs, including the modernizer, Abdur Rahman, had refused to build modern transport facilities in order to deter Russian and British incursions, as well as to avoid revolts against their authority. Road building along the peripheries had been strictly controlled.

The new Afghan leaders could not sequester the claims of development. Nationalism and the impulse to modernize demanded that they address Afghan integration and Afghan economic growth. The consolidation of state authority required that roads be built despite threats by local tribes, who still regarded such construction as attempts to control their territories. These new routes endangered tribal autonomy as well as their livelihood from the caravan traffic. Revolts resulted, but the road building did not stop. In Afghanistan, it was the main catalyst for the late 1959 revolt of the Mangal tribesmen of Khost (some of whom moved across the Durand Line into Pakistan), as well as in the Kandahar riot of 1960. In Pakistan, too, during the 1950s and early 1960s, the Mohmands, for example, "successfully opposed" road building.[113]

When Daoud first gained power in September 1953, his two main goals were to modernize the economy and the army. In fact, his dissatisfaction with the pace of economic development under his predecessor was a prominent reason for his takeover of power.[114] To achieve economic progress, Daoud, with his strongly pro-Pakhtunistan, anti-Pakistan views, turned to the Soviet Union for aid. During his second term in power, between 1973 and 1978, Daoud tried to reverse Afghan policies in the direction of the Muslim world, including Iran and Pakistan, but his efforts came too late to detach Afghanistan from the Soviet embrace.

Even as he began to mute the hostile rhetoric on Pakhtunistan, Daoud was overthrown. His Communist successors revived the propaganda for a Pakhtun state and for Baluch rights inside Pakistan. The permeability of the Durand Line, however, also posed difficulties for Kabul's new leaders: opponents of the regime had established bases of operation across the border, and a few hundred thousand Afghan refugees had fled to Pakistan. The Pakistanis, when asked to seal the border, responded that it was impossible. And their own 1978 effort to improve Afghan-Pakistan relations through assurance of uninterrupted transit facilities for Afghan goods met with no response from Kabul.[115]

The Afghans ignored all warnings about Soviet activities. When the U.S. ambassador told Daoud in 1956 that Soviet generosity was laying a "logistical infrastructure for invasion," the Afghan leader dismissed his words. In 1959, during discussions with U.S. representatives, members of the royal Afghan government made it clear they would continue down their chosen path of economic development, with assistance from the Soviet Union. They had few doubts regarding their ability "to maintain their independence despite increasingly deep involvement" with the Soviet Union. The Afghans suggested, in fact, that the United States was deliberately stalling on its aid commitments because it wanted Afghanistan to remain a "primitive buffer state."[116] When their Pakistani neighbors pointed to the potential dangers of Soviet road building inside Afghanistan, Daoud responded that the Pakistanis were "overconcerned about the strategic implications" of the roads.[117]

Throughout the 1950s and 1960s Afghans generally considered that roads—good roads—were essential for the expansion of trade and for the development of the domestic economy. But Afghan governments were unable to balance their aversion to Soviet domination with their requirements for development. The new roads did not adequately integrate the Afghan economy, nor did they unify Afghanistan's ethnically and tribally fragmented society. They did succeed, however, in providing access to the Soviet armored divisions that swept across the country in a few days in 1979–80. Afghanistan's high reliance on trade with the Soviet Union—about which its Communist leader, Najibullah, said in 1988: "Historic trade relations have in the past six or seven years undergone a qualitative change"—would ensure Soviet influence over Afghanistan's external economic relations for many years to come.[118]

Although Afghanistan's twentieth-century rulers could not neglect the demands of progress, they did have options: they could make critical choices in their dealings with neighbors. With their route of transit, Pakistan, however, the Afghans egregiously chose to quarrel. The dramatic increase in Afghanistan's dependence upon the Soviet Union was accompanied by a dramatic failure to achieve success in two areas, internal integration and foreign policy (particularly toward Pakistan). The Afghans failed to create Pakhtunistan—the goal for which they had sacrificed good relations with Pakistan. During the 1950s and 1960s they pursued a futile political and economic goal in the south which eventually contributed to a new war of routes along the Central and South Asian borderlands. (One of the reasons for the ouster of Daoud by King Zahir Shah in March 1963 was reportedly his obsessive pursuit of Pakhtunistan, which threatened to ruin the Afghan economy.)[119]

Vital security concerns in the north were sacrificed as a result, bringing the Red Army into Afghanistan. The Soviet Union had successfully manipulated the politics of access. Afghanistan's development translated into Soviet accessibility and the consequent relinquishment of the primary objective of security: national independence. Ironically, this little game of routes culminated in a decade-long Soviet triumph in the Great Game.

It was over the roads the Soviets had built that their troops rolled into Afghanistan in the winter months of 1979–80. Just as, a century ago, Russian motives for absorbing Central Asia and plans for the invasion of India were debated, so the Soviet Union's contemporary motives for invading Afghanistan have attracted endless dispute. The imputed motives range from ideological to strategic, from offensive to defensive, from accidental to inevitable. Thus, for example, Fred Halliday insists that "Russian policy was politically neutral throughout the postwar period, up to the 1978 crisis," when circumstances changed dramatically due to "Iranian interference." Other writers have subscribed to an opposing theory: in occupying Afghanistan, the Soviets were taking one more martial step in their historical march toward the Indian Ocean.[120]

Whatever Soviet motives may have been, the new physical accessibility of Afghanistan indisputably changed the Soviet Union's practical calculus of invasion (by "invitation" or otherwise) and occupation. Without the highway networks and tunnels that connect Soviet Central Asian with Afghan cities and Afghan cities with one another (through the added effect of U.S. aid in southern Afghanistan); without the crumbling of that ancient antiroute, the Hindu Kush—without, that is, the removal of the major obstacles to mobility, economic and political penetration, and conquest, the invasion of Afghanistan would have involved far more elaborate military and economic calculations for the Soviets.[121] These calculations would have more closely resembled those their Russian forebears had had to make in their Game with the British, involving perilous imponderables of logistics and supply and threatening potentially higher losses of manpower and great difficulties of communication.

Still, Afghanistan's difficult terrain did vitiate some of the advantages of Soviet proximity and access. "Mountains are our 'forests,'" said Gulbuddin Hekmatyar, leader of the fundamentalist mujahideen party, the Hezb-e-Islami. "Just as the Americans could not compete with the Vietnamese in the jungle, the Russians will fail in the mountains."[122] With more than a hundred thousand troops deployed in Afghanistan, and with the benefits of airpower and rapid resupply, the Soviets could not end mujahideen resistance. The war for Afghanistan has been primarily a war to protect or assail logistics and supply routes. Daily battles ensued along the Soviet-built highways, around the Salang Tunnel, and in the neighborhood of the Durand Line. According to the Soviets, one of their main tasks in occupied-Afghanistan was to "give assistance to the Afghan armed forces in protecting highways." Since all freight in the country is moved by road (the trucks are usually run by Afsotr, a joint Afghan-Soviet transport company established during the 1960s), convoys were the main targets for the mujahideen. When the Soviet troop withdrawal from Afghanistan began in 1988, the Salang Tunnel, and their highways from Kabul and from Kandahar, became critical exit ways. The political and military decisions of mujahideen commanders such as Ahmed Shah Massoud in the north and Ismael Khan in the west, who had focused their wartime strategy on ambushing Soviet access routes, would determine the ease with which the Soviets completed their withdrawal. In early 1989 Soviet and mujahideen forces warred over the safe northward passage of Soviet troops and the secure transport of food and relief supplies to Kabul along the Salang Tunnel route. Reportedly, the Soviets conducted air, artillery, and troops operations, including intensive bombing raids, which resulted in high Afghan casualties. Lt. Gen. Boris Gromov said, "We warned him [Massoud] what would happen if he blocked the highway. . . . The highway must operate. We had no other choice."[123]

Infrastructural aid gave the donor, the Soviet Union, the ability to reshape the economic, political, and military circumstances of these Central Asian borderlands, drawing them northward; to transform Pakistan's security environment; and to cast a longer shadow over the Persian Gulf, thereby generating Western concern. As President Carter's national security adviser, Zbigniew Brzezinski, saw it, the Soviet invasion was "not a local but a strategic challenge."[124] By carving a niche for themselves, by continuing to play the modern game of routes, the Soviets confounded both history and geography for nearly a decade in an important quarter of Asia.

The politics of routes still dominates the local affairs of these borderlands. A road through tribal territory is much more than an avenue of mobility. Here the laws of the state intersect with the laws of the tribe. A man involved in a traditional blood feud enters the protection of the state when he steps onto a national road; if a tribesman commits a crime on the Khyber road, for example, he can be fined by the state. On the territory adjoining the road, however, only tribal laws apply. The arrival of roads has had a significant economic impact on tribal life: many tribesmen, for example, Afridis and Shinwaris, have gained controlling interests in a trucking industry that operates throughout Pakistan and across the Khyber Pass into Afghanistan as well. Government road building in a barren area such as Waziristan, home to the powerful Mahsud tribe, can also prove lucrative to tribesmen through employment as road guards. And, as David Dichter has pointed out, the tribesmen often take down bridges and tear out road posts "just to make their presence felt, and to ensure that the government continues their subsidies and recognizes their independent nature."[125] As a result, the government must pay the tribes to repair the damage they have caused.

The illegal border trade between Afghanistan and Pakistan has continued to flourish during the years of the Afghan conflict. The Khyber Pass territory still performs as a free trade zone. Small Suzuki vans laden with illegal goods bought in the West, in Eastern Europe, and in South East Asia—often these are Soviet refrigerators—hurtle through the dusty, barren hills along the Khyber route toward one of the tribal markets or the larger bazaar in Peshawar. Weapons and narcotics take less public pathways in their journey to Pakistan.

In all the Afghan wars, including the most recent, tribal politics have become intertwined with state politics and with the conduct of the war. The Pakhtuns of southern Afghanistan and northwestern Pakistan are past masters in "selling" allegiance for cash. Today, Islamabad and Kabul must pay high prices for cooperation. In some areas the Pakistani government has tried to establish insurance premiums, which are forfeited if a tribe undertakes pro-Kabul activities. Smaller battles over the routes and passes into Afghanistan have been fought within the framework of the larger Afghan war. In July 1987 a deadly dispute for control of access routes broke out among the Turi, Mangal, and Bangash tribes in the environs of Parachinar in the Kurram Agency of Pakistan.[126] At times the Afghan government has successfully used tribesmen on the Pakistani side of the border to close the narrow passes to the mujahideen, to harass them, and to disrupt their supply routes. Tribal leaders have also accepted bribes and weaponry from one side of the border to stir up trouble on the other. One powerful Pakistani Afridi tribal leader, Wali Khan Kukikhel, has often indulged in pro-Kabul antics—such as leading his followers into

Afghanistan in 1985, accepting land, weapons, and payments from Kabul, and joining the Afghan frontier militia. (These Afridis returned to Pakistan in 1986.) Kukikhel's actions have led to armed confrontations with Pakistani and mujahideen forces.

Tribal recalcitrance keeps road building in the Pakistani borderlands a complicated endeavor. With almost predictable regularity, the advent of each new road project is greeted with a tribal protest that demonstrates the rivalry between tribal politics—which are conducted across borders—and the integrative and military demands of the individual nation-state. In 1987 the construction of an important 12.4-mile-long, 3.7-mile-wide paved road, which would link the roads from Khyber and Peshawar to a village in the Tirah Valley 30 miles southwest of Peshawar, spurred the competing politics of tribe and state.

The Pakistani government suggested that the road, by improving access to the valley, would tighten the ties between tribesmen and central government, and it gathered the Zakhakhel branch of the Afridi tribe to rally support for it. The Tirah road would reduce the isolation and underdevelopment of the area (the Zakhakhels have been without schools, hospitals, tubewells, and other important amenities). It would also have military utility for Pakistani and mujahideen units by easing vital frontier logistics and permitting the rapid transport of troops and equipment through the Khyber Agency to the Afghan border. The Afghan government opposed the project through a local tribal faction that was waging its own war with the Pakistanis. Wali Khan Kukikhel, the renegade Afridi chief, suggested the road would "invite foreign intervention" and argued that he and his men (who quarrel with the Zakhakhel leadership) did not want the Afghan mujahideen to enter the area. Some Afridis tried to block the road-building efforts: in January 1987, eleven people, including four tribal chiefs, were killed in the dispute over the road.[127]

The struggle over land routes is a central issue of progress during peace and a central issue of power during the wars, great and small, among the states and tribes of the borderlands. The events of the 1980s have a marked resemblance to those of the 1880s. Because of the new global rivals and a new set of international circumstances, the politics of these borderlands—after an interlude of less than fifty years—again appears on the mental maps of distant makers of global policy. In the U.S.-Soviet competition these faraway lands once again derive importance from the hazards posed by the potential access of one global competitor to lands valued by the other.

In these borderlands, natural routes have triumphed over artificial antiroutes. Like so many other colonial boundaries, the lengthy Durand Line has never transformed members of the same or related tribes into full citizens of separate states. Pakhtun tribesmen wander at will back and forth across the border, through more than two hundred passes between Quetta and northernmost Pakistan (ninety of which can accommodate vehicles). The arrival of Soviet troops sent millions of Afghan refugees southward and arms and mujahideen northward into Afghanistan. And the hundreds of natural paths and passes across the Afghanistan-Pakistan borderlands played a prominent part in saving the Afghan resistance to Soviet occupation.

The porous nature of the border zone and an inability to monitor it have been a mixed blessing for Pakistan. The honeycombed border has benefited the Afghan mujahideen, but it has also permitted the infiltration of the ugliness of war—weaponry, drugs, bombings, and death—into the Pakistani heartland. Neither the natural nor the manmade barriers—neither the Hindu Kush nor the Durand Line—have halted the movement of Central Asian dilemmas into the subcontinent. Since 1980 men have been at war from the Amu Darya to the Indus.

Pakistan has suffered because it could not shield its lands from the Central Asian war. The Soviets, too, have suffered the consequences of southern access. Although Najibullah has insisted that sealing the border of his land-locked country was the first and foremost political and military task of his state, neither the Afghans nor the Soviets have managed to close the border. Because of their inability to shut off mujahideen sources of resupply, they were unable to defeat the mujahideen. By 1988 the high costs of achieving a military victory had combined with the Soviets' new domestic agenda to make them seek a political peace.

4

The Karakoram and Himalayan Borderlands: The Consequences of Access

In 1962 the People's Republic of China launched a swift military strike across the Himalayan mountain barrier against India's northern borderlands. In 1978 a massive new highway, jointly built by the Chinese and the Pakistanis, pierced the neighboring Karakoram mountains, thereby cementing a fifteen-year-old informal regional partnership between their two countries. The Chinese incursions altered a centuries-old political and military relationship between Chinese Central Asia and South Asia and, in modest fashion, revived their economic intercourse. The rationales governing China's strategy in its southwestern borderlands, its penetration of the mountain barrier, and the consequences for South Asia are contained in the story of the region's routes.

The modern political history of the subcontinent may be read as the rivalry between two sets of friends; the areas bordering it, such as Afghanistan and Tibet (the buffers of an earlier era), have been embraced by one or another great land power. The mountainous anti-routes of the nineteenth century have today been pierced from the north; and since 1947 new restraints on movement have been imposed inside the subcontinent. The friendships evolved gradually: the signing, in 1963, of a border agreement between China and Pakistan heralded a new partnership. The Soviet Union and India formalized their extensive economic, military, and political ties in 1971, with the signing of the Indo-Soviet Treaty of Friendship and Cooperation. The antipathy between the two sets of partners was confirmed.

Territorial quarrels and border disputes—the pressures arising from antiroutes determined under the imperial aegis—remain eminent sources of political friction and military conflict in the region. The threat of border strife between India and China is omnipresent—as evidenced by frontier tensions in 1987. Similarly, clashes between India and Pakistan persist. The 1980s saw armed conflict along the Siachin Glacier, which lies in proximity to the Indo-Pakistani Line of Actual Control in Kashmir. Together with the Northern Areas—across which the Sino-Pakistani routes run—Kashmir remains the focus of territorial controversy.

The wars of the subcontinent have had their roots in competing interpretations of political and geographical identity, as in the secession of Bangladesh and the wars for Kashmir. These political controversies and martial disputes are captured in the politics of routes. A critical catalyst for the Sino-Indian War of 1962 (and a reason why the Sino-Indian border dispute continues unresolved) was the argument between China and India over ownership of the Aksai Chin, across which snakes a strategic Chinese road. The course of Sino-Indian and Sino-Pakistani relations, as well as of Sino-Soviet and Indo-Pakistani relations, has been affected by the development of the Karakoram Highway complex (also known by its acronym, the KKH).

My focus here is on the lands dominated by the high mountain peaks of the Himalayas and the Karakorams, where the desert lands of Central Asia and the river valleys of the subcontinent rudely meet. The Himalayas, the Karakorams or Black Gravel range, and the Pamirs all stretch across the northern rim of the subcontinent, culminating in a "quintessential barrier," the Pamir Knot. This massive arc of mountain ranges stretches for over two thousand miles across Asia, rising to heights of twenty thousand feet and more. Like that lesser range, the Hindu Kush, to their west, these ranges have been crossed for centuries. Unlike the Hindu Kush, however, the mountains have

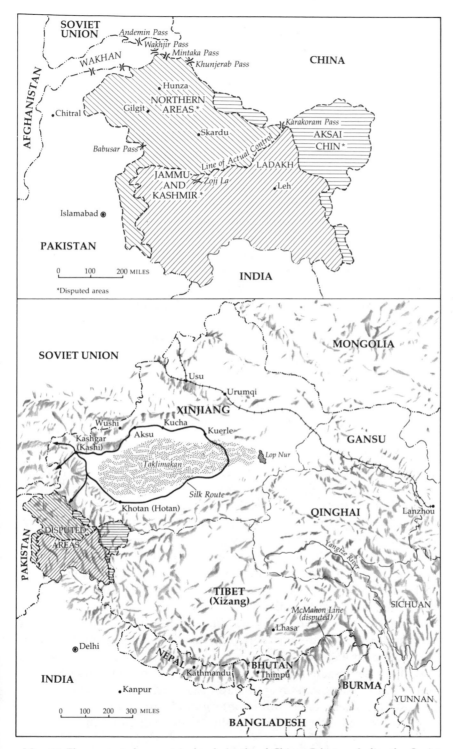

Map 10 The contested mountain borderlands of China, Pakistan, India, the Soviet Union, and Afghanistan

prevented invaders from launching a successful invasion southward until the second half of the present century.[1]

Today these ranges have been penetrated by roads. Major routes through passes that for centuries had been cut only by goat tracks have revolutionized the relationship between the states of the Karakorams and Himalayas and reduced dramatically the historical, political, and geographical distance between China and its southern neighbors. This is not to say, of course, that important routes have never traversed the ranges; the Silk Route, that legendary key to beauty, lucre, and glory, functioned as an international commercial and diplomatic highway in ancient times, and the mountain passes channeled an exchange of goods, political missives, and religious and cultural ideas. Still, when it reached the Himalaya-Karakoram region, the Silk Route became an extraordinarily arduous path. Contacts between Central and South Asia remained limited. Today, however, in the Northern Areas of Pakistan and the southwestern borderlands of China, a strand of the Silk Route has been revived as the Karakoram Highway.

An ancient caravan route flourished through the steep mountain passages, linking China with India, Syria, Iran, and Rome. The Silk Route, or rather routes, began in the modern Chinese province of Xinjiang. The inhabitants of the oasis towns of Xinjiang—formerly known as Chinese Turkestan, High Tartary, or the "Pivot of Asia"—were once the primary agents in the great commercial traffic between Central and South Asia and Europe.[2] Xinjiang is virtually surrounded by mountains: the Karakoram, the Pamir, the Altun Shan, Kunlun Shan, Tien Shan, and Altay Shan. Only a few routes linked it with lands to the west and south, to modern Afghanistan, northern Pakistan, Kashmir, and Tibet.

The trade routes from China began in the Tarim Basin and circumvented the Taklimakan Shamo, a purgatory of wind and sand. Here, in High Tartary, these perilous channels of access mixed men and their ideas. The routes marked the patterns of an ancient commingling in art, culture, and religion. Buddhism from India, Taoism and Confucianism from the heartland of China, Manicheanism from Iran, Islam from Arabia, and Christianity from Europe came together. The main oasis settlements of Xinjiang were on the northern and southern rims of the Taklimakan Shamo, across which threaded strands of the Silk Route. These oldest and longest trade routes known to man stretched across Asia and crossed the frontiers of vast empires.

The two main sections of the Silk Route swung in a wide arc around the Taklimakan desert, reuniting in a single road to the desert's east and to the west at Kashgar (Kashi), by the Pamirs. The geography of Xinjiang was conducive to the pursuit of commerce across the Silk Route. The combination of desert and oases eased passage for the traders: the desert dissuaded raiders from attacking the caravans, and the oases provided food and water. By the first century A.D., trade between China and India was extensive, and Chinese wares were to be found in the markets of the Roman Empire.[3]

The southern strand of the Silk Route—most traveled in the first centuries A.D.—traversed the base of the Altun Shan, passing through Shache (Yarkand), Hotan (Khotan), Yutian (Keriya), Minfeng (Niya), Qiemo (Qargan), and points beyond. The northern road reached Kashgar via the oasis towns of Aksu (Aqsu) and Kucha (Kuqa). From Kashgar the road crossed Ferghana, Soghdiana, Chorasmia, and northern Iran, branching off in a southerly direction toward Afghanistan and India. Smaller offshoots, tracks, branches, and transit areas combined to create a commercial and political network of routes which extended as far as Asia Minor, linked up with the roads of Iran and India, and then turned northward to the Black Sea. The highly organized caravan traffic that moved along these ways served to funnel both intraregional and transcontinental trade.[4]

A brisk exchange in luxury articles was carried on along the Silk Route. From Central Asia, silks and lacquerware were traded; from India and other parts, fine wool, cotton, linen, textiles, jewels, rugs, spices, incense, steel, copper, elephants, dwarfs, and dancers made their way back to the markets of China. This overland trade—the key to whose economic success lay in prevailing political and military relations between China, the Mongols, and the Turks—was of such importance that it directly affected the course of maritime trade. The prices of sea-transported goods in Baghdad, Constantinople, and Cairo, for example, fluctuated according to the deliveries expected from overland caravans.[5]

The old city of Kashgar in Xinjiang was a central link in the commercial chain. It was then, as it is today, a junction of the routes emerging from the south, from Gilgit and from Kashmir. The cultural, ethnic, economic, and political links between these northernmost parts of the subcontinent and Chinese Central Asia are of ancient origin. In the last half-century, they have been revived by Pakistan and China despite the extravagant obstacles posed by geography.

In the southwest, only a handful of passes provide entry into Xinjiang. The easternmost is the Karakoram Pass (18,290 feet). To its west lies the Khunjerab Pass (15,600 feet) and the Mintaka Pass (15,450 feet). In the modern history of the borderlands, these passes have played a leading role. Before the creation of the Karakoram Highway, commerce across the ranges was always a dangerous affair. Adventurous traders had to pass through terrain that was uninhabited and without fodder. Transport losses could run as high as 40 percent, and the old Karakoram passageway has been called "the most arduous trade route of importance in the world."[6] To reach Central Asia, eleven major passes had to be crossed at elevations of between 16,000 and 18,000 feet, and the cold vengeance of wind and ice endured. From Xinjiang, too, yak caravans carried silk, jade, salt, hemp, and wool along another old trade route, across the frozen Aksai Chin plateau to Tibet.

Despite the traders' travails, the Silk Route flourished. Only in the sixteenth century, as the sea trade between China and Europe grew in importance, did commercial activity along the Silk Route begin to wane. Toward the end of that century Xinjiang's routes ceased to be major arteries of international trade; the entire Central and West Asian region collapsed into political turmoil, leaving the routes cut or sporadically blocked. Landborne trade suffered. In a pattern that had repeated itself over many hundreds of years, trade moved out to sea. This time, however, the shift was to be more permanent.

Commerce between Europe and the Orient was captured by the nascent European mercantile powers. The Silk Route lapsed into anonymity, and to this day the oases of Xinjiang have not regained their earlier fame and importance.[7] It is unlikely that the Karakoram Highway will ever recapture for Xinjiang's towns the economic glory brought by the Silk Route. Still, the high mountain road has resuscitated the historical association between Kashgar and Khotan (Hotan) and the Northern Areas of the subcontinent. This new Silk Route supports new purposes and functions, however. Although men and goods do traverse the Karakoram Highway, their numbers and volume are not high. The rationales for construction of these new mountain routes are lodged more in the political and military purposes of the region's states than in their economic discourse.

The Borderlands in the Late Nineteenth Century

In the 1970s the Karakoram Highway definitively breached the mountain barrier, altering the balance of geographical politics in the subcontinent. To understand the historical relevance of the modern Sino-Pakistani decision to create access, we may briefly compare the purposes and efforts of these modern states with those of their imperial predecessors in the nineteenth century. Then, it was precisely the concern with such a breach of the mountain frontier that led to a series of occupations and boundary disputes between the British, Chinese, and Russian empires.

The Karakoram mountains became a nucleus of concern for the players of the Great Game. For the Chinese, then the weakest of the three contenders, whose memory of invasion had focused on their western frontiers, the controversies along the mountainous borderlands to the southwest were a less common experience. Xinjiang to the west and Tibet to the south had traditionally been considered China's "Inner Asian Frontiers," as Owen Lattimore calls them, or its "Inner Protectorates," in the language of Alastair Lamb.[8] Beyond these frontier regions lay the "Outer Protectorates," including Ladakh, below the Aksai Chin, and Hunza, which nestles high in the hug of the mountains controlled by contemporary Pakistan. With the expansion of British power into the subcontinent's northernmost reaches arguments inevitably developed between China and Britain over the control of these frontier principalities which guarded access through the Himalayan and Karakoram passes. Present, too, by the late nineteenth century were suspicions about Russian intentions toward Central and South Asia.

Chinese policies toward the subcontinent today make better sense when we recognize the old concerns about their most distant, and largest, territories, Xinjiang and Tibet. The Chinese fears of encirclement, and of loss of control over their peripheries, sponsored modern routing policy in the borderlands and along the subcontinent. South and Central Asia have long been a theater of contests between competing powers for control of the mountain ranges. The nineteenth century witnessed a shifting alignment of frontiers between Chinese, Russian, and British empires. In these parts, as Dorothy Woodman suggests, the game was necessarily a triangular one, since the disputed areas—Afghanistan, the Aksai Chin plateau, and Kashmir, the northernmost territories of India, Tibet, and Nepal—all lay on the fringes of the three empires and were claimed at different times by different players.[9] Russia applied constant pressure on Chinese interests in Xinjiang, and the potential for a Russian advance into India via Kashgar contributed to Britain's interest in the Central Asian squabble.

The pattern of imperial frontier rivalry between Russian, Briton, and Chinese illuminates China's road-building activities in the region nearly a century later. Imperial maneuvers over routes and territory stimulated—and then abandoned to the region's future rulers—the controversies over route and antiroute which came to define the territorial politics of modern Central and South Asia. The revival of the Silk Route was a contemporary response to geopolitical predicaments raised by the imperialists.

The Great Game itself began when the Russian movement into Central Asia along their rapidly expanding railroads captured the attention of India's British rulers and Xinjiang's Chinese overlords. The earliest British anxieties concerned their North West Frontier, the home of traditional invasion routes into the subcontinent. Yet by the late 1880s the British had become concerned that the Khyber Pass might not be Russia's sole line of approach. In 1888, one Captain Grombchevsky reached Hunza through a gap between the Pamirs and Xinjiang. As Mortimer Durand remarked, "The game had begun."[10]

The British began to discuss the defense not only of the Hindu Kush but of the Karakorams and the Himalayas, too. They fretted about a Russian menace to north India, to Xinjiang, to the Aksai Chin, and even to Tibet. Although explorers had shown that a large-scale invasion across the mountain ranges was not a likely event, trepidation abut Russian entry persisted. Since the routine complexities of defense and warfare in the imperial possessions were exacerbated by the terrain in these northern reaches, the British determined to improve their protective strategy in the borderlands.

Writing in 1898, for example, Captain George Younghusband highlighted the intractable nature of the mountain ranges and the adverse impact of the terrain on Britain's ability to defend the north. The harshest impact, of course, was on British logistics:

> On the frontiers of India . . . mere goat tracks, hardly passable for pack transport, take the place of roads. Rivers and mountain torrents are unabridged, or at best spanned by frail foot bridges. Railways often do not exist within several hundred miles of the point of attack. The countries . . . afford neither food nor shelter for the troops, nor forage

for the animals. Lastly . . . all operations . . . are rigidly bound down
by considerations of water.

Younghusband detailed the crises of supply and transport which
afflicted British troops when they took Chitral in 1895. In this most
remote northern segment of the Frontier, the land is surrounded by
mountains of over 20,000 feet. When the leading brigade arrived in
Chitral, he said, it took 28,000 pack animals—and when local crops
had been eaten, 38,000 pack animals—to keep the force supplied with
its daily requirements. As Younghusband put it, "The defeat of the
enemy in battle is by no means the most difficult task put before the
leader of an Indian frontier expedition."[11]

Of consummate interest to India's British rulers was the potential
access of a hostile power to the north Indian territory of Kashmir.
Apparently, even a barrier required a buffer: Kashmir was Britain's
territorial buffer behind the mountains. British policies toward the
smaller principalities that lay scattered around Kashmir were inti-
mately tied to the requirements of Kashmir's security. According to
the Imperial Gazetteer for the region: "From a strategic point of view,
the valley of Kashmir occupied a highly valuable position with reference to the safety of British India, for it could be looked upon as an
entrenched camp situated on the flank of any force attempting the
invasion of the empire from the west, while lying directly on the road
of an enemy advancing by the routes from Badakhshan, Kashgar, and
Yarkand."[12]

Taken by the Mughal emperor Akbar in 1587, Kashmir was subsequently captured by the Afghans (in 1752) and the Sikhs (1819). In
1846, following their defeat of the Sikhs, the British "sold" Kashmir to
the Dogra Raja of Jammu, Gulab Singh. He was adventurous: to
control trade between Tibet and Kashmir he conquered Ladakh in
1834. In 1840 he took glacier-bound Baltistan and thereafter began to
evince a keen interest in the petty principalities around Gilgit. The
tiny fiefdom of Hunza, for example, which had payed nominal allegiance to the rulers of Gilgit, transferred its tribute to Kashmir when
the Dogra king's forces took Gilgit in 1859. (Still, Hunza also continued to pay tribute to the rulers of Chinese Kashgar.) Gulab Singh's
attempts to subdue the tiny states were, however, only "partially
successful."[13] In the 1860s and 1870s his successors tried to push their
way into Chinese Turkestan.

Only during the nineteenth century did the term "Kashmir" come
to represent the populous Vale, Jammu, Poonch, Ladakh, Baltistan,

and the Gilgit region—including Gilgit, Gilgit Wazarat, Gilgit Agency, Chilas, Yasin, Ishkuman, Hunza, and Nagar. Each area was separated by differences in language, religion, or culture. (In Gilgit, for example, the people speak a variety of Dardic tongues; in Ladakh, the Buddhists speak Tibetan; in Baltistan, the people, of Tibetan origin, have converted to Islam; in the Vale of Kashmir, Kashmiri is spoken; in Jammu, mainly Dogri, a language related to Punjabi, is prevalent.)[14]

When Lord Lytton became viceroy of India in 1876, the potential for a Russian advance into Kashmir called for a realistic policy to control access through the mountains. Lytton saw the convergence of the Himalayas, Karakorams, and Hindu Kush as forming the natural northern boundary of India. He observed that "if a strong, independent and hostile power were established on the north of these mountains, the passes might become lines of a demonstration . . . which might at least be useful as a diversion to facilitate and support the flank of more serious operations in Afghanistan."[15] Lytton concluded that British influence must be made firm in the lands lying within the angle of the mountains, encompassing strategic zones between the frontier and the mountain routes. Where necessary, influence among the tribal chiefs and direct conquest were to be used to bolster the natural antiroute.

Gilgit became a British priority. Fought over by Tibetan and Chinese conquerors as early as the eighth century, Gilgit has a value that stems from its geographical location: it commands the mouth of the Hunza River and the Indus Valley. Where strategic needs are primary, as they were for the British in north India, location, of course, becomes the dominant factor. As an Englishman phrased it, the "three greatest Empires of the Earth met—Great Britain, Russia, and China" beside Gilgit; if Kashmir was the "northern bastion of India," then Gilgit was "her farthest outpost." After 1885, reported Russian pressure on northern Afghanistan and the Pamirs (near Wakhan) determined the British to take charge of the area. In 1889 they took Gilgit from the Dogra ruler of Kashmir. From their base at Gilgit, they infiltrated the rowdy ministates of Hunza and Nagar. Still, as late as 1935, the British continued to fret about full control of Gilgit; finally, they "leased" the area from Kashmir. The British built roads into Gilgit, and widened and realigned the old trade route that linked it with the southern Kashmiri town of Srinagar.[16]

The lower passes of Hunza, Yasin, and Chitral appeared especially vulnerable to incursions from the north. Hunza, which lies to Kashmir's northwest and has miniature terraced fields, sweet apricots and walnuts, poplars and willows, has long had an ambivalent political and territorial status. Since the mid-eighteenth century its rulers paid a yearly tribute of 1.5 ounces of gold to the power in Kashgar. Later, Hunza would be claimed by China "as an outlying district of the New Dominion [Xinjiang]." The Chinese spoke of incorporating it formally into a province. Captain Grombchevsky's arrival in Hunza made the British fret further about Russian inquisitiveness south of the Karakorams. In response, they took Gilgit and reached an agreement with the Mir of Hunza to prevent the passage of foreigners and guarantee the safe travel of Britons. The Mir also had to recognize British suzerainty. Still, he continued to flirt with the Russians. By 1891 Durand was wondering whether the Mir might allow the entry of Russian or Chinese forces across the Karakorams. (Through Hunza the Chinese would build the Karakoram Highway.) In that year the British finally took Hunza and set up posts to guard the routes to the lower valleys and across the Hindu Kush. They also improved communications in the area and linked it with Kashmir.[17]

The stalwart British defense of the northernmost, mountainous reaches of the subcontinent from Kashmir to Burma was the final unified defense of the subcontinent. Aggressive British frontier maneuvers were possible at the time because China was frail and unable to promote its territorial claims. Russian egress eastward and British activity in their southwestern borderlands discomfited the Chinese. In turn, uncertainty regarding the Chinese ability to keep Kashgar drove British debates about the level of Chinese contribution to a defense against Russia in the borderlands. The debates were between those who argued that China should shoulder the burden of defense north of the mountains—in Xinjiang, in the Aksai Chin, and in Tibet—and those members of the Forward School, led by Sir John Ardagh, the former director of military intelligence, who insisted that Manchu China was a "useless" buffer "between Russia and the Northern frontier of India." Ardagh advocated a northerly boundary along the Karakoram and Mustagh ranges, which would ensure British control over all the strategic mountain routes into the subcontinent (across the Kilik, Mintaka, Khunjerab, Shimshal, Mustagh, and Karakoram passes) and even of the Aksai Chin.[18] Ardagh's proposals were not wholly realized during his lifetime, and nearly a century later China would gain access through the mountain passes. For a newly strong China, these routes into the subcontinent were to become useful to its control of Xinjiang and Tibet, and to its political and military strategy in the subcontinent.

The territories contended over in the game included Xinjiang, the Aksai Chin, and Tibet. As Alastair Lamb has described it, "Nothing comes across Tibet; everything goes around it." Tibet stands at the eastern reaches of what is today a two-thousand-mile frontier between India and China. It became a Chinese protectorate in the eighteenth century, part of the system developed to supersede the Great Wall (which had repeatedly failed to serve its purpose).[19] As Russian influence began to permeate Tibet in the late nineteenth century, the British first encouraged China to hold the area, then increased their own presence there, and finally, in 1907, made a pact with the Russians. Another antiroute was erected, a buffer established.

Between Tibet and Xinjiang stands the Aksai Chin. A desolate, 17,000–19,000-feet-high, barren plateau, the Soda Plains, or "desert of white stones," became strategically significant in the late nineteenth century, because there the frontiers of Xinjiang, Tibet, and Kashmir met. Its location in relation to areas of importance to China made the Aksai Chin valuable then, and in a later era gave the remote plateau even more significance. At different times both the British and the Chinese claimed the Aksai Chin. In 1894 the British insisted that the Soda Plains were a part of Kashmir. In 1896 China claimed them. Disputing British maps, China incorporated the Aksai Chin into "Chinese Tibet." In 1918 the Cartographic Bureau of the Chinese army's General Staff produced a map again placing Aksai Chin inside China. This map and its successors have been thought by some students of regional strategy to signify a longstanding intention of the Chinese military to control the plateau.[20]

Of all the areas with which the imperial players were concerned, Xinjiang was the most vulnerable. It was part of Sir Halford Mackinder's "heartland" or, in his earlier formulation, of the "geographical pivot of history." Britain's initial interest in Xinjiang was motivated by the needs of commerce, and the early forays of British agents into the area were made to support a trading position in Chinese Turkestan.[21] For the Russians, Xinjiang presented opportunities first for trade, then for political interference. As they moved toward Xinjiang, however, the British became concerned that the Russians might enter Kashmir through the same region. Thus trade with Xinjiang soon took second place to British policies for frontier defense.

During this period, and well into the mid-twentieth century, the largest proportion of Xinjiang's trade was with the lands to its west—Russian territories—rather than with China. The Russians inherited geographical advantages: Xinjiang's richest areas lay along its western borders. They were quick to capitalize on these natural assets by developing the simple trade routes already in existence. Although political and military relations between Russia and China along the Xinjiang frontier were rarely harmonious, trade with China reached a peak when the Russians completed their conquest of the Central Asian khanates in the late 1880s. Earlier, Xinjiang had exported some of its raw products, such as silk and furs, along the lengthy, costly overland route to central China. Now, it traded animal fats, fruit, meat, and livestock with Russia in exchange for cotton and woolen fabrics. From 1881 onward, economic settlements and transport routes occupied Russian energies. With the building of the Turksib Railroad, connecting the Turkestan and Trans-Siberian railroads, the Russians created what Hans Weigart calls "a powerful instrument" for transmitting Russian economic and political influence to Xinjiang.[22]

The territorial controversies of the nineteenth century revolved around the requirements for, or the denial of, strategic access. Empires waned, but the disputes over entry ways remained unresolved. They were bequeathed to the contemporary successors of empire—Pakistan, India, China, and the Soviet Union. As the new China emerged after 1949, grew slowly in strength, and recaptured its ability to control its traditional Inner and Outer Protectorates, the geopolitical map of the region began to change. Earlier, the scorched deserts and the dizzying peaks had combined with a low Chinese capacity for overcoming distance to prevent effective territorial integration and credible defense against external intrusions. The key to Chinese weakness had been the inaccessibility of these outlying areas to Chinese power. Now, after the Communists had assumed power in Beijing, China set out to redress this deficiency.

The Modern Politics of Routes in the Central and South Asian Borderlands

In the postcolonial era the Soviet Union, China, India, and Pakistan faced one another in an environment where new political alignments exacerbated old crises. The boundaries defining the new states were the product of imperial exigencies and barters. Partition of the subcontinent killed the imperial concept of a unified defense along a single strategic line up to the Hindu Kush and the Himalayas. The ideological and political lines of defense created in 1947 split the subcontinent geographically into an Indian center with West and East Pakistani peripheries.

China simultaneously began to assert itself as a major regional power, extending its control over Xinjiang and Tibet; the Indians exercised de facto control over Sikkim and Bhutan. Land-locked Nepal, too, came to rely heavily on India. Kashmir became the venue of confrontation between India and Pakistan. The imperial buffer system ended. Xinjiang, Aksai Chin, and Tibet became a part of China's western and southwestern defense against the Soviet Union and India. Gilgit, Hunza, Nagar, Baltistan, and their environs became important to Pakistan's geopolitical flexibility in the subcontinent, while Ladakh, Nepal, Bhutan, and Sikkim were incorporated into India's frontier security plans against Pakistan and China. In 1979 the Soviet Union took Afghanistan, terminating the strategic notion of the Asian buffer.

Mountainous Kashmir, across which the Indus River races east to west, wedged between Pakistan and India, has been the cause of political discord, territorial division, and war between its claimants since 1947. Today the 478.5-mile Line of Actual Control runs from alongside the Karakoram Pass to about 81 miles northeast of Lahore. Pakistan controls about one-third of Kashmir while India controls the remaining two-thirds.

The strategic location of the disputed Northern Areas has ensured federal administration from Islamabad. Gilgit and Baltistan became administrative districts in 1974 while Hunza became part of the Northern Areas in 1975. The areas' representatives have a presence in Pakistan's national councils.[23] India has not welcomed these moves, insisting that the territories are disputed and their legal possession is linked to the status and ownership of Kashmir.

The border disputes between China and the Soviet Union and between China and India have yet to be resolved, although negotiations proceed. Troops are massed on borders. In the context of these new alignments, the construction of a Chinese road system within Xinjiang and Tibet, across the Aksai Chin, and into Pakistan's Northern Areas has had a significant impact upon political and military relations in Central and South Asia.

China's routing policies have been closely linked to its military posture along its western and southwestern borders. Because of China's earlier anxieties about the security of its inner Asian frontiers, which it could defend only by projecting central control across great distances, modern China's borderland highway projects address historical problems. In the past, terrain, physical inaccessibility, and inadequate logistics debilitated Chinese military and foreign policy, preventing intercourse with western lands and militating against the establishment of a unified and secure Chinese state. Since 1949, a persistent Chinese goal has been to alter these constraints through the creation of access. China's relations with the states of South Asia may be understood as a story of the search for, and conflict over, access.

China has created its strongest ties in South Asia with Pakistan. The geo-centerpiece of Chinese development aid to the region has been a joint Sino-Pakistani project: the Karakoram Highway complex. The Karakoram routes are joined to China's main strategic roads, which connect Xinjiang and Tibet. Within a broader system of borderland logistics, the Karakoram Highway has provided China with a logistical, political, and diplomatic asset.

China's own goals have impinged upon the security concerns of India, Pakistan, and the Soviet Union and have had an ancillary, material impact on the development of the borderlands. Economic, political, and social change has been prompted by the larger political and military rationales and interests of China. The politics of regional routes graphs the patterns of Chinese influence. For Pakistan, its collaboration with China in creating land corridors across untrodden—even uncharted—regions has been valuable in advancing its internal communications, its ability to control territory, its drive to develop the Northern Areas, its political and military stance in subcontinental affairs, and its enduring partnership with China.

CONTEMPORARY CHINESE ROUTING POLICIES

China's geography incorporates numerous, soaring mountain ranges, wide plains, deep basins such as the Tarim and Junggar Pendi in Xinjiang, and expansive deserts such as the forbidding Taklimakan, also in Xinjiang. High ranges traverse over two-thirds of China's 6 million square miles. There is little flat ground. The Altay range provides a northwestern barrier, and the Himalayas perform the same function in the southwest. Despite a lengthy coastline and excellent harbors, China has always oriented its perspective inland.[24] The natural environment insists on the importance of access and a connecting infrastructure for political and military control and economic growth.

The most striking feature of China's land-based strategy in Central and South Asia has been its route-building activities. Chinese projects have entailed high costs in manpower and lives and have been compounded by the difficulties of construction at average heights of over 10,000 feet. Two sets of reasons—economic and doctrinal, security and foreign policy—have together produced a rational, coherent routing policy.

Highway construction and highway assistance programs make economic sense for China, whose human assets and technological limitations match the capabilities required for such tasks. Highway construction is not technologically complex. China faces high technical, financial, resource, and capital constraints, but manpower is abundant—and highway construction is labor-intensive. China has mobilized its large reservoir of trained and organized Peoples Liberation Army (PLA) units, as well as surplus farm labor, for large-scale construction projects. Local governments at or below the administrative district level have been charged with organizing workers for construction: reportedly, over five million men were drafted to work on the Xinjiang-Tibet highway. The total investment by the government has involved mainly the costs of material and transportation and the user cost of equipment. The Chinese government also sometimes subsidizes the wages paid by the communes or brigades of peasants who work on road projects. The capital-output ratio is extremely low.[25]

Difficult topographical conditions, however, do affect significantly the cost of highway construction. Road-building projects in the southwest and northwest regions of China cost more. Thus, although the low expense on labor gives China a relative cost advantage, blasting assiduously away at the recondite rock faces of the Karakorams and Himalayas since the 1960s cannot be adequately explained from an economic perspective alone.

The economic perspective must be complemented by the strategic perspective. Chinese military doctrine favors the expansion of land-based logistics systems over other lines of communications. With about three million men, mainly infantry, under arms, China has stressed the value of numbers.[26] In an attempt to compensate for serious deficiencies in material, infantry provides the backbone of the PLA. In Korea in 1950, in India in 1962, and in Vietnam in 1979, Chinese footsoldiers formed the core of combat operations. This prominence of manpower over material, particularly over sophisticated hardware, in China's force structure and strategy supports the development of land routes. In any future conventional confrontation along the Himalayas or in Central Asia, adequate land-based logistics would be essential to the conduct of Chinese-style warfare.

China's internal crises have always been born of unvanquished distance. In numerous ways, ideological and bureaucratic and military, modern China—the People's Republic—must cope with the daily struggle between effective control and intransigent distance. To create and perpetuate accessibility in its vast territories must be a primary and routine goal of any Chinese central government. Communication and contact over vast distances are essential vehicles for state continuity, social cohesion, and economic strength. Route building in the borderlands responds to this urgent need to integrate China's farther regions more closely with the central provinces.

A Chinese writer, Wang Zhanyi, has argued that modern China focused on road building in the peripheries in order to end the "systematic isolation of minority areas in the old society." He cites as an example Tibet's lack of even a post road prior to China's entry into the region. New roads have also served as a deterrent against the potential encroachment of hostile neighbors (the Soviet Union, India) or as a preemptive vehicle in efforts to subdue them (Vietnam). In 1949 China possessed only about 46,600 miles of serviceable roads; 75 percent of them were located in the north, the northeast, and the east. In the 1950s, however, an assertive attempt began to build roads into the unruly, peripheral regions that touched on the Indochinese, Sino-Indian, and Sino-Soviet borderlands. Roads were cut into Xinjiang, Qinghai, Guangxi, and Yunnan. Important Chinese railroads were also built for political or military reasons in areas of low traffic density (below 6 million ton kilometers per route kilometer): in Yunnan (which borders Vietnam and Laos), in Inner Mongolia and Xinjiang (which border Outer Mongolia and the Soviet Union), in Qinghai (which borders Tibet), and in Fujian (which faces Taiwan).[27]

The building of roads and railroads outside the state's territory has formed a relatively inexpensive way for China to deliver economic and military aid to other states, to cement alliances, or to act as a part of China's "stadium diplomacy." To further foreign policy goals, China has granted infrastructural aid for development to a number of Asian and African states. In South Asia, the targets of Chinese munificence have been Nepal and Pakistan. The goals of Chinese development aid, particularly in the case of projects as long-term, expensive, and prodigious as the Karakoram Highway, are inseparable from those of broader Chinese foreign policy and, in the case of the subcontinent, from those of Chinese security policy. Large transport projects serve a number of purposes for China. They are an enduring and concrete demonstration of support for the economic development and the political-military stance of the recipient state; they confirm friendships; and they confer international prestige upon China. Its own small resources and large needs make participation in these highly visible projects look even more impressive. Since 1965 China has sent technicians and workers abroad to build over thirty roads and sixteen major bridges in more than twenty countries, including Pakistan, Nepal, Burma, Yemen, Iraq, Sudan, Zambia, and Mongolia.[28]

The donation of transport infrastructure to a contiguous state in a valued region (as with the Karakoram Highway) also serves specific security purposes. It can bolster frontier security; symbolize military cooperation; pose a threat to enemies in the region; channel aid and military equipment to the recipient state or, through it, to others; and serve the recipient state's internal security and its political and economic integration.

Why did China embark on a lengthy relationship with Pakistan, invest in the Karakoram Highway, and link its own borderland routes to those of Pakistan? Which Chinese concerns spurred antipathy toward India and friendship with Pakistan? The answers lie in three political and military situations, all of which sustained routing dilemmas: the meaning of the Sino-Soviet border dispute for Xinjiang; China's invasion of Tibet in 1949–50; and the Sino-Indian War of 1962, which began as a dispute over the barren lands of the Aksai Chin. In the evolution of these situations, which culminated in a favorable Chinese response to Pakistan's overtures of friendship, land routes played a focal role.

To grasp the nature of China's association with the subcontinent, we must understand the simple magnitude of its frontier lands and its broken fraternal relationship with the Soviet Union. China possesses over 12,428 miles of frontier, much of it bordering hostile states such as India, Vietnam, and, of course, the Soviet Union. The Sino-Soviet rift prompted Chinese dealings with Pakistan and disturbed ties with

India. In the years following 1949, the Soviet Union had relinquished its hold on Xinjiang and become China's pre-eminent benefactor. In the early 1950s the two ideological associates had tried jointly to develop Xinjiang. With the heightening of tensions in their relationship during the 1960s, however, Chinese perception of external threat changed, altering the timing, aims, and layout of Chinese route building along the borderlands. Attack was no longer feared from the sea alone; it could come over land, around the Xinjiang frontier from the Soviet Union. This change in threat perception spurred enormous road-building projects across the Himalayas during the 1960s and 1970s. With the opening of the mountain ranges and a new regional partnership through the Sino-Pakistani agreement of 1963, China began to create an apparatus for access and mobility. It would assist Chinese defenses against the Soviet Union and make India vulnerable in Kashmir.

XINJIANG UYGUR ZIZHIQU (XINJIANG UIGHUR AUTONOMOUS REGION)

Russia's historical access to Xinjiang and its own deficient links with the region posed a perennial problem for China and spurred China's road construction in its southwestern borderlands during the 1960s and 1970s. Xinjiang is modern China's largest political unit, comprising about 1,025,000 square miles, one-sixth of the country's total land area. Presently divided into three military districts (North, East, and South Xinjiang), the province is economically and strategically vital. In 1955, this "New Dominion" was formally incorporated into China as the Xinjiang Uyghur Autonomous Region. The Taklimakan desert, filled with rippling gravel and sand, dominates Xinjiang. North of the desert is Urumqi, the provincial capital, and to the south lie the cities of Kashi (old Kashgar) and Hotan. Vegetation and crops are confined to the oasis towns where mulberries, walnuts, pears, and apples can be grown. Xinjiang's past is the changing relationship between the nomad tribes of the steppe, who have triumphed over the terrain, and its settled agricultural communities.

Xinjiang shares a northeastern border with Mongolia, a 4,010-mile northwestern border with the Soviet Union, a southwestern border with Afghanistan and Pakistani and Indian Kashmir, a southeastern border with Tibet, and an eastern border with the Chinese provinces of Qinghai and Gansu. Until the mid-1970s it housed Chinese nuclear installations. This fact, combined with Xinjiang's location next to the Soviet Central Asian republics and its predominantly "non-Chinese" population (it is home to the Uyghur, Kazakh, Han, Hui, Kirghiz, Mongol, Sibo, Tajik, Uzbek, Tartar, Tahur, Manchu, and Russian peoples), has made Xinjiang extremely sensitive. Kashi is more than 2,000 miles from Beijing; controlling this periphery has long been an essential and difficult task for the Chinese.

Although the Soviet Union and China share a common frontier for several thousand miles, the fifteen hundred miles of border between Xinjiang and Kazakhstan are the most permeable segment of the Sino-Soviet borderland. Here, the frontier area is a broad strip of territory with crossnational ethnic and religious linkages between the citizens of the two states. In the nineteenth and early twentieth centuries this ethnic diversity, combined with weak Chinese central control, encouraged Russian incursions into Xinjiang. China had to conquer the region time and again. It has been estimated that central control was effective for only 425 years in the two millennia of Chinese "rule."[29] In the nineteenth century (between 1871 and 1881), anti-Chinese rebellions created the conditions for Russian occupation of the Ili region of Xinjiang. In the 1930s and 1940s discontent among the minorities once more provided an excuse for Russian interference.

In the early years after 1949, however, the Soviet Union and China were friends. In 1950 China reacted to the continuing problem of minority unrest, and to the need to exploit Xinjiang's mineral resources, by starting a process of Sinification, involving the PLA in both civil industrial and military activities, and building a highway network. During this era of Sino-Soviet collaboration, agreements were signed for economic and technical assistance. The most important was an accord to construct railway links between China and the Soviet Union through Mongolia and Xinjiang. The Friendship Railway would have linked the central lands of China through Xinjiang to Soviet Kazakhstan, connecting the industrial development of China's northwest with that of Soviet Central Asia. If completed, it would have established a Eurasian transcontinental line, permitting direct rail travel from East Berlin to Hanoi. By January 1961 the Soviets had built a spur from Aktogay to the Junggar Gate and set up a border settlement named Druzhba. With Sino-Soviet relations deteriorating rapidly, however, China halted construction at Ürümqi in 1962. By that time the Chinese had built the 1,176-mile rail line linking Ürümqi to Lanzhou in the province of Gansu. This line, which crosses the

Huanghe, snakes across a section of the Gobi desert and through the Tian Shan range, remains China's only major rail link to the far northwest. Although railways form the heart of the Chinese transport system, there are still too few in western China.[30]

By the early 1960s the Xinjiang frontier, always restless and often alive with anti-Chinese activity, was the eye of the storm gathering between China and the Soviet Union. Large troop movements were common, accompanied by charges and countercharges of subversion, border violations, territorial aggrandizement, and the instigation of minority unrest. These tensions in Xinjiang spurred China to further enhance access to its remote territories. Whereas Tibet was threatened only verbally by the Soviet Union, border incidents in Xinjiang took a dangerous turn around 1960. In 1963 China accused the Soviet Union of conducting disruptive activities in Xinjiang: the Soviet Union, it claimed, had carried out "large-scale subversive activities in the Ili region of Xinjiang and incited several tens of thousands of Chinese citizens into going to the Soviet Union"; further, it insisted that the Soviets had "systematically violated" China's border, with over five thousand violations in 1962 alone.[31]

By 1964 the Sino-Soviet argument had become muddled, ideologically, territorially, and militarily. China now perceived the main conventional military threat, as Francis J. Romance states, as coming overland in the guise of "highly mobile armor-heavy Soviet ground units supported by a panoply of tactical air assets" in the direction of Xinjiang.[32] China sent additional troops to the province, clearing and fortifying a twenty-mile-deep security zone along hundreds of miles of Soviet border. During this period, it was suggested that a continuing source of the relative weakness of the Chinese forces in Xinjiang (vis-à-vis the Soviet Union, whose troops were also operating at a great distance from the state's European core) remained the paucity of efficient land routes. The Chinese continued to lack transport equipment and, because of their primitive logistics apparatus, their forces had little strategic mobility.[33]

XIZANG ZIZHIQU (TIBET AUTONOMOUS REGION)

Tibet is the other great border territory, a vast plateau about half a million square miles in area over which China has kept constant vigil. Tibet lies at an average altitude of 15,000 feet. It is encircled by, and composed of, mountains including the northerly Min Shan, the Kunlun Shan and the Karakorams to the west, and the Himalayas to the south. Its northern regions hold white mountain peaks, endless plains, deep rivers, and lush forests. In the east lie virtually inaccessible lands, densely forested, filled with rugged gorges and the headwaters of Asia's powerful rivers, including the Nu Jiang (Salween), Lancang Jiang (Mekong), and Chang Jiang (Yangtze). In the south lie the dry, wide valleys of the upper Indus, Sutlej, and Brahmaputra rivers. Vast, flat salt plains characterize central Tibet, indented by blue lakes and icy rivers.[34] On the Nepalese-Tibetan border stands Mount Everest (29,028 feet).

The absorption of Tibet was likely from the moment that a strong authority established itself in Beijing. The Chinese have claimed Tibet for the past two centuries. Barely a year after the Communists came to power, this Inner Protectorate was transformed into a Chinese possession. The foremost Chinese objectives in the 1950 conquest of Tibet were strategic: control of the highest ground in Asia could translate into control of the Himalayan plateau. It promised to limit Indian incursions into the Himalayas and reduce the Soviet threat to China's western and southwestern flanks. By taking Tibet, China shut its mountain doors.

The Chinese have often insisted that their purpose in Tibet has been to "overcome its economic and cultural backwardness." But their early administrative and infrastructural efforts pointed to other aims as well. As soon as Tibet was occupied, Chinese forces began hastily to build roads and highways: as John Avedon notes, "Building roads capable of bearing seven-ton loads . . . [was] the army's major task during the fifties and the first half of the sixties." China's United Front Works Department reported that the "greatest part of the new highway construction throughout the country since Liberation has been located in the frontier regions." All of the highways listed in its report lay in Tibet or in the Xinjiang-Tibet borderlands. Almost all roads in these two regions are reportedly wide enough for two-way traffic and capable of carrying a minimum of seven-ton roads.[35]

By 1965, 90 percent of the districts in the Tibet Autonomous Region had been connected. China linked Tibet with Qinghai, Yunnan, Sichuan, and Xinjiang, reducing, for example, a two-to-three-month trek from Lhasa to Chengdu (in Sichuan) or to Xining (in Qinghai) to a journey of a few days. Among the massive road schemes the Chinese completed is the Sichuan-Tibet Highway (South Military

Road). Over four hundred miles long, built at an average height of 13,000 feet, and crossing fourteen mountain ranges and twelve rivers, it has a single, important offshoot that connects Xinjiang with Tibet. Into Tibet the Chinese also built the Qinghai-Tibet highway which runs from Xining to Lhasa and the Yunnan-Tibet highway which runs from Xiagnan to Markam. The Chinese concentrated on the borderland routes that linked their two most vulnerable regions, Xinjiang and Tibet, particularly the 793-mile-long Xinjiang-Tibet highway from Yecheng in southern Xinjiang to Pulan in western Tibet and eventually to Lhasa. Chinese sources describe this road as "located on the national defense line along China's western frontiers." Prior to construction, it took a camel service over a month to complete the round trip between Xinjiang and Tibet. Now it takes five days. Until the creation of the Karakoram Highway, the Xinjiang-Tibet highway was the highest road in the world. By 1981 the Chinese had built more than a hundred truck-capable roads in Tibet.[36]

Following the roads is an ambitious railroad, the 518-mile Qinghai-Tibet line, which has been called "the key to defending China's southwestern frontier against India, as well as to stabilizing the country and eventually exploiting its natural resources."[37] If and when it is completed, it will be the first railroad ever to penetrate Tibet. An oil pipeline has also been laid between China and Tibet and airfields in southern Tibet made fully operational all year round. PLA logistical support can now maintain twenty-one divisions in Tibet for approximately seventy days.[38]

Chinese access to Tibet has improved frontier security not only by speeding up troop mobility and the central government's physical control but by facilitating the penetration of Communist ideology and measures for the transfer of a Chinese population to Tibet.[39] In 1969 the first reports stated that China was shifting its major nuclear facility from Lop Nur (Lop Nor) in Xinjiang to Tibet. It was reported in 1976 that Nagchuka, a truck stop on the Xining-Lhasa Highway about 165 miles north of the capital, had become the location of the new nuclear sites.[40] The defense and supply of Tibet had become a military necessity, and the routes linking the interior to the southwest became critical to Chinese efforts to hold their frontier territories.

The security of China's borderlands, however, demanded a routing strategy broader than what China's domestic imperatives of integration, penetration, and control demanded. The linkage of routes between Xinjiang and Tibet would be supported by the construction of routes southward, into the subcontinent. Kashmir was viewed as a sensitive southern sector of the Xinjiang military frontier. In its vicinity, in 1962, China went to war with India over the Aksai Chin road. Then, in a move that ran contrary to Ardagh's wildest forward schemes, China began to build—at spectacularly high cost—a ground link with Pakistan, which broke through the mountains and pushed deep into the small state's northern property. In a brilliant effort that joined political, diplomatic, and military considerations, routes were cut into the subcontinent in order to provide greater flexibility for China in its territorial relations with the Soviet Union and India, and to counter joint Indo-Soviet politicking in South Asia.

Chinese roads have been built into Nepal and into the Northern Areas. In fact, in the mountain borderlands from Nepal to Pakistan, that is, along their border with India, the Chinese now possess a continuous, well-connected road system. These roads all lie within territory proximate to Xinjiang, Aksai Chin, or Tibet.

The Aksai Chin Road and the Sino-Indian War (1951– 1962): Conflict over Access

The Chinese decision to expand their access into Pakistan's Northern Areas followed the 1962 war with India. This conflict radically altered Chinese military calculations about their lengthy southwestern frontier with India and their political alignments in South Asia. Routes were at the center of the Sino-Indian dispute: specifically, the Aksai Chin sector of the Western Military Road complex that linked Xinjiang with Lhasa. China completed the 750-mile-long Aksai Chin sector of their road in 1957, apparently without India's knowledge. The Indians, when they discovered the road, claimed that 112 miles ran through Indian territory. The result was war.

One Indian writer has remarked that the war "can be explained almost exclusively in terms of China's determination not to give up the Aksai Chin and the strategic highway so vital for controlling the difficult provinces of Tibet and Sinkiang." Alastair Lamb suggests that the clash over the Aksai Chin road had the "profoundest consequences for the future of the Kashmir problem."[41]

Chinese troops first traversed the Aksai Chin during their conquest of Tibet. They discovered it contained the least taxing route of ac-

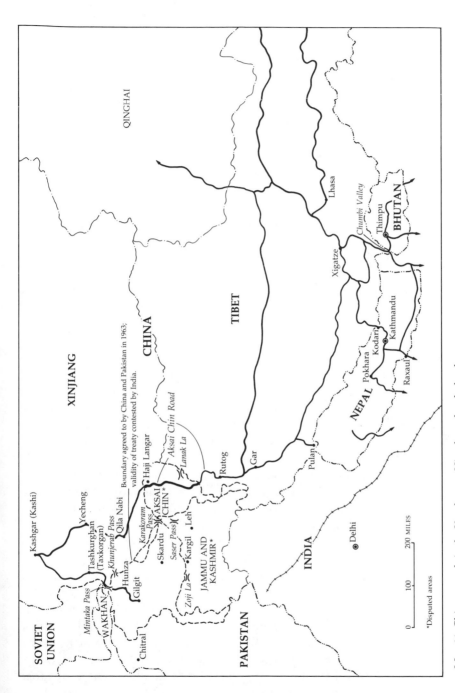

Map 11 Chinese roads in the Karakoram-Himalayan borderlands

SOVIET
UNION

Kashgar (Kashi)

Yecheng

XINJIANG

Tashkurghan (Taxkorgan)

Mintaka Pass
WAKHAN
Khunjerab Pass
Qila Nabi

Hunza

Karakoram Pass

Gilgit

Boundary agreed to by China and Pakistan in 1963;
validity of treaty contested by India.

CHINA

Haji Langar

Aksai Chin Road

AKSAI CHIN*

•Skardu

Saser Pass

•Leh

Lanak La

Rutog

Gar

•Chitral

Zoji La

Kargil

JAMMU AND
KASHMIR*

PAKISTAN

QINGHAI

TIBET

Lhasa

Chumbi Valley

Xigatze

Thimpu

BHUTAN

Pulan

Kodari

Kathmandu

NEPAL

Pokhara

Raxaul

INDIA

⊚Delhi

0   100   200 MILES

*Disputed areas

cess—by the standards, of course, of the Himalaya-Karakoram borderlands—between Xinjiang and Tibet. Work on a road along the
track began shortly thereafter. It was completed in 1957 and ran
southward from Hotan in Xinjiang, across the Soda Plains to Rutog in
Western Tibet, and wound its way to Lhasa.

While the Indians languished in ignorance, the Chinese exploited
the Aksai Chin to the fullest. The road they built crossed a flat plateau
and was serviceable in the winter, whereas direct routes from the
center of China into Tibet would have encountered even more hazardous terrain and climatic conditions. During the invasion of Tibet,
the Chinese had used the Aksai Chin as a route for the movement of
troops and supplies from Xinjiang. Again, in 1955, the Aksai Chin
route had been particularly useful for the suppression of the Khampa
rebellion in the eastern parts of that newly acquired region.

The historical origins of the Sino-Indian war are to be found in
imperial frontier rivalry. The belated Indian discovery of the Aksai
Chin road in 1958 spurred competing Chinese and Indian claims—
based upon nineteenth-century arguments—to the area through
which it ran. A simultaneous border dispute made war more likely.
The McMahon Line marks India's northeastern boundary; China
claims never to have accepted this imperial line of division. Drawn up
during the Simla Conference of 1913–14, the McMahon Line runs
along the Himalayan peaks for seven hundred miles. It originally
demarcated territory owned by British India and China. The Chinese
initialed the boundary agreement but never signed it, and after 1949
they rejected the McMahon Line altogether.

The Indian argument about rights to, and control of, the remote
highlands continued British arguments for a forward command line
in the region. In 1947 the Indians had modified their maps to accord
with a British decision of 1927 to relinquish "most claims to a boundary north of the main Karakoram watershed," permitting China to
maintain a position across Xinjiang. But these Indian maps had retained the Aksai Chin as Indian territory, exactly as Sir John Ardagh
had proposed.[42]

For its part, China considered as "undetermined," and disputed,
the lengthy boundary between Xinjiang and Tibet and Kashmir, that
is, the Aksai Chin, as well as the McMahon Line in the northeastern
Himalayas. Zhou Enlai first raised the boundary issue with India in a
letter to Nehru dated 23 January 1959, in which he pointed out that
there was no mutually acceptable, fixed Sino-Indian boundary line.

The Chinese Ministry of Foreign Affairs made its firm views known to the Indian government in 1959. Of the Aksai Chin, it maintained:

> This area is the only traffic artery linking Sinkiang and western Tibet, because to its north east lies the great Gobi of Sinkiang through which direct traffic with Tibet is practically impossible. . . . From March 1956 to October 1957, the Chinese government built along the customary route a motor-road from Yeycheng of Sinkiang to Gartok of Tibet of a total length of one thousand two hundred kilometres, of which a section of the one hundred and eighty kilometres runs through this area, and over three thousand civilian workers took part in its construction.[43]

Having expended so much effort, and with an important stake in the retention of the route, the Chinese were unwilling even to contemplate relinquishing the Aksai Chin to India.

Since the invasion of Tibet, on the other hand, the Indian government had concentrated on a possible Chinese advance along the McMahon Line in the North East Frontier Agency (NEFA). Not until the discovery of the Aksai Chin road was serious consideration given to the territory through which the road passed. Before being alerted to the presence of the Chinese road, the Indians had paid scant attention even to Ladakh. Once a crossroads for caravans on the trade routes between Tibet, Kashmir, and Xinjiang, Ladakh stands under the Aksai Chin. At its main town, Leh, once converged the high routes from the Zoji La and Himachal Pradesh passes, the Indus road into Tibet, and the route through the Saser and Karakoram passes into Xinjiang.[44] Ladakh is Buddhist, with 200,000 people.

Ladakh first drew the attention of the Indian government during the 1948 Kashmir conflict with Pakistan. When the Pakistanis captured Kargil, and cut off the 200-mile mule track that connected Srinagar with Leh across the 11,580-feet-high Zoji La Pass, the Indian Army was forced to improvize an airstrip at Leh and to construct hastily an alternate and less vulnerable land route to Leh from Manali in the East Punjab.[45] When Kargil was recaptured in November 1948, Ladakh came under renewed Indian control. Still, only an infantry battalion with support was stationed there. A few additional posts were established after Chinese intrusions in the post-1954 period.

The Aksai Chin, however, was ignored. India still considered it a "very difficult area of access"; besides, "the government was busy elsewhere." The Aksai Chin was "much more difficult to reach, through the Karakorams or the Ladakh mountains, and more importantly, it leads nowhere."[46] The Soda Plains were simply not as pertinent to India's strategic interests as they were to those of China. Only after the war was lost did the creation of better borderland routes near the Aksai Chin, in Ladakh, and in NEFA, become an Indian priority.

Stalled negotiations and major border incidents in 1959 at Longju and the Kongka Pass, heightened the illwill between China and India. China's refusal to give up its rights to the Aksai Chin and India's stubborn reluctance to permit Chinese use of the territory resulted in a Chinese military strike in 1962. When the Soviet Union failed to support China unconditionally, Sino-Soviet relations worsened.

The impact of the linkage between the Sino-Soviet and Sino-Indian disputes on Beijing's subcontinental perspective should not be underestimated. Before the dispute with India, China had begun to expand accessibility within its frontiers along the Kashi-Lhasa nexus. As Soviet and Indian interests converged, and Soviet and Chinese interests diverged, China's border routing system became inadequate to deal with the new strategic facts. Not only did China view Tibet as insecure; Xinjiang, too, was now at risk. The Aksai Chin road became irreplaceable.

Between 1958 and 1962 China's difficulties with India were exacerbated by the disintegration of its alliance with the Soviet Union. After the Longju incident in August 1959, the Soviet Union merely expressed regret at the squabbling between two states with which it maintained friendly relations. This was tantamount, according to Alfred D. Low, "to a formal proclamation of Soviet neutrality." The Soviet response to the next major border clash between India and China further strained Chinese goodwill. The clash at the Kong ka Pass in Ladakh in October 1959 was reported in the Soviet press without editorial comment. The Indian and Chinese versions of the story were printed side by side. This even-handed treatment of a Communist ally and its noncommunist neighbor was bitterly resented in China. In an editorial in the *People's Daily* titled "What Is the Cause of the Dispute?" the many-faced quarrel with the Soviet Union was even attributed to the "Soviet failure to give unconditional support to China's stand in the Himalayan conflict." When China launched its military campaign into NEFA and Ladakh on 20 October 1962, the Soviets did not applaud. This was a final disappointment. When the Sino-Soviet rift became public knowledge, China maintained that "the difference on the Sino-Indian boundary question figured large [sic] in the unfurling of the dispute."[47]

Soviet neutrality in the Himalayan conflict, combined with violations of the Chinese border and general unrest in Xinjiang, had two route-related effects. Soviet actions reaffirmed the need to maintain the Aksai Chin road, upon which rested China's ability to control the lengthy lines of communication between Xinjiang and Tibet. They also highlighted a logistical vulnerability in China's reliance on the Aksai Chin. In response, the Chinese waged a sharp, successful war against India. They also welcomed the possibility of routing ties with Pakistan. In these ways Chinese strategy in South Asia was a stepchild of Sino-Soviet discord.

In the 1962 war, China revealed the flexibility and utility of a sophisticated road network in mountainous terrain. Without aircraft the Chinese mounted a quick attack across barriers previously thought to be impenetrable by a large fighting force. They were able to maintain efficient supply routes. Small unit operations were undertaken, preassault artillery was effectively deployed, and despite long supply lines, Chinese forces did not suffer shortages in equipment or supplies.[48] By 1962 the Chinese had redressed their earlier strategic disability in the southwest.

The Chinese possessed one important logistical advantage in the Tibet-NEFA zone: whereas their troops had to climb only 5,000 feet from the Tibetan plateau to reach the mountain crests, the Indians had to hike over 20,000 feet at some points. The steep hills, mountains, and gorges of NEFA, combined with its heavy rains and snow, had made road building a difficult task and logistics the "most difficult" problem for the Indians to surmount: as Som Dutt notes, "Any given item of equipment which starts its journey by rail has to be transferred first to road transport vehicles of three-ton, one-ton, and jeep capacity, then to pack mules, and lastly to porters on a man-pack basis. Add to this the complexities of finding adequate local labor at the transfer points."[49]

The borderland routes in NEFA differed little from those a century earlier. In Neville Maxwell's words, "No roads reached more than a few miles from the plains into the foothills, and there were no lateral roads in NEFA at all—the north-south lie of the great ridges running down from the Himalayas made lateral movement almost impossible, and access to the different sectors of the McMahon Line was from the Brahmaputra Valley."[50] In logistical disarray, the Indians were speedily broken, and China, having made its point, then retired.

India's premier, Jawaharlal Nehru, drew a broad strategic lesson from the war. The Himalayan barrier, he said, "has proved to be vulnerable. If it is breached, the way to the Indian plains and the ocean beyond would be exposed."[51] The Indian refrain about the danger to plains and oceans was to become common after the Chinese began their road-building program inside Pakistani territory.

The Aksai Chin road acted as a catalyst for perhaps the most consequential war in the modern history of the subcontinent. The conflict soured Sino-Indian relations and made more attractive a Sino-Pakistani regional association that would create another route of access: the Karakoram Highway. The 1962 war drastically changed India's regional security environment, and it contributed to a realignment in India's defense posture. Sino-Pakistani collaboration would worsen the new reality; Indian strategic doctrine had to be "radically reoriented."[52] No longer did the threat come from the west and the east, from Pakistan alone; China's reach now matched its southward grasp.

The war altered India's earlier notions about the number of fronts on which, and the number of players against which, its troops might have to do battle, and revised the Indian Army's attitudes and organization with regard to high frontier defense, logistics, and resupply. Most importantly, the '62 war prompted India's decision to seek a nuclear weapons capability that could deter a Chinese attack in the future. In its turn, Pakistan would try to match India's nuclear progress, and a new and dangerous sphere of rivalry would emerge on the subcontinent.

Sino-Indian Competition in the Himalayan
Borderlands: A Brief Consideration of Nepal, Bhutan,
and Sikkim

China's primary concern in South Asia has always been with India. Both states are vast, populous, and modernizing, each wants to symbolize the power and progress of Asia, and both compete for regional and international status. Along their borderlands, this rivalry has been encapsulated in territorial clashes, border disputes, and in the building of routes in Nepal, Bhutan, Sikkim (annexed by India), and, most dramatically, Pakistan.

Strategic conduct in the Himalayan borderlands, it can be argued, has always revolved around Tibet, and it is the proximity of Nepal, Bhutan, and Sikkim to Tibet which has determined Chinese and

Indian policy toward these lands. When it became necessary to reinforce Tibet in the late 1950s and early 1960s, when the Dalai Lama fled to India in 1959 and Indian interference in Tibet was suspected, the Chinese built the first roads across the Himalayas, into Nepal. Like Afghanistan to its west, Nepal is mountainous, land-locked, and one of the world's poorest states. Northern Nepal contains six peaks over 26,000 feet while, a hundred miles away, the southern fields and jungles fall to only 600 feet above sea level. Tibet stands to Nepal's north, and India to its east, south, and west. Once the enormous Tibetan buffer disappeared, this Himalayan state became the new intermediate zone between China and India. Nehru declared that the security of India and of Nepal was indivisible.[53] Because of the proximity of India's major population centers, railroads, and communication sites to Nepal's southern borders, and Chinese proximity to Nepal's north, India has been unable to ignore the dangers of Chinese penetration into the mountain kingdom.

Nepal has ancient cultural and political ties with India. Since 1947 it has been economically and militarily dependent on its neighbor, upon whom it relies for about 85 percent of its total trade, transit facilities, a seaport at Calcutta, and economic progress. It is, as Nepalis sometimes say, "India-locked." Since 1950 the two states have signed (renewable) treaties of trade, transit, and commerce. Substantial amounts of rice, timber, and luxury consumer goods are also smuggled from Nepal into India.[54]

Nepal's ties to Tibet are also old: the historical relationship dates back at least as far as the seventh century A.D. The two countries had long conducted a trade in Tibetan salt which was restricted to the early summer and autumn, when the mountain passes permitted movement.[55]

Stuck between two sprawling land powers, Nepal has pinned its politics on its location. When possible, it has tried to play China and India against each other. The physical map of Nepal vividly reflects the patterns of Sino-Indian competition. Prior to 1969 India and Nepal forged defense agreements through which the former controlled Nepalese arms purchases. Indian radio operators and other personnel were stationed at checkpoints along the Nepalese-Tibetan border. In 1969, however, the Nepalese government, wounded by an Indian insistence on bilateral trade and transit treaties that made Nepal dependent upon Indian markets, canceled these agreements and asked for a withdrawal of Indian military personnel.[56]

Chinese aid to Nepal began in 1956. On 25 September 1961 King Mahendra of Nepal traveled to Beijing to discuss a Sino-Nepali boundary treaty. He came home with a boundary settlement as well as an agreement to permit China to build a road inside Nepal. It is likely, according to Leo Rose, that the Chinese tied their interest in a territorial accommodation to Nepal's permission to build the road.[57] The Chinese offered financial aid for the construction of a Kathmandu-Lhasa link, the first Chinese road to breach the Himalayan barrier. They contributed $10 million for a section of the highway inside Nepal and provided engineers, machines, and material. Reportedly, the Chinese did not adhere to the letter of the highway contract: the Nepalese had specified a road with bridges capable of carrying eight metric tons, but the Chinese built bridges to accommodate heavier vehicles. A Chinese defector who worked on the road between 1962 and 1964 later complained that the construction work had been used for the "placement of political agents." On this and other projects Chinese units reportedly showed propaganda movies and distributed literature and Mao buttons.[58]

The 70.8-mile Arniko highway starts at Kathmandu and ends at the "Friendship Bridge" near Kodari. Built during 1962–67, it provides China with one of its best routes across the Himalayas into the subcontinent. It has had "limited" economic impact and is "lightly" used. The Chinese interest in this road is readily understandable. At the time of construction, China was finding it hard to supply its garrisons in Tibet across the difficult, costly, and controversial routes from Qinghai, Sichuan, and Xinjiang. (The Aksai Chin route from Xinjiang was more secure and less tyrannical than the others but it was then the subject of violent controversy with India.) The new road not only cut through the Himalayas, it also increased China's ability to supply its military units in Tibet with rice from Nepal's Terai, a surplus production region, and with cheaper manufactured goods.[59] Between 1966 and 1973 China also built the 108-mile Prithvi highway linking Kathmandu and Pokhara.

Reports in 1975 indicated that the Chinese were building the Pokhara-Surkhet Highway which linked points on the Nepalese-Tibetan border with Nepalese centers and veered southwest toward the Indian state of Uttar Pradesh. The road made the Indians uneasy. In March 1975 they warned Nepal "not to allow anti-Indian activities by China on Nepali soil."[60]

From the start of its own development aid program to Nepal,

India's main goals were to secure a forward line of communications in the Himalayas and to curb the growth of Chinese influence. After the Chinese entered Tibet, Nehru said "We are interested in the economic development of Nepal. . . . One of the immediate needs, of course, is communications—a road to Nepal from India as well as roads within Nepal."[61] Indian Army engineers built Kathmandu airport, and, between 1952 and 1956, they completed the 118.7-mile Tribhuvan highway linking the Nepalese capital with Raxaul on the Indo-Nepalese border. This arduous route would support Nepal's trading priorities as well as India's strategic concerns.

Nepal has tried to capitalize on its many infrastructural suitors. In 1958–59 it proposed a 646.3-mile east-west route that would transmit the control of the center to the peripheries and provide a means of crossing Nepal without once having to enter Indian territory. The United States and India rejected Nepal's requests for funding on the grounds of economic infeasibility. The Soviet Union remained undecided. In 1962 Nepal's government tried to make the road a grand national venture, a symbol of Nepal's independence under the guidance of the king. It failed. In late 1963, however, Nepal asked for—and of course got—Chinese aid for a portion of the route. For China it was a welcome way of locating men near the Indian border. The strategy of exploiting the regional rivalry worked: in the wake of the 1962 Sino-Indian war, India promptly pressured Nepal into abandoning the agreement with China and offered to build not only the proposed Chinese section but an additional section of the east-west route. The Nepalese Ministry of Economic Planning stated on 29 March 1965 that India had agreed to build over 400 miles of the 600-mile east-west highway across Nepal. It announced that the Chinese government had accepted Nepal's wishes that it "divert resources previously earmarked for the Ithari-Dhalkewar section of the east-west highway and the Kamala irrigation project to other more useful projects to be agreed upon by both Governments." These projects were sited near the Indo-Nepalese border. Ultimately, India, the Soviet Union, and Britain built portions of the east-west highway.[62]

In the case of Nepal during the 1960s and 1970s, as Aran Schloss argues, development planning and implementation in the transport sector were highly influenced by the political and strategic motives of donor states, especially those of China and India, as well as of Nepal. For example, in one case, Nepal asserted its independence by choosing a road alignment that did not connect with Indian road or rail, "despite greater economic justifications." Without the Indian road program Nepal could not have reached even its present, low level of economic development. Still, the program has been a controversial symbol of dependence: many Nepalis and non-Nepalis view it as advancing "India's strategic interests"; and, it has been noted, India did not pursue industrial or other projects that "did not have some obvious military or political value to India." Nepal's road map also reflects the interests of other donor states. A road built by the British Army during 1954–58 had "almost no viable economic justification" in the context of Nepal's needs; rather, it provided access to a Gurkha recruitment center.[63] To the extent that it was better able to exploit donors' needs and the Sino-Indian rivalry, Nepal progressed in its capacity to determine and accomplish its own routing requirements.

In the tiny neighboring states of Bhutan and Sikkim, the Indians took the forward approach. Land-locked Bhutan, with an area of only 18,000 square miles, perches below Tibet with Indian territory on its western, southern, and eastern borders. The terrain is almost wholly mountainous, with a few broad, heavily forested river valleys in the middle and south of the country. The climate ranges from the ice and snow of the high Himalayas to the subtropical heat and humidity of the southern lands. As a result, human contacts, trade (internal and external), transport, and communications have historically been kept to a minimum. What little contact the Bhutanese had with the outside world prior to the 1960s was through trade caravans that traveled to and from Tibet. After independence the Indians were quick to push their line of control northward: in 1949 they signed a Treaty of Friendship with Bhutan (similar to a 1910 treaty signed with the British), which placed the state's foreign affairs and strategic defense in Indian hands. Until that time, Bhutan had maintained extensive trade and cultural ties with Tibet to the north (because, surprising though it might seem, it was somewhat easier to pass across the Himalayan routes than through the lowland valleys and forests to the south), while British India had restricted its foreign policies. With Tibet, Bhutan had traded rice for salt, wool, tea, soda, and precious metals.[64]

Bhutan is a strategically valuable high ground for India. Access to Bhutan by a hostile power would threaten rich areas of West Bengal and Assam and jeopardize the road and rail route across the thirty-mile corridor that is India's only land link with its northeastern states. When Tibet was taken by the Chinese, Nehru declared that "from time immemorial the Himalayas have provided us with magnificent barriers. . . . We cannot allow that barrier to be penetrated because it is also the principal barrier to India." For India, new and direct road links with Bhutan had become essential. At this time the only sensible way to enter Bhutan was across Sikkim and Tibet and China's sharp and lean sliver of southern land, the Chumbi Valley. Transport involved first jeeps but then ponies and yaks. After the Chinese takeover of Tibet, permission was needed to use this route.[65]

On a visit to Bhutan in 1958, Nehru stressed the indivisibility of Bhutanese and Indian security and offered development aid. The outbreak of the Khampa revolt in Tibet in 1959 and the Dalai Lama's escape to India unnerved the Bhutanese. As one source puts it, these "were important factors in Bhutan's decision to stop relying on seclusion as the country's cheapest and best defensive measure." The Bhutanese closed their northern border, terminating ten centuries of relations with Tibet, and accepted India's offers of trade and transit, economic aid and military succor. India would use development aid to ensure its security in the Himalayan battleground. It offered to build Bhutan's first road and undertook to train the Royal Bhutan Army.[66]

Until 1960 Bhutan did not possess a single mile of paved road. The staggering physical obstacles to roadbuilding combined with the political decision of Bhutan's rulers to keep their land closed to outsiders. The Bhutanese had followed a conscious policy of denying their country good roads in order to keep Bhutan inaccessible and therefore safe. Like the Afghans, they had turned down British road-building offers. (The British had wanted to build better links to Tibet through Bhutan.) Today, too, the Bhutanese government strictly limits the entry of foreigners through visa controls.

In Bhutan, about half of the total outlay in each of the first three development plans was for road building. The Indian Border Roads Organization (BRO), a construction firm under the Ministry of Transport and made up mainly of military personnel, took control of Bhutanese road projects. Together with the Bhutan Engineering Services, it built and improved a road from the Indian border to Paro and northwestward to the capital, Thimpu. This was Bhutan's first road, and its first direct link with the world beyond its borders. Given Bhutan's peculiar labor constraints, its road network would have progressed slowly without Indian assistance. The BRO and its contract laborers rapidly opened up Bhutan through a series of new routes, and India acquired improved access to Tibet. The BRO has continued to maintain the Bhutanese highway system, which, because of the terrain, requires extraordinarily large expenditures. The BRO controls the three militarily significant north-south access roads and an east-west road. Central and eastern Bhutan have been linked to India. The road from Paro and Thimpu to Tashigang in the east traverses five hundred miles of perilous terrain and has bridges that stand at 11,000 feet.[67]

Sikkim's geographical location tolled the death knell for its territorial independence. The country was tucked in tightly between Bhutan and Nepal, and its northern border abutted Tibet, the land that has most influenced Sikkim's historical development and cultural identity. Because Tibet was absorbed by China, the Indians eventually took Sikkim, which had been a protectorate since 1947. The Indian government held the right to "construct and maintain communications for strategic purposes and to take such measures as it considered necessary for the defense of Sikkim and the security of India." Before 1962 Sikkim had traded clothing and utensils for Tibetan wool, yaks, and salt and benefited from the Indo-Tibetan trade that had crossed the country.[68] Following the conflict of that year, the Sikkim-Tibet border was sealed, and trade was redirected toward India.

Sikkim is a sensitive area for both India and China. During the 1965 Indo-Pakistan war, China suddenly warned India that it must dismantle its installations on the border with Sikkim within three days. The threat was China's contribution to Pakistan's war efforts.

Sikkim was annexed in 1975, largely because of its location beside the strategic Chumbi Valley. An offshoot of China's Sichuan-Tibet Highway leads to Nathula in this junction between Tibet, Bhutan, and Sikkim. The Chinese have long maintained permanent garrisons in the Chumbi Valley, as well as an airstrip at Yatung. In 1971 they began to expand their airbases and road complex, increasing Indian anxieties about this borderland. Sikkim remains a point of contention today. China continues officially to attack its "illegal" annexation by India.[69]

The Emergence of Sino-Pakistani Ties

The common animosity of the Soviet Union and India toward China prompted an obvious partnership in the subcontinent. China struck up a friendship with its southwestern neighbor, Pakistan, and with it proceeded to perfect its borderland routes. Yet it was not until the fracas over the Aksai Chin that China evinced much interest in border negotiations. The Indo-Pakistani regional rivalry, as well as American support for India during the 1962 Sino-Indian war, urged Pakistan to increase its efforts to seek closer ties with China. The Sino-Pakistani border agreement of 1963 heralded fast-improving, wide-ranging, relations, an extensive Chinese military and economic aid commitment to Pakistan, and a secure southern outlet for Xinjiang which, though readily penetrable from north and west, had been blocked in the southwest by the tall Pamir and Karakoram ranges. This new Sino-Pakistani amity would also be hazardous to India in its northern territories.

Since 1962, Indian enmity and Soviet encroachment had led China to adopt a unified defense in the Sino-Soviet and Sino-Indian borderlands. It amounted to a northern variant of the British idea of an integrated frontier defense for India along the Hindu Kush and the Himalayas. It advocated the establishment and maintenance of efficient land lines of communication between Xinjiang and Tibet. With such a long, vulnerable frontier to defend—from the tip of Mongolia to Burma—a breathing space, an exit route, could only be welcome. Friendship with Pakistan would provide this relief.

Yet Pakistan's relations with China had not always been harmonious. The turning point was 1961. The signing of the 1963 border treaty marked nothing less than a reorientation of Pakistan's foreign and security policy. In 1959, when China and India clashed and China laid claim to thousands of square miles of the Aksai Chin, the Pakistani reaction paralleled that of earlier British overlords. President Ayub Khan adopted the mental map of his mentors (and, of course, played classic politics) in making a grand gesture toward India: he proposed a joint defense pact between the two subcontinental rivals. The primary antiroute, he said, ought to be erected in the north. Ayub viewed Chinese advances toward the Himalayas as yet another attempt by a northern power to penetrate the subcontinent. He voiced skepticism about both Soviet and Chinese intentions, and he asked India to join with Pakistan in reaffirming the mountain line of defense propounded by the British Raj:

> As a student of war and strategy, I can see quite clearly the inexorable push of the north in the direction of the warm waters of the Indian Ocean. This push is bound to increase if India and Pakistan go on

squabbling with each other. If, on the other hand, we resolve our problems and disengage our armed forces from facing inwards, as they do today, and face them outwards, I feel we shall have a good chance of preventing a recurrence of the history of the past, which was that whenever this sub-continent was divided—and often it was divided—someone or the other invited an outsider to step in.

(India promptly rejected this Pakistani offer to jointly defend the mountain ridges.) Moreover, sporadic Chinese border violations around Hunza had been reported since 1953. On 23 October 1959, Ayub announced that "any Chinese intrusions into Pakistani territory"—he was thinking specifically of Hunza, where China had traditionally been active—"would be repelled by Pakistan with all the force at her command."[70]

As he watched Sino-Indian ties worsen, however, Ayub changed his stance: in late 1959 he stated that Pakistan would like to resolve all Karakoram border issues with China. China, however, did not open talks with Pakistan according to the latter's timetable. It was only on 15 January 1961, as Sino-Indian relations were deteriorating rapidly, that Pakistan's foreign minister could say that China had agreed to demarcate their common border. On 3 May 1962, China and Pakistan agreed to negotiate a boundary alignment between Xinjiang and Pakistan's northern lands. An accord on the precise alignment of the boundary was reached in December 1962.

The unsettled border between China and Pakistan traveled along Pakistan's Northern Areas. Although initially hesitant to discuss demarcation of territories also claimed by India, by late 1961 China was ready to start talks with Pakistan. The 1962 Sino-Pakistani agreement included the territory of Xinjiang and "the contiguous area of Hunza the defence of which is under the actual control of Pakistan." The treaty was said to be provisional: China had negotiated with the party in actual control of Kashmiri territory, and the treaty was subject to renegotiation upon resolution of the Kashmir dispute. Technically, therefore, China was willing to reopen talks with any party that ultimately gained lawful ownership of these disputed lands. Still, the very signing of this agreement, and the later signing of secret agreements to construct highways through the disputed territories, complicated China's stand on the Kashmir problem. In effect, China recognized Pakistan's practical control over the Northern Areas. And in its highways China made a discrete physical investment in the region. The Kashmir dispute remains frozen and the status quo has long been observed there. China's concrete investments in the region have retained their original importance. Despite its protestations, in a brilliant illustration of the enduring meaning of access China had insinuated itself into the Kashmir quarrel.

The Sino-Pakistani border treaty permitted each signatory increased accessibility to the other's mountain borderlands. The new border alignment conformed closely to the historic boundaries between the two states, although the Indians repeatedly accused Pakistan of relinquishing territory to China. On 2 March 1963 the frontier running westward from the Karakoram Pass—encompassing Gilgit and Hunza and ending at the trijunction of Pakistan, Xinjiang, and Afghanistan—was officially delimited. China relinquished control over 750 square miles of land beyond the main watershed of the Karakoram range and, most important, gave up its historical claims to Hunza, which if exercized could have brought Chinese forces through the Karakorams toward Gilgit.

Immediately there were political repercussions: India challenged the legality of the treaty and attacked Pakistan for not trying to settle their own dispute. China's entry into the Kashmir dispute was an injurious setback for India. It protested Chinese interference with Indian sovereignty over all the lands of Kashmir. Indians argued that since Kashmir was theirs, there could be no common border between China and Pakistan. Therefore the border treaty had no legal standing. The border treaty was a prelude, however, to the strengthening of a regional concordat whose most visible symbol would be the Karakoram Highway.

In the wake of the border treaty, routes at sea and in the air were agreed upon, and trade agreements were signed by China and Pakistan. In 1963 Pakistan International Airlines became the first airline belonging to a noncommunist state to be granted landing rights in major Chinese cities in return for Chinese landing rights in East and West Pakistan. China also assisted in the expansion of Karachi airport. A further agreement was signed to permit China's air carrier to establish a new route through Karachi to East Africa. Finally, predating the opening of the grand land routes, a shipping accord was signed in 1965.[71]

Pakistan was a strong proponent of jointly built Sino-Pakistani routes. Alone it lacked the resources and the know-how to open up its frontier lands. The proposed routes would run across the Northern Areas, furthering Pakistan's territorial consolidation as well as its political, economic, and military purposes in Gilgit, Hunza, Nagar, and Baltistan. The introduction of Sino-Pakistani roads would also complicate Indian intentions in the borderlands.

The locational importance of the Northern Areas to Pakistan is primarily a function of the locational importance of Kashmir. Without these territories a roughly 150-mile common land boundary would arise between India and Afghanistan, leaving Pakistan vulnerable to their concerted military actions. With the partition of the subcontinent, Kashmir itself became of even greater strategic value than in imperial times. Its military relevance for both India and Pakistan lay in its location and in its usefulness for each state's defense posture. For India, control of the Kashmir Valley, in particular, became essential for the protection of remote Ladakh, next to the Chinese borderlands. In a war with Pakistan, too, India could be vulnerable to a fast penetration of Kashmir by Pakistani armor and tactical airpower aiming to sever the territory off from India proper. Kashmir, however, had numerous links to Pakistani territory: its partition had meant economic disruption, since its waters were essential to the irrigation and power supplies of (Pakistani) west Punjab; its timber resources were rafted down west Punjab's rivers; its willow and resin were used in Pakistani industry; and the natural access routes from Kashmir led mainly to west Punjab.[72]

Pakistanis have always argued strongly for Kashmir's economic and strategic importance to their country. Sir Zafrullah Khan once said: "The possession of Kashmir can add nothing to the economy of India or to the strategic security of India. On the other hand, it is vital for Pakistan. If Kashmir should accede to India, Pakistan might as well, from both the economic and the strategic points of view, become a feudatory of India, or cease to exist as an independent sovereign state."[73] In the brutal and destructive Pakistani civil war of 1971, India intervened and won the surrender of Pakistani troops at Dhaka; thereafter Pakistan retained few illusions about its military strength relative to India. With the loss of its eastern wing, Pakistan was psychologically broken and physically truncated. The retention of a claim to Kashmir for ideological reasons however remained necessary. Although there has not been a major war involving Kashmir since the 1960s, the area continues to be sensitive for Pakistan and India. Even today, a mini-war persists around the Siachin Glacier. It has been difficult to resolve because it is linked to the ideological-territorial dispute over Kashmir.

As Sino-Pakistani discussions progressed, it became apparent that a joint Sino-Pakistani route through these contentious territories would act as a firm antiroute. The codevelopment of a logistical apparatus in the Northern Areas forced the Indians and the Soviets to contend with an increased sense of insecurity about joint Sino-Pakistani maneuvering in the area.

THE KARAKORAM HIGHWAY NETWORK

Over many thousands of years the economy and the society of the Northern Areas had changed but little. The lives and work of its people had remained isolated from the modernization of the Indus Valley. Rulers from the plains—including the British and the Chinese from across the mountains—had come and gone, but material conditions were relatively unaltered. Local kings worried about the impact of roads and schools on their feudal lordship as much as on the ancient ways of their people; they resisted economic and social change. Occasionally the frontier concerns of lowland powers brought men up to the mountains, but when these concerns faded, the outsiders departed. In general, the political tussles of the borderlands were geographically confined affairs. After 1959, however, the central government of Pakistan came forward with plans to develop the Northern Areas and to integrate them with the heart of Pakistan.

The government's program for the 27,000 square miles of the Northern Areas focused on routes. A sparse population and high altitude had isolated these areas from early development efforts in Pakistan. An average height of 8,000 feet and an extreme climate, together with the government's resource constraints, made reliance on airlift for economic, political, and military communication neither convenient nor efficient. Without a rudimentary system of land routes, very little could move in and out of these areas.

Although the new Pakistani state, aspiring to nationhood, desired the extention of its territorial and economic grasp into the peripheries, it could also justify their integration by political and military necessity. With India standing prepared in Kashmir, Afghanistan next door, and the Soviet Union only a few score miles away across Wakhan, it was to Pakistan's military advantage to increase the center's physical links with the Northern Areas. The proximate danger

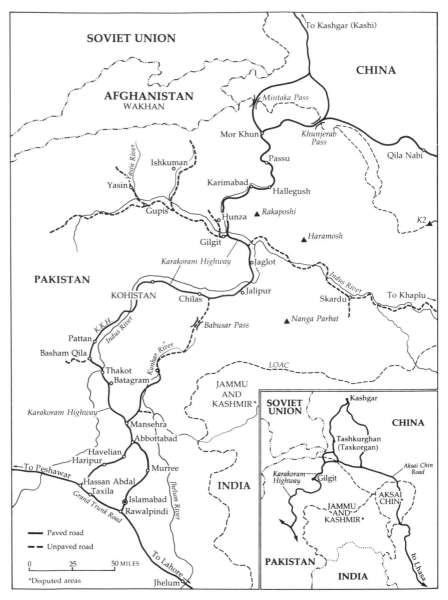

Map 12 The Karakoram Highway. Adapted from a Government of Pakistan drawing.

from India, Afghanistan, and the Soviet Union was increased by the distance of the Northern Areas from the Pakistani center.

The Indus Valley road—the first major route to strike out toward the highlands—was begun in 1959. It was the forefather of the Karakoram Highway. The road made access to Kohistan possible across the 13,690-feet-high Babusar Pass. The 525-mile-long all-weather road linked Pakistan's major cities with Gilgit. It met an existing Gilgit-Hunza track, making feasible access across the Karakorams and rough travel into Kashi in Xinjiang. In the highlands the two-lane road replaced a narrow pony track open for only three months in the year.[74]

The Pakistan Army Engineers were inducted to build the all-weather road. Twenty-three men died during its construction, many in rock falls started by blasting operations. The Army Engineers built the section from Havelian up to Chilas, and the Public Works Department built the 89.5 miles from Chilas to Gilgit. From Thakot to Gilgit, however, the terrain posed so many obstacles that by 1965, only a natural-surface route had been completed.[75] Later this route would be upgraded and incorporated into the Karakoram Highway.

In a broadcast on Radio Pakistan on 3 March 1964, the state's communications secretary announced that when completed, the Indus Valley road would dramatically advance the economy of the Northern Areas and connect Rawalpindi with Beijing by land. Rawalpindi was already linked to Karachi by over a thousand miles of road and rail. The new route would improve the center's communications with its furthermost periphery, "revolutionize" the economy in that "remote, sheep breeding" area, and stimulate increased trade with Xinjiang.[76]

As late as 1964, however, Pakistan was officially denying any collaboration between China and Pakistan in road building. The Foreign Office denied a statement made by the minister of works to the press earlier that year: "The Pakistan government has at present no plan to build an all-weather road between Pakistan and China." Yet the next stages of road building in the Northern Areas clearly involved Sino-Pakistani cooperation and extensive Chinese infrastructural aid. In 1966 and 1967 Sino-Pakistani accords had already been signed regarding "the assistance and the supply of bridging equipment and construction machinery by China."[77]

On 21 October 1967 the two governments announced their agreement to build highways.[78] The text of the agreement has never been published. But official Pakistani publications did portray the new road system as a reopening of the Silk Route, which would increase border trade and general communication between neighboring Sino-Pakistani territories.

The old mountain route had lain in relative disuse since the Communist revolution of 1949. After the Sino-Soviet rift began to widen in 1959, it became dormant. In 1967 it was reopened to facilitate overland trade, and in 1968 it was rebuilt. The road is thirty-two-feet wide and, for twenty-four miles, it is suitable for heavy jeeps. In winter, it is blocked by snow.[79] On 24 August 1969, after a twenty-year border closure, a fifty-camel caravan from China crossed the mountains at the Mintaka Pass with goods to trade at Hunza and Gilgit. (Mintaka means "a thousand sheep." This is the same route reputedly taken by Marco Polo seven centuries ago.) The sixty-member delegation brought silk, carpets, pressure cookers, and jasmine tea. Pakistani and Chinese citizens bartered goods worth Rs. 3 lakhs ($16,667).[80] On the Chinese side, the road taken by the trade delegation began at Kashi and, passing twenty-four posts at intervals of six to twenty-eight miles, wound its way southward through the Mintaka Pass toward Gilgit. It was completed by May 1968. On the Pakistani side, the way leading from the Indus Valley road followed the river, eliminated the 12,000-feet climb of the ancient track, and reduced a journey of two weeks to nine hours.[81]

At about this time another routing venture was initiated. A five-ton road was built that forked off at Mor Khun, ninety miles north of Gilgit, and traveled seventy miles northeast to the Khunjerab Pass. (In Wakhi, the language of northern Hunza, Khunjerab means "Valley of Blood.") Together Chinese and Pakistani workers completed the two-lane passage from Thakot to Khunjerab Pass. Seven battalions of the Pakistan Army engineers worked on the route between Thakot and Hallegush while Chinese workers completed the route between Hallegush and the Khunjerab Pass.

From the start, road construction proved taxing. It involved many improvisations in the supply of men and building materials. The tiny mountain towns lay at distances of 90 to 160 miles from each other with no connecting roads capable of carrying heavy machinery. The Pakistan Air Force was called in to lift thousands of tons of building machinery and material.

These areas had not been surveyed prior to the creation of plans to build the highway. Reliable hydrological and meteorological data were wanting. Airstrips had to be devised deep in the Karakoram range, at Chilas and at Gilgit. C-130s ferried heavy equipment to the road builders. Seven battalions of Army Engineers of the Pakistan Army spearheaded the venture, and a new corps of workers—the Frontier Works Organization, whose ten thousand men were headquartered in Gilgit—was raised specifically to advance the road projects. Other army corps enlisted to work on the project included the signals, army service corps, ordnance, electrical and mechanical engineers, and army aviation.[82] On 16 February 1971 the new road was formally inaugurated.

In 1973 the momentous decision was taken to convert existing routes into the highest international highway in the world, the five-hundred-mile Karakoram Highway. A two-lane, metaled highway suitable for heavy traffic, it would consolidate the economic, political, and military links between Pakistan's center, the Northern Areas, and Chinese Xinjiang. Along with about fifteen thousand Pakistanis, twelve thousand Chinese workers were moved into the Northern Areas to work on the great mountain road; between Thakot and Hunza, 9,500 Chinese were employed. The blue-uniformed Chinese worked on the Karakoram Highway until 1980, when they were withdrawn. These men, required to serve a minimum of two years on the road project, were drawn mainly from Xinjiang (and included many Muslims). Skilled workers were also brought from as far away as Shaanxi, Shanxi, and Hunan.[83] Chinese experts in mountain road-building and geologists were also imported. At the peak of construction, over twenty-five thousand men were at work on the highway.

The new metaled highway follows the route from Mor Khun, off the Gilgit-Xinjiang road, and runs across the Khunjerab Pass to form another improved link with Kashi. The highway follows a perilous route, skirting the eastern and southern flanks of Wakhan. It crosses the peaks of Hunza's twelve massive glaciers, including the infamous 35-mile-long Batura Glacier. It was routed across the treacherous Khunjerab Pass, rather than the lower Mintaka Pass, because Mintaka is only twenty miles from the eastern tip of Wakhan, dangerously near the Russian border and impassable when closed by winter snows.[84] The Chinese guard the Khunjerab Pass (which, until recently, was closed to foreign travelers). Outsiders were forbidden entry to the pass without a permit and allowed to drive only as far as the Batura Bridge, forty miles from Karimabad in Hunza. On 1 May

1986, however, the entire length of the highway was opened to third-country travelers, from Rawalpindi across the Khunjerab Pass, past Taxkorgan (Tashkurghan) and the homes of Kirghiz and Tajiks, to Kashi.

Even before the completion of the new Karakoram Highway, China had built a 118-mile-long highway from the Khunjerab Pass to Qila Nabi, which lies on their main strategic supply route between Xinjiang and Tibet. The road connects the Karakoram Highway with China's own frontier routes, the Western Military Complex. This was a vital link. The route runs approximately perpendicular to the Aksai Chin road and connects Mor Khun on the Gilgit-Kashi route with Qila Nabi in eastern Xinjiang on the Kashi–Aksai Chin–Lhasa highway. This particular land link further reduces the distance between China and Pakistan. It also improves China's ability to deter attempts to intercept military equipment and supplies traveling to or from southern Xinjiang.

The Karakoram Highway was completed in 1978. The route has twenty-four major bridges and seventy smaller ones, in whose construction the Chinese, with their age-old expertise in high-altitude construction, specialized. The main bridges are at Thakot, Hayni, Hallegush, Raikot, and Gilgit. A rash of natural hazards—deep gorges, high flood levels, and rushing rivers—required that each bridge be constructed to individual specifications. The Karakoram Highway has prestressed bridges, plate girder bridges, reinforced concrete arched bridges, and suspension bridges. All are of traditional Chinese design, with arches and slender pillars, carved lanterns and fountains along the rails, and butterflies and floral patterns in pastel shades along the side walls. The highway has 1,708 high-class culverts and a carriage width of 19.7 feet.[85]

Karakoram Highway maintenance units, culled from a ten-thousand-strong Pakistani engineer formation, function throughout the year. Each is comprised of about fifty men who patrol and reconstruct a thirty-mile stretch. Between the old capital of Hunza and the Sino-Pakistani border the highway, which moves across uninhabited and bleak territory, is to remain under the permanent control of the Pakistan Army Engineers. The highway's construction data are impressive: China and Pakistan used over 8,000 tons of dynamite to move thirty million cubic yards of earth and rock. Eighty thousand tons of cement, 35,000 tons of coal, and 1,000 trucks were consumed in the endeavor.[86]

Liu Mauqing, the chief Chinese engineer on the Karakoram Highway—he had also worked on the massive Xinjiang-Tibet Highway—said that "no road anywhere had been more difficult to build than the Karakoram Highway." It has been called the Canadian Pacific of road-building, requiring China and Pakistan to overcome immense obstacles. It also entailed the sacrifice of more than 400 Pakistani and Chinese lives, as well as 314 casualties. (At the confluence of the Indus and Gilgit rivers, the town of Gilgit houses a large Chinese cemetery). One member of the scientific International Karakoram Project has called the Karakoram Highway an "engineering miracle," the "eighth wonder of the world"; in comparison to the Karakoram Highway, the Khyber Pass is but a "safe roadway up and over a few low hills."[87]

The difficulties entailed in construction were staggering. The terrain is harsh and rugged, strewn with ravines and gorges. Portions of the range consist of crumbling slate. The altitudes at which the road builders had to work varied dramatically, from a low of 2,513 feet to a high of 15,400 feet. Climatic conditions varied as well; temperatures ranged from a minimum of 20° Fahrenheit to a high of 118° in the lower Gilgit Valley during the summer months.

Road building in the Northern Areas did not come to a standstill with the inauguration of the Karakoram Highway. Shortly afterward, work began on a 104-mile road running along the Indus to link the Karakoram Highway with Skardu to the southeast. The all-weather road begins at Jaglot (on the Karakoram Highway, about twenty-four miles before Gilgit) and crosses the longest gorge in the world, the Indus gorge between Jaglot and Skardu, before it reaches Skardu. It has a three-ton capacity, with twenty-four bridges and 400 culverts. Ninety-two men died in its construction; 4.2 million cubic meters of rock were blasted; 25,000 tons of cement and 1,000 trucks were employed. These efforts opened up the 10,000-square-mile area of Baltistan, which since 1947 had had no land links with the rest of the world. Before partition a track linked Skardu via Kargil to Srinagar in Kashmir. Srinagar had lain in Indian hands, however, for more than four decades. On 1 September 1980, for the first time since the creation of Pakistan, a bus belonging to the National Tourism Company of Pakistan, NATCO, reached Skardu.[88]

Zia ul-Haq's military government continued to emphasize the expansion of infrastructure in the far north. In 1983, for example, the martial law administrator for Zone "E," Major-General Pir Dad, announced that the government was assigning top priority to the construction of roads and bridges in the Northern Areas, to link these regions with the trade and traffic on the Karakoram Highway.[89]

The Chinese, too, have maintained an interest in building Pakistani roads. For example, Chinese public-sector construction organizations have tendered bids for World Bank–funded projects such as a $300 million scheme to construct dual carriageways along Pakistan's N5 national highway near Karachi and Lahore. Chinese road builders in South Asia reportedly submit low tenders for road projects in such countries as Nepal and Pakistan. One official from an international aid agency voiced his concern that such Chinese bidding for sensitive road projects could create a political dilemma for his organization.[90]

Allegations about secret Sino-Pakistani road building also continued to flourish, and the "highway bogey" became an inflamed issue in the politics of South and Central Asia. Chinese access across the mountain divide symbolized a transformation of the historical separation between these Asian regions. The "psycho-strategic" dynamics of the situation cannot be ignored. In August 1980, *Tass* reported that troops were being moved along the Karakoram Highway; that Pakistan was receiving arms across it; and that "China, with the knowledge of the Pakistani authorities, is building the second highland highway, parallel to the Karakoram Highway." The Indian news tabloid *Blitz* (heavily quoted in the Soviet press) also reported that China was "stepping up the construction of a new road that will duplicate the existing strategic Karakoram Highway" and will then link up with the warm-water port of Karachi.[91]

In March 1981 Indian sources reported plans for a Sino-Pakistani road project to link the Karakoram Highway with forward lines in Kashmir. For example, a bridge was reportedly being built across the river at Azad Pattan via Hazara which would connect the Karakoram Highway with Dara Haipeer and finally with Muzzafarabad. Bridge construction was being supervised by Chinese and Pakistani engineers. Although there has been no independent verification of Chinese participation, the Pakistanis have been expanding their road links in Kashmir. In 1985 New Delhi was said to be again concerned about Chinese plans to upgrade parts of the Karakoram Highway to carry 30-ton trucks and to build a rail line in the Sino-Pakistani borderlands. The *Times of India* also reported that Chinese and Pakistani military leaders have discussed plans to upgrade the Karakoram Highway over a period of years.[92]

THE POLITICS OF THE KARAKORAM
HIGHWAY: REGIONAL DEBATES ABOUT
SECURITY AND DEVELOPMENT

The Sino-Pakistani alliance of access across the Karakorams has altered the geopolitics of the area. In an earlier decade, the ancient trade between Xinjiang and Kashmir—which the inhospitable marches of the Karakoram could not kill—had died as a result of the Sino-Indian border quarrel. The 1970s witnessed an expansion of access. The mountains that had earlier been the subcontinent's natural barrier to invasion from the north were breached by a route, and the physical distance between China and Pakistan was lessened. Where passage had been rare and difficult, the Karakoram Highway permitted an unprecedented ease of movement. Within Pakistan the construction of these routes advanced the conquest of physical distance, the extension of central control, and economic and political integration.

Pakistan's leaders claimed the Karakoram Highway as the tool of economic development in the Northern Areas. That was its declared purpose. Certainly the highway has brought change to the highlands. When the British guarded India's frontiers, they had no concern for the economic or political development of the Northern Areas, whose economies and societies remained virtually untouched until the third quarter of the twentieth century. Yet when economic progress and political change finally came, they stemmed in large part from the pursuit of regional political and military goals by the successors of empire.

The Karakoram valleys had been so inaccessible before the introduction of the highway that they developed separate spoken tongues. In Hunza and Nagar, Brusheski is spoken; in the environs of Gilgit, Shina; in the northernmost reaches near Afghanistan, Wakhi; and in Chitral, Khowar. The new Karakoram Highway has the potential to serve as the backbone of a network of integrative routes in the area. As of 1979 the Northern Areas had—apart from the highway itself—only 248.5 miles of metaled, jeepable roads, 30 miles of unmetaled truck roads, and 1,332 miles of unmetaled roads. (When completed, the new roads opened these sparsely populated areas to trucks and lorries and reduced bulk transportation costs on average by about 50 percent, from about $6.00 to $3.00 per 80 pounds.)[93]

Technological progress accompanied the new mountain routes. The Northern Areas saw the introduction of a telecommunications system and telegraph and telephone lines, which the army set up for its own purposes, and improved tourist facilities in the form of rest houses used to lodge engineers and others working on the highway.[94] In Hunza a few schools and simple medical clinics were built; a bank was even established. Trade ties, previously developed through the small barter trade with China, are being cultivated with the Pakistani center. A market economy is being introduced.

Life has slowly begun to change in these parts. Gilgit is now about two hours away from Hunza by jeep; it used to be three days away by horse. According to its ruler, the Mir of Hunza, who appears to have embraced change more readily than his peers, "the Karakoram Highway has changed our lives and brought us into Pakistan. . . . We now get whatever we need and things are much cheaper." Added his wife, "New ideas are coming to Hunza."[95]

In Pattan, along the route of the Karakoram Highway, new schools and subsidized food have arrived. Baltistan, too, has been aided by the Highway. Kohistan, in the NWFP, another beneficiary of newly acquired access, had previously owned only a few footpaths and mountain trails. Until October 1976 it did not even have an official Pakistani administrator. The people were impoverished, and there were no schools or medical facilities.

Still, progress has brought its own difficulties: an old socioeconomic order has been disrupted. New pressures travel up the Karakoram Highway. Whereas earlier the Hunzakuts used to grow their own food, they are now dependent on food imports. The traditional, egalitarian system of land distribution has been shaken by outsiders wanting to purchase property. Until the late 1970s agricultural lands were not sold. Now they are becoming marketable commodities that can turn a profit. Inevitably, the opening up of the region has encouraged some of its inhabitants either to enter the tourism industry or to migrate to Pakistani cities.[96]

As these areas have become more integrated with lowland Pakistan, and as business, transport, and the sale of fruit have replaced subsistence farming, so have their traditional cultures become vulnerable to the intrusions of modernity. The oral histories of the high valleys are threatened. As one of the few literate men in Hunza said: "The highway is opening things up so fast. . . . Our life, our culture, our traditions will disappear if it doesn't get written down. We need to be able to take from our past like they do in Europe, to write not for now but for fifty years from now."[97]

The new routes permit private organizations to help develop the

Northern Areas. The most important of these is the Aga Khan Foundation, which has focused on building collective institutions. It has become increasingly involved in the provision of education and health facilities and in construction and rural development programs. Its largest investment, made in 1982, has been in the Aga Khan Rural Support Programme (AKRSP). This private, nonprofit company aims to raise agricultural incomes and production by nurturing village-level organizations. These, it is hoped, might eventually sustain the development process initiated by AKRSP's management and technical personnel. In its first five years of operation the AKRSP focused on family farm and village-level resources: on "irrigation, roads, flood protection, land, crops, livestock." The next phase is targeted at a broader, more integrated development strategy, incorporating the need to link economic systems at the level of farm, village, and valley or watershed. (Still, increased agricultural production in the Northern Areas will always be hampered by the inhospitable terrain, whereas the expansion of community-based resources such as forestry will be hampered by the absence of any concept of communal property.)[98]

Thus, the highway projects of the Pakistani center have indeed promoted social and economic development in the Northern Areas. In contrast with the modest scale of government development activities in other peripheries, however, economic progress in the north does not alone appear to warrant the extraordinarily high financial and human costs of creating and maintaining the Karakoram Highway and its associated routes. Inside Pakistan, the decision to spend scarce funds and hundreds of human lives chasing a grand road venture convinces nobody if the sole purpose is to benefit the tiny population of the Northern Areas. The economic benefits expected to accrue hardly cover the burden of regular maintenance—reportedly ten thousand Pakistani troops and tens of millions of dollars annually.[99] Baluchistan, a far larger and more populous area, received a relative fraction of this attention before the 1973 insurgency and the 1979 Soviet invasion of Afghanistan. In fact, it is noteworthy that private foundations, not only the government of Pakistan, are fashioning progress in the Northern Areas. One writer has critically noted:

> Since the government is not concerned about sustainable development, and more interested in the fact that the Northern Areas lies [sic] in a "geopolitically sensitive" region . . . roads and other infrastructure oriented to military purposes take precedence in its budget allocations and planning. . . . While the government has concentrated its development

efforts on the military and bureaucratic infrastructure required to expand its control of the area, it has left social and economic development
largely to the Geneva-based Aga Khan Foundation.[100]

Commercial reasons for the joint Sino-Pakistani endeavor are not
entirely convincing, either. The centuries-old reason for the decline of
the Silk Route still holds true: the sea route from Chinese ports to
India and Pakistan, though long, is still far cheaper than the resurrected overland route. Officially, the Karakoram Highway was intended both to improve the economic and social lot of the people in
the Northern Areas and to expand tourism and trade with China. It
has been called a restoration of the Silk Route, conjuring up visions of
intense economic activity and the exchange of precious goods between Central and South Asia. The prospects for trade and economic
cooperation were said to motivate this huge investment in men,
material, and money. At the time of the highway's creation it was
suggested that the volume of Pakistan's trade with China would
increase and that Chinese trade with the Middle East would expand
through Karachi. Kashi was now about fifteen hundred miles from
Karachi—a shorter distance than that between Kashi and China's own
eastern ports.

China's principal reasons for financing and building the network of
Karakoram routes were neither the development of the remote Northern Areas nor the development of Xinjiang. Expectations for tourism
remain high, but these roads into Pakistan have not been an economic
boon for China, not even in Xinjiang.[101] Although China has long
been eager to exploit Xinjiang's oil, gas, and coal reserves, investment
and recovery have been very slow. Internal distance remains China's
first enemy. For economic progress, the province still needs vast
improvements in its internal transport network. The Chinese have
built the Ürümqi-Kuerle highway, which runs north-south, and are at
work on another network of routes in southern Xinjiang which will
link up with Ruoqiang from Qinghai province. A railway along the
Silk Route from Wushi to Kashi has been completed. Another 147-
mile line is being built from Ürümqi to Usu, as is the Southern
Xinjiang Railway from Turpan to Korla. Still, Xinjiang today has too
few roads and, more important, too few railroads. There is also a
paucity of good routes linking the province with distant central
China. China's Sixth Five Year Plan, approved in 1982, described
transport as a "particularly weak link" in the economy.[102]

Furthermore, China has never had a significant economic interest in Pakistan. The two countries have not had extensive trade ties. In 1977, for example, Pakistan's imports from China totaled 3 percent of its total imports, and the figure for exports to China was only 1 percent. In 1981, 9.4 percent of the value of all Pakistani exports and 3.2 percent of the value of all Pakistani imports were to and from China. As of 1985 Sino-Pakistani bilateral trade—in cash, barter, and border terms—totaled a mere $200 million. Although the Chinese have tried to increase commerce with Pakistan, their neighbor has little to offer apart from a few promising possibilities: fruits and vegetables, iron and steel products, and urea. It has been suggested that even Chinese efforts to expand trade in these commodities have been motivated by political and not economic concerns.[103]

The Chinese have been far more forthcoming about economic aid: between 1956 and 1979 Pakistan received 13 percent, $620 million, of China's aid to Asia and the Middle East. Large-scale aid began in 1964, after the border treaty had been signed. Chinese-assisted projects include a textile mill in Pakistani Kashmir, a sports complex, a glass sheets factory, and a hydroelectric plant. China has also directed economic aid to projects in Pakistan's less developed, strategically important frontier regions—to the North West Frontier Province and Baluchistan.[104]

The Karakoram Highway project did spur some trade ventures. Pakistan was to deliver wool and leather goods, clothing, cutlery, and jute bags; it would receive teas, hides, skins, electrical equipment, hardware, and silk. Through 1982, however, only two truck convoys had made the long, rough journey each year between Pakistan and Xinjiang. This was called a "merely symbolic operation." To be sure, such convoys can occasionally be sighted traveling the Karakoram Highway and crawling across the Khunjerab Pass. They carry fish and dried fruit to Xinjiang, and simple consumer goods (such as bicycles, textiles, and household appliances) from Xinjiang to Pakistan's Northern Areas. Transparent silks from Pakistan are sold in the stores and towns of western and southern Xinjiang, which Pakistani traders occasionally visit. Silks from Hotan are also exported to Pakistan. All these transactions occur in small volumes.[105]

The old border trade between the inhabitants of Hunza and those of Xinjiang has risen as a result of improvements in access, but the figures quoted by Chinese foreign trade officials—$250,000 in 1985— remain low.[106] Although annual border trade agreements have been signed, these exchanges of cheap hardware, cigarettes, and gadgets do not make the Karakoram Highway an economic successor to the

Silk Route. True, thirty-thousand tourists are now expected to trek annually from Rawalpindi via Taxkorgan to Kashi, but it will take many decades before revenues match the original investment in, and the yearly maintenance costs of, the Karakoram Highway.

It seems clear that grander, less immediately lucrative rationales based on regional politics and national security created access in these borderlands. As early as July 1964, during the construction of the Indus Valley road, it was predicted that the road would "prove to be of great strategic importance for Pakistan."[107] In the twenty years that followed, this road and its many successors proved to be economic as well as political and military assets for Pakistan.

The Karakoram Highway extends the control of Pakistan's central government into previously inaccessible frontier regions. Pakistani troops now possess greater operational flexibility along the northernmost frontier. After 1947 Pakistan exercised only nominal control over the Northern Areas, and compounding this difficulty was the Indian claim to the territories. Only through the development of a road network could the Pakistani center effectively integrate these remote borderlands. Today Pakistani troops stand guard to the north of the Karakoram Highway, watching Wakhan, and to the south, along the Line of Actual Control in Kashmir, watching India.

The Karakoram Highway has interfered in the political and military relationships between Central and South Asia. No single highway has run through such sensitive territory, through an area where the borders of Pakistan, India, China, the Soviet Union, and Afghanistan come close together. By traversing these lands, the Karakoram Highway and its associated routes have posed threats and presented opportunities to all the states of the region.

These routes have balanced the Soviet Union's close relations with India with a stronger Sino-Pakistani tie. The Karakoram Highway has been the geocenterpiece of Chinese economic and military aid to Pakistan, a massive demonstration of support and commitment completed at a time when the Pakistanis were growing more worried about Soviet activities inside Afghanistan. On a trip to China after completion of the highway, Zia applauded the Sino-Pakistani venture: "The Karakuram Highway is an outstanding example of such cooperation between our two peoples. I take this opportunity of paying tribute to the dedication of the Chinese workers many of whom have sacrificed their precious lives while engaged in the construction of this monument of Sino-Pakistan friendship."[108]

Sino-Pakistani political and security ties have been extensive and mutually beneficial. Chinese military and economic aid, and political support for Pakistan in regional affairs, have been reciprocated by Pakistan's role as critical intermediary in the Sino-American relationship during the early 1970s, by its support of Chinese diplomatic positions, and by its reported transfer to China of sophisticated Western weaponry. A Chinese Foreign Ministry official has described the ties thus: "China's military relationship with Pakistan is one of the closest (China has with another country). Since we are very good friends we have helped to build their defense."[109]

For twenty years China has supplied Pakistan with tanks, aircraft, armored vehicles, and small arms. By 1982, according to the International Institute for Strategic Studies, about 75 percent of Pakistan's tank forces and about 65 percent of its military aircraft came from China.[110] China has provided technical and financial aid for Pakistan's defense-related projects, such as a heavy foundry, a heavy mechanical complex, and a heavy equipment overhaul factory at Taxila; it has given expert advice in making anti-aircraft rockets at the Pakistan Ordinance Factories at Wah and in maintaining fighter aircraft at the Kamra Aeronautical Complex; and, according to some reports, it has collaborated with Pakistan in the design and testing of nuclear weapons. Finally, Pakistani officials attach great significance to the most conspicuous Sino-Pakistani joint-venture, the Karakoram Highway. In 1981 Zia confirmed that Pakistan's "relationship with China is the cornerstone of our foreign policy. . . . It is purely based on mutual interest, friendship and understanding that has developed over the past thirty years. . . . China has been with us through thick and thin . . . they have been very liberal with us, so far, with their military assistance programme."[111] During the 1965 Indo-Pakistani war, China warned India to stop the fighting; and in the 1971 Indo-Pakistani war it continued to supply weapons to Pakistan. Still, China has hesitated to intervene directly on Pakistan's behalf. The signing of the 1971 Indo-Soviet treaty of amity reinforced this Chinese reluctance.

China's own broad political and military purposes in South Asia resulted in the development of the Northern Areas. China has used the Karakoram Highway as a form of "stadium diplomacy" and simultaneously strengthened ties with the enemy of its enemy. Although the route has yet to be used in wartime, Pakistan and China have used it to send strong messages to their rivals and neighbors. Upon completion of the highway China's deputy premier, Li Xiannian, said publicly that the Karakoram Highway "allows us to give military aid to Pakistan." During the official inauguration ceremony, Chinese vice-premier Geng Biao took the opportunity to say that China "firmly supported" Pakistan's stand on Kashmir and its proposal to turn South Asia into a nuclear-free zone.[112]

In 1971 the Karakoram Highway was reportedly used to ferry military supplies to Pakistan from China. During the Indo-Pakistani War of 1971—when Chinese material support for Pakistan was not especially forthcoming—President Yahya Khan of Pakistan ordered sections of the Karakoram Highway closed to foreigners. This move was regarded, in Robert Jackson's words, as a "gesture which was intended to draw a veil of concealment across the overland route."[113] Travelers point out that the highway's cement bridges were constructed to support the passage of heavy tanks: according to one writer, the Karakoram Highway, contrary to Chinese and Pakistani claims, has "strategic military implications."[114] These writers challenge the Pakistani assertion that the highway is capable only of carrying five-ton vehicles.

Still, despite its physical impressiveness, its many political attractions, and its diplomatic versatility, the Karakoram Highway network is not an ideal system for military logistics. It is a solitary, narrow route without alternatives. The highway is ill-suited to the rapid movement of troops or supplies between China and Pakistan in wartime. (In peacetime, however, it can support such functions at a slower rate). Further, although the high altitudes at which these routes have been built are not conducive to the most effective use of airpower, the Karakoram Highway is vulnerable to interdiction from the air. Precisely because it is so valuable to its builders, the highway has been described as "one of the world's most attractive targets for air interdiction."[115]

The difficulties involved in traversing the Karakoram Highway, moreover, make it unreliable in any major campaign. The problems are most serious in the northernmost sections of the highway, as Nazir Kamal notes: "high winds, extreme variations in temperature . . . and seismic activity . . . combine to bring down massive debris from steep heights without detection. . . . Glacial shifts, heavy mudflows . . . as well as indiscriminate rockfalls are a constant threat. . . . In the winter the formation of ice sheets on the road surface [and] the slope of the valley walls and glaciers" together make the route perilous and unreliable.[116]

Accidents are not infrequent. Numerous trucks and workers have driven off the edges into the deep ravines and gorges below. In December 1974 an earthquake at Pattan caused landslides that blocked the road for two weeks. Glaciers knocked out concrete bridges and created massed mudflows that chewed up much of the highway.[117]

Although objectively the Karakoram Highway may not be an ideal logistics route, it has been important to foreign and security policy makers. Its presence has put India on the psychological defensive in Kashmir; brought China into the Kashmir quarrel on Pakistan's side; and enhanced Sino-Pakistani military cooperation. The decision to construct these northern routes, and the angry responses of the Soviet Union and India, suggest the regional political significance of the Karakoram Highway.

Both India and the Soviet Union have lodged loud protests about this Sino-Pakistani joint venture. Indian and Soviet officials have charged that the roads are offensive in nature and that China has expansionist goals in the subcontinent. Until the 1962 war China had not been perceived as a direct military threat to India.[118] Its defense and security planners had considered a trans-Himalayan military strike infeasible. Their damaging defeat in the war caused the Indians to reconsider Sino-Pakistani cooperation along the borderlands and in Kashmir.

After 1962 the Indians also came to fear Chinese encroachments upon Ladakh. This historical Central Asian marketplace had once witnessed a small but steady traffic from Xinjiang. One old merchant described the journey to Leh's marketplace in Ladakh from his home in Xinjiang across the treacherous Karakoram Pass, in the years before the Chinese closed their southern borders in 1949: "It took thirty-four days, the march from my home in Yarkand down to Leh. . . . It was a backbreaking trail, long and high. We had to slit the noses of some of the mules and ponies so they could suck enough air into their lungs. But there was no danger of getting lost. Bleached bones of animals and men regularly marked the trail."[119]

Concerns about possible Chinese military infiltration led to the development of this distant highland. When Indian forces discovered the Aksai Chin road, they established themselves along Ladakh's frontiers and began to supervise a road-building program. A 271-mile motorable road was rushed through Kashmir, from Srinagar up to Leh. It reduced a sixteen-day trip to two days. At Khardung La (18,380 feet) one of the highest motor roads in the road—open only three months each year—was built. These new routes brought some economic relief to the impoverished Ladakhis, who provided the labor for the army's roads and cantonments.[120]

From an Indian perspective, according to Som Dutt, a Chinese seizure of Ladakh would have enabled China "to push her border in the west far enough out to ensure the complete security of her communications with Sinkiang." This view prevailed before the construction of the Karakoram Highway—an event that raised the stakes for Indian planners watching Sino-Pakistani reconnoitering around Kashmir. Despite Chinese reticence during the 1960s and 1970s to become directly involved in a subcontinental war, since 1962 Indian military planners have had to prepare for such an eventuality. When the Indo-Pakistani war of 1965 broke out in Kashmir, the Indians' first move was to occupy two Pakistani military positions near Kargil. Thus they disallowed any collaboration between Chinese and Pakistani forces near the Karakoram Pass and secured the route to the Ladakh-China border.[121]

India also took steps to improve communications and transport facilities throughout the northeast, where in 1950 only about a hundred miles of road existed. An integrated plan for new airfields, motor and jeep roads, and trails for porters, horses, and mules was quickly put forward. Troops and border security forces were trained for mountain warfare; modern communications and early warning radar were installed; and civil and military transport systems were unified.[122]

With the Karakoram Highway network completed in the Northern Areas, India found its part of Kashmir doubly threatened. It lodged numerous protests with both Pakistan and China. (Earlier Indian remonstrances had come shortly after the completion of the Indus Valley road in mid-1965, when Pakistan and China were demarcating their border. The Indians were concerned then about the potential for Chinese use of the road as an entrance into the subcontinent.) On 19 April 1968 India complained again. It alleged that a road designed to serve offensive military purposes had been built through its territory. India stated the Sino-Pakistani border treaty itself was invalid as "Pakistan has no *locus standi* whatsoever to enter into negotiations or to conclude any agreements with any country which would affect in any way Indian territory illegally occupied by Pakistan in this area." A second protest note, sent on 23 November 1968, accused Pakistan of desiring more than overland trade with China. In 1969, upon the improvement of a Gilgit-Xinjiang route across the Mintaka Pass, the Indian minister of state for external affairs, B. R. Bhagat, said the route "seeks to interfere with Indian sovereignty in Kashmir." India refused to accept the argument that it merely reopened a strand of the Silk Route.[123]

When China sent thousands of workers to work on the highway, the Indians were quick to protest the introduction of hostile personnel close to the ceasefire line. On 25 June 1969 India accused China of supporting Pakistan's illegal occupation of Kashmir, thereby "willfully complicating Indo-Pakistani relations," and of threatening the "peace and tranquility in the region" by building routes as part of a "calculated and co-ordinated plan." According to India, the "construction of this road demonstrates China's collusion with Pakistan to undermine the sovereignty of India"; the road could be explained only on the grounds of "military expansionism."[124]

The Indian government repeatedly claimed sovereignty over the areas through which the routes ran. It protested the "construction of a road in a territory lawfully belonging to India." The Indian note to Pakistan stated:

> Pakistan cannot be unaware that this road will help to extend the Chinese road network in the Tibet-Sinkiang areas into northern Kashmir. Indeed, this new road will give easier access to Chinese troops from the areas which they have illegally occupied in north-east Kashmir and from Tibet to the Gilgit area in Pakistani-occupied Kashmir, which lies immediately to the north of the cease-fire line dividing the armed forces of India and Pakistan in Kashmir.[125]

The Indians accused China of developing "a strategic network of roads, with the connivance of Pakistan to subserve China's ambitions in the region. . . . "It is quite evident from such activities," continued the Indian note "that China, an 'external force' in Kashmir," was deliberately disrupting Indo-Pakistani relations and "adding new tensions." The note to China reiterated points made to Pakistan: India felt the road through the Khunjerab Pass was "clearly designed to provide a link with the Chinese network of roads in Sinkiang and Tibet."[126]

On 26 June 1969 an Indian government spokesman said in New Delhi that the new road was "a militarily sinister move directed against India"; the fledgling route would "enable China to move troops from Tibet and the Ladakh front to Gilgit, directly cutting the distance from 1,000 to 200 miles." The Pakistani response, also contained in a diplomatic note, said: "The State of Jammu and Kashmir is not, and has never been, recognized as a part of Indian territory; and therefore the Government of India have no *locus standi* to lodge any protest with the Government of Pakistan in respect of the matter referred to in their Note." In 1978 the Indian foreign minister noted that the Karakoram Highway had "serious strategic implications" for the region; and in August 1982, when China and Pakistan signed a protocol to open the Khunjerab Pass to commercial traffic, India lodged a formal protest with Beijing and Islamabad which stated that the agreement was made regarding an area under "illegal" Pakistani occupation.[127]

Since the inception of the Karakoram Highway, some Indian military leaders have argued that it was necessary to sever the leading mountain road between Pakistan and its most important ally. In 1979 the Indian minister of foreign affairs announced on a visit to China that prospects for improvement in Sino-Indian relations would be hindered by such Sino-Pakistani actions as China's endorsement of Pakistan's stand on Kashmir and the construction of the Karakoram Highway.[128]

This unreliable road so visibly perturbs a few Indian writers on security affairs that they list it, along with Pakistan's erstwhile membership in Western alliances (and its more recent association with the United States) and the Chinese takeover of Tibet, as prime evidence of the belligerence of the routing partners in subcontinental affairs. Another improbable refrain is that the Karakoram Highway will provide China with access to the Indian Ocean.[129] The immediate Indian fear, however, remains the threats of Chinese access to their lines of communication from Kargil to Leh, and of the road into Xinjiang being coupled with the Aksai Chin road to form a pincer movement around Indian Kashmir.

India's concerns cannot be wholly discounted. The location of the Karakoram Highway has strategic and political meaning. An English-language Pakistani newspaper, the *Morning News,* once described the Karakoram Highway as "primarily a defense project built by the Pakistan Army with substantial Chinese assistance." Further, Pakistani military planners know well that China is a key factor in Indian calculations of Pakistani capabilities; they expect the Indians to make war moves toward Pakistan between December and March, when the Karakoram passes are blocked by snow and China's ability to aid its friend is retarded.[130]

A principal Chinese goal in the Sino-Indian borderlands is the retention of the Aksai Chin. Successive border negotiations with India—for decades a close friend of the Soviet Union and now a friend, too, of another of China's hostile neighbors, Vietnam—have not borne fruit. Bilateral relations began to improve in 1976 when China and India exchanged ambassadors, but over a decade later no agreement on the border had been reached. The borderlands remain a zone of tension. As recently as 1987, the Indian and Chinese armies raised their troop and air-based strengths at the junction of Tibet, Bhutan, and India's newly established northeastern state of Arunachal Pradesh. The Chinese accused Indian troops of repeated border violations and of "nibbling away" at Chinese territory.[131] They also continue to claim about 34,000 square miles in Arunachal Pradesh as well as 14,500 square miles of the Aksai Chin.

The western sector of the border in the Aksai Chin is the most strategically valuable to China. According to one Indian source, S. Nihal Singh, the Chinese proposed a package deal to the Indian foreign minister in 1979: Chinese claims to a traditional line of control in the eastern sector (which runs further south than the McMahon Line) would be abandoned in return for de jure Chinese possession of the Aksai Chin territory. Nothing came of this overture. China continues to rely on its Xinjiang-Tibet routes and the routes into the Northern Areas to protect Xinjiang and Tibet (where political unrest persists) and to conjure up the threat of a third front against India. These routes have eased Chinese troop and supply movements through the Aksai Chin, Xinjiang, Tibet, and Kashmir. Before the Karakoram Highway network, China could pressure India in Kashmir only by pulling troops away from the border with the Soviet Union to 220 miles south of the Mintaka Pass or by moving its troops from India's northern border all the way up the Aksai Chin road to Kashi and then southward to the Mintaka Pass.[132] The connection of the MorKhun–Khunjerab section, which linked the Xinjiang-Tibet road with the Gilgit-Xinjiang highway, considerably lessened the distances involved.

The spread of China's logistical system in these borderlands could also be useful to China's defenses against the Soviet Union. In the nineteenth century the British had emphasized the value of Gilgit's location on the frontiers of Kashmir as a base from which to monitor any Russian moves into the subcontinent, as well as forays into Xinjiang. The Karakoram Highway has given China potential access to Gilgit, helping monitor Soviet movements near Xinjiang or any

Indian or Soviet attempt to cut the lines of communication between Xinjiang and Tibet. In theory the Gilgit airfield could be used in different ways by different states: to threaten the Soviet Pamirs and Central Asia, or to counter anti-Soviet troop deployments from Kashi, or to threaten Chinese supply lines from Xinjiang in the event of renewed conflict with India. Still, this fixed wing, 4,770-feet-high airfield (as well as Skardu's, which lies at 7,600 feet) is surrounded by mountain peaks and is often shut owing to clouds and rain, even at the height of the summer. It cannot be relied upon for the efficient movement of military supplies or for tactical maneuvers.[133] Airstrips cannot substitute for the utility of the new roads in these Northern Areas, which became of special concern to China and Pakistan after the Soviet invasion of Afghanistan in 1979.

Gilgit lies 140 miles south of the valuable Wakhan corridor in Afghanistan's Badakhshan province. This is a 185-mile-long—and, in parts, only six-and-a-quarter-mile-wide—sliver of Afghan land that stands at an average altitude of 14,750 feet, rising to over 19,000 feet in the Pamirs. Wakhan holds numerous passes of entry to the south and north. In ancient times this was the most direct route from Bactria to the oases on the southern rim of the Tarim Pendi (in Xinjiang). Wakhan shares a northern border with Soviet Tajikistan, an eastern border with Xinjiang, and a southern border with Pakistan's Northern Areas. Its easternmost parts are only thirty miles from the Karakoram Highway.

Soviet forces reportedly entered Wakhan in 1978. After 1980 they occupied the territory and sealed it off from the rest of Afghanistan. Wakhan's current status is uncertain. Some analysts claim that the Soviets annexed it in 1981. Lawrence Ziring (citing a report prepared for a Pakistani newspaper) has said that the Wakhan corridor was ceded to Moscow in an Afghan-Soviet agreement signed on 16 June 1981. Logistics troop support, and, according to Chinese reports, the basic facilities for medium-range ballistic missiles have been installed here. (Western analysts will not confirm the Chinese reports.) A new highway has been built from Murghab in Soviet Tajikistan to the northeast Wakhan corridor; a tunnel on this route runs under the Andemin Pass (15,130 feet) and permits the Soviets to approach the Karakoram Highway. The Soviets have upgraded the main track through Wakhan, which has branches leading to the Wakhjir Pass into China and assorted passes into Soviet Central Asia, into an all-weather road and built feeder roads, helipads, and a fixed-wing airstrip. The headman of the Kirghiz tribe, Rakhman Gul, whose men and animals were driven out of the area, into Gilgit (and who were later settled in the Lake Van region of Turkey), also reported that the Soviets were furbishing the road near Qala Panja (which runs into Pakistan), building airfields, other new roads, and installing telephone and telex cables inside Wakhan.[134]

The Chinese have consistently opposed the Soviet invasion of Afghanistan. In February 1981 China also accused the Soviets of having annexed the Afghan corridor. The *Peking Review* announced that four thousand Soviet troops stood in Wakhan, patrolling the passes to China and Pakistan and building bunkers, barracks, underground missile sites, and strategic roads.[135] All this Soviet activity in the vicinity of the Karakoram Highway made Wakhan's eastern and southern neighbors anxious. During the 1980s, a few miles north of the Hunza Valley, Pakistani troops watched Wakhan from their high military lookouts.

The Soviet Union, too, has not been unaware of the political and military reality created by the Sino-Pakistani routes. Since 1969 Moscow has voiced its loud opposition to these cooperative projects. The Soviets argued that the new highways would assist Chinese troop movements to Xinjiang. In 1978 *Tass* referred to the Karakoram Highway as the "Road of Danger." It "actually linked with Peking's plans of military interference in Asia and particularly on the border with Afghanistan."[136]

In 1979 *Pravda* attacked the Karakoram Highway, noting that Chinese troops were involved in its development and repair. The roads, said the newspaper, were built to serve the "expansionist plans of the Chinese leadership" and caused justifiable concern in India. *Pravda* also reported that the Chinese had been enabled to concentrate their armed forces on India's borders; that they were using the road system to mount subversive activities against both India and Afghanistan; and that Chinese specialists were training sabotage groups for operations in Kashmir and using the Karakoram Highway to funnel arms to Afghan "counterrevolutionaries," that is, the Afghan mujahideen. In the two years preceding the invasion of Afghanistan, the Soviet press reiterated time and again the threat posed by the roads. Moscow's harangues stressed the far-fetched possibility that the Chinese might use the Karakoram Highway to link up with the western military and naval presence in the Indian Ocean.[137]

One commentator has even suggested that the building of the road was a factor in the timing of the 1978 coup in Afghanistan. Shahram Chubin writes: "One explanation for the Soviet decision to acquire a new client state is to be found in Sino-Soviet rivalry, which had become more extensive throughout Asia. The decision to consolidate Soviet dominance in Afghanistan may be viewed as a decision to forestall any extension of Chinese influence and to deny China any new area in which to operate. The imminent completion of the Karakoram Highway from Pakistan to China may indeed have been an additional influence on the timing of the coup."[138]

Prior to their invasion of Afghanistan, Lawrence Ziring noted that the Soviets condemned not only Pakistan's support for the mujahideen but also the Karakoram Highway as a "principal artery for the flow of Chinese weapons to the insurgents." After the invasion, the Soviets continued to oppose China's use of the Karakoram route. According to *Pravda* (and also the Press Trust of India), China was moving "large supplies of weapons and ammunition into Pakistan over the all-weather Karakoram Highway."[139] The alleged Chinese use of the highway to transport arms to the Afghan mujahideen was seen as an unwelcome entrance into Soviet affairs. Western military analysts, meanwhile, suggested that if the Afghan war broadened in geographical scope, "given the high percentage of rebel arms which are of Chinese origin, the Soviets may also feel compelled to interdict the most conspicuous route of supply." The Karakoram Highway was deemed a highly probable target of any joint Indo-Soviet moves. *Foreign Report*, a British news bulletin, asserted that "a department of the Soviet Communist Party's central committee requested an assessment of the pros and cons of a Soviet military intrusion into northern Pakistan. The aim: to destroy Afghan bases in the region and to cut the Karakoram highway in the Pakistani part of Kashmir, used by China to send military supplies to the rebels."[140]

In 1982 the Kabul government itself, through the official *Kabul New Times*, charged China with "cartographic aggression." The editorial drew a parallel between China's present activities in the Pamir-Karakoram region and the situation in the Aksai Chin in 1962. The present-day Chinese "emperors," said the paper, would like to turn Afghanistan into another Xinjiang, in order to "head on to the Indian Ocean."[141]

The road building in the Karakorams may also have encouraged concerns about the creation of a more extensive military apparatus in the area. In February 1981 India's minister of state for defense, Shivraj

Patel, told the Indian Parliament that China was "assisting Pakistan in building new airbases and repairing old ones."[142] Following a visit to China by U.S. secretary of state Alexander Haig, the Soviet Union accused the Chinese and the Americans of having begun a covert project—"Karakoram-80"—along with the British and the Pakistanis. According to reports, listening posts were being located in the Karakorams in order to "monitor activities in the Soviet Union, Afghanistan and India."[143]

By 1984 the environs of the Karakoram Highway were witnessing sporadic skirmishes, tempted by their location. Indo-Pakistani hostilities broke out around the Siachin Glacier. Situated to the north of the Indo-Pakistani Line of Actual Control in Kashmir, the Siachin Glacier rests near the Aksai Chin and the Sino-Pakistani border; it also controls passage into Ladakh.

Intermittent clashes continue in the world's highest battleground. Hundreds of mountains troops, operating at altitudes as high as 22,000 feet, have died in the mountain war between India and Pakistan. The war, fought with heavy artillery and machine guns, has been small and slow, because it has been waged at heights that prevent the use of helicopters and in terrain where resupply by trekking can take forty days. It has also been expensive, with an estimated cost of about $1.6 million per day. More casualties have resulted from the pernicious environment than from the skirmishes: in a breakdown of Indian casualties in 1985, ten out of fifty men had died in combat, the remaining forty from frostbite or avalanches.[144]

The disputed ownership of the lands around the Siachin Glacier spurred the conflict. Pakistan claims the glacier as being inside Pakistani-controlled territory, whereas India claims it as part of Indian-controlled Kashmir. The boundary line near the glacier has never been demarcated. It is an extension—from grid reference point NJ9842—of the Line of Actual Control in Kashmir, which Pakistan says runs in a northeasterly direction to the Karakoram Pass. India says the line has a northwesterly alignment along the 22,000-feet-high Saltoro Range, a sheet of rock west of the Siachin Glacier. (The *Times Atlas* and the *Readers Digest Atlas* have sided with Pakistan in the cartographic feud.)

Since 1984 India has held about 1900 square miles claimed by Pakistan. Indian troops have captured points on the gargantuan glacier, which is 18,000 feet high, about 46 miles long, and between one and five miles wide, and have held the four passes that provide entry to the glacier from Indian-controlled Kashmir. It has been suggested that India's moves into the region reflected its objections to the Karakoram Highway, about 155 miles away: its interest in the glacier stems from its high environs, which provide superior posts from which to observe Chinese and Pakistani activities along a section of the route. At the time of Indo-Pakistani combat in the region, reports were also surfacing of a Chinese military build-up in the neighboring Aksai Chin.[145] In May 1988, Gilgit itself became the site of violence and death when fighting began between rival Shia and Sunni sects. The tribesmen were armed with the weapons of the Afghan war, including rocket launchers, machine guns, and mortars. While the Shias blocked the highway in the north, the Sunnis cut it in the south. Many hundreds were killed. Because of the importance of Gilgit as a staging post for troops fighting the war in Siachin, and of the Karakoram Highway, Pakistani soldiers were flown in to restore calm and reopen the mountain way.[146]

China and India have not fought each other since 1962. Both sides are trying to improve relations; in June 1980 Deng Xiaoping announced that the Kashmir dispute was a bilateral, Indo-Pakistani issue that should be settled by peaceful means.[147] Still, the border controversy, and specifically the Chinese intention to keep the Aksai Chin, remains a fundamental obstacle to the improvement of Sino-Indian relations. China has persistently called for a comprehensive settlement along the lines of the existing boundaries, while India has demanded a sector-by-sector approach. During the first round of Sino-Indian border talks, which occurred in Beijing on 10–14 December 1981, China insisted that India surrender all claims to the Aksai Chin. Indeed, the resolution of the Sino-Indian boundary controversy still hinges on China's decision about how best to secure its frontier routes.

In the Sino-Indian borderlands, about four hundred thousand troops stand within striking distance of each other. India's improved logistical capabilities in the mountains have helped balance the Chinese advantage of 1962. Defeat in that year led the Indians to build roads, airfields, and helipads and to raise additional, better-supplied mountain divisions. Currently eleven army divisions (each of 17,500 men) are deployed. These are backed by paramilitary units such as the Ladakh Scouts and the Indo-Tibetan Border Police. On the other side the Chinese, because of their sophisticated network of routes, have access to troops headquartered in both Sichuan and Xinjiang. In the Southwestern Military Region based at Chengdu in Sichuan, the Chinese keep eight infantry divisions (each of 12,700 men), six local force divisions, and two or three border-force divisions. One division based at Urumqi can also be brought to the border rapidly.[148] Both sides can now bring airpower to bear in the mountains. Still, the Chinese, in Tibet, hold the higher—though politically unsteady— ground. During 1987, tensions rose along the eastern sector of the Sino-Indian border. In Tibet, significant disturbances occurred as recently as October 1987, and March and December 1988. Lhasa has remained tense.[149] This combination of events does not augur well for the resolution of the border dispute (Tibetan troubles reinforce the conviction of the Chinese that they must retain the Aksai Chin road), nor for improved Sino-Indian relations. Despite the Chinese offer of 23 September 1988 to hold direct talks on Tibet's future with the Dalai Lama (the leader of the Tibetan Buddhists who heads a government-in-exile sheltered by India), China will never discuss the full independence of this icy plateau, its most strategic southwestern territory.

Indeed, the importance of South Asia to the Soviet Union and China has been grounded in its adjacence to Soviet Central Asia, Xinjiang, and Tibet, distant, insecure peripheries that are home to minority populations and difficult to control from the center.[150] Each state has carved high roads across the mountains to subdue the terrain, to open new channels of communication and development, and, most important, to advance its presence and its own forms of control in tenuous borderlands.

Yet changes in political strategy, like changes in technology, can transform the meaning of geography. Under Mikhail Gorbachev, the Soviet Union has made domestic economic and political restructuring a priority, and it has begun to disengage itself from regional conflicts across the world. The Chinese had set three conditions for an improvement in Sino-Soviet relations: the withdrawal of 115,000 Soviet troops from Afghanistan, a reduction of Sino-Soviet border tensions, and the removal of 120,000 Vietnamese troops from Cambodia. The Soviets have withdrawn their troops from Afghanistan on schedule, and they have announced troop reductions along the Sino-Soviet border. Tensions there are lower than in the past two decades. Soviet willingness to hold talks with senior Chinese officials on a Cambodian settlement has also been tested: vice-ministers of the two countries met for five days of talks in August 1988.

The Soviets have initiated improvements in both U.S.-Soviet and Sino-Soviet relations. In 1986, and again in the fall of 1988, Gorbachev called for Sino-Soviet dialogue at the highest levels of leadership. (There have been no such talks since 1969.) A summit meeting between the two Communist powers became a possibility. By September 1988 the Soviets had already suggested that "we are ready for a summit, but they are not ready for one yet." On 28 September 1988 it was announced that the Chinese foreign minister would visit Moscow to met Gorbachev. And on 14 October 1988 Deng Xiaoping stated that the first Sino-Soviet summit meeting in thirty years was likely to be held soon, in mid-May 1989.[151] The conditions for a tentative Sino-Soviet accommodation have been created. Still, Sino-Soviet differences on geographical and ideological issues run deep. There have been many years of bitterness and a reconciliation that would cause a material restructuring of Chinese and Soviet strategies towards Xinjiang, Tibet, Afghanistan, India, and Pakistan would take a long time to mature. These are neighboring and competitive land powers with insecure peripheries, which may find it difficult to easily embrace one another's views on Central and South Asia. China's geographical encirclement by Soviet friends and properties, by Vietnam, India, Afghanistan (the Wakhan corridor), Soviet Central Asia, and Mongolia, will remain an important fact in its strategic planning.

A radical improvement in relations between China and the Soviet Union could diminish Chinese concerns for their southwestern borderlands and affect Chinese political, economic, and military policies toward Pakistan and India. The mere hint of Sino-Soviet camaraderie has prompted political and strategic reevaluation by China's neighbors. Stronger Sino-Soviet ties could resolve India to seek a rapprochement with China, especially along the borderlands. Rajiv Gandhi has already visited Beijing at the end of 1988. The trip was the first by an Indian prime minister since Jawaharlal Nehru visited China thirty-four years ago. India has begun to stress the need for normalization of Sino-Indian relations and to resolve the border controversy. Its resolution would, however, require India to accept Chinese strategic interests in the Aksai Chin. As the Soviet Union pursues friendship with China, too, India will likely seek a reaffirmation of its own bonds with Moscow.

Sino-Soviet intimacy could lessen China's interest in Pakistan as a political and physical wedge between Indian and Soviet policies and lands; and a new political accord between the Communist land powers could alter the pivotal meaning of Pakistan's location. Yet, so long as the Sino-Soviet and Sino-Indian territorial disputes remain unsolved, and so long as India threatens Pakistan, both China and Pakistan have reason to pursue their partnership. In the Sino-Pakistani relationship the constancy of geography should overshadow the fickleness of history.

The states of South Asia, however, must closely watch the evolution of Sino-Soviet political relations. From their point of view, new turns in this relationship could reorient the military, political, and economic realities of the subcontinent and its environs. For decades, a cycle of territorial disputes and negotiations over legitimate ownership of, and access to, the borderlands has occupied much of the political life of Central and South Asia. The nature of conflict and the direction of progress in the Karakoram and Himalayan borderlands will continue to be determined by the mingling of politics with geography.

5

The Politics of Routes

The development of the land routes of the South, Central, and West Asian borderlands amounts to a pivotal point of regard from which a regional biography may be written.[1] Routes remain historically important factors and analytically viable tools for grasping regional evolution. As physical facts they can "map" history—provide an X-ray of political-geographical changes—as well as move it along. Geographical factors such as sheer physical distance have retained their importance in the study of state and regional politics in the developing world.

One important reason for our failure to appreciate the full importance of routes in the developing world has been the segregated study of security and development. A proper study of the politics of routes evokes the image of a systemic entanglement. Indeed, a dynamic of national choices emerges from such an integrated view of security and development. Historically, security and development have both been factors in the infrastructure policies of empires and states; analytically, with regard to the major routes we have explored, calculations of security were contemporaneous with calculations of development, compromising the definitional purity of the two categories. Of course, contemporaniety always takes a specific form, and in the region under study the claim of security has tended to predominate over that of development.

In the borderlands the politics of routes has been intertwined in political and military games great and small. The routes from Kashi across the mountains into Tibet, Nepal, and the Northern Areas; the routes encircling Afghanistan's ancient cities, branching northward into Soviet Central Asia and southward into Pakistan's North West Frontier and Baluchistan; the sparse routes that have pulled Baluchistan toward Iran, Afghanistan, and now the core areas of Pakistan—all draw together the historical currents that have shaped the region. Their patterns reflect the commingling of diverse interpretations of state interest. The decline of particular avenues of movement and communication, such as the Silk Route for example, foretold the demise of the cities and towns that had flourished with it. And the creation of new routes permitted the evolution of new political, economic, and strategic realities in Afghanistan while they broke the isolation of the Northern Areas and brought to them the lures and controls of Pakistan's lowland civilization. Finally, the primary cause of insecurity in South Asia emerged from that bloodiest and firmest of all manmade antiroutes, the Indo-Pakistan border.

At every level of state life, from small feuds between peripheral tribes and central authorities through insurgencies and regional wars to grand Russian and Chinese geopolitics, routes have occasioned controversy and conflict. It is important not to underestimate the unexplored, the unmastered, the unknown. In most developing states, access remains a fundamental aspiration and a contested goal. Processes of achieving security and development are, in a rigorous and fundamental way, processes of controlling—expanding or restraining—access.

We may make several observations about the paramountcy of the politics of access, and about the relationship between security and development, in the borderlands of South, Central, and West Asia.

1. The politics of access has dominated the conduct of insurgency and war, whether in Baluchistan, the wars of the nineteenth century, or the latest round of Afghan war fought in an environment with nuclear potential. But that new potential has not vitiated the importance of traditional assets. Because of the nature of the terrain and the limited avenues of movement the Afghan war has been, in the stark-

est sense, a war for logistics. The struggle between Afghan mujahideen and Soviet and Communist Afghan troops has been primarily to control access. Roads have been the focus of mujahideen attack and Soviet defense. In 1988, the Soviet roads and tunnels built in the 1960s and 1970s served as essential exit routes for Soviet troops departing Afghanistan.

The failure of the Durand Line, an artificial antiroute, has had weighty consequences. The inability to control access during the 1980s has meant that the Afghan conflict has entered Pakistan, contributing through the presence of Afghan mujahideen and refugees to terrorism and bombings on Pakistani soil; to the destruction of Pakistan's pasture lands and forests; to the restructuring of its frontier economy; and to the spread of drugs and guns, of heroin and Kalashnikovs, rocket-launchers, assault rifles, landmines, and such, across Pakistan.[2]

The success of the groups that organize this killing commerce depends on an ability to control the highways running between the poppy fields and the arms caches in the NWFP and the retail outlets and the port in Karachi (where, among other nearby locales, CIA-supplied arms for the mujahideen have been dropped off). In Pakistan, local Pakhtuns and Afghan truckers control most of the heavy vehicles that ply the national highways, easing the carriage of contraband.

The border zone has played a crucial role in the successes and failures of the Afghan war. For so long the bane of Afghan rulers in Kabul, the Durand Line has continued to perform its traditional role as a flawed antiroute. It has had a sorry history: the Durand Line has been ignored in peacetime and during war, and it has been a continuing source of friction between Afghanistan and Pakistan. The dispute over the validity of this antiroute, in the form of the Afghan claim for Pakhtunistan, was raised in the Geneva talks for an Afghan settlement. In March 1988, Najibullah's government announced that the parties to negotiation had to settle the matter of the legitimacy of the Durand Line before proceeding. This Afghan stance annoyed the Soviet Union, which by then was intent on a removal of its military personnel from Afghanistan. Pakistan responded by insisting that the accord incorporate a reference to "internationally recognized frontiers" between itself and Afghanistan.[3] Although the Afghans were unsuccessful in this round of the dispute, the revival of the Durand

Line controversy reinforced Pakistani fears about future Afghan claims for Pakhtunistan.

During the years of the Soviet occupation of Afghanistan, the idea of Pakhtunistan has lost support. Afghan Pakhtuns, who comprised over 90 percent of the refugee population, required shelter, arms, and humanitarian aid from Pakistan. For nearly a decade they lived in, and fought their anti-Soviet war from, Pakistani territory. The question of Pakhtunistan became moot. As the Soviets leave Afghanistan, however, Pakistan can have no guarantee that the Pakhtunistan issue will not reappear once again in Afghanistan's domestic politics and regional policies.

If the 1989 withdrawal results in the triumph of Afghan groups in Kabul who revive calls for erasure of the Durand Line (and for Baluch rights), the Afghanistan-Pakistan borderlands could see persistent instability. With the NWFP and Baluchistan weakened by the flood of refugees, guns, drugs, and terrorism since 1979, Pakistan will have a reduced capacity to contend with any future inflammation by Afghanistan of ethno-territorial disputes south of the Durand Line.

In the 1980s the Durand Line has been a predictable failure. In its inefficacy however, it has shaped the Soviet inability to win a clear military victory in Afghanistan. The Afghan war has also been fought from across the Khyber, and the Soviet Union and its Afghan allies have suffered the consequences of the permeability of the border. Time and again they have been unable to enforce the barrier function of the Durand Line. Northwards, across the line, have traveled thousands of mujahideen who oppose Soviet occupation from their bases in the frontier lands and cities of Pakistan. With them have gone animals, weapons, ammunition, medical supplies, trainers, healers, and journalists, and help from the United States, China, the Arab states—this traffic has kept the war alive. The old, natural ways that slice into Afghan territory have challenged the control the Soviets established along their own manmade routes.

The traditionally porous Afghan-Pakistani border zone has permitted the crucial movement and resupply of men from bases inside Pakistan; Afghanistan's tyrannical terrain has given cover to the mujahideen; and the continuing struggle of the communist Afghan state with the tribes (the difficulties it has incurred in trying to extend control across a fragmented country and tribal society)—all have combined to deny a Soviet triumph in Afghanistan. Inability to seal the southern access routes prevented the Soviet Union from achieving a clear military victory over the externally supported Afghan mujahideen. The costs, however, have not been small: nearly one million Afghans are dead.

The politics of access will remain fundamental to any resolution of the Afghan conflict. From this perspective, the full, long-term meaning of a Soviet troop withdrawal from Afghanistan will depend in large part on a continued, balancing pressure from the south upon Soviet interests in Afghanistan. Pakistan alone cannot provide that pressure, especially as long as the Afghan refugees remain inside its borders, and it must again be concerned with the potential for an Afghan revival of the Pakhtunistan issue. Since 1980 the Soviets have been expanding the infrastructure of strategic and economic access to Afghanistan. A new Afghan regime cannot be "neutral" or genuinely "non-aligned" nor can it be a "buffer." Where geography grips history, no buffer exists with only one power, the possessor of commanding access, supporting its neutrality. Those states with an interest in the control of Soviet access in the borderlands of Central and South Asia might recall the old British strategy of alerting the Russians that a concerned power stands resolutely to the south of the Hindu Kush.

2. The borderlands have undergone speedy socio-economic development precisely where and when states have perceived a high degree of insecurity. In central regions, political power assures that demands upon economic resources receive responses. In peripheries the impetus for progress is different; here insecurity fosters development. When there are fears about internal dangers to the state's political center, when an external threat (real or perceived) exists, where the integrity of territory is undermined—there the need for access becomes important in the peripheries. Routes lead the developmental advance.

Consider Baluchistan. In its early history, it was not strategically valuable to neighboring empires, and so it suffered economic neglect and sporadic invasion. Its hot lands remained overwhelmingly an antiroute. In the nineteenth century the requirements of imperial security dominated the routing policies of the British in Baluchistan and its environs: antiroutes were established to prevent Russian encroachment, the proposals for railways and roads leading into the Persian Gulf and Iran were quashed because they posed potential hazards to western India's security, and routes were built inside Baluchistan whose timing, location, and number testified to their strategic purpose. Roads and railroads were constructed to link the fort towns and cantonments (themselves built to guard the routes across the ranges) with one another and with the interior. Quetta's rise is instructive. There the requirements of movement for troops and commodities gave rise to a flourishing city. Quetta was developed; major routes radiated from it; the rest of Baluchistan was neglected.

The legacy of empire was uneven development. Even within the new state of Pakistan, Baluchistan received scant attention during the early years. Apart from routes built to extract resources and help quell brushfire skirmishes, and the lagging RCD highway project, few major road-building programs were initiated until the insurrection of 1973–77. Again, the location, timing, and effort indicate that not only an interest in oil, gas, and coal but an interest in security propelled the construction of routes. It was Bhutto's (and the Shah's) concerns for internal and regional security that they addressed with roads, electricity and, in Pakistan's case, schools. A similar phenomenon occurred in 1980. Immediately following the Soviet invasion of Afghanistan, when fears for the external defense of Pakistan and of Soviet-inspired subversion within Baluchistan proliferated, the Pakistani center produced a development plan for Baluchistan. The largest component of this plan was a road and rail construction program. Although economic and social benefits must accrue from such a massive investment, the costly development of Baluchistan, especially of its long-neglected coastal areas, followed the outbreak of a regional war.

As an instrument of foreign and security politics, routes have spearheaded socio-economic change. China's concern for the security of its borderlands and its political and military strategy in the subcontinent created accessibility in the most remote peripheries of Pakistan and India. Indo-Chinese competition also led to the creation of access in the states of the Himalayan borderlands. In Baluchistan, the center used roads as military instruments as well as means by which to break the traditional tribal order. Economic and social changes were stimulated by military competition, insurgency, war, and strategic partnerships.

In the subcontinent's northern reaches, British policies for the protection of strategic access had improved the few trade routes that wound through Kashmir and its neighboring territories. Still, no large-scale movement was possible across the Karakorams; the mountains retained mastery. Only in the third quarter of the twentieth century was the massive barrier disturbed. For Britain's successor,

Pakistan, the Karakoram Highway and the alliance it symbolizes meant important gains in state security.

The origination of routes in the borderlands has generally required a strong rationale of security. In the Sino-Pakistani and Sino-Indian borderlands road building has been instigated by crises of security, such as the rude awakening of India occasioned by the 1962 war; by the needs of military conquest and occupation; or by the political and military advantages accruing from cooperative road building. In the mountain peripheries of the subcontinent, in Ladakh, the Indian northeast, Sikkim, Bhutan, and Nepal, strategic competition and conflict have spurred routes and regional development.

The Karakoram Highway and its affiliated routes have made a concrete statement about the strength and intended longevity of Sino-Pakistani friendship. Ancillary benefits have followed in the development of the Karakoram lands. Routes, of course, are also the long arm of government, and the lumbering vehicle for development. Advances in mountain road building have transformed the technology of transport on the new highways: mules and other pack animals have been replaced by cars, jeeps, buses, trucks, and, potentially, armored vehicles. For the inhabitants of the highlands the meaning of space and the meaning of time have been transformed.

The Karakoram network and its associated tracks have meant increases in and new modes of economic activity and trade in the Northern Areas and the arrival of lowlanders and their culture. The impetus for construction, however, was not the demand of the economy or of commerce alone. Trade across the thousands of miles from Kashi to Karachi would have to be of high volume and value to justify the enormous risks and costs of transportation, let alone those of construction.

3. During the nineteenth century, in Afghanistan and Bhutan—two land-locked states hemmed in by stronger powers—considerations of ruler (regime) and state security prevented the creation of routes that might facilitate trade and enhance economic and political integration. Both states consciously denied access, relinquishing potential economic gains in order to maintain their territorial integrity. Afghanistan, for instance, once hosted great routes of trade and routes of conquest. By the nineteenth century, however, the country was militarily weak and no longer home to powerful centers of trade. The Russian railroad advance across Central Asia and British advances in India had started the Great Game. The British built roads

inside India's North West Frontier (to control the tribes and maintain access to Afghanistan) and sought to create a buffer—an antiroute—inside Afghanistan. This confirmation of Afghanistan's inaccessibility had dire consequences for the country's economic development.

Accessibility was the major policy question in Afghan affairs in the nineteenth and twentieth centuries. Amir Abdur Rahman, caught between two encroaching powers, carefully calculated Afghan needs on the basis of two considerations: the defense of his country's territorial integrity against Britain and Russia, and the needs of internal (i.e. ruler) security. He also had to take care not to overly offend the tribes, which resisted the insertion of routes into their lands. Abdur Rahman decided to promote Afghanistan's natural antiroutes and gave them political and strategic endorsement. He pursued a deterrent strategy of access denial, explicitly forbidding the economic progress that the expansion of access might have spurred.

In the modern era, it was the creation of access in Afghanistan for the purposes of development which helped destroy state security. Contrary to the argument made by scholars, on the basis of quantitative analyses, that advances in development will lead to advances in security, a study of the politics of routes reveals that the political, social, and strategic dimensions of development should be considered before such a simple conclusion is reached. Historically, improved economic conditions have not necessarily improved the security of states. Further, neither security nor development policies involve an appraisal of economic costs alone. Indeed, in the case of Afghanistan, the claim of security gave way completely to that of development. The result was the forfeiture of security. The traditional routing orientation of Afghanistan suffered a dramatic reversal founded in a changed Afghan attitude toward national development and foreign policy.

Economic progress became a governmental imperative. The purposeful pursuit of Pakhtunistan in the south, the consequent sporadic closure of the routes into Pakistan, and the welcome accorded to new northern routes built by the Soviets resulted in the steady erosion, and finally in the loss of Afghanistan's territorial integrity. The years between the 1950s and the 1970s witnessed a tussle between Afghanistan and Pakistan over the southern trade routes and potential economic channels to the Arabian Sea, the severance of these routes, and Afghan acceptance of infrastructural aid from the Soviet Union. Because of the impact of terrain on the country's political and economic fragmentation, the Afghans saw new trunk routes as essential to the pursuit of development. Kabul's leaders banked on their ability to keep Soviet military influence at bay. They failed. The construction of these very routes helped end Afghanistan's independence in 1979.

4. Without access, there can be no political cohesion. Governments and rulers of nascent nation-states have used the expansion of access to dominate the geographical periphery and to advance political integration. The inhabitants of the periphery, to preserve traditional ways, have often restricted access. Everywhere in the borderlands roads are a potent symbol of politics. In Baluchistan, before the British came, the lack of routes was a prime factor conditioning the ability of indigenous Baluch tribal federations to exercise control and to wield authority over all Baluchistan. In the Pakhtun frontier regions of Pakistan, a road through tribal territory is much more than an avenue of mobility, because here the laws and the "iconography" of the modern state intersect with the laws and the iconography of the tribe.

The forging of routes has been a focal point in the tussle between tribe and state for control over the destiny of the periphery. The mandate of all aspiring nation-states, to create a cohesive national entity amid the chaos of competing peoples, threatens the tribes. Specifically, the tribes have viewed governmental road building as intrusion by an artificial political center. The center's increased access represents new national ideas that threaten old forms of identity; at the same time the changes in economic, social, and political relationships brought about by the road threaten old systems of control over the distribution of local resources and over laws. Routes are nothing less than infringements upon tribal independence.

In the areas considered here, the contest over routes has been at the heart of the political, social, economic, and ideational struggle between new centers and old peripheries. Zulfiqar Ali Bhutto, for example, well understood the power of routes. He saw a reduction in Baluchistan's inaccessibility as a way to reinforce the strength of the center and to disrupt Baluch sociopolitical organization. He used routes to carry the ideas and social system of the political center. Today, Pakistani authorities still attempt to assert their control over peripheries through route construction; much bargaining and negotiation precede the construction of each major artery. The centuries-old pattern of tribal resistance to the center's road building continues.

5. For a small, populous, and poor state such as Pakistan it is

external economic and technical assistance which facilitates the creation of physical access, promoting the integration and development of its borderlands. The broader geopolitical and security interests of great powers have led to the development of national peripheries and regional borderlands. U.S., Iranian, and Arab interests in Baluchistan expanded links between the Pakistani center and Baluch lands and within Baluchistan. A Chinese interest in Pakistan's Karakoram lands likewise helped fulfill Pakistan's integrative requirements. The space within which Pakistan carries out administrative policies has been increased, as has its freedom of movement and its territorial cohesion. Clearly, no central control is effective if communication and transport links with the peripheries are tenuous. The new land routes have also improved the internal security of the Pakistani state. Perhaps the most important benefit for Pakistan is the physical integration of and effective control over strategically vulnerable territories whose status India disputes.

6. The fashioning of channels of access has been a focus of the regional maneuvers of friendly states. Nestled in the furthermost reaches of the highest mountains on earth, the Karakoram Highway has linked two modern political and military partners in a region where, historically, access has been always sought, but seldom attained. The earliest rationale for carving out what would become known as the Silk Route was a Chinese search for political allies in their defense against harassment by borderland foes, predecessors of the Huns. With the Karakoram Highway the Chinese have repeated an ancient policy: they have fashioned a bond with Pakistan against their common rivals, India and the Soviet Union.

Consider the contemporary implications of the Karakoram Highway. The construction of the world's highest international road has provided a powerful, visible centerpiece for the Sino-Pakistani partnership. It benefits both China and Pakistan in their political and military maneuvering in the subcontinent. Though not an ideal offensive strategic system, the Karakoram network has unnerved and discomfited its builders' rivals. It has put India on the psychological defensive in Kashmir, where to the west India now faces Pakistan, to the north, China. By connecting their own transport system with that of the Chinese the Pakistanis have complicated potential Indian infringements on the Northern Areas.

7. Quarrels about valuable routes and regions of access caused two regional conflicts that had dramatic consequences for the political and

military evolution of South and Central Asia. First, Afghanistan's quest for Pakhtunistan, which can be read partly as a search for economic autarky and enhanced security through the acquisition of physical access, led to bitter conflict with Pakistan in the 1950s and 1960s.

It is in the context of the quarrel over Pakhtunistan that the urgency of Pakistan's efforts in the late 1980s to influence the composition of a future Afghan regime in Kabul, and return the Afghan refugees to their own lands after a Soviet withdrawal, might be understood. Pakistanis have an interest in seeing a friendly, representative regime in Kabul—one that will draw the refugees homeward, end the historically hostile drift in Afghan-Pakistani relations, reduce the spillage of war into the NWFP and Baluchistan. Although the Afghan mujahideen have neither the interest nor the ability to pursue claims to Palistani territory at present, the potential for Afghan irridentism will continue to cast a shadow over Pakistani political, tribal, and trade relations.

Second, the 1962 Sino-Indian war was a struggle over access. In large measure China went to war with India to retain control of that portion of the Aksai Chin through which ran its road linking Xinjiang and Tibet. Today, Sino-Indian border negotiations are stalled because of disagreement over ownership and control of the Aksai Chin. And the consequences of the '62 war are writ large in the current nuclear rivalry between Pakistan and India.

8. In the sprawling regional designs of the Soviet Union, and China too, land routes stretching beyond their political boundaries retain their traditional importance. Both states are land powers with millions of soldiers under arms. Naval supremacy has been the American forte, and despite the Soviet Union's recent improvement in maritime capabilities, in central, South and West Asia, the Soviets continue to see themselves as a land power. The Chinese are even weaker in the water. In the forseeable future, China, with its vast reserves of manpower and its time-honored concern about land frontiers, will continue to emphasize the manipulation of frontier access routes. China is a developing country and a great Asian nuclear power. It has ambition, but it lacks routes. The lack of accessibility within China—the inadequacy of links between the heartland of Chinese power and its crucial frontier territories of Xinjiang and Tibet—has always hampered Chinese power. The familiar dangers of unvanquished dis-

tance, both internal and external, will have to be conquered before the Chinese can achieve status as a world power.

When the global interests of great powers intersect with the regional interests of local states, their exchanges have nearly always involved access. American military and economic aid to Pakistan, an expression of a keen interest in Pakistan's location in relation to Central Asia and the Persian Gulf, manifest U.S. requirements for regional access. The Soviets and Americans, in their competition on the playing field of Third World states, have founded their strategy on the need for military and political access. And access is precisely what small states have found themselves offering, or selling, to enhance their own military strength and economic progress through association with an outside power.

Strident confrontations over the acquisition and denial of access have occurred between the United States and the Soviet Union. During the Cold War years and again during the Soviet takeover of Afghanistan, the United States has tried to prevent the Soviet Union from pushing forward its political and geographical frontiers in West, South, and Central Asia. In the coming years perceived U.S. strategic interests in the Persian Gulf, and the attendant needs for assured access (especially for CENTCOM, and especially during times of emergency) should result in the retention of U.S. interests in South and West Asia.

While Soviet access to Third World facilities has increased, U.S. access has become more complicated and more costly. Developing countries increasingly insist that deals for access be done differently. The Panama Canal Treaty, for example, insists on the closure of U.S. installations there by the end of 1999, while the government of the Philippines has extracted a hefty sum—$481 million per year—from the United States after protracted negotiations for retention of American facilities at Clark Air Force Base and Subic Bay.

The Sino-Indian territorial competition in the Himalayan borderlands has also manifested itself in a struggle for access to Nepal's, Bhutan's, and Sikkim's territories, as well as to Kashmir. For China, each new north-south route leading from Tibet or Xinjiang across the mountains into the subcontinent is a logistical asset. Route construction in the Himalayan borderland states provides similar assets for India, another land power that perceives its principal political and military threat as emerging across its northern frontiers, from China. Financial and technical aid for route building has been disbursed by both countries to the smaller states of the borderlands (including Pakistan) in exchange for strategic access.

9. Global political change impinges on a region's rivalries and on the meaning of its geography. The Soviet Union's new, more conciliatory, foreign and security policies during the late 1980s have served to reduce tensions between the great powers as well as to ameliorate Third World conflicts. This could alter the geographical relationships between the states of Central and South Asia. Old regional wars are seeing sudden resolution. U.S.-Soviet relations are improving, and, despite Chinese reticence, Sino-Soviet talks on matters of mutual concern, such as troops reductions on their Central Asian border and the Vietnamese military presence in Cambodia, proceed. The Soviets have also taken their troops from Afghanistan.

If consolidated, these great power rapprochements, when joined with the Soviet withdrawal from Afghanistan, could lessen U.S. and Chinese commitments to Pakistan. Such a process would force the South Asian state to become more self-reliant when addressing the future status of the Afghan-Pakistani and Indo-Pakistani borderlands. Regional territorial and boundary disputes could become invested with greater local, and lesser global significance. Still, given Pakistan's pivotal location next to Iran, near the Persian Gulf, and between India and Afghanistan, it is unlikely that American and Chinese interests will ever entirely erode. Instability in, and access to, Pakistan will always concern both powers.

The status of the Karakoram-Himalayan borderlands could also become hostage to the changing tenor of Sino-Soviet relations and of Soviet attitudes toward the Sino-Indian mountain rivalry. Enhanced ties between the Communist powers could lead to the reformulation of Indian political and military strategy in the Aksai Chin and in its northeastern properties. Of course, any long-term reconciliation of Sino-Indian interests would transform their borderlands as well as the Himalayan states from zones of hectic military and development activity to zones of greater stasis.

In this book, I have made comparisons not merely across space but across time. I have suggested that significant continuities exist in the region between the strategic conceptions of past and present. But we must be careful not to simplify: there have been important geographical and political discontinuities as well. Indeed, it is precisely the contrast between what has changed and what has remained constant that makes apparent the full importance of geographical politics.

Two discontinuities are noteworthy. First, the geographical barriers that established the region's strategic identity for centuries have been breached. In the modern period the Himalayas, the Karakorams, the Hindu Kush, and the wastelands of Baluchistan have all been penetrated. Despite this revolution in the regional system of access, however, the routes are still few and far between, difficult and hazardous. The natural antiroute has not been wholly neutralized or made obsolete. That limitation accounts for the special valence that the politics of routes retains in borderlands and state peripheries.

There have been definitive changes in the conditions of access. What has not changed is the predominance of the problems of access. Where the geopolitics of the premodern period was more circumscribed by antiroutes, modern geopolitics has been both freed and obsessed by routes. The creation of new avenues of access has not removed or (in some cases) even greatly reduced the strategic dilemmas of the past.

Another comparison across time concerns the economic dimension of routing policy in the imperial and postimperial periods. Plainly, routes in this region have existed for economic reasons since ancient times; the Silk Route owes its name to such a reason. Yet a distinction must be drawn between the economic character of such traditional routes and the economic character of their modern equivalents. Under empire, of course, there was no notion of development comparable to our own. The new states, by contrast, bear full responsibility for socioeconomic, political, and regional development within their territories. The demands placed upon governments by their peoples now are qualitatively and quantitatively different. This aspect of the transformation of the international order has been much stressed, but a study of routes shows that the heavy new responsibilities of development have not overtaken—and seem unlikely to overtake—the requirements of security, especially in the peripheries. The strategic quandaries that these states face are often the same as those faced by predecessor empires, or have been compounded by imperial policy. The three cases demonstrate, indeed, that considerations of security often play a major role in matters of development.

Although I have restricted my focus to routes across land—those routes which have most directly affected the evolution of the region— I note that across this entire territory, the real and perceived importance of land routes derives in part from their relationship to the sea. The commercial ventures and military adventures that span the history of the routes of the Indian Ocean make up another great tale. Just as the pattern of land routes and the fairs, market towns, and imperial and national cities that have evolved alongside them once fashioned the strategies and goals of seafaring merchants and mercenaries, so the life of the oceans has assigned political, military, and economic value to particular land routes in South, West, and Central Asia, despite sometimes immense distances from the Indian Ocean and the Persian Gulf.

Land routes and corridors have been prized not least for the access they provide to the sea. They have also competed with sea routes for the intercontinental trade. In ancient and early medieval times, strife on land—conflict between imperial systems or chaos within them—pushed trade out to sea. And during certain periods, in particular at the height of the Silk Route's success, the sea trade and the very survival of port cities were directly affected by the terms of overland trade. Only with the rapid transformation in the technology of seapower in the sixteenth century did sea routes overtake those on land as major carriers of intercontinental trade.

During the nineteenth and early twentieth centuries the British developed a lingering fear that the Russians would link overland routes with port facilities along the Persian Gulf. They felt threatened by what they saw as Russia's momentum southward, through Afghanistan to the Indian Ocean. Similar trepidations galvanized a Pakistani government and its foreign friends to secure land access along the Makran Coast of Baluchistan.

The Great Game asserted in strong terms this connection between land and sea routes. It may be described, in fact, as a contest over land routes for the sake of the open ocean. Russia's rapid railroad advance across Central Asia, in the direction of Afghanistan, kept the British pressing forward, northward, and westward, on their guard for half a century. Afghanistan, too, in the nineteenth century, and in the twentieth, has promoted the idea of a land corridor across Baluchistan—which Afghan proponents of Pakhtunistan argue, will provide the future state with valuable access to the sea. Even the Karakoram Highway, which runs many thousands of miles away from Beijing and Karachi, has been described by Soviet and Indian writers as the way by which the Chinese mean to reach the Indian Ocean.

The relationship to sea routes has long been a factor in evaluating the importance of land routes for security. This point has been apparent in the impact of contemporary Soviet routing policies in the region. Indeed, as the control of the sea lanes and points of strategic egress has become increasingly pertinent to the global military rivalry between today's superpowers, changes in the pattern, structure, and direction of land routes (and their acquisition and control) have also become of more immediate concern. The Soviet occupation of Afghanistan, for example, altered the strategic situation in the entire northwestern quadrant of the Indian Ocean.

The consequences of an absence of access to sea routes and a reliance on land routes beyond the territories of the state are nowhere more visible than in the interaction between the security and development policies of land-locked states. Their territorial politics, economic transactions, and military security are highly dependent on their relationships with neighboring transit states. As the history of these Asian borderlands shows, the search for access to the sea, in the guise of Pakhtunistan to the south, and new routes to the north, toward the Soviet Union and its seaports, which the Afghans needed for economic development, ultimately robbed them of their independence. The right of transit to the Arabian Sea trade routes that began at the port of Karachi (from Kabul or Kandahar) was used not merely as an economic but as a political and a military weapon by Pakistan in its arguments with Afghanistan. This manipulation of transit trade had critical consequences for South, Central and West Asia. In the northeastern mountains, Nepal was forced to surrender control of its foreign and security policies to New Delhi because its economic lifelines run southward to the Indian Ocean port of Calcutta.

In assessing the contemporary meaning of land routes for developing states, one must consider not only the sea but also the skies. The Soviets, during their tenure in Afghanistan, rapidly improved its airports and military airfields and expanded their use of helicopters and swift aerial attack, thereby improving their capacity to project power across Afghan land routes and sea lanes in the region. Inside Baluchistan the Pakistanis embarked on an ambitious scheme of airport construction along the Makran Coast. Such advances in aerial transportation have now reached the most distant parts of the region. Movement through the air is providing an active supplement to movement across the earth's surface. But like modern technologies of communication such as radios and space satellites, air power has not diminished the primary and unique relevance of roads and railroads to the developing world. Roads support the daily interactions of developing countries and make up the connective tissue of their societies. They remain pivotal in the theater of development and in the theater of war. Travel and transport across land in times of conflict, though slower, is also cheaper than by air. Trucks are more readily replaced than expensive air transport planes. And as the invasion of Afghanistan demonstrated, while air power is profitable for a surprise attack, and seeking out the mujahideen, land lines of communication remain essential to consolidate an invasion, and support occupying as well as retreating forces.

Finally, the study of Asian routes reveals certain ironies that illuminate the essentially ambiguous nature of infrastructural aid for both donor states and recipient states or regions. Foreign development aid is usually colored by the broader political, military, or economic interests of the donor state. Still, the mix of motives—to foster security or development—is nowhere more evident than in the sphere of infrastructure. Such development aid projects (which are particularly important to Third World states in the early stages of economic progress, which possess rugged topography, inadequate resources, or remote, unexploited peripheries) can readily support the regional or international security requirements of the donor while they address the domestic needs of the recipient state. Soviet road building in Afghanistan, Chinese road building in Pakistan, and Indian road building in Nepal and Bhutan supply vivid testimony to the primacy of political and strategic interests in the provision of foreign aid.

A state may have many motives for giving or receiving infrastructural aid. It may provide such aid for reasons of geopolitics, for the projection of power, to enhance the security of an ally, to increase its economic or political dependence on the donor, as a form of stadium diplomacy, for the socioeconomic development of the recipient, or for the purposes of trade. It may consider denying assistance because of a potential threat from a competing state (often the recipient's neighbor), or if the political costs are too high, or if the project is of no strategic value to itself.

The recipient state may have as many motives as the donor. A state may desire or accept such assistance for reasons of its own internal security requirements, to improve its external military posture, to promote a policy of alliance, to reduce its economic and political dependence on another state, or to promote political integration, social or economic development, and trade. It may deny itself infrastructure if it views the project as detrimental to its internal security; as increasing the threat from an external source (usually a neighbor); if the political costs of accepting aid are too high; if its share of the financial costs are too high; and if it has inadequate resources for the task. The interests and objectives of donor and recipient in a specific project may not coincide.

Routes have many different real or perceived functions for a state through whose territory they run, and for a state (particularly a donor state) toward which they run. The cases studied in this book disclose a variety of unintended or unanticipated consequences of routing policy, in the areas of both security and development. The most striking of these consequences, of course, were the repercussions of Soviet route building inside Afghanistan. In that case, the aid of the donor state was eventually turned against the recipient. What was intended as a boon to development culminated in a disaster for security. It is worth noting that infrastructural aid may also be turned against the donor state. Examples of such a reversal are legion in the Third World: the Soviet and Vietnamese use of American-built facilities in Vietnam, for instance, or the Soviet use of such facilities in Ethiopia. In the region I have studied, a similar fate befell American road-building efforts in Afghanistan; and should the Indians ever move beyond the Siachin Glacier toward the Northern Areas, the Chinese could discover a similar vulnerability regarding the Karakoram Highway. The road to hell is not the only road paved with good intentions. Moreover, unintended and unanticipated consequences nicely illustrate the difficulties confronting policy makers who wish to distinguish neatly between aid for security and aid for development. At the most advanced technological level, this difficulty presents itself intractably in the case of nuclear reactors. My case studies demonstrate, however, that the problem exists even at the oldest and most prosaic level, that of land routes and transport infrastructure.

If this book is pledged to a single, over-arching idea, it is the idea of the persistent autonomy of geography in the politics of the developing world—the idea of the independence of routes as a category of analysis and as a carrier of history. I have tried to warn throughout of the risk of a geographical reductionism. Obviously, the broad and complicated questions of state and regional politics, and of security and development, cannot be narrowed merely to questions of geography, of arterial geography in particular. Nor can geopolitical explanations predict the future in any region of the world. Still, there remains a fundamental sense in which the risk for scholars and strategists is not geographical reductionism, but its opposite—the failure fully to appreciate geographical features such as routes, which are irreducible to their various political, economic, military, geographical, and ideational contexts. Elements of geography should not be merely preludes to analysis. They are, or deserve to become, vital and integral components of political analysis.

Routes function in many spheres. Military planners have often remarked upon their purpose and value as logistical arteries; transportation economists note their contribution to specific patterns of growth and distribution; and social engineers attend to their role in the improvement of educational or electoral amenities. Routes are essentially overdetermined in their use and their meaning. Yet these discrete qualities, functions, and disciplines notwithstanding, I argue that routes are in some sense larger than any specific sphere of state policy. Over and above their importance in a state's specific domestic and foreign policies, its security and development policies, and over and above their relevance to particular disciplines or subdisciplines, routes stubbornly retain a more substantial importance. They constitute a fundamental and essential condition in developing countries, enabling or disabling through their presence or their absence. Braudel calls distance "the first enemy" of communication, of administration, of commerce, and of economic organization in the Mediterranean region during the sixteenth century.[4] Throughout the developing world today, routes challenge this enemy and sometimes defeat it. They are, for that reason, primary agents of human history.

Such an approach to state and regional politics can be applied to other developing regions. One such area is Southern Africa. Here the political, diplomatic, and military attempts of the local states to effect change internally and regionally have been severely hampered by their traditional dependence on South Africa's routes, communication facilities, and ports. In recent years, in fact, a cornerstone of regional cooperation between the states banded together in the Organization of Front Line States (Angola, Mozambique, Zimbabwe, Zambia, Botswana, and Tanzania) has been the development of transportation routes to circumvent South African territory and forge direct links among themselves. A road and rail map of their historical economic dependence on South African routes and their contemporary endeavors to escape that dependence tells us a good deal about the ties that bind them to their southern neighbor; about the manner in which such ties have circumscribed the political, economic, and military measures they can afford; and about their prospects for internal integration and development.

In the developing world, where colonial rule has been and gone, leaving a legacy of arbitrary territorial division and a physical infrastructure tailored to imperial rivalries rather than local economic and political needs, where diverse peoples and forms of social organization have been bound together, with few resources, little technology, and on terrain that militates against movement, the story of routes and antiroutes can map the ways in which states trade off their interests in power and in progress, and can trace the course of the rivalries and partnerships that shape a region's geopolitics.

Notes

Chapter 1   Routes and States

1. Jean Gottmann, *The Significance of Territory* (Charlottesville: University of Virginia Press, 1973), 27.

2. George N. Curzon, *Frontiers* (1908; rpt. Westport, Conn.: Greenwood, 1976), 23–26.

3. See Jean Gottmann, "The Political Partitioning of Our World: An Attempt at Analysis," *World Politics* 4 (July 1952), 515.

4. Indeed, routes need not have a concrete physical manifestation at all—they may be intangible channels of access.

5. After the 1745 Scottish rebellion, for example, the British initiated road-building projects in the Scottish Highlands. See William H. McNeill, *The Pursuit of Power: Technology, Armed Forces and Society since A.D. 1000* (Chicago: University of Chicago Press, 1982), 163.

6. Alan K. Henrikson, Fletcher School of Law and Diplomacy, Tufts University, letter to the author, 28 May 1985.

7. For an interesting discussion of the symbolic, "cosmological," or "supernatural" qualities attached to ideas of geographical distance (and exclusionary, social, and moral distance) see Mary W. Helms, *Ulysses' Sail: An Ethnographic Odyssey of Power, Knowledge, and Geographical Distance* (Princeton: Princeton University Press, 1988).

8. Gottmann, *Significance of Territory*, 9.

9. McNeill, *Pursuit of Power*, 57.

10. Brooks Adams, *The New Empire* (1902; rpt. New York: Bergman, 1969), 2.

11. See D. I. N. Bovill, I. G. Heggie, and J. L. Hine, *A Guide to Transport Planning within the Roads Sector for Developing Countries* (London: Ministry of Overseas Development, 1978), 1; also see Rolf Hofmeier, "The Political Economy of Transport Projects," *Intereconomics* 2 (March–April 1980), 95.

12. See, for example, Robert H. T. Smith, "The Development and Function of Transport Routes in Southern New South Wales, 1866–1930," *Australian Geographic Studies* 2 (April 1964), 47–65.

13. See "Supporting U.S. Strategy for Third World Conflict," *Report of the Regional Conflict Working Group Submitted to the Commission on Integrated Long-Term Strategy*, The Pentagon, Washington, D.C., June 1988, pp. 36–37; and "Commitment to Freedom: Security Assistance as a U.S. Policy Instrument in the Third World," *A Paper by the Regional Conflict Working Group Submitted to the Commission on Integrated Long-Term Strategy*, The Pentagon, Washington, D.C., May 1988, pp. 45, 51.

14. Edward N. Luttwak, *The Grand Strategy of the Roman Empire* (Baltimore: Johns Hopkins University Press, 1976), 67.

15. McNeill, *Pursuit of Power*, 9, 243.

16. Geoffrey Kemp and John Maurer, "The Logistics of Pax Britannica: Lessons for America," paper presented at a conference on Projection of Power: Perspectives, Perceptions, and Logistics, Fletcher School of Law and Diplomacy, Tufts University, Medford, Mass., April 1980, p. 8.

17. Martin Ira Glassner, "Transit Rights for Land-Locked States and the Special Case of Nepal," *World Affairs* 140 (Spring 1978), 304–305.

18. See Kemp and Maurer, "Logistics of Pax Britannica," 5–7.

19. A road has also been called as much an educational institution as a business venture, particularly in "underdeveloped countries where road communications are lacking. . . . It is only through a reasonably good system of main highways and rural roads, particularly in a country such as Pakistan, where nearly 90 percent of the population lives in villages, that mobile libraries, public health units, livestock control units and agricultural services can be made available to the people." Accordingly, "in road projects the intangible and indirect benefits so outweigh the tangible ones" that it would be "unfair to consider their merits from a purely cost standpoint." Pakistan Road Engineers Association, "The Economic and Social Justifications for Road Development in Pakistan," in International Road Federation, *Roads—Social, Economic and Financial Aspects* (Washington, D.C.: International Road Federation, 1973), 22.

20. Norman J. G. Pounds, *Political Geography*, 2d ed. (New York: McGraw-Hill, 1972), 12.

21. Richard Hartshorne, "The Functional Approach in Political Geography," *Annals of the Association of American Geographers* 40 (June 1950), 104. See also Martin I. Glassner and Harm de Blij, eds., *Systematic Political Geography*, 3d ed. (New York: John Wiley, 1980), 477.

22. Stein Rokkan, "Cities, States, and Nations: A Dimensional Model for the Study of Contrasts in Development," in S. N. Eisenstadt and Rokkan, eds., *Building States and Nations: Models and Data Resources*, vol. 1 (Beverly Hills: Sage, 1973), 74–75.

23. See Saul B. Cohen, *Geography and Politics in a World Divided* (New York: Random House, 1963), 16–19.

24. For the meanings of geopolitics see Harold Sprout, "Geopolitical Hypotheses in Technological Perspective," *World Politics* 15 (January 1963), 187–212. Ladis K. D. Kristof, "The Origin and Evolution of Geopolitics," *Journal of Conflict Resolution* 4 (March 1960), 15–52; and Robert Strausz-Hupé, *Geopolitics: The Struggle for Space and Power* (1942; rpt. New York: Arno, 1972), 1–7.

25. Colin S. Gray, *The Geopolitics of the Nuclear Era: Heartland, Rimland and the Technological Revolution* (New York: Crane Russak, 1977), 5.

26. Halford J. Mackinder, *Democratic Ideals and Reality*, 2d ed. (New York: Holt, 1942), 109.

27. Nicholas J. Spykman, "Geography and Foreign Policy I," *American Political Science Review* 32 (February 1938), 34, 36–37, 40.

28. See the argument in Colin S. Gray, "Across the Nuclear Divide—Strategic Studies, Past and Present," *International Security* 2 (Summer 1977), 24–46.

29. John Herz, "Rise and Demise of the Territorial State," *World Politics* 9 (July 1957), 473–93; in 1968 Herz reformulated his ideas in "The Territorial State Revisited—Reflections on the Future of the Nation-State," *Polity* 1 (January 1968), 11–34. See also Harold Sprout and Margaret Sprout, "Geography and International Politics in an Era of Revolutionary Change," in W. A. Douglas Jackson, ed., *Politics and Geographic Relationships* (Englewood Cliffs, N.J.: Prentice-Hall, 1964), 42.

30. Albert Wohlstetter, "Illusions of Distance," *Foreign Affairs* 46 (January 1968): 242–255, 244, 248. A brilliant work on the interaction between technology, geography, and political and military interests is Carlo M. Cippola, *Guns, Sails and Empires: Technological Innovation and the Early Phases of European Expansion, 1400–1700* (New York: Pantheon, 1965). See also *Discriminate Deterrence: Report of the Commission on Integrated Long-Term Strategy* (Washington, D.C. USGPO, 1988), whose deliberations were cochaired by Albert Wohlstetter and Fred C. Iklé. The chapter "Wars on the Soviet Periphery" discusses American-Soviet capabilities and competition for access to air and land bases.

31. Geoffrey Kemp, "The New Strategic Map," in Uri Ra'anaan, Robert L. Pfaltzgraff, Jr., and Kemp, eds., *Arms Transfers to the Third World: The Military Buildup in Less Industrial Countries* (Boulder, Colo.: Westview, 1978), 5.

32. See "Supporting U.S. Strategy for Third World Conflict."

33. Zulfiqar Ali Bhutto, *The Myth of Independence* (London: Oxford University Press, 1969), 11.

34. One writer has argued that "despite their obvious importance for other areas of development policy, military acquisition and production programs have been largely overlooked" by development scholars and practitioners. Janne E. Nolan, *Military Industry in Taiwan and South Korea* (London: Macmillan, 1986), 3.

35. F. E. I. Hamilton, "Location Factors in the Yugoslav Iron and Steel Industry," *Economic Geography* 40 (January 1964), 60.

36. Extract from the "United Nations Report of the Group of Experts on the Economic and Social Consequences of Disarmament" (1972), in Richard Jolly, ed., *Disarmament and World Development* (New York: Pergamon, 1978), 126; Independent Commission on Disarmament and Security Issues, *Common Security: A Blueprint for Survival* (New York: Simon & Schuster, 1982). The Commission argues (p. 7) that competitive arms acquisition policies of developing countries result in the diversion to the military sector of scarce resources required for development. The econometric study used in the Commission's report—a survey of sixty-nine countries during the 1950s and 1960s—concluded that "increases in military spending had significant negative effects on the rates of growth" (p. 91). See also Nicole Ball, "Defense Expenditures and Economic Growth: A Comment," *Armed Forces and Society* 11 (Winter 1985), 297.

37. See Emile Benoit, *Defense and Economic Growth in Developing Countries* (Lexington, Mass.: D. C. Heath, 1973), 19.

38. P. C. Frederiksen and Robert E. Looney, "Defense Expenditures and Economic Growth in Developing Countries," *Armed Forces and Society* 9 (Summer 1983), 643. (This study was criticized by Ball in her "Defense Expenditures"); David K. Whynes, *The Economics of Third World Military Expenditure* (Austin: University of Texas, 1979), 143; and A. F. Mullins, Jr., *Born Arming: Development and Military Power in New States* (Stanford: Stanford University Press, 1987), 106, 118.

39. Syed Shaukat Ali, "Defence and Development," *Defence Journal,* January–February 1984, pp. 37, 38.

40. K. Subrahmanyam, *Defense and Development* (Calcutta: Minerva Associates, 1973), 4, 30, 31.

41. Stephanie Neuman, "A Talking Paper: The Relationship between Military Expenditures and Socio-Economic Development," paper presented at the conference on Security and Development in the Indo-Pacific Arena, Fletcher School of Law and Diplomacy, Tufts University, Medford, Mass., April 1978, p. 27.

42. Stephanie Neuman, "Security, Military Expenditures and Socio-Economic De-

velopment: Reflections on Iran," *Orbis* 22 (Fall 1978), 589, 590. Benoit, too, comments on the potentially favorable effects of military spending on growth: "Dual-use infrastructure, such as roads, airfields, ports, and communications networks, . . . may sooner or later be used in part by civilians, especially in outlying areas." Benoit, *Defense and Economic Growth*, 17. And Subrahmanyam (*Defense and Development*, 20) has taken the problem of routes to demonstrate the importance of a holistic approach to the making of policy: "Vast sums of money have been spent on the construction of border roads; but again because they are treated as non-plan expenditure, adequate attention has not been paid to evaluating the ancillary economic development that can be undertaken along these roads and to the optimisation of the returns from these investments. Similarly, our troops are deployed in sparsely populated frontier areas, most of which are inhabited by tribal populations. The development of cantonments for our forces and the urbanisation and integration of the tribal populations in the mainstream of national life can be viewed as an integrated problem."

43. Neuman, "Security, Military Expenditures," 570, 584, 594. Neuman maintains (p. 570) that analyzing "the percentage of GNP spent on the military is an inconclusive test of military spending."

44. An intensive analysis of a few cases may be more instructive than a superficial analysis of many. This view, held by Arendt Lijphart ("Comparative Politics and Comparative Method," *APSR* 65 [September 1971], 685), is commended by Alexander George in "Case Studies and Theory Development: The Method of Structured, Focused Comparison," in Paul Gordon Lauren, ed., *Diplomacy: New Approaches in History, Theory, and Policy* (New York: Free Press, 1979). George argues that historical, comparative case studies are neither competitive with nor a substitute for quantitative analysis. The methods are complementary. Still, the former should precede the latter (p. 61).

45. In Chapter 4, I discuss briefly the routes of Nepal, Bhutan, and Sikkim as they relate to China's southwestern routing strategy and Sino-Indian competition in the Himalayan borderlands.

46. Alastair Lamb, *Asian Frontiers: Studies in a Continuing Problem* (New York: Praeger, 1968), 17.

47. The geographical material in this section is based on W. G. East, O. H. K. Spate, and Charles E. Fisher, *The Changing Map of Asia*, 5th ed. (London: Methuen, 1971); Spate, *India and Pakistan*, 2d ed. (London: Methuen, 1957); George B. Cressey, *Crossroads: Land and Life in Southwest Asia* (Chicago: J. B. Lippincott, 1960); and A. Tayyeb, *Pakistan: A Political Geography* (London: Oxford University Press, 1966).

Chapter 2   Baluchistan and Its Environs

1. The term "Baluchistan" here refers to those Baluch territories which conform to the provincial boundaries of Baluchistan in Pakistan. References to Baluch lands other than those within Pakistan (for example, in Iran) so specify. Pakhtuns are also called Pushtuns or Pathans.

2. An estimated 100,000 Baluch live in Soviet Turkmenistan.

3. Richard F. Nyrop, ed., *Pakistan: A Country Study* (Washington, D.C.: USGPO, 1984), 93.

4. Oskar H. K. Spate and A. T. A. Learmonth, *India and Pakistan: A General and Regional Geography*, 3d ed. (London: Methuen, 1967), 480.

5. Imperial Gazetteer of India, Provincial Series, *Baluchistan* (1908; rpt. Lahore: Oriental Publishers, 1976), 10; Spate and Learmonth, *India and Pakistan*, 482.

6. Thomas Hungerford Holdich, *The Indian Borderland* (London: Methuen, 1901), 10. For the climate in these parts, see George P. Tate, *The Frontiers of Baluchistan* (1909; rpt. Lahore: East & West Publishing, 1976), 162–175.

7. Quoted in *Pakistan: Past and Present* (London: Stacey International, 1977), 154.

8. For Alexander's disaster-ridden incursion into Baluchistan see Donald W. Engels, *Alexander the Great and the Logistics of the Macedonian Army* (Berkeley: University of California Press, 1978), 110–118.

9. See Mohammed Sardar Khan Baluch, *History of the Baluch Race and Baluchistan* (Quetta: Gosh-e-Adab, 1977), 62, 230, and Imperial Gazetteer, *Baluchistan*, 12.

10. For a sampling of the diverse theories about the origins of the Baluch see Sardar Khan Baluch, *History of the Baluch Race*; M. Longworth Dames, *The Baloch Race: A Historical and Ethnological Sketch* (London: Royal Asiatic Society, 1904); and Richard N. Frye, "Remarks on Baluchi History," *Central Asiatic Journal* 4 (1961), 44–50. For the theory that the Baluch come from Aleppo see Mir Khuda Bux Bijarani Marri Baloch, *Searchlight on Baloches and Balochistan* (Karachi: Royal Book, 1974), 11.

11. Brian Spooner, "Tribal Ideal and Political Reality in a Cultural Borderland: Ethnohistorical Problems in Baluchistan" (1978), discussed in Selig S. Harrison, *In Afghanistan's Shadow: Baluch Nationalism and Soviet Temptations* (New York: Carnegie Endowment for International Peace, 1981), 19–20. I am grateful to this excellent work by Harrison—especially the interviews he conducted—for data on Iranian and Pakistani Baluchistan during the 1970s. Sardar Khan Baluch, *History of the Baluch Race*, 72, 86. In 1758 Nasir Khan did defeat the Afghans in battle, and for nearly a century afterward Kalat (established in 1686) was virtually its own master. Still, even during this period of "self-rule" the writ of Kalat remained confined to the northern parts of Baluchistan and remained only "nominal" beyond.

12. Imperial Gazetteer, *Baluchistan*, 51, 56, 57.

13. The potential for a Russian advance across Afghanistan towards Baluchistan was a central consideration in British defense policy along the Baluch frontier. This consideration I discuss in Chapter 3. For an interesting examination of the concept of "mental map" or "cognitive framework" in its relationship to policy making, see Alan K. Henrikson, "The Geographical 'Mental Maps' of American Foreign Policy Makers," *International Political Science Review* 1 (1980), 495–530. Henrikson defines a "mental map" as "an ordered but continually adapting structure of the mind—alternatively conceivable as a process—by reference to which a person acquires, codes, stores, recalls, reorganizes, and applies, in thought or action, information about his or her large-scale geographical environment, in part or in its entirety" (p. 498).

14. In an oft-quoted remark, Curzon referred to Persia as a critical piece on a "chessboard upon which is being played out a game for the dominion of the world." Curzon, *Persia and the Persian Question*, 2 vols. (1892; rpt. New York: Barnes & Noble, 1966), 1:3–4. See also Firuz Kazemzadeh, *Russia and Britain in Persia, 1864–1914: A Study in Imperialism* (New Haven: Yale University Press, 1968), 156.

15. Firuz Kazemzadeh, "Russian Imperialism and Persian Railways," in Hugh Mclean, Martin E. Malia, and George Fischer, eds., *Russian Thought and Politics*, Harvard Slavic Studies 4 (Cambridge: Harvard University Press, 1957), 358. I am indebted to this fine article for material on Russian attitudes toward Persian railways prior to World War I.

16. Kazemzadeh, I. A. Zinov'ev, the director of the Asiatic Department, and Russian Foreign Ministry official quoted in "Russian Imperialism and Persian Railways," 362; also see 279, 359, 363.

17. Memorandum quoted in Kazemzadeh, "Russian Imperialism and Persian Railways," 371–372; also see 373.

18. Curzon, *Russia in Central Asia in 1889 and the Anglo-Russian Question* (1889; rpt. New York: Barnes & Noble, 1967), 377. For British views see Valentine Chirol, *The Middle Eastern Question; or, Some Political Problems of Indian Defence* (London: John Murray, 1903), 287–289.

19. Curzon, *Russia in Central Asia*, 379–380. For Russian objections see Kazemzadeh, *Russia and Britain in Persia*, 592, and Chirol, *The Middle Eastern Question*, 287.

20. See the excellent study by Edward Mead Earle, *Turkey, the Great Powers and the Bagdad Railway* (New York: Macmillan, 1923), 71, 75. For quote see Chirol, *The Middle Eastern Question*, 288.

21. See Briton Cooper Busch, *Britain and the Persian Gulf, 1894–1914* (Berkeley: University of California Press, 1967), chap. 4.

22. Earle, *Bagdad Railway*, 75.

23. Paul Rohrbach quoted in ibid., 128.

24. The views of the Russian military are in Kazemzadeh, *Russia and Britain in Persia*, 593; for Curzon's policies see Earle, *Bagdad Railway*, 198.

25. Earle, *Bagdad Railway*, 198–199, 264.

26. Olaf Caroe, *Wells of Power: The Oilfields of South-Western Asia* (London: Macmillan, 1951), xvi, xvii, 32.

27. See Ainslee T. Embree, "Editor's Introduction" (xvii) and "Pakistan's Imperial Legacy" (37–40), in Embree, ed., *Pakistan's Western Borderlands: The Transformation of a Political Order* (Durham, N.C.: Carolina Academic Press, 1977). For imperial frontier dilemma, see ibid., 38. On Sir Robert Sandeman's career see Imperial Gazetteer, *Baluchistan*, 1, 19. Also see Caroe, *The Pathans, 550 B.C.–A.D. 1951* (London: Macmillan, 1951), 376–378.

28. Quotation from Caroe, *The Pathans*, 378. Also see the leftist writer Aijaz Ahmed, "The National Question in Baluchistan," in Feroz Ahmed, ed., *Focus on Baluchistan and the Pushtoon Question* (Lahore: People's Publishing, 1975), 20; Inayatullah Baloch, "Afghanistan-Pashtunistan-Baluchistan," *Aussenpolitik* 31 (3d Quarter 1980), 294; and Imperial Gazetteer, *Baluchistan*, 70.

29. Holdich, *Indian Borderland*, 49. See also C. Collin Davies, *The Problem of the North-West Frontier, 1890–1908*, 2d ed. (London: Curzon Press, 1975), 8–17.

30. Ainslee T. Embree, "Pakistan's Imperial Legacy," in Embree, *Pakistan's Western Borderlands*, 36; for Quetta's status see Chirol, *Middle Eastern Question*, 270; and Mohammad Rizwanullah, *Lonely Guardian of the Khojak Pass* (Rawalpindi: n.p., 1965), 40.

31. See A. L. P. Tucker, *Sir Robert G. Sandeman* (New York: Macmillan, 1921), 49, and Edwin A. Pratt, *The Rise of Rail-Power in War and Conquest, 1833–1914* (London: P. S. King, 1951), 359–365.

32. P. S. A. Berridge, *Couplings to the Khyber* (London: David & Charles, 1969), 136. The railways were built at "immense cost"; by 1905, for example, 481 miles of rail had been laid at a cost of £7.3 million. See Imperial Gazetteer, *Baluchistan*, 54, 56. Also see Chirol, *Middle Eastern Question*, 287–288. The rush to build the routes was so obvious that one of the stations along the route was named "Jhatpat" (Jhutpat) or "Hurry."

33. Imperial Gazetteer, *Baluchistan*, 53, and Government of Pakistan, *Special Development Plan for Baluchistan* (Islamabad, 1980), 2 (hereafter cited as *SDP*). In the 1930s and 1940s progress in road building in Baluchistan was poor, and World War II caught the British with weak communications along their western frontier. See Khalifa Afzal Hussain, *The Development of Roads and Road Transport in Pakistan* (Lahore: Transport Construction Corporation, 1973), 60–61.

34. Brian Spooner, "Tribal Ideal and Political Reality," quoted by Harrison, *In Afghanistan's Shadow*, 20.

35. Sibi had 3 percent urbanization and 6 percent literacy rates, compared to 45.6 percent urbanization and 22.9 percent literacy rates in the Quetta-Pishin district. "Baluchistan," in Ahmed, *Focus on Baluchistan*, 1–3.

36. Shirin Tahir-Kheli, "Defense Planning in Pakistan," in Stephanie G. Neuman, ed., *Defense Planning in Less-Industrialized States* (Lexington, Mass.: D. C. Heath, 1984), 212.

37. In the view of Sardar Ataullah Mengal, a radical leader of the Baluch revolt, Kalat had the same direct relationship with Whitehall as had Nepal. It thus differed from India's other princely states in its arrangements with the British government. The Kalat Assembly initially rejected accession to Pakistan. No one heeded it, and the Baluch, according to Mengal, were forced to join Pakistan. Yet, he said, "we are not going to accept it in our hearts." Sardar Ataullah Mengal, interview with Anthony Mascarenhas, Boreham Wood, England, printed in Foreign Broadcast Information Service (FBIS) South Asia, 10 September 1982, pp. F-2–F-4.

38. Government of Pakistan, *SDP*, 3, and Government of Pakistan, *Report on the Progress Achieved in Baluchistan, 1972–1975* (Lahore, 1975), 59. A brief tour of some Baluch routes during the early 1960s indicated the general condition of transport routes: the roads along the Makran Coast—gradually refurbished after the events of December 1979—were shabby and hazardous. When entering Makran by jeep one was advised to keep extra tires in reserve, since the trip across the "rough unmetalled roads" could cause "these and other parts of your vehicle" to "get out of order." Between the port towns of Gwadar and Pasni the coastal route was described as "difficult to drive as it is not metalled and here and there sand storms obstruct the road." See "Special Section on Baluchistan," *Pakistan Quarterly* 8 (Winter 1963), 53.

39. The Regional Cooperation for Development (RCD), an on-again, off-again venture, was formed by Iran, Turkey, and Pakistan in 1964. Afghanistan did not join. Apart from a score of minor joint-ventures the RCD has had little substantive success, either political or economic.

40. See Sylvia Matheson, *The Tigers of Baluchistan* (London: Arthur Barker, 1967), 64.

41. See Louis Dupree, *Afghanistan* (Princeton: Princeton University Press, 1980), 492.

42. Government of Pakistan, *White Paper on Baluchistan* (Rawalpindi, 1974), 3, 4.

43. See Inayatullah Baloch, "Afghanistan-Pushtunistan-Baluchistan," *Aussenpolitik* 31 (Third Quarter 1980), 300; and Inayatullah Baloch and Hans Frey, "Pakistan and the Problems of Sub-Nationalism," *Journal of South Asian and Middle Eastern Studies* 5 (Spring 1982), 67. For a description of the rise of these movements see Baloch, "Afghanistan-Pushtunistan-Baluchistan," and Harrison, *In Afghanistan's Shadow*, 71–92.

44. See *Foreign Report* (London), 14 February 1973, p. 5, and Lawrence Ziring, "Bhutto's Foreign Policy, 1972–1973," in J. Henry Korsen, ed., *Contemporary Problems of Pakistan* (Leiden: E. J. Brill, 1974), 64.

45. During the Cold War—an era of U.S. land pacts against Soviet expansion—Pakistan had joined SEATO in 1954, by virtue of the location of its eastern wing, and CENTO in 1955, by virtue of the location of its western wing at the junction of West, South, and Central Asia.

46. Quoted in Ziring, "Bhutto's Foreign Policy," 63.

47. To diffuse the potential rebelliousness of the Baluch, the Shah incorporated their lands into the new province of Sistan va Baluchistan as well as into other neighboring provinces.

48. Quoted in Harrison, *In Afghanistan's Shadow*, 158–159. See also p. 98.

49. See ibid., 100, 101. Also see Robert M. Burrell and Alvin J. Cottrell, *Iran, Afghanistan, Pakistan: Tensions and Dilemmas*, Washington Papers vol. 2 (Beverly Hills, Calif.: Sage, 1974), 8.

50. Quoted in Harrison, *In Afghanistan's Shadow*, 97.

51. Quoted in C. L. Sulzberger, "Belief in Crude Reality," *New York Times*, 22 April 1973, and in "The Shah on War and Peace," *Newsweek*, 14 November 1977, p. 70.

52. See Selig S. Harrison, "After the Afghan Coup: Nightmare in Baluchistan," *Foreign Policy* 32 (Fall 1978), 156–57.

53. On 14 May 1973 the Shah and Bhutto issued a joint communiqué in Tehran

which stated they would "resolutely stand by each other in all matters bearing on their national independence and territorial integrity." Quoted in Ziring, "Bhutto's Foreign Policy," p. 64.

54. Burrell and Cottrell, *Iran, Afghanistan, Pakistan,* 16. The RCD Highway starts at Zahedan in Iran and enters Pakistan at Taftan on the Iran-Pakistan border. It runs 3,215 miles via Dalbadin, Nushki, Quetta, Kalat, Khuzdar, and Bela all the way to Karachi.

55. See Abdur Rahman Pazhwak, *Pakhtunistan: The Khyber Pass as the Focus of the New State of Pakhtunistan* (London: Afghan Information Bureau, 1952). See Chapter 3 below for a discussion of the Pakhtunistan issue.

56. Amin quoted in Harrison, *In Afghanistan's Shadow,* 144; Karmal quoted in Yossef Bodansky, "Soviet Military Involvement in Afghanistan," in Rosanne Klass, ed., *Afghanistan: The Great Game Revisited* (New York: Freedom House, 1987), 273.

57. The British were wont to cite the will of Peter the Great, which reputedly recommended the Russian conquest of India and the Gulf coastline. The relevant article in the will is as follows: "To approach as near as possible to Constantinople and India. Whoever governs there will be the true sovereign of the world. . . . And in the decadence of Persia, penetrate as far as the Persian Gulf, re-establish if it be possible the ancient commerce with the Levant, advance as far as India, which is the depot of the world." Quoted in Percy Sykes, *A History of Persia,* 2 vols. (London: Macmillan, 1921), 245.

58. Both quotes in Inayatullah Baloch, "Afghanistan-Pushtunistan-Baluchistan," 293–294. Also see staff article, "The Soviet Attitude to Pashtunistan," *Central Asian Review* 8 (1960), 310–315. During World War II, the British Post-Hostilities Planning Sub-Committee postulated that the Soviet Union—with its expanding industrial base— would eventually chase Middle Eastern oil and therefore retain an interest in the Gulf coastline. The Soviets, it was anticipated, would show "a permanent interest in the Trans-Persian railways and in the ports of the Arabian Gulf," which would provide them with "access to the sea from Turkestan and Central Asia, thus easing the strain on [their] internal transport system." Quoted in Habibur Rahman, "British Post-Second World War Military Planning for the Middle East," *Journal of Strategic Studies* 5 (December 1982), 51.

59. See Inayatullah Baloch, "Afghanistan-Pushtunistan-Baluchistan," 287; and staff article, "The Baluchis of Pakistan and Persia" (a review of M. G. Pikulin's *Beludzhi* [Moscow, 1959]), *Central Asian Review* 8 (1960), 307.

60. See Anwar H. Syed, *China and Pakistan: Diplomacy of an Entente Cordiale* (Amherst: University of Massachusetts Press, 1974), 48.

61. Mir Ahmed Yar Khan Baluch, *Inside Baluchistan: A Political Autobiography* (Karachi: Royal Book, 1975), 161; *Times* quoted in Norman D. Palmer, "South Asia and the Indian Ocean," in Alvin J. Cottrell and Robert M. Burrell, eds., *The Indian Ocean: Its Political, Economic and Military Importance* (New York: Praeger, 1972), 246–247.

62. Pakistan has accepted Soviet assistance in other areas: the Soviets have provided both plans and expertise for Pakistan's first integrated iron and steel works near Karachi. Construction began in 1976.

63. T. B. Miller, *Soviet Policies in the Indian Ocean Area* (Canberra: Australian National University Press, 1970), 16; and Syed Abdul Quddus, *Afghanistan and Pakistan* (Lahore: Ferozsons, 1982), 172–173; and Syed, *China and Pakistan,* 237.

64. See Shirin Tahir-Kheli, "External Dimensions of 'Regionalism' in Pakistan," *Contemporary Asia Review* 1 (1977), 91.

65. See Syed, *China and Pakistan,* 237, and Geoffrey Jukes, *The Indian Ocean in Soviet Naval Policy,* Adelphi Paper no. 87 (London: International Institute for Strategic Studies, 1972), 3.

66. In February 1975 Bhutto banned the NAP. Its leaders were tried for high treason and jailed.

67. See Robert G. Wirsing, *The Baluchis and the Pathans,* Minority Rights Group Report no. 48 (London: Minority Rights Group, 1981), 11.

68. Quoted in *Keesings Contemporary Archives* (hereafter *Keesings*), 17–23 March 1975, p. 27016.

69. Harrison, "After the Afghan Coup," 139. Khair Buksh Marri, sardar of the 120,000-strong Marri tribe, eventually exiled himself to Kabul where he and some of his supporters have been housed, fed, and trained by the Soviet Union. In the late 1980s he called upon all his followers to leave Baluchistan and migrate to Afghanistan. According to a 1988 report, between 9,000 and 15,000 tribesmen have done so. See *Far Eastern Economic Review* (Hongkong), 14 January 1988, p. 30. A Soviet withdrawal from Afghanistan, however, might adversely affect the plans of these Marri Baluch.

70. *Far Eastern Economic Review,* 28 May 1976, p. 33.

71. See Satish Kumar, *The New Pakistan* (New Delhi: Vikas Publishing, 1978), 183.

72. See *Far Eastern Economic Review,* 28 May 1976, pp. 34–38.

73. For guerilla tactics see ibid. Marri quoted in Harrison, *In Afghanistan's Shadow,* 47. See also ibid., 167, 172–173.

74. Among the most prominent Baluch leaders in opposition were Khair Buksh Marri, Ghaus Buksh Bizenjo, and Ataullah Mengal. Baluch student organizations were also participants in the anticenter movement.

75. Quoted in Harrison, *In Afghanistan's Shadow,* 156.

76. See Government of Pakistan, *Report on Progress,* 60.

77. Government of Pakistan, *White Paper,* 33. In the 1960s the investment in Baluchistan amounted to less than Rs. 30 million each year ($1.7 million); in 1972–73 alone, however, Bhutto's government spent Rs. 120 million ($6.5 million). The sum rose to Rs. 180 million ($10.0 million) in 1973–74 and to Rs. 210 million ($11.7 million) the following year. Added to these sums were Rs. 150 million ($8.3 million) spent by federal agencies in Baluchistan. (All dollar conversions are at 1988 average rates.)

78. Ibid., 29.

79. Ibid.

80. See L. F. Rushbrook-Williams, *Pakistan under Challenge* (London: Stacey International, 1975), 196.

81. Construction was undertaken in the Marri-Bugti areas on the following routes: the Sibi-Talli Tangi-Kahan road; the Sibi-Mawand-Fazilchel-Kohlu-Barkhan-Rakhni road, which moves on to Dera Ghazi Khan; the Kashmor-Sui-Dera Bugti-Kahan-Fazilchel road; the Bellpat-Lehri road, to be joined with the Sangsila-Dera Bugti road; and roads for the Oil and Gas Development Corporation and other foreign drilling companies: the Mohammad Lath-Dera Bugti-Kahan road, the Barkhan-Spring Brackish road, and another road from Fort Munro to an oil-exploration site in the mountains. Among other road projects undertaken were routes linking Baluchistan to the Punjab and Sind and to Iran. These included the Loralai-Dera Ghazi Khan road and the Bela-Arawan road, which, when completed, would provide a direct link with the Shah's Iran. See Government of Pakistan, *White Paper,* 31.

82. See Robert G. Wirsing, "South Asia: The Baluch Frontier Tribes of Pakistan," in Wirsing, ed., *Protection of Ethnic Minorities: Comparative Perspectives* (New York: Pergamon, 1981), 298.

83. Bhutto's government quoted in Harrison, *In Afghanistan's Shadow,* 166; story retold in Rushbrook-Williams, *Pakistan under Challenge,* 197.

84. Marri quoted in Harrison, *In Afghanistan's Shadow,* 46–47; for Harrison's own assessment, see 167.

85. Harry V. Hodson, *Twentieth Century Empire* (London: Faber & Faber, 1948), quoted in Caroe, *Wells of Power*, 158.

86. See "Defending the Gulf: A Survey," *Economist*, 6 June 1981, p. 10; Buckley quoted in *Far Eastern Economic Review*, 11 December 1981, p. 17.

87. Thomas H. Moorer and Alvin J. Cottrell, "The Search for U.S. Bases in the Indian Ocean: A Last Chance," *Strategic Review* 8 (Spring 1980), 36.

88. Francis Fukuyama, *The Security of Pakistan: A Trip Report* (Santa Monica, Calif.: RAND Corporation, 1980), 31–34. The Rapid Deployment Force (RDF) was renamed the Rapid Deployment Joint Task Force (RDJTF) and in January 1983 again renamed the Central Command (CENTCOM).

89. Quoted in FBIS, *South Asia*, 23 October 1981, p. F–1.

90. Quoted in William S. Ellis, "Pakistan under Pressure," *National Geographic*, May 1981, pp. 685–686.

91. Government of Pakistan, *SDP*, i.

92. Quoted in Harrison, *In Afghanistan's Shadow*, 150.

93. See *Economist*, 12 June 1982, p. 30.

94. Government of Pakistan, *The New Face of Baluchistan* (Islamabad: Pakistan Publications, 1980), 23.

95. Government of Baluchistan, *White Paper on the Budget, 1981–1982* (Quetta, 1982), 82.

96. Government of Pakistan, *SDP*, 15–16. Out of a total projected outlay of Rs. 19,392.26 million ($1.08 billion), with a foreign exchange component of Rs. 4,657.86 million ($258.8 million), Rs. 9,634.77 million ($535.2 million) with a foreign exchange component of Rs. 1,294.70 million ($71.9 million) was to be devoted to the transport and communications sector. The second-highest priority was accorded to the industry and minerals sector at Rs. 5,550 million ($308.3 million) with a foreign exchange component of Rs. 2,630 million ($146.1 million). There followed, in descending order of priority, water, energy, physical planning and housing, education (at Rs. 326.90 million—$18.16 million—with a foreign exchange component of Rs. 43.15 million or $2.4 million), and agriculture. Ibid., 18.

97. For the government's justifications of individual road schemes and a comprehensive listing of proposals, see Government of Pakistan, *SDP*, 37–54.

98. Tahir-Kheli, "Defense Planning in Pakistan," 227.

99. See "Baluchistan Diary III," *Muslim* (Islamabad), 10 July 1984.

100. Ibid.

101. International aid organization, staff report, 25 November 1980, pp. 4–5.

102. *Refugees*, May 1987, p. 29.

103. For example, the creation of access—in this case, airports—became a contentious regional issue. The rapid development of airfields along the coast of Baluchistan has been perceived as part of Pakistan's military integration into the Gulf Cooperation Council (GCC). When General Zia was accused of building bases for the RDF, he responded that, in fact, the construction was associated with the GCC. *Economist*, 12 June 1982, p. 33.

104. *Middle East* (London), 4 April 1983, p. 34; Jamal Rashid "Pakistan and the Central Command," *Middle East Report*, July–August 1986, p. 33; and *Dawn Overseas Weekly*, 17 December 1987, p. 4.

105. "Defending the Gulf," *Economist*, 6 June 1981, pp. 10–11.

106. Fukuyama, *Security of Pakistan*, 29.

107. "Baluchistan Diary III," *Muslim*, 10 July 1984; official quoted in *Los Angeles Times*, 1 December 1985.

108. *Independent* (London), 20 June 1987.

109. "Baluchistan Diary III," *Muslim*, 10 July 1984; aid workers quoted in *Los Angeles Times*, 1 December 1985.

110. *Daily News* (Karachi), weekend ed. 1 October 1987.

111. See Lifschultz, *Far Eastern Economic Review*, 18 December 1986, p. 26.

112. *Washington Times*, 18 February 1988; *Independent*, 20 June 1987; *Observer* (London), 12 July 1987; and Rashid, "Pakistan and the Central Command," 29. According to news reports General George Crist, commander of CENTCOM, has often visited Pakistan to discuss military matters, and the United States has sought better intelligence-gathering facilities inside Baluchistan—near Iran. An article written by Pakistan's *Defence Journal* staff, which made the argument for Pakistan acquiring U.S. AWACs, emphasized the strategic importance of the Makran Coast at the outset: "The lack of sufficient early warning also poses a severe problem in the coastal region of Pakistan. Air defence of Karachi, the country's only sea-port, and the adjoining coastal belt, which is located in one of the most sensitive strategic areas, has also been a source of concern for this reason." See "AWACs for Pakistan: Relative Merits and Employment Issues," *Defence Journal* 13 (1987), 3. Discussing Pakistan's navy, Keith Jacobs has written that "training is also undertaken in Karachi harbor and at Gwadar port facility on two ex-British frigates, which now serve as stationary training and accommodation ships." Jacobs, "Pakistan's Navy," *United States Naval Institute Proceedings*, 110 (March 1984), 149. (According to Lord Curzon, Gwadar had sometimes been "spoken of as the possible maritime terminus of a railway line from Seistan, or British Baluchistan"; *Persia and the Persian Question*, 2:431.)

113. Robert L. Hardgrave, Jr., "Why India Matters," *Asian Affairs: An American Review* 2 (Spring 1984), 47–48. According to Rashid, "Pakistan and the Central Command," 33, the Pakhtun and Baluch politicians, Khan Abdul Wali Khan and Bizenjo, publicly claim that Gwadar is already a U.S. base.

114. Pakistani officials insist there have been no conversations or agreements regarding naval facilities. See Selig S. Harrison, "Fanning Flames in South Asia," *Foreign Policy* 45 (Winter 1981), 91–92, and *New York Times*, 2 June 1981, p. A–14. Indian sources, however, have made much of the bases issue. The left-wing Indian daily *Patriot* wrote that the U.S. wanted access to Gwadar in exchange for weapons aid to Pakistan, and the Indian magazine *Blitz* suggested that America and Pakistan were planning joint operations against Iran. In 1987 India's *National Herald* quoted a Soviet Army publication as asserting that Pakistan had agreed to turn Gwadar into the headquarters for one division of the Central Command. In response to such accusations, the Pakistani Foreign Office categorically denied it would ever agree to grant bases or permit the deployment of foreign forces on Pakistani soil. See *Current Digest of the Soviet Press*, 28 October 1981, p. 18, and FBIS, *South Asia*, 26 January 1982, p. F–1.

115. Minister of Information, Embassy of Pakistan, London, Letter to the Editor, *Independent*, 6 January 1987; State Department position quoted in *Far Eastern Economic Review*, 18 December 1986, p. 27; Raphel quoted in *Dawn*, 16 October 1987; and Japan International Cooperation Agency, "Basic Design Report on The Coastal Fisheries Development Project in the Islamic Republic of Pakistan," Tokyo, March 1980.

116. FBIS, Near East and South Asia, 9 March 1989, 55, 57.

Chapter 3   Afghanistan, Pakistan, and the Soviet Union

1. Of the approximately three million Afghan refugees in Pakistan in 1988, the majority were Pakhtun. They have been settled in camps in the NWFP and Baluchistan, as well as in the Punjab. Some have made their way south to Sind. About two million refugees fled to Iran where they have lived mainly in Zahedan, Birjand, Mashad, and

Tehran. Another 150,000 scattered elsewhere. Pakhtun territory straddles the lands of Afghanistan and Pakistan. Inside Pakistan about two-thirds of Pakhtun lands are incorporated into the North West Frontier Province while the remaining areas are divided, for administrative purposes, into tribal agencies and "special areas." Before 1980 Afghanistan's Pakhtuns occupied between one-fourth and one-third of that country.

2. These data are taken from Louis Dupree, *Afghanistan* (Princeton: Princeton University Press, 1980), 57–65; and Richard F. Nyrop, *Afghanistan: A Country Study* (Washington: USGPO, 1986), xxi, 85–87.

3. This thesis is best argued by W. K. Fraser-Tytler, *Afghanistan: A Study of Political Developments in Central and Southern Asia* (London: Oxford University Press, 1967), 3–46.

4. See David Dichter, *The North West Frontier of West Pakistan: A Study in Regional Geography* (Oxford: Clarendon Press, 1967), 3.

5. Olaf Caroe, *The Pathans, 550 B.C.–A.D. 1957* (London: Macmillan, 1965), 208, 249.

6. Dietmar Rothermund, *Asian Trade and European Expansion in the Age of Mercantilism* (New Delhi: Manohar, 1981), 69.

7. See Valentine Chirol, *The Middle Eastern Question; or, Some Problems of Indian Defence* (London: John Murray, 1903), 336; and Olaf Caroe, *Soviet Empire* (London: Macmillan, 1953), 85–87. Prince Gortchakov's circular, dated 21 November 1864, argued that the Russian position in Central Asia was that of all civilized states which come into contact with half-savage nomad populations. In such cases, "the more civilised state is forced in the interest of the security of its frontier, and its commercial relations, to exercise a certain ascendancy over their turbulent and undesirable neighbours." Such civilized states "have been forced by imperious necessity into this onward march, where the greatest difficulty is to know where to stop." Quoted in Alexis S. Krausse, *Russia in Asia, 1558–1899* (1899; rpt. London: Curzon Press, 1973), 224–225.

8. See David Dicks, *Curzon in India* (New York: Taplinger, 1969), 152, and Krausse, *Russia in Asia*, 152.

9. H. Sutherland Edwards, *Russian Projects against India* (London: Remington, 1885), 56–58.

10. Curzon, *Russia in Central Asia in 1899 and the Anglo-Russian Question* (1899; rpt. New York: Barnes & Noble, 1967), 48–55, and Francis H. Skrine and Edward D. Ross, *The Heart of Asia* (London: Methuen, 1899), 306–319.

11. See Chirol, *Middle Eastern Question*, 335; quotation from Dicks, *Curzon in India*, 165.

12. Edwards, *Russian Projects*, 268.

13. See Ludwig W. Adamec, *Afghanistan, 1900–1923: A Diplomatic History* (Berkeley: University of California Press, 1967), 15, and Curzon, *Russia in Central Asia*, 330.

14. See Vartan Gregorian's excellent history, *The Emergence of Modern Afghanistan* (Stanford: Stanford University Press, 1969), 152.

15. Memorandum by the Secretary, A. J. Balfour, 30 April 1903, quoted in Raju G. C. Thomas, "The Afghan Crisis and South Asian Security," *Journal of Strategic Studies* 4 (December 1981), 418.

16. See Adamec, *Afghanistan*, 29. The Forward School was opposed by the Stationary School, which recommended that no railroads or roads be built toward, or in, Afghanistan: Afghan underdevelopment was seen as the key to British security. The Forward School, however, urged the construction of good routes that could ease the dispatch of troops in the event of an invasion through Afghanistan. See C. Collin Davies, *The Problem of the North-West Frontier, 1890–1908*, 2d ed., (London: Curzon Press, 1975), 3–7.

17. See Gregorian, *Emergence of Modern Afghanistan*, 152. Other suggestions to build

railroads included an Alexandria-Egypt-Karachi line, a Trans-Mesopotamian line, and another Afghan line that would link Quetta and Kandahar to Herat and Mashad. See Arthur C. Yate, "The Proposed Trans-Persian Railway," *Proceedings of the Central Asian Society,* February 1911, p. 7. For the views of *Novoe Vremya* see Adamec, *Afghanistan,* 68.

18. Curzon, *Russia in Central Asia,* 13.

19. Quoted in Gregorian, *Emergence of Modern Afghanistan,* 202.

20. Louis Dupree has argued (like Olaf Caroe) that Ahmed Shah Durrani created an Afghan "empire not a nation-state." *Afghanistan,* xix. Olivier Roy, however, has distinguished between types of states and argued that the Durranis established a "dynastic state." *Islam and Resistance in Afghanistan* (Cambridge: Cambridge University Press, 1986), 13.

21. For a discussion of the Wakhan corridor see Chapter 4.

22. Robert Issaq Bruce, *The Forward Policy* (1900), 2d Pakistani ed. (Quetta: Nisa Traders, 1979), 262.

23. See Leon B. Poullada, "Pushtunistan: Afghan Domestic Politics and Relations with Pakistan," in Ainslee T. Embree, ed., *Pakistan's Western Borderlands: The Transformation of a Political Order* (Durham, N.C.: Carolina Academic Press, 1977), 136. Quotation from Charles Miller, *Khyber: British India's North West Frontier* (New York: Macmillan, 1977), 159.

24. See Mir Sultan Mahomed Khan Munshi, ed., *The Life of Abdur Rahman: Amir of Afghanistan,* 2 vols. (London: John Murray, 1900), 2:150.

25. Roy, *Islam and Resistance,* 14.

26. Gregorian, *Emergence of Modern Afghanistan,* 203.

27. Ibid., 161.

28. Ibid., 143.

29. See Martin van Creveld, *Supplying War: Logistics from Wallenstein to Patton* (Cambridge: Cambridge University Press, 1977), 82.

30. Quotation from Munshi, *Life of Abdur Rahman,* 2:154. See also Chirol, *Middle Eastern Question,* 345, and Adamec, *Afghanistan,* 22.

31. Quoted in Munshi, *Life of Abdur Rahman,* 2:209–210.

32. Habibullah quoted in Adamec, *Afghanistan,* 90, and see Gregorian, *Emergence of Modern Afghanistan,* 204; Rees quoted in Gregorian, *Emergence of Modern Afghanistan,* 203.

33. On Curzon's policy see Davies, *North-West Frontier,* 102. Lord Roberts, in his 7 March 1898 speech to the House of Lords on the subject of the Forward Policy, said: "Throughout the last Afghan war so persistently were we harassed by the tribesmen that the greater number of the troops employed were occupied in keeping open the lines of communication." Quoted in Bruce, *Forward Policy,* 326.

34. On British road building, see Khalifa Afzal Hussain, *The Development of Roads and Road Transport in Pakistan* (Lahore: Transport Construction Corp., 1973), 32.

35. Quoted in Ludwig W. Adamec, *Afghanistan's Foreign Affairs to the Mid-Twentieth Century* (Tucson: University of Arizona Press, 1974), 92.

36. Davies, *North West Frontier,* 186.

37. Lovat Fraser, *India under Curzon and After* (London: William Heinemann, 1911), 75–76.

38. Quoted in Akbar S. Ahmed, *Pukhtun Economy and Society* (London: Routledge & Kegan Paul, 1980), 339.

39. See Mujtaba Razvi, *The Frontiers of Pakistan* (Karachi: National Publishing House, 1971), 149. Leon B. Poullada argues that Afghan promotion of the Pakhtunistan scheme has been rooted in the complex politics of Pakhtun nationalism inside Afghanistan. See "Pushtunistan: Afghan Domestic Politics and Relations with Pakistan," 126–151.

40. See Mujtaba Razvi, "Pak-Afghan Relations since 1947: An Analysis," *Pakistan Horizon* 32 (June 1980), 86.

41. Abdur Rahman Pazhwak, *Pakhtunistan: The Khyber Pass as the Focus of the New State of Pakhtunistan* (London: Afghan Information Bureau, 1952), 8, 26, 27. See also Lawrence Ziring, "Pakistan's Nationalities Dilemma," in Ziring, ed., *The Subcontinent in World Politics* (New York: Praeger Special Studies, 1982), 110.

42. Quoted in Munshi, *Life of Abdur Rahman*, 2:211–212.

43. See Adamec, *Afghanistan*, 103.

44. See G. S. Bhargava, *South Asian Security after Afghanistan* (Lexington, Mass.: Lexington Books, 1983), 68. This deal was being discussed at the same time as Joachim von Ribbentrop was offering the Soviets opportunities "south of the territory of the Soviet Union in the direction of the Indian Ocean."

45. Quotation from *Statesman* (Delhi), 22 June 1947. The British government argued that the lands claimed by the Afghans had been recognised as an integral part of India by the Anglo-Afghan treaty of 1921. See S. M. Burke, *Pakistan's Foreign Policy: An Historical Analysis* (London: Oxford University Press, 1973), 72.

46. See Razvi, *Frontiers of Pakistan*, 146. Quotations from Burke, *Pakistan's Foreign Policy*, 74.

47. Quoted in staff article, "The Soviet Attitude to Pushtunistan," *Central Asian Review* 8 (1960), 313; see also Mohammed Ahsen Chaudhri, "Afghanistan and Its Neighbours," in Mohammed Ayoob, ed., *The Middle East in World Politics* (New York: St. Martin's Press, 1981), 145. For a period following the signing of the Indo-Pakistani peace accord at Tashkent in 1966, the Soviet Union avoided any mention of Pakhtunistan.

48. See *Central Asian Review* staff article "The Soviet Attitude," 314, and *New York Times*, 23 March 1988.

49. See Poullada, "Pushtunistan," 150.

50. See Ghani Mohammed Khan, *Afghanistan's Transit Trade through Pakistan and the Unrecorded Transactions at Landi Kotal*, Board of Economic Enquiry no. 70 (Peshawar: University of Peshawar, 1972), 3, and Dichter, *North West Frontier*, 180.

51. Mohammed Khan, *Afghanistan's Trade*, 25; and Fry, *Afghan Economy*, 224.

52. Quoted in Mike W. Edwards, "An Eye for an Eye: Pakistan's Wild Frontier," *National Geographic*, January 1977, p. 122.

53. Quoted in ibid.; see also Mohammed Khan, *Afghanistan's Trade*, 27.

54. James W. Spain, *The Way of the Pathans*, 2d. ed. (Karachi: Oxford University Press, 1972), 117.

55. See Maxwell Fry, *The Afghan Economy* (Leiden: E. J. Brill, 1974), 216, and Peter G. Franck, *The Economics of Competitive Coexistence: Afghanistan between East and West* (Washington, D.C.: National Planning Association, 1960), 16.

56. Dichter, *North West Frontier*, 179, citing statistics provided by the Central Statistical Office of Pakistan. Note the low figures for 1955 and 1956. Prior to 1955, 80 percent of Afghanistan's exports and 79 percent of its imports moved through Pakistan. By 1977 the average had dropped to 30 percent. For details, see Harvey H. Smith et al., *Area Handbook for Afghanistan*, 4th ed. (Washington, D.C.: USGPO, 1973), 346.

57. See Anthony Hyman, *Afghanistan under Soviet Domination, 1964–81* (New York: St. Martin's Press, 1982), 31, 32.

58. Hasan Ali Shah Jafri, *Indo-Afghan Relations, 1947–1967* (New Delhi: Sterling, 1976), 72.

59. See Louis Dupree, "Afghanistan's Big Gamble, Part II: The Economic and Strategic Aspects of Soviet Aid," *American Universities Field Staff [AUFS] Reports*, South Asia ser. 4, 4 (Hanover, N. H.: AUFS, 1960), 7.

60. Smith et al., *Area Handbook*, 346.

61. See Nyrop, *Afghanistan: A Country Study*, 61–62.

62. Quoted in Leon B. Poullada, "Afghanistan and the United States: The Crucial Years," *Middle East Journal* 35 (1981), 187.

63. U.S. Bureau of Budget, "Analysis of India, Pakistan and Afghanistan and Suggestions for U.S. Policy, 2 December 1959," item 000995 in *The Declassified Documents 1983 Collection* 9, 3 (Washington, D.C.: Carrollton Press, 1983); Ayub Khan quoted in *Pakistan Times* (Lahore), 13 December 1959; and Pakistani government quoted in Louis Dupree, "Pushtunistan: The Problem and Its Larger Implications, Part I," *AUFS Reports*, South Asia ser. 5, 2 (Hanover, N.H.: AUFS, 1961), 10.

64. See Louis Dupree, "Pushtunistan: The Problem and Its Larger Implications, Part II," *AUFS Reports* 5, 3 (Hanover, N.H.: AUFS, 1961), 8. Also see Selig S. Harrison, "George Washington Ayub," *New Republic*, 30 October 1961, p. 7, and Dupree, *Afghanistan*, p. 169.

65. Dupree, "Pushtunistan II," 3, and Mohammed Khan, *Afghanistan's Trade*, 18.

66. John C. Griffiths, *Afghanistan* (New York: Praeger, 1967), 48–49.

67. Peter G. Franck, "Economic Progress in an Encircled Land," *Middle East Journal* 10 (Winter 1956), 58.

68. U.S. Office of the President, "Memo of Conversation between President John F. Kennedy and Prince Naim, 27 September 1962," item 110B in *The Declassified Documents 1977 Collection* 3, 2 (Washington, D. C.: Carrollton Press, 1977).

69. Estimates in 1977 showed that the overland routes through Iran and Turkey cost about $110–125 per ton as compared to about $100 per ton on the Soviet container route. See David Shirreff, "Landlocked Exporters Aim for New Markets," *Middle East Economic Digest*, 27 May 1977, p. 12.

70. Robert M. Burrell and Alvin J. Cottrell, *Iran, Afghanistan, Pakistan: Tensions and Dilemmas*, Washington Papers, vol. 2 (Beverly Hills, Calif.: Sage, 1974), 42.

71. See Henry S. Bradsher, *Afghanistan and the Soviet Union* (Durham: Duke University Press, 1983), 62; Shirin Tahir-Kheli, "Iran and Pakistan: Cooperation in an Area of Conflict," *Asian Survey* 17 (May 1977), 485; and *Asia Yearbook, 1981* (Hongkong: Far Eastern Economic Review, 1981), 99.

72. Neumann quoted in Thomas T. Hammond, *Red Flag over Afghanistan* (Boulder, Colo.: Westview Press, 1984), 26. In 1954 Dulles told Afghanistan's Prince Naim that "extending military aid to Afghanistan would create problems not offset by the strength it would generate. Instead of asking for arms, Afghanistan should settle the Pushtunistan dispute with Pakistan." Quoted in Leon B. Poullada, "The Road to Crisis, 1919–1980: American Failures, Afghan Errors and Soviet Successes," in Rosanne Klass, ed., *Afghanistan: The Great Game Revisited* (New York: Freedom House, 1987), 43.

73. U.S. Joint Chiefs of Staff, "Program of Assistance for General Area of China, 10 January 1950," item 33A in *The Declassified Documents 1979 Collection* 5, 1 (Washington, D.C.: Carrollton Press, 1979).

74. U.S. National Security Council, "U.S. Policy towards Afghanistan, NSC 5409, 1954" item 280B in *The Declassified Documents 1980 Collection* 6, 3 (Washington, D.C.: Carrollton Press, 1980).

75. U.S. National Security Council, "Expansion of Soviet Influence in Afghanistan and U.S. Countermeasures, NSC 5409, 11 May 1956," item 280C in *The Declassified Documents 1980 Collection* 6, 3 (Washington, D.C.: Carrollton Press, 1980).

76. See U.S. Bureau of Budget, item 000995, *Declassified Documents 1983 Collection*.

77. U.S. National Security Council, item 280B, *Declassified Documents 1980 Collection*.

78. Poullada, "Road to Crisis," 50.

79. U.S. Department of State, "Elements in U.S. Policy towards Afghanistan, 27 March 1962," item 65B in *The Declassified Documents 1978 Collection* 4, 1 (Washington, D.C.: Carrollton Press, 1978). For data on U.S. aid and U.S. roads see Dupree, *Afghanistan*, 630–631, and Nancy Peabody Newell and Richard S. Newell, *The Struggle for Afghanistan* (Ithaca: Cornell University Press, 1981), 51.

80. See Louis Dupree, "Red Flag over the Hindu Kush, Part IV," *AUFS Reports*, Asia ser. no. 27 (Hanover, N.H.: AUFS, 1980), 9. See also Bradsher, *Afghanistan and the Soviet*

Union, 29–30; Arthur Bonner, *Among the Afghans* (Durham: Duke University Press, 1987), 268; Nyrop, *Country Study,* 169; and Griffiths, *Afghanistan,* 47.

81. *Financial Times,* 3 September 1986.

82. Dichter, *North West Frontier,* 47.

83. See Adamec, *Afghanistan,* 143.

84. Fry, *Afghan Economy,* 12.

85. See Franck, "Economic Progress," 58.

86. Anthony Arnold, *Afghanistan: The Soviet Invasion in Perspective* (Stanford: Hoover Institution Press, 1985), 34.

87. See U.S. Department of State, "Sino-Soviet Bloc Economic Activities in Underdeveloped Areas 5 March 1956," item 242C in *The Declassified Documents 1977 Collection* 3, 3 (Washington, D.C.: Carrollton Press, 1977).

88. See Gunther Nollau and Hans J. Wiehe, *Russia's South Flank: Soviet Operations in Iran, Turkey and Afghanistan* (New York: Praeger, 1963), 109–110.

89. Patrick J. Reardon, "Modernization and Reform: The Contemporary Endeavor," in George Grassmuck and Ludwig W. Adamec, eds., *Afghanistan: Some New Approaches* (Ann Arbor: University of Michigan Press, 1969), 158.

90. Arnold, *Afghanistan: The Soviet Invasion,* 39; and Griffiths, *Afghanistan,* 45.

91. Smith et al., *Area Handbook,* 33, and Dupree, *Afghanistan,* 644.

92. Nikita Khrushchev, *Khrushchev Remembers,* trans. Strobe Talbott (Boston: Little, Brown, 1974), 298–299.

93. See Dupree, "Afghanistan's Big Gamble, Part II," 19.

94. See Marshall Goldman, *Soviet Foreign Aid* (New York: Praeger, 1967), 117, and Dupree, *Afghanistan,* 645.

95. See Smith et al., *Area Handbook,* 33; Nollau and Wiehe, *Russia's South Flank,* 122; and Goldman, *Soviet Foreign Aid,* 118.

96. Goldman, *Soviet Foreign Aid,* 115. For World Bank report see Basil G. Kavalsky cited in Bradsher, *Afghanistan and the Soviet Union,* 263. Arnold J. Toynbee, *Between Oxus and Jumna* (New York: Oxford University Press, 1961), 4; and Toynbee, "Impressions of Afghanistan and Pakistan's North-West Frontier," *International Affairs* 37 (April 1961), 163.

97. See Arnold, *Afghanistan: The Soviet Invasion,* 39–40.

98. See *Time,* 14 January 1980, p. 15.

99. Dupree, "Red Flag over the Hindu Kush," 6.

100. Quotation from *Pakistan, Bangladesh, and Afghanistan, Quarterly Economic Review,* 1st quarter (London: Economist Intelligence Unit, 1982), 22. See John F. Schroder and Abdul Tawab Assifi, "Afghan Mineral Resources and Soviet Exploitation," in Klass, *Afghanistan: The Great Game Revisited,* 126; and Nyrop, *Country Study,* 170.

101. U.S. Department of State, item 242C, *Declassified Documents 1977 Collection;* and Nollau and Wiehe, *Russia's South Flank,* 127.

102. Louis Dupree, "Afghan Studies," *AUFS Reports,* South Asia ser. 20, 4 (Hanover, N.H.: AUFS, 1976), 9; National Foreign Assessment Center, *Communist Aid Activities in Non-Communist Less Developed Countries, 1979 and 1954–1979* (Washington, D.C.: Central Intelligence Agency, October 1980), 35; and Bradsher, *Afghanistan and the Soviet Union,* 25.

103. See Ludwig W. Adamec, "Germany, Third Power in Afghan Foreign Relations," in Grassmuck and Adamec, *Afghanistan: New Approaches,* 253, and Nollau and Wiehe, *Russia's South Flank,* 106–107.

104. For these figures see Dupree, "Afghanistan's Big Gamble, Part II," 2; Vassili Vassilev, *Policy in the Soviet Bloc on Aid to Developing Countries* (Paris: Organisation for Economic Co-operation and Development, 1969), 68, 96, 97; Dupree, *Red Flag over the Hindu Kush,* 7; and Mohammed Khan, *Afghanistan's Trade,* 15.

105. Vassilev, *Policy in the Soviet Bloc*, 65, 68, 77. Through 1975 Afghanistan remained the third-largest recipient of Soviet aid to developing countries. See Orah Cooper and Carol Fogerty, "Soviet Economic and Military Aid to the Less Developed Countries, 1954–1978," *Fourth Economic Committee of the U.S. Congress*, 10 October 1979, pp. 648–662.

106. By 1975 Afghanistan owned about 10,625 miles of roads, 5,750 of which were all-weather capable. There were, however, only about 1,562 miles of paved highways—from Sheberghan to Herat and Kabul. See Nyrop, *Afghanistan: A Country Study*, 167. On trade see Fry, *Afghan Economy*, 57.

107. See Nyrop, *Afghanistan: A Country Study*, 164.

108. See Fry, *Afghan Economy*, 57, 60, and Robert R. Nathan Associates, "Economic Advisory Services Provided to the Ministry of Planning, Royal Government of Afghanistan, September 1961–June 1972: Final Report," mimeo. (Washington, D.C., July 1972), 46.

109. Donald N. Wilber, ed., *Afghanistan* (New Haven: Human Relations Area Files, 1956), 162.

110. Louis Dupree, "Afghanistan 1977: Does Trade Plus Aid Guarantee Development?" *AUFS Reports*, Asia ser. 21, 3 (Hanover, H.H.: AUFS, 1977), 2.

111. See Dupree, "Red Flag over the Hindu Kush," 7.

112. See Schroder and Assifi, "Afghan Mineral Resources," 111. In 1979–81, for example, the Soviet Union paid $48.00 per thousand cubic meters of Afghan gas when the international price was $114.78. See M. Siddieq Noorzoy, "Long-Term Soviet Economic Interests and Policies in Afghanistan," in Klass, *Great Game Revisited*, 89. Thus Afghanistan was deprived of cheap gas while the Soviet Union's own supplies were freed for export.

113. See Fry, *Afghan Economy*, 56; Dupree, *Afghanistan*, 492; and Reardon, "Modernization and Reform," 160.

114. See discussion in ibid., 155, and in Dupree, *Afghanistan*, 507.

115. Bradsher, *Afghanistan and the Soviet Union*, 122.

116. See ibid., 27; and U.S. Bureau of Budget, item 000995, *Declassified Documents 1983 Collection*.

117. Daoud's views are discussed in Dupree, "Afghanistan's Big Gamble, Part II," 16.

118. Quoted in *Washington Post*, 21 January 1988.

119. See Nyrop, *Afghanistan: A Country Study*, 62.

120. Fred Halliday, *Soviet Policy in the Arc of Crisis* (Washington, D.C.: Institute for Policy Studies, 1981), 88. For a recent example of the opposing interpretation see Yossef Bodansky, "Soviet Military Involvement," 229–285.

121. The Salang Tunnel is an example of the practical relevance of earlier Soviet infrastructural efforts to the 1979 invasion, occupation, and 1988–89 retreat. It was the main land artery of resupply during the war and the site of daily attempts by the mujahideen to disrupt Soviet lines of communication. In 1982 it was also the location of a ghastly accident during which a fire caused the asphyxiation of 700 Soviet troops and 400 Afghan civilians. See *Boston Globe*, 10 November 1982.

122. Interview with Anthony Paul, *Far Eastern Economic Review*, 15 September 1988, p. 47.

123. See *Asiaweek*, 10 August 1986, p. 26, and *Washington Post*, 1 February 1989.

124. For Brzezinski see U.S. House Committee on Foreign Affairs, Subcommittee on Europe and the Middle East, *NATO After Afghanistan* (Washington: USGPO, 1980), 7. On 25 May 1980 an article in *Pravda* argued that all foreign military bases in the Indian Ocean and the Persian Gulf would have to be eliminated before Soviet troops could consider a withdrawal from Afghanistan. It said that both the Afghan and the Soviet governments believed that "in the process of settlement, the present-day situation in

the Indian Ocean and Persian Gulf zone" and the "military-political activity of the states which do not belong to the region" should be considered. Quoted in *Keesings*, 1 August 1980, p. 30383.

125. Dichter, *North West Frontier*, 154. Within the framework of the Pakistani state the tribes have maintained a remarkable degree of independence. Some of their territory is self-administered through tribal assemblies. They still do not pay taxes to the Pakistani government—in fact, some tribes continue to receive subsidies. Political Agents appointed by the governor of the NWFP attempt to enforce a modicum of state-level negotiating and legal authority in tribal territories.

126. *Independent*, 29 July 1987. Between sixty and two hundred persons were reported killed, and at least two villages were destroyed.

127. See *Independent*, 29 July 1987; *Far Eastern Economic Review*, 5 March 1987, pp. 20–22; and *Herald* (Karachi), February 1987, p. 48.

Chapter 4   The Karakoram and Himalayan Borderlands

1. See Roy Wolfe, *Transportation and Politics* (Princeton: D. Van Nostrand, 1963), 15. In the fourteenth century one of the sultans of Delhi did attempt an attack across the Himalayas—with disastrous consequences. This was to be the last large-scale attempt to ford the ranges until the British crossed over into Tibet in 1904. See Alastair Lamb, *Asian Frontiers: Studies in a Continuing Problem*, (New York: Praeger, 1968), 47.

2. See Owen Lattimore, *Pivot of Asia* (1950; rpt. New York: AMS Press, 1975).

3. See Phillip D. Curtin, *Cross-Cultural Trade in World History* (Cambridge: Cambridge University Press, 1984), 93–94.

4. See K. N. Chaudhuri, *Trade and Civilisation in the Indian Ocean* (Cambridge: Cambridge University Press, 1985), 169, 173, and Mario Bussagli, *Central Asian Painting* (New York: Rizzoli, 1979), 13, 14.

5. See Curtin, *Cross-Cultural Trade*, 94; Jack Chen, *The Sinkiang Story* (New York: Macmillan, 1977), 61; and Chaudhuri, *Trade and Civilisation*, 172.

6. S. Shahid Hamid, *Karakuram Hunza* (Karachi: Ma'aref, 1979), 28, and Prithiwas C. Chakravarti, *The Evolution of India's Northern Borders* (London: Asia Publishing House, 1971), 119.

7. See Chen, *Sinkiang Story*, 128–130. For a description of the old cities of Xinjiang see Sir Aurel Stein, *On Central Asian Tracks: A Brief Narrative of Three Expeditions in Innermost Asia and Northwestern China* (1933; rpt. Chicago: University of Chicago Press, 1974).

8. See Lamb, *Asian Frontiers*, 25–38.

9. See Dorothy Woodman's fine history of the region, upon which I have relied, *Himalayan Frontiers: A Political Review of British, Chinese, Indian and Russian Rivalries* (London: Barrie & Rockliff, Cresset Press, 1969), 72.

10. Quoted in ibid.

11. George J. Younghusband, *Indian Frontier Warfare* (London: Kegan Paul, Trench, Trubner, 1898), 6, 7.

12. Charles Ellison Bates, *A Gazetteer of Kashmir* (1872; rpt. New Delhi: Light & Life, 1980), 1.

13. See Alastair Lamb, *The Kashmir Problem: A Historical Survey* (New York: Praeger, 1966), 26.

14. Ibid., 19.

15. Quoted in Woodman, *Himalayan Frontiers*, 87.

16. Edward F. Knight, *Where Three Empires Meet* (1896; rpt. Karachi: Indus, 1978), ix. Lamb has said that from 1935 the Gilgit area "passed right out of the orbit of the Kashmir and Jammu State Government. . . . The British certainly considered that they

had acquired rights over the whole Gilgit region and not merely the leased area" (*Kashmir Problem*, 26). See also P. M. K. Bamzai, *Kashmir and Central Asia* (New Delhi: Light & Life, 1980), 3.

17. Woodman, *Himalayan Frontiers*, 53, 90. The British appointed an "Officer on Special Duty" there, responsible for watching the southern access routes across the mountain passes leading to the three areas. His duties included furnishing "reliable intelligence of the progress of events beyond the Kashmir border." See F. M. Hassnain, *Gilgit: The Northern Gate of India* (New Delhi: Sterling, 1978), 85. Also see India Office Memoranda (25 January 1892 and 24 March 1904) cited in Zubeida Mustafa, "The Sino-Pakistani Border: Historical Aspect," *Pakistan Horizon* 25 (Second Quarter 1972), 44–45.

18. Quoted in Woodman, *Himalayan Frontiers*, 73. See also ibid., 360–363.

19. Lamb, *Asian Frontiers*, 16.

20. See Chakravarti, *Evolution of India's Northern Borders*, 124, Francis Watson, *The Frontiers of China* (London: Chatto & Windus, 1966), 103, and Woodman, *Himalayan Frontiers*, 66.

21. See Woodman, *Himalayan Frontiers*, 18–83.

22. Lattimore, *Pivot of Asia*, 170; M. I. Sladkovsky, *The Long Road: Sino-Russian Economic Contacts from Ancient Times to 1917* (Moscow: Progress, 1974), 228–230; and Hans W. Weigart et al., *Principles of Political Geography* (New York: Appleton-Century-Crofts, 1957), 167.

23. The terms and boundaries applied here to disputed lands refer only to the territorial status quo and do not imply any judgment on their final legal status.

24. See Frederica M. Bunge and Rinn-Shup Shinn, eds., *China: A Country Study* (Washington, D.C.: USGPO, 1981), 46–50.

25. See Ronald Hsia, *The Role of Labor-Intensive Investment Projects in China's Capital Formation* (Cambridge: Center for International Studies, MIT, 1954), 2, 4, 16; also see Wei Min, "Rural Highways," *Beijing Review*, 9 November 1981, p. 26.

26. *The Military Balance* (London: International Institute for Strategic Studies), 143–145, for 1987–88 suggests that the total number of persons under arms is being gradually reduced. In 1983 the Chinese maintained a force level of 4,100,000 (including 300,000 railway construction troops). The construction units were transferred to a civilian ministry, and by 1987 there appeared to have been a total reduction of forces of 730,000.

27. See Wang Zhanyi, "From Coastal Plains to the Roof of the World," *Beijing Review*, 9 November 1981, p. 21; Bunge and Shinn, *China*, 279; and Thomas P. Lyons, "Transportation in Chinese Development, 1952–1982," *Journal of Developing Areas* 10 (April 1985), 321.

28. The relationship between Chinese aid for the Tanzania-Zambia railway and Chinese foreign policy raises these issues; see George T. Yu, "The Tanzania-Zambia Railway: A Case Study in Chinese Economic Aid to Africa," in Warren Weinstein and Thomas H. Henrikson, eds., *Soviet and Chinese Aid to African Nations* (New York: Praeger Special Studies, 1980). Also see Wang Zhanyi, "From Coastal Plains," 23.

29. See Owen Lattimore, *Inner Asian Frontiers of China*, American Geographical Society Research Series no. 21 (London: Oxford University Press, 1940), 171.

30. See W. A. Douglas Jackson, *The Russo-Chinese Borderlands* (Princeton, N.J.: D. Van Nostrand, 1968), 91. In 1979 railroads carried 53.6 percent of total freight and 61.7 percent of total passenger traffic. See Bunge and Shinn, *China*, 278.

31. See Ram Rahul, "Struggle for Central Asia," *International Studies* 18 (January 1979), 7–12. Quotations from *The Sino-Soviet Dispute*, Keesings Research Report no. 3 (New York: Charles Scribner's Sons, 1969), 111, 113.

32. Francis J. Romance, "Modernization of China's Armed Forces," *Asian Survey* 20 (March 1980), 303.

33. *New York Times*, 13 November 1964.

34. This description is based on material in John F. Avedon, *In Exile from the Land of Snows* (New York: Alfred A. Knopf, 1984), 12–13. I have referred to this region, known in China as Xizang, by its old, commonly recognized name, Tibet, throughout.

35. *Beijing Review*, 27 May 1985, quoted in Michael C. van Walt van Praag, *Population Transfer and the Survival of the Tibetan Identity* (New York: U.S.-Tibet Committee, 1986), 18; Avedon, *In Exile from the Land of Snows*, 317; Chinese authorities quoted in Dawa Norbu, "Strategic Development in Tibet," *Asian Survey* 19 (March 1979), 246–247, 251.

36. Avedon, *In Exile from the Land of Snows*, 317; quotation from Chung Chih, *An Outline of Chinese Geography* (Beijing: Foreign Languages Press, 1978), 178–179. See also Norbu, "Tibet," 248–249, and Wang Zhanyi, "From Coastal Plains," 22.

37. Avedon, *In Exile from the Land of Snows*, 233.

38. See Qi Wen, *China: A General Survey* (Beijing: Foreign Languages Press, 1979), 135, and Bunge and Shinn, *China*, 279. However, according to Paul Theroux, who recently traveled the railways of China and tried to reach Lhasa, the Chinese have "abandoned" the line at Golmud in Qinghai because they were "faced by the impenetrable Kunlun Mountains." Theroux, "China Passage," *National Geographic*, March 1988, p. 298; also Theroux, *Riding the Iron Rooster: By Train through China* (New York: G. P. Putnam's Sons, 1988). See also *Far Eastern Economic Review*, 9 April 1987, p. 38.

39. According to Avedon, *In Exile from the Land of Snows*, 315, China's 1982 census put the number of Chinese settlers in Tibet at 96,000, while Tibetan sources estimated that 600,000 Chinese had been systematically settled in Central Tibet alone. For higher figures see van Praag, *Population Transfer*, 10, 13.

40. See Avedon, *In Exile from the Land of Snows*, 318.

41. C. N. Satyapalan, "The Sino-Indian Border Conflict," *Orbis* 8 (Summer 1964), 389, and Alastair Lamb, *Crisis in Kashmir, 1947–1956* (London: Routledge & Kegan Paul, 1966), 93.

42. Alastair Lamb, *The China-India Border* (London: Oxford University Press, 1964), 112. According to Lamb, the "key section of the Aksai Chin, that through which the Chinese road now runs, seems to have remained cartographically within India almost by default" (114).

43. Note given by the Ministry of Foreign Affairs of China to the Embassy of India in China, 26 December 1959, quoted in Woodman, *Himalayan Frontiers*, 254.

44. See Oskar H. K. Spate and A. T. A. Learmonth, *India and Pakistan: A General and Regional Geography*, 3d ed. (London: Methuen, 1967), 445.

45. See Lorne J. Kavic, *India's Quest for Security: Defense Policies, 1947–1965* (Berkeley: University of California Press, 1967), 50–51.

46. Ibid., 51, and Neville Maxwell, *India's China War* (New York: Pantheon, 1970), 87.

47. Quoted in Alfred D. Low, *The Sino-Soviet Dispute: An Analysis of the Polemics* (Cranbury, N.J.: Associated University Presses, 1976), 98, 100, 102.

48. See Jonathan Pollack, "China," in Pollack and Onkar Marwah, eds., *Military Power and Policy in Asian States* (Boulder, Colo.: Westview Press, 1980), 64. Woodman, discussing the war, says: "Communications were far more developed by Chinese than Indians, with roads much nearer the Chinese forward posts giving them greater mobility and regroupment facilities." *Himalayan Frontiers*, 293.

49. Som Dutt, *The Defense of India's Northern Borders*, Adelphi Papers no. 25 (London: International Institute for Strategic Studies, 1966), 8.

50. Maxwell, *India's China War*, 182.

51. Jawaharlal Nehru, "Changing India," *Foreign Affairs* 41 (April 1963), 458–459.

52. See W. Patel, "The Situation of India," *Survival*, November 1962, p. 255.

53. See Mira Sinha, "Nepal's Role in Sino-Indian Relations, 1949–1969," *Institute for Defense Studies and Analysis Journal* (New Delhi), April 1970, p. 461.

54. Martin Ira Glassner, "Transit Rights for Land-locked States and the Special Case of Nepal," *World Affairs* 140 (Spring 1978), 307, 311.

55. George L. Harris et al., *Area Handbook for Nepal, Bhutan, and Sikkim*, 2d ed. (Washington, D.C.: USGPO, 1973), 275.

56. *Keesings*, 11–18 October 1969.

57. See Leo Rose, *Nepal: Strategy for Survival* (Berkeley: University of California Press, 1971), 213; also see Hemen Ray, "Communist China's Strategy in the Himalayas," *Orbis* 11 (Fall 1967), 834.

58. See Harris et al., *Nepal, Bhutan, and Sikkim*, 233; defector quoted in Ray, "Communist China's Strategy," 845; and Rose, *Nepal: Strategy for Survival*, 263.

59. See Aran Schloss, *The Politics of Development: Transportation Policy in Nepal*, Monograph Series no. 22 (Berkeley: University of California, Center for South and Southeast Asia Studies; Lanham, Md.: University Press of America, 1983), 29, 102; also see Rose, *Nepal: Strategy for Survival*, 240.

60. Indian warning quoted in Marcus F. Franda, "North Eastern India, In the Wake of Vietnam," *AUFS Reports* 19, 13 (Hanover, N.H.: AUFS, 1975), 8.

61. Nehru quoted in Mohammed Ayoob, "India and Nepal: Politics of Aid and Trade," *Institute for Defence Studies and Analyses Journal* 3 (October 1970), 129.

62. See Aran Schloss, "Stages of Development and the Uses of Planning: Some Nepali Experiences," *Asian Survey* 23 (October 1983), 1120–1122. Ministry announcement in *Keesings*, 8–15 May 1965, p. 20735.

63. Views on Indian aid quoted in Ayoob, "India and Nepal," 132–133. For the discussion of Nepal's transport planning see the thorough studies by Aran Schloss to which I am indebted, *The Politics of Development* and "Stages of Development," esp. 1119.

64. See Harris et al. *Nepal, Bhutan, and Sikkim*, 351, and see World Bank, *Bhutan: Development in a Himalayan Kingdom*, A World Bank Country Study (Washington, D.C., 1984), 20. For obvious reasons there exists a very limited literature on Bhutan, particularly on development and security issues. This World Bank study is the most exhaustive of its kind.

65. See Harris et al., *Nepal, Bhutan, and Sikkim*, 365; Nehru quoted in World Bank, *Bhutan*, 9; and Harris et al., *Nepal, Bhutan, and Sikkim*, 366.

66. Harris et al., *Nepal, Bhutan, and Sikkim*, 365; see also World Bank, *Bhutan*, 10; and Seymour Scheinberg, "Strategic Developments in Bhutan," *Military Review* 58 (January 1978), 48.

67. See World Bank, *Bhutan*, 71, 73. Bhutan's labor constraints result from the involvement of a large proportion of its work force in family agricultural production. A controversial law of the early 1960s enforced compulsory labor for building roads. In efforts to avert dependence upon India, Tibetan refugees were recruited but found unsuited to the task, and 25,000 Nepali road workers were imported. See Scheinberg, "Strategic Development," op cit, p. 49.

68. For Indian policy towards Sikkim see Lorne J. Kavic, *India's Quest for Security*, 52. See also Harris et al., *Nepal, Bhutan, and Sikkim*, 400.

69. China "absolutely does not recognize India's illegal annexation of Sikkim and firmly supports the people of Sikkim in their just struggle for national independence and sovereignty against Indian expansionists." Chinese position cited in S. P. Seth, "Sino-Indian Relations: Problems and Prospects," *Asia Pacific Community* 28 (Spring 1985), 82.

70. Mohammed Ayub Khan, "Pakistan Perspective," *Foreign Affairs* 38 (July 1960), 556; second quotation from Lamb, *Crisis in Kashmir*, 100.

71. See Yaacov Vertzberger, *The Enduring Entente: Sino-Pakistani Relations, 1960–1980,* Washington Papers no. 95 (Washington, D.C.: Praeger and Center for Strategic and International Studies, Georgetown University, 1983), 82. For the Sino-Pakistani boundary agreement see Mustafa, "The Sino-Pakistani Border," 48.

72. See Spate and Learmonth, *India and Pakistan,* 439.

73. Quoted in Michael Brecher, *The Struggle for Kashmir* (New York: Oxford University Press, 1953), 48.

74. See Jagdish P. Jain, *China, Pakistan and Bangladesh* (New Delhi: Radiant, 1974), 143.

75. See Hamid, *Karakuram Hunza,* 165, and Nazir A. Kamal, "Karakoram Highway: A Nation-Building Effort," *Strategic Studies* 2 (Spring 1979), 19.

76. Jain, *China, Pakistan and Bangladesh,* 142.

77. Ibid., 143, and Kamal, "Karakoram Highway," 19.

78. See Syed, *China and Pakistan,* 135, and *Keesings,* 21–31 December 1968, p. 23104. There is a discrepancy in the dates ascribed by various sources to the first joint Sino-Pakistani infrastructural venture. The Pakistani government's own Tourism Development Corporation said that the Karakoram Highway project was born in 1965 and a joint Sino-Pakistani agreement to build a two-lane paved highway for heavy traffic up to the Khunjerab Pass was signed in 1966. See Pakistan Tourism Development Corporation (PTDC), *Karakoram Highway: A Twentieth Century Miracle* (Karachi: Ferozsons, 1982). Other reports give 1964 as the year in which China offered to assist Pakistan in constructing a ninety-mile stretch of highway from the Khunjerab Pass down to Hallegush, which was completed in 1968. See Mohsin Ali, "Special Report on the Karakoram Highway," *Mag* (Karachi), 12 May 1983, p. 47, and Hamid, *Karakuram Hunza,* 166.

79. See Syed, *China and Pakistan,* 139; S. B. Guha, "The Silk Road," *Institute of Defence Studies and Analyses Journal* 2 (January 1970), 258; and *Keesings,* 21–31 December 1968, p. 23104. Zubeida Mustafa gives August 1970 as the date for the reopening of the route. See "The Sino-Pakistani Border," 50.

80. See Seymour Topping, "Opening the High Road to China," *New York Times,* 2 December 1979, sec. 6, p. 142, and Guha, "Silk Road," 256.

81. *Keesings,* 21–31 December 1968, p. 23104.

82. See Hamid, *Karakuram Hunza,* 166.

83. See Topping, "Opening the High Road," 137.

84. Ibid., 142.

85. See Kamal, "Karakoram Highway," 21; PTDC, *Karakoram Highway;* and Topping, "Opening the High Road," 124.

86. Figures from Hamid, *Karakuram Hunza,* 169, 173–174.

87. Liu Mauqing quoted in Topping, "Opening the High Road," 126. The normal Chinese practice is cremation: cemeteries are viewed as a waste of space. But in central Sichuan, too, there is a graveyard for soldiers and prisoners who died during the twelve years it took to build the Chengdu-Kunming railway. See Theroux, "China Passage," 312. See also K. J. Miller, "The International Karakoram Project 1980: A First Report," *Geographical Journal* 47 (July 1981), 167.

88. See "The Skardu Highway," *Strategic Studies* 4 (Spring 1981), 19–23.

89. *Dawn Overseas Weekly* (Karachi), 3 November 1983.

90. *Financial Times* (London), 3 September 1986, and conversation with international aid agency official (1987).

91. *Tass in English,* 11 August 1980, in British Broadcasting Corporation, *Summary of World Broadcasts, Soviet Union,* 13 August 1980; *Blitz* quoted in *News of the Week,* 13 August 1980, p. III/C.

92. See *Statesman Weekly,* 28 March 1981; *Times of India* (Delhi), 9 October 1982; *Far Eastern Economic Review,* 15 August 1985, p. 32; and *Times of India,* 22 October 1985.

93. Figures from Kamal, "Karakoram Highway," 20, 25.

94. Hamid, *Karakuram Hunza,* 161.

95. Interviewed in Topping, "Opening the High Road," 139.

96. Ameneh Azam Ali, "Beyond the Next Mountain," *Herald* (Karachi), January 1988, p. 73.

97. Quoted in *Wall Street Journal,* 15 December 1987.

98. See Azam Ali, "Beyond the Next Mountain," 74–75.

99. Neither China nor Pakistan will officially disclose the costs of building and maintaining the highway. Reports suggest, however, that maintenance alone costs as much as $10 million. See "On an Asian Road Linking Worlds and Ages," *New York Times,* 25 May 1986.

100. Azam Ali, "Beyond the Next Mountain," 73.

101. The Karakoram Highway has revived one aspect of Silk Route travel: Chinese Muslims from Xinjiang now travel across the Khunjerab Pass into Pakistan. From here they leave to perform their religious duty—Hajj—at Mecca in Saudi Arabia. In 1985, 1,483 men used this route. See Latif Ahmed Sherwani, "Review of Sino-Pakistani Relations (1981–1985)," *Pakistan Horizon* 39 (1st Quarter 1986), 105.

102. See Lyons, "Transportation in Chinese Development," 305. Also see *Washington Post,* 13 January 1985, p. A-31; *Asiaweek* (Hong Kong), 2 August 1985, p. 46; and Qi Wen, *China: A General Survey,* 138.

103. Statistics from William J. Barnds, "China's Relations with Pakistan: Durability amidst Discontinuity," *China Quarterly* 63 (September 1975), 466; *International Herald Tribune,* 5 February 1979; and Yaacov Vertzberger, "The Political Economy of Sino-Pakistani Relations: Trade and Aid, 1963–82," *Asian Survey* 23 (May 1983), 641. See also *Far Eastern Economic Review,* 12 December 1985, p. 25.

104. See National Foreign Assessment Center, *Handbook of Economic Statistics* (Washington, D.C.: Central Intelligence Agency, 1980), 107–108, and Yaacov Vertzberger, "China's Diplomacy and Strategy toward South Asia: From Benign Neglect to Prominence," *Jerusalem Journal of International Relations* 8 (June 1986), 108.

105. See Syed, *China and Pakistan,* 139; *Far Eastern Economic Review,* 2 July 1982, p. 32; and Jan Myrdal, *The Silk Road* (New York: Pantheon, 1979), 121.

106. See Carroll Bogert, "Letter from Karakorum Highway," *Far Eastern Economic Review,* 25 September 1986, p. 102.

107. *Pakistan Times* (Lahore), 19 July 1964.

108. Quoted in Hamid, *Karakuram Hunza,* 167.

109. Quoted in *Far Eastern Economic Review,* 12 December 1985, p. 25. The same article quotes a Western diplomat to the effect that Pakistan was suspected of supplying China with the model for the Exocet missile: "France is restricted by COCOM" from "selling military technology to China but Pakistan is not a communist country so it is a good bridge for China to the Western arms market."

110. *Military Balance, 1981–82.*

111. Sherwani, "Review of Sino-Pakistani Relations," 99; interview with General Zia ul-Haq, *Far Eastern Economic Review,* 16 October 1981, p. 46.

112. Chinese officials quoted in Topping, "Opening the High Road," 54, and Raju G. C. Thomas, "Indian Defense Policy: Continuity and Change under the Janata Government," *Pacific Affairs* 53 (Summer 1980), note 4, 225.

113. See Robert Jackson, *South Asian Crisis: India, Pakistan and Bangladesh* (New York: Praeger, 1975), 49, 105.

114. See Topping, "Opening the High Road," 50; also Vertzberger, *Enduring Entente,* 83; *Pakistan, Bangladesh and Afghanistan, Quarterly Economic Review,* 4th Quarter (London:

Economist Intelligence Unit, 1978), 10–11; and William S. Ellis, "Pakistan under Pressure," *National Geographic*, May 1981, p. 695.

115. James B. Curren and Phillip A. Karber, "Afghanistan's Ordeal Puts a Region at Risk," *Armed Forces Journal International*, March 1985, p. 103.

116. Kamal, "Karakoram Highway," 23–24.

117. Described in Topping, "Opening the High Road," 137. Another traveler described the hazards of the highway: "It can take an hour to travel just one mile on the Karakoram, and only a second to depart it." Ellis, "Pakistan under Pressure," 694.

118. See G. S. Bhargava, *India's Security in the 1980s*, Adelphi Papers no. 125 (London: International Institute for Strategic Studies, 1976), 14.

119. Quoted in Thomas J. Abercrombie, "Ladakh: The Last Shangri-La," *National Geographic*, March 1978, p. 346.

120. See ibid., 349.

121. Quotation from Dutt, "Defense of India's Northern Borders," 4; see also Woodman, *Himalayan Frontiers*, 311.

122. See Onkar S. Marwah, "India's Military Power and Policy," in Pollack and Marwah, *Military Power and Policy in Asian States*, 113. U.S. aid to India included equipment for six mountain divisions and road-building, railroad, and communications equipment. Sudhakar Bhat, *India and China* (New Delhi: Popular Book Services, 1967), 164.

123. See Woodman, *Himalayan Frontiers*, 310; Indian protest quoted in Jain, *China, Pakistan and Bangladesh*, 145; Bhagat quoted in *Keesings*, 21–31 December 1968, 23104, and *Far Eastern Economic Review*, 15 August 1985, p. 32.

124. Jain, *China, Pakistan and Bangladesh*, 146.

125. *Asian Recorder*, 27 August 1978, p. 14479.

126. Ibid.

127. For notes see *Keesings*, 1–8 November 1969, p. 23652. For 1982 protest see Jerrold F. Elkin and Brian Fredericks, "Sino-Indian Border Talks: The View from New Delhi," *Asian Survey* 23 (October 1983), 1134. Also see *Asian Recorder*, 27 August–2 September 1978, p. 14479.

128. See Shashi Bhushan, *Karakoram Road* (New Delhi: Secretariat of the Congress Socialist Forum, 1978); see also Zalmay Khalilzad, "The Security of South West Asia," in Khalilzad et al., *Security in Southern Asia* (New York: St. Martin's Press, 1984), 107, and Timothy George, "Sino-Indian Relations," in Khalilzad et al., *Southern Asia*, 13.

129. See, for example, Bhushan, *Karakoram Road*, 3, and B. L. Kak, *Kashmir: Problems and Politics* (New Delhi: Seema, 1981), 145.

130. *Morning News* quoted in Goswami, *Pakistan and China*, 147, and see Tahir-Kheli, "Defense Planning in Pakistan," 213.

131. *Far Eastern Economic Review*, 1 January 1987, p. 22.

132. S. Nihal Singh, "India's Restraint over Incursions by China Is Wise," *International Herald Tribune*, 9 September 1986. See also Russell Brines, *The Indo-Pakistani Conflict* (London: Pall Mall, 1969), 147–149, 184, 201–206.

133. See *Keesings*, 1–8 November 1969, p. 23652; *Jane's Defence Weekly*, 9 February 1985, p. 216; and Syed, *China and Pakistan*, 138.

134. See Lawrence Ziring, "Buffer States on the Rim of Asia: Pakistan, Afghanistan, Iran and the Superpowers," in Hafeez Malik ed., *Soviet-American Relations with Pakistan, Iran, and Afghanistan* (New York: St. Martin's, 1987), 121. He refers to a report by Azmat Hyat Khan written for the *Muslim*, 27 September 1984. Ziring also points out the significance of Wakhan's proximity to the Karakoram Highway for the Soviet Union. See also John F. Schroder and Abdul Tawaf Assifi, "Afghan Mineral Resources and Soviet Exploitation," in Klass, *Afghanistan: The Great Game Revisited*, 126. For reports on ballistic missile installations see *Asiaweek*, 10 June 1988, p. 16. On Rakhman Gul see Fahmida Ashraf, "The Strategic Wakhan," *Pakistan Times Overseas Weekly*, 25 May 1986, p. 6.

135. Reuters Report and *Peking Review* quoted in Ashraf, "Strategic Wakhan."
136. See Jain, *China, Pakistan and Bangladesh,* 147, and *Tass in English* (Dateline London), 20 November 1978.
137. *Tass in English* (Dateline London), 23 April 1979, and Dev Murarka, "Geopolitics of Brezhnev's Visit," *Mainstream* (New Delhi), 13 December 1980.
138. Shahram Chubin, *Soviet Policy towards Iran and the Gulf,* Adelphi Papers no. 157 (London: International Institute for Strategic Studies, 1980), 6.
139. See Ziring, "Buffer States," 111; and *Keesings,* 9 May 1980, p. 30231. In January 1980 the *Daily Telegraph* (London) reported that China was moving supplies of arms and ammunition across the Karakoram Highway for the Afghan mujahideen in Pakistan, 5 January 1980.
140. Curren and Karber, "Afghanistan's Ordeal," 102, 103, and *Foreign Report,* 10 October 1984, pp. 1–2. Another source suggests, however, that the Chinese have not used the Karakoram Highway to move weapons to the Afghan mujahideen. Instead, arms have been shipped to Karachi and overland to the frontier. Using the Karakoram route for this purpose was deemed "too difficult and provocative to the USSR." D. Bonavia, "More Bricks in China's Wall," *Far Eastern Economic Review,* 5 June 1981, pp. 14–15, quoted in Vertzberger, "China's Diplomacy," 137, 40.
141. Quoted in *Far Eastern Economic Review,* 12 March 1982, p. 16.
142. *Dawn Overseas Weekly,* 7 March 1981.
143. *New York Times,* 18 June 1981, p. A-3.
144. *Daily Telegraph,* 12 October 1987; and *Independent,* 10 January 1987.
145. See *Herald,* January 1986, p. 32. See also Edgar O'Ballance, "The Karakoram Highway," *Armed Forces,* February 1987, pp. 60–61, and *Daily Telegraph,* 7 October 1987. A number of news reports on the Siachin conflict referred to Indian concerns about the Karakoram Highway. For example, see *Times,* 24 August 1984, and 17 January 1985; and *India Abroad,* 9 October 1987. *Jane's Defence Weekly* reported on 30 April 1988 that Indian advances across Siachin in early 1988 had brought them to a point roughly 120–125 miles from the Karakoram Highway. Some Indian analysts, however, discount the importance of the highway as a factor in the Siachin war. See for example, Air Commodore Jasjit Singh's article "No Pak Claim to Siachin" in *Times of India,* 19 May 1988.
146. See *Independent,* 25 May 1988.
147. Cited in Rosemary Foot, "The Sino-Soviet Complex in South Asia," in Barry Buzan and Gowher Rizvi, eds., *South Asian Insecurity and the Great Powers* (New York: St. Martin's Press, 1986), 197.
148. *Far Eastern Economic Review,* 9 April 1987, p. 38.
149. See *Washington Post,* 24 and 26 September, and 11 December 1988.
150. Foot, "Sino-Soviet Complex," 188.
151. Soviet spokesman quoted in *New York Times,* 29 September 1988; also see *New York Times,* 14 October 1988.

Chapter 5   The Politics of Routes

1. Fernand Braudel was struck by the fact that the Mediterranean region "has no unity but that created by the movements of men, the relationships they imply, and the routes they follow." Routes, he observed, "have always both reflected the range of Mediterranean economic systems and civilizations, and governed their fate." Braudel, *The Mediterranean and the World in the Age of Philip II,* trans. Sian Reynolds, 2 vols. (Glasgow: Fontana/Collins, 1975), *Mediterranean* 1:276, 1:281.
2. See Mahnaz Ispahani, "The Perils of Pakistan," *New Republic,* 16 March 1987.
3. *New York Times,* 23 March 1988.
4. Braudel, *Mediterranean,* 1:355.

Selected Bibliography

Books

Adamec, Ludwig W. *Afghanistan, 1900–1923: A Diplomatic History.* Berkeley: University of California Press, 1967.
——. *Afghanistan's Foreign Affairs to the Mid-Twentieth Century.* Tucson: University of Arizona Press, 1974.
Adams, Brooks. *The New Empire.* 1902; rpt. New York: Bergman, 1969.
Adler, J. G. *British India's Northern Frontier, 1865–95.* London: Longmans, 1963.
Agarwal, Rajesh K. *Defense Production and Development.* New Delhi: Arnold Heinemann for Birla Institute, 1978.
Ahmad, Kazi. *A Geography of Pakistan.* 2d ed. Karachi: Oxford University Press, 1969.
Ahmed, Akbar S. *Pakhtun Economy and Society.* London: Routledge & Kegan Paul, 1980.
Ahmed, Feroz, ed. *Focus on Baluchistan and the Pushtoon Question.* Lahore: People's Publishing House, 1975.
Arnold, Anthony. *Afghanistan: The Soviet Invasion in Perspective.* Stanford: Hoover Institution Press, 1985.
Arnold, Guy, and Ruth Weiss. *Strategic Highways of Africa.* London: Julian Friedman, 1977.
Avedon, John F. *In Exile from the Land of Snows.* New York: Alfred A. Knopf, 1984.
Ayoob, Mohammed, ed. *The Middle East in World Politics.* New York: St. Martin's Press, 1981.
Baloch, Mir Khuda Bux Bijarani Marri. *Searchlights on Baloches and Balochistan.* Karachi: Royal Book, 1974.

Balochistan through the Ages. 2 vols. Quetta: Nisa Traders/Gosh-e-Adab, 1979.

Baluch, Mir Ahmed Yar Khan. *Inside Baluchistan: A Political Autobiography.* Karachi: Royal Book, 1975.

Baluch, Mohammed Sardar Khan. *The Great Baluch.* Quetta: Baluchi Academy, 1965.

———. *History of the Baluch Race and Baluchistan.* Quetta: Gosh-e-Abad, 1977.

Bamzai, Prithivi Nath. *Kashmir and Central Asia.* New Delhi: Light & Life, 1980.

Bates, Charles Ellison. *A Gazetteer of Kashmir.* 1872; rpt. New Delhi: Light & Life, 1969.

Benoit, Emile. *Defense and Economic Growth in Developing Countries.* Lexington, Mass.: D. C. Heath, 1973.

Berliner, Joseph S. *Soviet Economic Aid: The New Aid and Trade Policy in Underdeveloped Countries.* New York: Praeger, 1958.

Berridge, P. S. A. *Couplings to the Khyber.* London: David & Charles, 1969.

Bhargava, G. S. *India's Security in the 1980s.* Adelphi Papers, no. 125. London: International Institute for Strategic Studies, 1976.

———. *South Asian Security after Afghanistan.* Lexington, Mass.: Lexington Books, 1983.

Bhushan, Shashi. *Karakoram Road.* New Delhi: Secretariat of the Congress Socialist Forum, 1978.

Bhutto, Zulfiqar Ali. *The Myth of Independence.* London: Oxford University Press, 1969.

Bovill, D. I. N., I. G. Heggie, and J. L. Hine. *A Guide to Transport Planning within the Roads Sector for Developing Countries.* London: Ministry of Overseas Development, 1978.

Bradsher, Henry S. *Afghanistan and the Soviet Union.* Durham: Duke University Press, 1983.

Braudel, Fernand. *The Mediterranean and the Mediterranean World in the Age of Philip II.* 2 vols. Trans. Sian Reynolds. Glasgow: Fontana/Collins, 1975.

Brecher, Michael. *The Struggle for Kashmir.* New York: Oxford University Press, 1953.

Brines, Russell. *The Indo-Pakistani Conflict.* London: Pall Mall, 1969.

Bruce, Richard Issaq. *The Forward Policy.* 1900; 2d Pakistani ed., Quetta: Nisa Traders, 1979.

Bunge, Frederica M., and Shinn Rinn-Shup, eds. *China: A Country Study.* Washington, D.C.: USGPO, 1981.

Burrell, Robert M., and Alvin J. Cottrell. *Iran, Afghanistan, Pakistan: Tensions and Dilemmas.* Washington Papers, no. 95. Beverly Hills, Calif.: Sage, 1974.

Busch, Briton Cooper. *Britain and the Persian Gulf, 1894–1914.* Berkeley: University of California Press, 1967.

Bussagli, Mario. *Central Asian Painting.* New York: Rizzoli, 1979.

Caroe, Olaf. *Wells of Power: The Oilfields of South-Western Asia.* London: Macmillan, 1951.

———. *Soviet Empire.* London: Macmillan, 1953.

———. *The Pathans, 550 B.C.–A.D. 1957.* London: Macmillan, 1965.

Chakravarti, Prithivas C. *The Evolution of India's Northern Borders.* London: Asia Publishing House, 1971.

Chaudhuri, K. N. *Trade and Civilisation in the Indian Ocean*. Cambridge: Cambridge University Press, 1985.

Chen, Jack. *The Sinkiang Story*. New York: Macmillan, 1977.

Chih, Chang. *An Outline of Chinese Geography*. Beijing: Foreign Languages Press, 1978.

Chirol, Valentine. *The Middle Eastern Question; or, Some Political Problems of Indian Defence*. London: John Murray, 1903.

Chubin, Shahram. *Soviet Policy towards Iran and the Gulf*. Adelphi Papers, no. 157. London: International Institute for Strategic Studies, 1980.

Cipolla, Carlo M. *Guns, Sails and Empires: Technological Innovation and the Early Phases of European Expansion, 1400–1700*. New York: Pantheon, 1965.

Cohen, Saul B. *Geography and Politics in a World Divided*. New York: Random House, 1963.

Cooley, Charles H. *The Theory of Transportation*. Baltimore: American Economic Association, 1894.

Cottrell, Alvin J., and Robert M. Burrell, eds. *The Indian Ocean: Its Political, Economic and Military Importance*. New York: Praeger, 1972.

Cox, Kevin R., David D. Reynolds, and Stein Rokkan, eds. *Locational Approaches to Power and Conflict*. New York: John Wiley, 1974.

Cressey, George B. *Crossroads: Land and Life in Southwest Asia*. Chicago: J. B. Lippincott, 1960.

Curtin, Phillip D. *Cross-Cultural Trade in World History*. Cambridge: Cambridge University Press, 1984.

Curzon, George N. *Persia and the Persian Question*. 2 vols. 1892; rpt. New York: Barnes & Noble, 1966.

——. *Russia in Central Asia in 1889 and the Anglo-Russian Question*. 1889; rpt. New York: Barnes & Noble, 1967.

——. *Frontiers*. 1908; rpt. Westport, Conn.: Greenwood Press, 1976.

Dames, M. Longworth. *The Baloch Race: A Historical and Ethnological Sketch*. London: Royal Asiatic Society, 1904.

Davies, C. Collin. *An Historical Atlas of the Indian Peninsula*. London: Oxford University Press, 1959.

——. *The Problem of the North-West Frontier: 1890–1908*. 2d ed. London: Curzon Press, 1975.

Deutsch, Karl W., and William J. Folz, eds. *Nation Building*. New York: Atherton Press, 1963.

De Vree, Johan K. *Political Integration: The Formation of Theory and Its Problems*. The Hague: Mouton, 1972.

Dichter, David. *The North West Frontier of West Pakistan: A Study in Regional Geography*. Oxford: Clarendon Press, 1967.

Dicks, David. *Curzon in India*. New York: Taplinger, 1969.

Dobson, George. *Russia's Railway Advance into Central Asia: Notes on a Journey from St. Petersburg to Samarkand*. 1890; rpt. London: W. H. Allen, 1970.

Downs, Roger M., and David Stea. *Maps in Minds: Reflections on Cognitive Mapping*. New York: Harper & Row, 1977.

Dupree, Louis. *Afghanistan's Big Gamble, Part II: The Economic and Strategic Aspects of*

Soviet Aid. American Universities Field Staff Reports, South Asia Series, vol. 4, no. 4. Hanover, N.H.: American Universities Field Staff, 1960.

——. *The Mountains Go to Mohammed Zahir: Observations on Afghanistan's Reaction to Visits from Nixon, Bulganin, Eisenhower and Khrushchev*. American Universities Field Staff Reports, South Asia Series, vol. 4 no. 6. Hanover, N.H.: American Universities Field Staff, 1961.

——. *Pushtunistan: The Problem and Its Larger Implications, Part I*. American Universities Field Staff Reports, South Asia Series, vol. 5, no. 2. Hanover, N.H.: American Universities Field Staff, 1961.

——. *Pushtunistan: The Problem and Its Larger Implications, Part II*. American Universities Field Staff Reports, South Asia Series, vol. 5, no. 3. Hanover, N.H.: American Universities Field Staff, 1977.

——. *Afghanistan, 1977: Does Trade Plus Aid Guarantee Development?* American Universities Field Staff Reports, Asia, vol. 21, no. 3. Hanover, N.H.: American Universities Field Staff, 1977.

——. *Afghanistan*. Princeton: Princeton University Press, 1980.

——. *Afghan Studies*. American Universities Field Staff Reports, South Asia Series, vol. 20, no. 4. Hanover, N.H.: American Universities Field Staff, 1980.

——. *Red Flag over the Hindu Kush, Part IV*. American Universities Field Staff Reports, Asia Series, no. 27. Hanover, N.H.: American Universities Field Staff, 1980.

Durand, Algernon. *The Making of a Frontier*. London: John Murray, 1899.

Dutt, Som. *The Defense of India's Northern Borders*. Adelphi Papers, no. 25. London: International Institute for Strategic Studies, 1966.

Earle, Edward Mead. *Turkey, the Great Powers and the Bagdad Railway*. New York: Macmillan, 1923.

East, W. G., and J. R. V. Prescott. *Our Fragmented World*. London: Macmillan, 1975.

East, W. G., O. H. K. Spate, and Charles E. Fisher. *The Changing Map of Asia*. 5th ed. London: Methuen, 1971.

Edwards, H. Sutherland. *Russian Projects against India*. London: Remington, 1885.

Eisenstadt, S. N., and Stein Rokkan. *Building States and Nations*. 2 vols. Beverly Hills, Calif.: Sage, 1973.

Elphinstone, Mountstuart. *An Account of the Kingdom of Caubul and Its Dependencies in Persia, Tartary, and India*. London: Longman, Hurst, Rees, Orme & Brown, 1815.

Embree, Ainslee T., ed. *Pakistan's Western Borderlands: The Transformation of a Political Order*. Durham, N.C.: Carolina Academic Press, 1977.

Engels, Donald. *Alexander the Great and the Logistics of the Macedonian Army*. Berkeley: University of California Press, 1978.

Fisher, Charles A., ed. *Essays in Political Geography*. London: Methuen, 1968.

Franck, Peter G. *The Economics of Competitive Coexistence: Afghanistan between East and West*. Washington, D.C.: National Planning Association, 1960.

Franda, Marcus F. *North Eastern India in the Wake of Vietnam*. American Universities Field Staff Reports, vol. 19 no. 13. Hanover, N.H.: American Universities Field Staff, 1975.

Fraser, Lovat. *India under Curzon and After*. London: William Heinemann, 1911.

Fraser-Tytler, W. K. *Afghanistan: A Study of Political Developments in Central and Southern Asia.* 3d ed. London: Oxford University Press, 1967.

Fry, Maxwell. *The Afghan Economy.* Leiden: E. J. Brill, 1974.

Fukuyama, Francis. *The Security of Pakistan: A Trip Report.* Santa Monica, Calif.: RAND Corporation, 1980.

Glassner, Martin I. *Transit Problems of Three Asian Land-Locked Countries: Afghanistan, Nepal and Laos.* Baltimore: University of Maryland, School of Law, 1983.

Glassner, Martin I., and Harm de Blij, eds. *Systematic Political Geography.* 3d ed. New York: John Wiley, 1980.

Goldman, Marshall. *Soviet Foreign Aid.* New York: Praeger, 1967.

Gopalakrishnan, R. *The Geography and Politics of Afghanistan.* New Delhi: Concept Publishing, 1982.

Goswami, Birendra Nath. *Pakistan and China: A Study in Their Relations,* Bombay: Allied Publishers, 1971.

Gottmann, Jean. *The Significance of Territory.* Charlottesville: University Press of Virginia, 1973.

Gottmann, Jean, ed. *Center and Periphery: Spatial Variation in Politics.* Beverly Hills, Calif.: Sage, 1980.

Gould, Peter. *Mental Maps.* Harmondsworth: Penguin, 1974.

Grassmuck, George, and Ludwig W. Adamec, eds. *Afghanistan: Some New Approaches.* Ann Arbor: University of Michigan Press, 1969.

Gray, Colin S. *The Geopolitics of the Nuclear Era: Heartland, Rimland and the Technological Revolution.* New York: Crane Russak, 1977.

Gregorian, Vartan. *The Emergence of Modern Afghanistan.* Stanford: Stanford University Press, 1969.

Griffiths, John C. *Afghanistan.* New York: Praeger, 1967.

——. *Afghanistan: Key to a Continent.* Boulder, Colo.: Westview Press, 1980.

Haefele, Edwin T., ed. *Transport and National Goals.* Washington, D.C.: Brookings, 1969.

Halliday, Fred. *Soviet Policy in the Arc of Crisis.* Washington, D.C.: Institute for Policy Studies, 1981.

Hamid, S. Shahid. *Karakuram Hunza.* Karachi: Ma'aref, 1979.

Hammond, Thomas T. *Red Flag over Afghanistan.* Boulder, Colo.: Westview Press, 1984.

Harkavy, Robert E. *The Security Policies of Developing Countries.* Lexington, Mass.: Lexington Books, 1982.

——. *Great Power Competition for Overseas Bases: The Geopolitics of Access Diplomacy.* New York: Pergamon, 1982.

Harrison, Selig S. *In Afghanistan's Shadow: Baluch Nationalism and Soviet Temptations.* Washington, D.C.: Carnegie Endowment for International Peace, 1981.

Hassnain, F. M. *Gilgit: The Northern Gate of India.* New Delhi: Sterling, 1978.

Helms, Mary W. *Ulysses' Sail: An Ethnographic Odyssey of Power, Knowledge, and Geographical Distance.* Princeton: Princeton University Press, 1988.

Herz, John M. *The Nation-State and the Crisis of World Politics.* New York: D. McKay, 1976.

Hodson, Harry V. *Twentieth Century Empire.* London: Faber & Faber, 1948.

Holdich, Thomas Hungerford. *The Indian Borderland*. London: Methuen, 1901.
——. *India*. New York: Appleton, 1905.
——. *The Gates of India*. London: Macmillan, 1916.
Hoskins, Halford L. *British Routes to India*. New York: Octagon, 1966.
Hsia, Ronald. *The Role of Labor-Intensive Investment Projects in China's Capital Formation*. Cambridge: Center for International Studies, Massachusetts Institute of Technology, 1954.
Huntington, Ellsworth. *The Pulse of Asia: A Journey in Central Asia Illustrating the Geographic Basis of History*. Boston: Houghton Mifflin, 1907.
Huntington, Samuel P. *Political Order in Changing Societies*. New Haven: Yale University Press, 1968.
Hussain, Khalifa Afzal. *The Development of Roads and Road Transport in Pakistan*. Lahore: Transport Construction Corp., 1973.
Hyman, Anthony. *Afghanistan under Soviet Domination, 1964–1981*. New York: St. Martin's Press, 1982.
Imperial Gazetteer of India, Provincial Series. *Baluchistan*. 1908; rpt. Lahore: Oriental Publishers, 1976.
Independent Commission on Disarmament and Security Issues. *Common Security: A Blueprint for Survival*. New York: Simon & Schuster, 1982.
Innes, H. A. *Empire and Communication*. Oxford: Clarendon Press, 1950.
International Road Federation. *Roads—Social, Economic and Financial Aspects*. Washington, D.C.: International Road Federation, 1973.
Jackson, Robert. *South Asian Crisis: India, Pakistan and Bangladesh*. New York: Praeger, 1975.
Jackson, W. A. Douglas. *The Russo-Chinese Borderlands*. Princeton: D. Van Nostrand, 1968.
Jackson, W. A. Douglas, ed. *Politics and Geographic Relationships*. Englewood Cliffs, N.J.: Prentice-Hall, 1964.
Jafri, Hasan Ali Shah. *Indo-Afghan Relations, 1947–1967*. New Delhi: Sterling Publishers, 1976.
Jain, Jagdish P. *Soviet Policy toward Pakistan and Bangladesh*. New Delhi: Radiant Publications, 1974.
——. *China, Pakistan and Bangladesh*. New Delhi: Radiant Publications, 1974.
Japan International Cooperation Agency. "Basic Design Report on the Coastal Fisheries Development Project in the Islamic Republic of Pakistan." Tokyo, March 1980.
Jolly, Richard, ed. *Disarmament and World Development*. New York: Pergamon Press, 1978.
Jukes, Geoffrey. *The Indian Ocean in Soviet Naval Policy*. Adelphi Paper no. 87. London: International Institute for Strategic Studies, 1972.
Kamrany, Nake M. *Peaceful Competition in Afghanistan: American and Soviet Models of Economic Aid*. Washington, D.C.: Communication Service Corp., 1969.
Kavic, Lorne J. *India's Quest for Security: Defense Policies, 1947–1965*. Berkeley: University of California Press, 1967.
Kazemzadeh, Firuz. *Russia and Britain in Persia, 1864–1914: A Study in Imperialism*. New Haven: Yale University Press, 1968.
Keay, John. *The Gilgit Game*. London: John Murray, 1979.

Kerner, R. J. *The Urge to the Sea: The Course of Russian History: The Role of Rivers, Portages, Ostrogs, Monasteries and Furs.* New York: Vanguard, 1942.

Khalilzad, Zalmay, T. George, R. Litwak, and S. Chubin. *Security in Southern Asia.* New York: St. Martin's Press, 1984.

Khan, Dilawar. *Baluchistan.* Islamabad: English Book House, 1977.

Khan, Ghani Mohammad. *Afghanistan's Transit Trade through Pakistan and the Unrecorded Transactions at Landikotal.* Board of Economic Enquiry, no. 70. Peshawar: University of Peshawar, 1972.

Khan, Mohammed Ayub. *Friends Not Masters: A Political Autobiography.* New York: Oxford University Press, 1967.

Khrushchev, Nikita. *Khrushchev Remembers.* Trans. Strobe Talbott. Boston: Little, Brown, 1974.

Klass, Rosanne, ed. *Afghanistan: The Great Game Revisited.* New York: Freedom House, 1987.

Knight, Edward F. *Where Three Empires Meet.* 1896; rpt. Karachi: Indus, 1978.

Korson, J. Henry, ed. *Contemporary Problems of Pakistan.* Leiden: E. J. Brill, 1974.

Krausse, Alexis S. *Russia in Asia, 1558–1899.* 1899; rpt. London: Curzon Press, 1973.

Kumar, Ravinder. *India and the Persian Gulf Region, 1858–1907: A Study in British Imperial Policy.* London: Asia Publishing House, 1965.

Kumar, Satish. *The New Pakistan.* New Delhi: Vikas Publishing House, 1978.

Lamb, Alastair. *The China-India Border.* Chatham House Essays. London: Oxford University Press, 1964.

——. *Crisis in Kashmir, 1947–1966.* London: Routledge & Kegan Paul, 1966.

——. *The Kashmir Problem: A Historical Survey.* New York: Praeger, 1966.

——. *Asian Frontiers: Studies in a Continuing Problem.* New York: Praeger, 1968.

Lattimore, Owen. *Inner Asian Frontiers of China.* American Geographical Society Research Series, no. 21. London: Oxford University Press, 1940.

——. *High Tartary.* 1930; rpt. New York: AMS Press, 1975.

——. *Pivot of Asia.* 1950; rpt. New York: AMS Press, 1975.

Lattimore, Owen, and Lattimore, Eleanor. *Silks, Spices and Empire.* New York: Delacorte Press, 1968.

Lauren, Paul Gordon. *Diplomacy: New Approaches in History, Theory, and Policy.* New York: Free Press, 1979.

Low, Alfred D. *The Sino-Soviet Dispute: An Analysis of the Polemics.* Cranbury, N.J.: Associated University Presses, 1976.

Lowe, John C., and S. Moryades. *The Geography of Movement.* Boston: Houghton Mifflin, 1975.

Luttwak, Edward N. *The Grand Strategy of the Roman Empire.* Baltimore: Johns Hopkins University Press, 1976.

Mackinder, J. Halford. *Democratic Ideals and Reality.* 2d ed. New York: Henry Holt, 1942.

Mcmillen, Donald H. *Chinese Communist Power and Policy in Xinjiang, 1949–1977.* Boulder, Colo.: Westview Press, 1979.

McNeill, William H. *The Pursuit of Power: Technology, Armed Forces and Society since A.D. 1000.* Chicago: University of Chicago Press, 1982.

Malik, Hafeez ed. *Soviet-American Relations with Pakistan, Iran and Afghanistan.* New York: St. Martin's, 1987.

Matheson, Sylvia. *The Tigers of Baluchistan.* London: Arthur Barker, 1967.

Maxwell, Neville. *India's China War.* New York: Pantheon, 1970.

Mayer, Lawrence. *Comparative Political Inquiry.* Homewood, Ill.; Dorsey Press, 1972.

Military Balance. London: International Institute for Strategic Studies, annual.

Millar, Charles. *Khyber: British India's Northwest Frontier.* New York: Macmillan, 1977.

Millar, T. B. *Soviet Policies in the Indian Ocean Area.* Canberra: Australian National University Press, 1970.

Mullins, A. F., Jr. *Born Arming: Development and Military Power in New States.* Stanford: Stanford University Press, 1987.

Muni, S. D. *Arms Build-Up and Development: Linkages in the Third World.* Canberra: Australian National University Press, 1980.

Munshi, Mir Sultan Mahomed Khan. *The Life of Abdur Rahman: Amir of Afghanistan.* 2 vols. London: John Murray, 1900.

Myrdal, Jan. *The Silk Road.* New York: Pantheon, 1979.

Neuman, Stephanie G., ed. *Defense Planning in Less Industrialized States.* Lexington, Mass.: Lexington Books, 1984.

Nolan, Janne E. *Military Industry in Taiwan and South Korea.* London: Macmillan, 1986.

Nollau, Gunther, and Hans J. Wiehe. *Russia's South Flank: Soviet Operations in Iran, Turkey and Afghanistan.* New York: Praeger, 1963.

Nyman, Hans-Erik. *Great Britain and Chinese, Russian, and Japanese Interests in Sinkiang, 1918–1934.* Stockholm: Esselte Studium, 1977.

Nyrop, Richard F. *Area Handbook for Pakistan.* Washington, D.C.: USGPO, 1971.

———. *Afghanistan: A Country Study.* Washington: USGPO, 1986.

———, ed. *Pakistan: A Country Study.* Washington, D.C.: USGPO, 1984.

Owen, Wilfred. *Distance and Development.* Washington, D.C.: Brookings, 1968.

Pakistan: Past and Present. London: Stacey International, 1977.

Pazhwak, Abdur Rahman. *Pakhtunistan: The Khyber Pass as the Focus of the New State of Pakhtunistan.* London: Afghan Information Bureau, 1952.

Pollack, Jonathan, and Onkar Marwah, eds. *Military Power and Policy in Asian States.* Boulder, Colo.: Westview Press, 1980.

Pounds, Norman J. G. *An Introduction to Economic Geography.* London: John Murray, 1970.

———. *Political Geography.* New York: McGraw-Hill, 1972.

Pratt, Edwin A. *The Rise of Rail-Power in War and Conquest: 1833–1914.* London: P. S. King, 1915.

Prescott, J. R. V. *The Geography of State Policies.* Chicago: Aldine, 1968.

———. *Political Geography.* London: Methuen, 1972.

———. *Boundaries and Frontiers.* London: Croom Helm, 1978.

Qi Wen. *China: A General Survey.* Beijing: Foreign Languages Press, 1979.

Quddus, Syed Abdul. *Afghanistan and Pakistan.* Lahore: Ferozsons, 1982.

Ra'anaan, Uri, Robert L. Pfaltzgraff and Geoffrey Kemp, eds. *Arms Transfers to the*

Third World, The Military Buildup in Less Industrial Countries. Boulder, Colo.: Westview Press, 1978.

Rahul, Ram. *The Himalayan Borderland.* New Delhi: Vikas Publications, 1970.

——. *Struggle for Central Asia.* New Delhi: Vikas Publications, 1982.

Rawlinson, Henry. *England and Russia in the East.* London: John Murray, 1875.

Razvi, Mujtaba. *The Frontiers of Pakistan.* Karachi: National Publishing House, 1971.

Rizwanullah, Mohammed. *Lonely Guardian of the Khojak Pass.* Rawalpindi: n.p., 1965.

Rose, Leo. *Nepal: Strategy for Survival.* Berkeley: University of California Press, 1971.

Rothermund, Dietmar. *Asian Trade and European Expansion in the Age of Mercantilism.* New Delhi: Manohar Publishers, 1981.

Rowland, John. *A History of Sino-Indian Relations.* Princeton: D. Van Nostrand, 1967.

Roy, Olivier. *Islam and Resistance in Afghanistan.* Cambridge: Cambridge University Press, 1986.

Rushbrook-Williams, L. F. *Pakistan under Challenge.* London: Stacey International, 1975.

Schloss, Aran. *The Politics of Development: Transportation Policy in Nepal.* Monograph Series no. 22. Berkeley: University of California, Center for South and Southeast Asia Studies, and Lanham, Md.: University Press of America, 1983.

Showalter, Dennis E. *Railroads and Rifles.* Hamden, Conn.: Archon, 1975.

Sidky, M. H. *The Conduct of Chinese Foreign Policy in Afghanistan and Pakistan.* Ann Arbor: University of Michigan Press, 1980.

Singer, Andre. *Lords of the Khyber: The Story of the North-West Frontier.* London: Faber & Faber, 1984.

The Sino-Soviet Dispute. Keesings Research Report, no. 3. New York: Charles Scribner's Sons, 1969.

Skrine, Francis H., and Edward D. Ross. *The Heart of Asia: A History of Russian Turkestan and the Central Asian Khanates from the Earliest Times.* London: Methuen, 1899.

Sladkovsky, M. I. *The Long Road: Sino-Russian Economic Contacts from Ancient Times to 1917.* Moscow: Progress Publishers, 1974.

Smith, Harvey H., et al. *Area Handbook for Afghanistan.* Washington, D.C.: USGPO, 1973.

Soja, Edward W. *The Political Organization of Space.* Commission on College Geography Resource Paper, no. 8. Washington, D.C.: Association of American Geographers, 1971.

Spain, James W. *The Way of the Pathans.* 2d. ed. Karachi: Oxford University Press, 1972.

Spate, O. H. K. *India and Pakistan: A General and Regional Geography.* 3d ed. London: Methuen, 1967.

Stein, Aurel. *On Ancient Central Asian Tracks: Brief Narrative of Three Expeditions in Innermost Asia and Northwestern China.* 33; Chicago: University of Chicago Press, Phoenix Edition, 1974.

Stokes, Charles J. *Transportation and Economic Development in Latin America.* New York: Praeger, 1968.

Strausz-Hupé, Robert. *Geopolitics: The Struggle for Space and Power.* 1942; rpt. New York: Arno Press, 1972.

Subrahmanyam, K. *Defense and Development.* Calcutta: Minerva Associates, 1973.

Syed, Anwar H. *China and Pakistan: Diplomacy of an Entente Cordiale.* Amherst: University of Massachusetts Press, 1974.

Sykes, Percy. *A History of Afghanistan.* 2 vols. London: Macmillan, 1921.

Tate, George P. *The Frontiers of Baluchistan.* 1909; rpt. Lahore: East & West Publishing, 1976.

Tayyeb, A. *Pakistan: A Political Geography.* London: Oxford University Press, 1966.

Theroux, Paul. *Riding the Iron Rooster: By Train through China.* New York: G. P. Putnam's Sons, 1988.

Tilly, Charles, ed. *The Formation of National States in Western Europe.* Princeton: Princeton University Press, 1975.

Toynbee, Arnold. *Between Oxus and Jumna.* New York: Oxford University Press, 1961.

Trivedi, Ram Naresh. *Sino-Indian Border Dispute and Its Impact on Indo-Pakistan Relations.* New Delhi: Associated Publishing House, 1977.

Tucker, A. L. P. *Sir Robert G. Sandeman.* New York: Macmillan, 1921.

United Nations. Expert Group on the Transport Infrastructure for Land-Locked Developing Countries. *A Transport Strategy for Land-Locked Developing Countries.* New York: United Nations, 1974.

Van Creveld, Martin. *Supplying War: Logistics from Wallenstein to Patton.* Cambridge: Cambridge University Press, 1977.

van Walt van Praag, Michael C. *Population Transfer and the Survival of the Tibetan Identity.* New York: U.S.-Tibet Committee, 1986.

Vassilev, Vassili. *Policy in the Soviet Bloc on Aid to Developing Countries.* Paris: Organisation for Economic Co-operation and Development, 1969.

Vertzberger, Yaacov. *China's South Asian Strategy: Encirclement and Counterencirclement.* New York: Praeger, 1985.

———. *The Enduring Entente: Sino-Pakistani Relations, 1960–1980.* Washington Papers, no. 95. Washington, D.C.: Praeger, and Center for Strategic and International Studies, Georgetown University, 1983.

Watson, Francis. *The Frontiers of China.* London: Chatto & Windus, 1966.

Weigart, Hans, et al. *Principles of Political Geography.* New York: Appleton-Century-Crofts, 1957.

Weinstein, Warren, and Thomas H. Henrikson. *Soviet and Chinese Aid to African Nations.* New York: Praeger Special Studies, 1980.

Wheeler, Geoffrey. *The Modern History of Soviet Central Asia.* Westport, Conn.: Greenwood Press, 1964.

Whynes, David K. *The Economics of Third World Military Expenditure.* Austin: University of Texas Press, 1979.

Wilber, Donald N., ed. *Afghanistan.* New Haven: Human Relations Area Files, 1956.

Wirsing, Robert G. *The Baluchis and the Pathans.* Minority Rights Group Report, no. 48. London: Minority Rights Group, 1981.

———. *Protection of Ethnic Minorities: Comparative Perspectives.* New York: Pergamon Press, 1981.

Wolfe, Roy. *Transportation and Politics*. Princeton: D. Van Nostrand, 1963.

Woodman, Dorothy. *Himalayan Frontiers: A Political Review of British, Chinese, Indian and Russian Rivalries*. London: Barrie & Rockliff, Cresset Press, 1969.

World Bank. *Bhutan: Development in a Himalayan Kingdom*. A World Bank Country Study. Washington, D.C., 1984.

Younghusband, George J. *Indian Frontier Warfare*. London: Kegan, Paul, Trench, Trubner, 1898.

Younghusband, George J., and Francis Younghusband. *The Relief of Chitral*. 1895; rpt. Lahore: English Book House, 1976.

Zagoria, Donald. *The Sino-Soviet Conflict, 1956–1961*. Princeton: Princeton University Press, 1962.

Ziring, Lawrence, ed. *The Subcontinent in World Politics*. New York: Praeger Special Studies, 1982.

Articles

Abercrombie, Thomas J. "Ladakh: The Last Shangri-La." *National Geographic*, March 1978, pp. 332–358.

Adamec, Ludwig W. "Germany, Third Power in Afghan Foreign Relations." In George Grassmuck and Ludwig W. Adamec, eds. *Afghanistan: Some New Approaches*. Ann Arbor: University of Michigan Press, 1969, pp. 204–259.

Ahmed, Akbar. "Afghanistan and Pakistan: The Great Game of the Tribes." *Journal of South Asian and Middle Eastern Studies* 3 (Summer 1980), 23–41.

Ali, Mohsin. "Special Report on the KKH." *Mag* (Karachi), 12 May 1983, pp. 8–10, 47–48.

Ali, Syed Shaukat. "Defence and Development." *Defence Journal*, January–February 1984, pp. 37–40.

Aloys, Michel A. "Foreign Trade and Foreign Policy in Afghanistan." *Middle Eastern Affairs* 12 (January 1961), 7–16.

Ashraf, Fahmida. "The Strategic Wakhan." *Pakistan Times Overseas Weekly*, 25 May 1986.

Ayoob, Mohammed. "Indo-Iranian Relations: Strategic, Political, and Economic Dimensions." *India Quarterly* 33 (January–March 1977), 1–19.

———. "India and Nepal: Politics of Aid and Trade." *Institute for Defence Studies and Analyses Journal* 3 (October 1970), 127–156.

Azam Ali, Ameneh. "Beyond the Next Mountain." *Herald* (Karachi), January 1988, pp. 70–76.

Ball, Nicole. "Defense Expenditures and Economic Growth: A Comment." *Armed Forces and Society* 11 (Winter 1985), 291–297.

Baloch, Inayatullah. "Afghanistan-Pashtunistan-Baluchistan." *Aussenpolitik* 31 (3d Quarter 1980), 283–301.

"The Baluchis of Pakistan and Persia." Staff review article of M. G. Pikulin's *Beludzhi* (Moscow, 1959). In *Central Asian Review* 8 (1960), 299–309.

Barnds, William J. "China's Relations with Pakistan: Durability amidst Discontinuity." *China Quarterly* 63 (September 1975), 463–489.

Bodansky, Yossef. "Soviet Military Involvement in Afghanistan." In Rosanne

Klass, ed. *Afghanistan: The Great Game Revisited*. New York: Freedom House, 1987, pp. 229–287.

Bogert, Carroll. "Letter from the Karakoram Highway." *Far Eastern Economic Review*, 25 September 1986.

Burns, John F. "Karakoram Highway Links Two Worlds." *International Herald Tribune*, 2 June 1986.

Canfield, Robert L. "Soviet Gambit in Central Asia." *Journal of South Asian and Middle Eastern Studies* 5 (Fall 1981), 10–30.

Chaudhri, Mohammed Ahsen. "Strategic and Military Dimensions in Pakistan-China Relations." *Pakistan Horizon* 39 (Fourth Quarter 1986), 15–28.

Child, John. "Geopolitical Thinking in Latin America." *Latin American Research Review* 14 (1979); 89–111.

Codrington, K. De B. "A Geographical Introduction to the History of Central Asia." *Geographical Journal* 104 (July 1944), 29–91.

Conner, Walker. "Self-Determination: The New Phase." *World Politics* 20 (October 1967), 30–53.

Curren, James B., and Phillip A. Karber. "Afghanistan's Ordeal Puts a Region at Risk." *Armed Forces Journal International*, March 1985, pp. 78–105.

Defence Journal staff. "AWACs for Pakistan: Relative Merits and Employment Issues." *Defence Journal* 13 (1987), 3–8.

Deutsch, Karl. "The Growth of Nations." *World Politics* 5 (January 1953), 168–195.
——. "Social Mobilization and Political Development." *American Political Science Review* 55 (September 1961), 493–514.

Edwards, Mike W. "An Eye for an Eye: Pakistan's Wild Frontier." *National Geographic*, January 1977, pp. 111–138.

Elkin, Jerrold F., and Brian Fredericks. "Sino-Indian Border Talks: The View from New Delhi." *Asian Survey* 23 (October 1983), 1128–1140.

Ellis, William S. "Pakistan under Pressure." *National Geographic*, May 1981, pp. 668–700.

Finer, Samuel E. "State Building, State Boundaries and Border Control." *Social Science Information* 13 (1974), 79–126.

Foot, Rosemary. "The Sino-Soviet Complex in South Asia." In Barry Buzan and Gowher Rizvi, eds. *South Asian Insecurity and the Great Powers*. New York: St. Martin's Press, 1986, pp. 181–204.

Franck, Dorothea Seelye, "Pakhtunistan—Disputed Disposition of a Tribal Land." *Middle East Journal* 6 (Winter 1952): 49–69.

Frederickson, P. C., and Robert E. Looney. "Defense Expenditures and Economic Growth in Developing Countries." *Armed Forces and Society* 9 (Summer 1983), 633–645.

Fromkin, David. "The Great Game in Asia." *Foreign Affairs* 58 (Spring 1980), 936–951.

Frye, Richard N. "Remarks on Baluchi History." *Central Asiatic Journal* 4 (1961), 44–50.

Garver, John W. "The Sino-Soviet Territorial Dispute in the Pamir Region." *China Quarterly* 85 (March 1981), 107–118.

George, Alexander. "Case Studies and Theory Development: The Method of

Structured, Focused Comparison." In Paul Gorden Lauren, ed. *Diplomacy: New Approaches in History, Theory, and Policy*. New York: Free Press, 1979, pp. 43–68.

Glassner, Martin I. "Transit Rights for Land-Locked States and the Special Case of Nepal." *World Affairs* 140 (Spring 1978), 304–314.

Gray, Colin S. "Across the Nuclear Divide—Strategic Studies, Past and Present." *International Security* 2 (Summer 1977), 24–46.

Guha, S. B. "The Silk Road." *Institute for Defense Studies and Analyses Journal* 2 (January 1970), 255–262.

Halliday, Fred. "The Limits of Russian Imperialism." *New Statesman*, 5 December 1980, pp. 10–12.

Hamilton, F. E. I. "Location Factors in the Yugoslav Iron and Steel Industry." *Economic Geography* 40 (January 1964), 46–64.

Hardgrave, Robert L., Jr. "Why India Matters." *Asian Affairs: An American Review* 2 (Spring 1984), 45–56.

Harrison, Selig S. "George Washington Ayub." *New Republic*, 30 October 1961, p. 7.

———. "After the Afghan Coup: Nightmare in Baluchistan." *Foreign Policy* 32 (Fall 1978), 136–160.

———. "Baluch Nationalism and Superpower Rivalry." *International Security* 5 (Winter 1980–81), 152–163.

———. "Fanning Flames in South Asia." *Foreign Policy* 4–5 (Winter 1981), 84–102.

Hartshorne, Richard. "The Functional Approach in Political Geography." *Annals of the Association of American Geographers* 40 (June 1950), 95–130.

Henrikson, Alan K. "The Geographical 'Mental Maps' of American Foreign Policy Makers." *International Political Science Review* 1 (1980), 495–530.

Herz, John. "Rise and Demise of the Territorial State." *World Politics* 9 (July 1957), 473–493.

"Highway Construction in China." Staff article in *Beijing Review*, 9 November 1981, pp. 21–27.

Hofmeier, Rolf. "The Political Economy of Transport Projects." *Intereconomics* 2 (March–April 1980), 94–99.

Horn, Robert C. "Afghanistan and the Soviet-Indian Influence Relationship." *Asian Survey* 23 (March 1983), 244–260.

Ispahani, Mahnaz. "Alone Together: Regional Security in Southern Africa and the Arabian Gulf." *International Security* 8 (Spring 1984), 152–175.

———. "The Perils of Pakistan." *New Republic*, 16 March 1987.

Jacobs, Keith. "Pakistan's Navy." *United States Naval Institute Proceedings* 110 (March 1984), 148–150.

Kamal, Nazir A. "Karakoram Highway: A Nation-Building Effort." *Strategic Studies* 2 (Spring 1979), 18–31.

Kapil, Ravi L. "Political Boundaries and Territorial Instability." *International Review of History and Political Science* 5 (August 1968), 46–78.

Kazemzadeh, Firuz. "Russian Imperialism and Persian Railways." In Hugh Mclean, Martin E. Malia, and George Fischer, eds. *Russian Thought and Politics*, Harvard Slavic Studies no. 4. Cambridge: Harvard University Press, 1957, pps. 355–373.

——. "Afghanistan: The Imperial Dream." *New York Review of Books*, February 1980, pp. 10–14.

Khan, Mohammed Ayub. "Pakistan Perspective." *Foreign Affairs* 38 (July 1960), 547–556.

Kristof, Ladis K. D. "The Origins and Evolution of Geopolitics." *Journal of Confict Resolution* 4 (March 1960), 15–52.

Lipjhart, Arend. "Comparative Politics and the Comparative Method." *American Political Science Review* 65 (September 1971), 682–693.

Luttwak, Edward N. "After Afghanistan, What?" *Commentary*, April 1980, pp. 40–49.

Lyons, Thomas P. "Transportation in Chinese Development, 1952–1982." *Journal of Developing Areas* 19 (April 1985), 305–328.

Marwah, Onkar. "India's Military Power and Policy." In Marwah and Jonathan Pollack, eds. *Military Power and Policy in Asian States: China, India, Japan*. Boulder, Colo.: Westview Press, 1980.

Miller, K. J. "The International Karakoram Project 1980: A First Report." *Geographical Journal* 47 (July 1981), 153–163.

Moorer, Thomas H., and Alvin J. Cottrell. "The Search for U.S. Bases in the Indian Ocean: A Last Chance." *Strategic Review* 8 (Spring 1980), 30–38.

Mustafa, Zubeida. "The Sino-Pakistani Border: Historical Aspect." *Pakistan Horizon* 25 (Second Quarter 1972), 43–50.

Nehru, Jawaharlal. "Changing India." *Foreign Affairs* 41 (April 1963), 453–465.

Neuman, Stephanie. "Security, Military Expenditures and Socio-Economic Development: Reflections on Iran." *Orbis* 22 (Fall 1978), 569–594.

Newell, Richard. "Afghanistan: The Dangers of Cold War Generosity." *Middle East Journal* 23 (Spring 1969), 168–178.

Noorzoy, M. Siddieq. "Long-Term Soviet Economic Interests and Policies in Afghanistan." In Rosanne Klass, ed. *Afghanistan: The Great Game Revisited*. New York: Freedom House, 1987, pp. 71–95.

Norbu, Dawa. "Strategic Development in Tibet." *Asian Survey* 19 (March 1979), 245–259.

O'Ballance, Edgar. "What of Baluchistan." *Army Quarterly and Defence Journal* 4 (October 1981), 399–407.

Partem, M. G. "The Buffer Zone in International Affairs." *Journal of Conflict Resolution* 27 (March 1983), 3–26.

Patel, W. "The Situation of India." *Survival* 4 (November 1962), 255–258.

Poullada, Leon B. "Pushtunistan: Afghan Domestic Politics and Relations with Pakistan." In Ainslee Embree, ed. *Pakistan's Western Borderlands: The Transformation of a Political Order*. Durham, N.C.: Carolina Academic Press, 1977.

——. "Afghanistan and the United States: The Crucial Years." *Middle East Journal* 35 (Spring 1981), 178–190.

——. "The Road to Crisis, 1919–1980: American Failures, Afghan Errors and Soviet Successes." In Rosanne Klass, ed. *Afghanistan: The Great Game Revisited*. New York: Freedom House, 1987, pp. 37–71.

Rahman, Habibur. "British Post–Second World War Military Planning for the Middle East." *Journal of Strategic Studies* 5 (December 1982), 511–530.

Rahul, Ram. "Struggle for Central Asia." *International Studies* 18 (January 1979), 1–12.

Rashid, Jamal. "Pakistan and the Central Command." *Middle East Report*, July–August 1986, pp. 28–34.

Ray, Hemen. "Communist China's Strategy in the Himalayas." *Orbis* 11 (Fall 1967), 826–845.

Razvi, Mujtaba. "Pak-Afghan Relations since 1947: An Analysis." *Pakistan Horizon* 32 (June 1980), 34–51.

Reardon, Patrick J. "Modernization and Reform: The Contemporary Endeavor." In George Grassmuck and Ludwig W. Adamec, eds. *Afghanistan: Some New Approaches*. Ann Arbor: University of Michigan Press, 1969, pp. 155–201.

Rokkan, Stein. "Cities, States and Nations: A Dimensional Model for the Study of Contrasts in Development." In S. N. Eisenstadt and Rokkan, eds. *Building States and Nations: Models and Data Resources*. Vol. 1 Beverly Hills, Calif.: Sage, 1973.

Romance, Francis J. "Modernization of China's Armed Forces." *Asian Survey* 20 (March 1980), 298–310.

Satyapalan, C. N. "The Sino-Indian Border Conflict." *Orbis* 8 (Summer 1964), 374–390.

Sayeed, Khalid bin. "Pathan Regionalism." *South Atlantic Quarterly* 63 (Autumn 1964), 478–507.

Scheinberg, Seymour. "Strategic Developments in Bhutan." *Military Review* 58 (January 1978), 47–55.

Schloss, Aran. "Stages of Development and the Uses of Planning: Some Nepali Experiences." *Asian Survey* 23 (October 1983), 1115–1127.

Schroder, John F., and Abdul Tawab Assifi. "Afghan Mineral Resources and Soviet Exploitation." In Rosanne Klass, ed. *Afghanistan: The Great Game Revisited*. New York: Freedom House, 1987, pp. 97–135.

Segal, Gerald. "China and Afghanistan." *Asian Survey* 21 (November 1981), 1158–73.

Seth, S. P. "Sino-Indian Relations: Problems and Prospects." *Asia Pacific Community* 28 (Spring 1985), 67–85.

"The Shah on War and Peace." *Newsweek*, 14 November 1977, p. 70.

Sherwani, Latif Ahmed. "Review of Sino-Pakistani Relations, 1981–85." *Pakistan Horizon* 39 (1st Quarter 1986), 92–106.

Shirreff, David. "Landlocked Exporters Aim for New Markets." *Middle East Economic Digest*, 27 May 1977, pp. 12–14.

Singh, Air Commodore Jasjit. "No Pak Claim to Siachin." *Times of India*, 19 May 1988.

Singh, S. Nihal. "India's Restraint over Incursions by China Is Wise." *International Herald Tribune*, 9 September 1986.

"The Skardu Highway." *Strategic Studies* 4 (Spring 1981), 16–23.

Smith, Robert H. T. "The Development and Function of Transport Routes in Southern New South Wales, 1866–1930." *Australian Geographic Studies* 2 (April 1964), 47–65.

"The Soviet Attitude to Pashtunistan." Staff article in *Central Asian Review* 8 (1960), 310–315.

"Special Section on Baluchistan." *Pakistan Quarterly* 8 (Winter 1963), 32–76.

Sprout, Harold. "Geopolitical Hypotheses in Technological Perspective." *World Politics* 15 (January 1963), 187–212.

Sprout, Harold, and Margaret Sprout. "Geography and International Politics in an Era of Revolutionary Change." In W. A. Douglas Jackson, ed. *Politics and Geographic Relationships*. Englewood Cliffs, N.J.: Prentice-Hall, 1964.

Spykman, Nicholas J. "Geography and Foreign Policy, I." *American Political Science Review* 32 (1938), 28–50.

Sulzberger, C. L. "Belief in Crude Reality." *New York Times,* 22 April 1973.

Syed, Anwar H. "The Politics of Sino-Pakistani Agreements." *Orbis* 11 (Fall 1967), 798–825.

Tahir-Kheli, Shirin. "External Dimensions of 'Regionalism' in Pakistan." *Contemporary Asia Review* 1 (1977), 85–95.

——. "Iran and Pakistan: Cooperation in an Area of Conflict." *Asian Survey* 17 (May 1977), 474–490.

——. "Defense Planning in Pakistan." In Stephanie G. Neuman, ed. *Defense Planning in Less Industrialized States*. Lexington, Mass.: Lexington Books, 1984, pp. 209–230.

Theroux, Paul. "China Passage." *National Geographic,* March 1988, pp. 298–328.

Thomas, Raju G. C. "Indian Defense Policy: Continuity and Change under the Janata Government." *Pacific Affairs* 53 (Summer 1980), 223–244.

——. "The Afghan Crisis and South Asian Security." *Journal of Strategic Studies* 4 (December 1981), 415–434.

Topping, Seymour. "Opening the High Road to China." *New York Times Magazine,* December 1979, sec. 6.

Toynbee, Arnold. "Impressions of Afghanistan and Pakistan's North-West Frontier." *International Affairs* 37 (April 1961), 161–169.

Valenta, Jiri. "The Soviet Invasion of Afghanistan: The Difficulty of Knowing Where to Stop." *Orbis* 24 (Summer 1980), 201–218.

Vertzberger, Yaacov. "Sino-Afghan Relations, 1949–1978." *Journal of South Asian and Middle Eastern Studies* 6 (Spring 1983), 32–43.

——. "The Political Economy of Sino-Pakistani Relations: Trade and Aid, 1963–82." *Asian Survey* 23 (May 1983), 637–652.

——. "China's Diplomacy and Strategy towards South Asia: From Benign Neglect to Prominence." *Jerusalem Journal of International Relations* 8 (June 1986), 100–141.

Wohlstetter, Albert. "Illusions of Distance." *Foreign Affairs* 46 (January 1968), 242–255.

Wolf, Charles, Jr. "Defense and Development in Developing Countries." *Journal of the Operations Research Society of America* 10 (November 1962), 828–838.

Wolf, John B. "The Diplomatic History of the Baghdad Railroad." Dissertation presented to the graduate school of the University of Minnesota, July 1933.

Yu, George T. "The Tanzania-Zambia Railway: A Case Study in Chinese Economic Aid to Africa." In Warren Weinstein, and Thomas H. Henrikson. *Soviet and Chinese Aid to African Nations*. New York: Praeger Special Studies, 1980, pp. 117–144.

Zingel, Wolfgang-Peter. "Pakistan's Economic Development." *Journal of South Asian and Middle Eastern Studies* 5 (Spring 1982), 70–82.

Ziring, Lawrence. "Soviet Policy on the Rim of Asia: Scenarios and Projections." *Asian Affairs* 9 (January 1982), 135–146.

Government Publications

A Perspective on the Pinyin Romanization of Chinese Characters. Washington, D.C.: Central Intelligence Agency, 1981.
Government of Baluchistan. *White Paper on the Budget, 1981–1982*. Quetta, 1982.
Government of Pakistan. *White Paper on Baluchistan*. Rawalpindi, 1974.
——. *Report on the Progress Achieved in Baluchistan, 1972–1975*. Lahore, 1975.
——. *The New Face of Baluchistan*. Islamabad: Pakistan Publications, 1980.
——. *Special Development Plan for Baluchistan*. Islamabad, 1980.
Pakistan Tourism Development Corporation. *Karakoram Highway: A Twentieth Century Miracle*. Karachi: Ferozsons, 1982.
Regional Conflict Working Group Paper Submitted to the Commission on Integrated Long-Term Strategy. "Commitment to Freedom: Security Assistance as a U.S. Policy Instrument in the Third World." Washington, D.C.: Pentagon, May 1988.
Regional Conflict Working Group Report Submitted to the Commission on Integrated Long-Term Strategy. "Supporting U.S. Strategy for Third World Conflict." Washington, D.C.: Pentagon, June 1988.
U.S. Bureau of Budget. "Analysis of India, Pakistan and Afghanistan and Suggestions for U.S. Policy, 2 December 1959." Item 000995 in *The Declassified Documents 1983 Collection*, vol. 9, no. 3. Washington, D.C.: Carrollton Press, 1983.
U.S. Congress. Senate. Committee on Foreign Relations. Sub-Committee on Near Eastern and South Asian Affairs. *U.S. Security Interests and Policies in Southwest Asia*. 96th Cong., 2d. sess. Washington, D.C., 1980.
U.S. Department of Defense. *Soviet Military Power, 1984*. Washington, D.C., 1984.
U.S. Department of State. "Sino-Soviet Bloc Economic Activities in Underdeveloped Areas, 5 March 1956." Item 242 C in *The Declassified Documents 1977 Collection*, vol. 3, no. 3. Washington, D.C.: Carrollton Press, 1977.
——. "Elements of U.S. Policy towards Afghanistan, 27 March 1962." Item 65 B in *The Declassified Documents 1978 Collection*, vol. 4, no. 1. Washington, D.C.: Carrollton Press, 1978.
U.S. House Committee on Foreign Affairs. Subcommittee on Europe and the Middle East. *NATO after Afghanistan*. Washington, D.C.: USGPO, 1980.
U.S. Joint Chiefs of Staff. "Program of Assistance for General Area of China, 10 January 1950." Item 33 A in *The Declassified Documents 1979 Collection*, vol. 5, no. 1. Washington, D.C.: Carrollton Press, 1979.
U.S. National Foreign Assessment Center. *Handbook of Economic Statistics*. Washington, D.C.: Central Intelligence Agency, 1980.
——. *Communist Aid Activities in Non-Communist Less Developed Countries, 1979 and 1954–1979*. Washington, D.C.: Central Intelligence Agency, October 1980.
U.S. National Security Council, "U.S. Policy towards Afghanistan, NSC 5409, 1954" Item 280 B in *The Declassified Documents 1980 Collection*, vol. 6, no. 3. Washington, D.C.: Carrollton Press, 1980.
——. "Expansion of Soviet Influence in Afghanistan and U.S. Countermeasures,

NSC 5409, 11 May 1956." Item 280C in *The Declassified Documents 1980 Collection*, vol. 6, no. 3. Washington, D.C.: Carrollton Press, 1980.

U.S. Office of the President. "Memo of Conversation between President John F. Kennedy and Prince Naim, 27 September 1962." Item 110B in *The Declassified Documents 1977 Collection*, vol. 3, no. 2. Washington, D.C.: Carrollton Press, 1977.

Wohlstetter, Albert, and Fred C. Ilké. *Discriminate Deterrence: Report of the Commission on Integrated Long-Term Strategy.* Washington, D.C.: USGPO, 1988.

Unpublished Materials

International Aid Organization. Staff Report. 25 November 1980.

Kemp, Geoffrey, and John Maurer. "The Logistics of Pax Britannica: Lessons for America." Paper presented at the Conference on Projection of Power: Perspectives, Perceptions, and Logistics, Fletcher School of Law and Diplomacy, Tufts University, Medford, Mass., April 1980.

Neuman, Stephanie. "A Talking Paper: The Relationship Between Military Expenditures and Socio-Economic Development." Paper presented at the Conference on Security and Development in the Indo-Pacific Arena, Fletcher School of Law and Diplomacy, Tufts University, Medford, Mass., April 1978.

Index